Inclusive Learning and Educational Equity

Volume 7

Series Editor
Lani Florian, School of Education, Charteris Land Room 4.11,
University of Edinburgh, Moray House, Edinburgh, UK

Editorial Board Members
Mel Ainscow, University of Manchester, Manchester, UK
Petra Engelbrecht, North-West University, Potchefstroom, South Africa
Humberto J. Rodríguez, Escuela Normal Especialización, Monterrey, Mexico
Roger Slee, School of Education, Magill Campus, University of South Australia, Adelaide, Australia
Elizabeth Walton, University of Nottingham, Nottingham, UK

Aims and Scope:

This book series reflects on the challenges of inclusive education as a strategy for improving educational equity. The series addresses issues of diversity in support of the UN Sustainable Development Goals (SDGs) which set the global education agenda for 2030 in SDG 4: Ensure inclusive and quality education for all and promote lifelong learning.

Although considered an important aspect of a global human rights agenda ensuring education for all is a complex endeavour that is subject to the forces of globalization, and the exclusionary pressures associated with migration, mobility, language, ethnicity, disability, and intergenerational poverty. Acknowledgement of the reciprocal links between these markers of diversity and educational underachievement has led to an increasing interest in the development of inclusive education as a strategy for improving educational equity.

By addressing these and related diversity issues, this series aims to contribute important advances in knowledge about the enactment of inclusive education. The development of educational processes and pedagogical interventions that respond to the tensions between education policies that promote competition and those designed to promote inclusion at individual, classroom, school, district, national, and international levels are explored by the contributors to this series.

This series:

- Offers a critical perspective on current practice.
- Stimulates and challenges further developments for the field.
- Explores global disparities in educational provision and compares developments.
- Provides a welcome addition to the literature on inclusive education.

Lawrence Meda • Jonathan Chitiyo
Editors

Inclusive Pedagogical Practices Amidst a Global Pandemic

Issues and Perspectives Around the Globe

Editors
Lawrence Meda
Sharjah Education Academy
University City
Sharjah, United Arab Emirates

Jonathan Chitiyo
University of Pittsburgh Bradford
Bradford, PA, USA

ISSN 2512-1499 ISSN 2512-1510 (electronic)
Inclusive Learning and Educational Equity
ISBN 978-3-031-10644-6 ISBN 978-3-031-10642-2 (eBook)
https://doi.org/10.1007/978-3-031-10642-2

© The Editor(s) (if applicable) and The Author(s), under exclusive license to Springer Nature Switzerland AG 2022
This work is subject to copyright. All rights are solely and exclusively licensed by the Publisher, whether the whole or part of the material is concerned, specifically the rights of translation, reprinting, reuse of illustrations, recitation, broadcasting, reproduction on microfilms or in any other physical way, and transmission or information storage and retrieval, electronic adaptation, computer software, or by similar or dissimilar methodology now known or hereafter developed.
The use of general descriptive names, registered names, trademarks, service marks, etc. in this publication does not imply, even in the absence of a specific statement, that such names are exempt from the relevant protective laws and regulations and therefore free for general use.
The publisher, the authors, and the editors are safe to assume that the advice and information in this book are believed to be true and accurate at the date of publication. Neither the publisher nor the authors or the editors give a warranty, expressed or implied, with respect to the material contained herein or for any errors or omissions that may have been made. The publisher remains neutral with regard to jurisdictional claims in published maps and institutional affiliations.

This Springer imprint is published by the registered company Springer Nature Switzerland AG
The registered company address is: Gewerbestrasse 11, 6330 Cham, Switzerland

Series Editor's Preface

The COVID19 pandemic has resulted in an unprecedented disruption to education systems around the world and is widely reported to have hit the most vulnerable students the hardest. Reports from international non-governmental organisations bear this out. On 4 April 2020, the UNESCO Institute of Statistics reported 81.8% of learners enrolled at pre-primary, primary, lower-secondary, and upper-secondary levels of education in 151 countries were affected by country-wide school closures.[1] Just over a week later, on 16 April 2020, the OECD reported 91% of enrolled learners from 191countries were affected by school closures, with children and youth in need of additional support less likely to obtain it as a result.[2] These dates and these numbers, representing well over a billion learners, are important because they reflect the intensity of a rapidly changing and uncertain global situation that contributors to this book address in this volume.

The chapters in this volume focus on pedagogical practices employed in real time to meet the diverse learning needs of students during the early phases of the COVID-19 pandemic. As such, the volume adds to a growing body of literature that documents the disruptions and the responses to the disruptions caused by the pandemic on national education systems, the widening gaps in educational access, and concerns about the effects on equity and educational outcomes. Though many of these concerns pre-date the pandemic, the disruption to education caused by school closures intensified them. Yet, educators around the world have continued their work, and many have responded to the challenges of the pandemic with innovation. As the International Task Force on Teachers for Education 2030[3] noted:

> During the crisis, teachers around the world led the efforts to connect students and their families to schools digitally (and in other ways) by ensuring access, sharing ideas with other teachers and with parents, and by creating partnerships. Many teachers demonstrated resourcefulness during the crisis leading content design, facilitating capacity building as peer leaders, mentoring and readily adopting and catalysing change within their schools.

---

[1] https://en.unesco.org/covid19/educationresponse
[2] https://oecdedutoday.com/coronavirus-school-closures-student-equity-inclusion/
[3] https://teachertaskforce.org/blog/teachers-innovating-education-transformation

The documentation of this work contained in this volume places a particular focus on special education supports as they were applied in different contexts during the uncertain early phase of the COVID-19 pandemic. Studies and accounts from Poland, Northern Ireland, South Africa, the United Arab Emirates (UAE), the United States of America (USA), Canada, Malawi, Jordan, Turkey, Latin America, and the Caribbean region document challenges as well as opportunities in responding to diverse learning needs while coping with effects of the pandemic. It is useful to reflect on the upheaval caused by the pandemic when considering these accounts.

The rapid move to online teaching enabled a form of schooling to reach many learners with both positive and negative intended and unintended consequences. This produced a shift in circumstances that redrew the boundaries of learner (and teacher) vulnerability. What can be learned from these changes in perception? How can the lessons learned help to develop twenty-first-century practices that restructure education systems to respond to the inequities laid bare by national and regional differences in resources as well as commitments to education for all?

An argument put forth in this volume suggests more adequate preparation of teachers to respond to diverse learning needs during both online and in-person teaching is needed. The European Agency for Special Needs and Inclusive Education has recently called for an alignment of teacher competences to support the development of sustainable practices that link inclusive practices to recent developments in the science of learning.[4] Connecting competences for inclusion, with its emphasis on participation, belonging, and well-being,[5] to science of learning findings about learning as a social act that depends on human relationships[6] represents a hopeful activity with implications for both online and in-person teaching. As hybrid models take form, we are reminded that preparing teachers for an uncertain future helps create a path to a better one.

University of Edinburgh   Lani Florian
Edinburgh, UK

---

[4] European Agency for Special Needs and Inclusive Education, 2021. *Aligning competence frameworks for Teacher Professional Learning for Inclusion: Conceptual Working Paper.* (L. Florian, ed.). Odense, Denmark

[5] Florian, L., Black-Hawkins, K. and Rouse, M., 2017. *Achievement and Inclusion in Schools.* second edition. London: Routledge

[6] Darling-Hammond, L. and Cook-Harvey, C. M., 2018. *Educating the Whole Child: Improving School Climate to Support Student Success.* Palo Alto, CA: Learning Policy Institute

Acknowledgments

This book project would not have been a success if it was not for the effort of people whom we would like to acknowledge in this section. First and foremost, we would like to thank Almighty God for granting us editors the knowledge, capacity, and skills needed to guide this project.

Second, we would like to express our heartfelt appreciation to all chapter contributors. We would not have completed this book without contributions from these authors. The double-blind peer-review process was rigorous, and some contributors were requested to revise and resubmit their work to the satisfaction of reviewers. Contributors did not despair, but hung on up to the logical end. For that, the editors would like to thank and congratulate them for a job well done.

Third, book editors would like to say a big thank you to all reviewers who were drawn from different universities across the globe. Their expertise in making this project a success was invaluable. Each reviewer reviewed a chapter twice, first when it was submitted and a second time to check if previous comments raised were addressed to their satisfaction. It required a lot of dedication and commitment to spare time to review one chapter twice.

Fourth, we would like to express our sincere gratitude to Prof. Candice Livingston from the Cape Peninsula University of Technology in South Africa. She served as a language editor and critical reviewer of all the chapters. She conducted her critical review after each chapter was subjected to a double-blind review process. She was very critical and thorough, and she provided constructive feedback which was accepted and valued by all chapter contributors. The editors greatly appreciate her herculean efforts to ensure that all the chapters are of high quality and will make benchmark contributions to the field of education.

We would also like to thank Mr. Akewak Biru Kebede, a student at Zayed University, who agreed to work as a research assistant on this project. He checked all the work to ensure that authors adhered to APA guidelines. Last but not least, we would like to thank Zayed University for supporting this project through funding.

Contents

1 **Introducing the Road to Inclusion During the COVID-19 Global Pandemic** 1
Lawrence Meda and Jonathan Chitiyo

2 **Students with Disabilities in Inclusive Educational Settings in Poland** 7
Joanna Głodkowska, Barbara Marcinkowska, and Emilia Wojdyła

3 **Inclusion of Economically Deprived Secondary School Children in Virtual-Based Learning During COVID-19 in Malawi** 33
Louis Okon Akpan and Omolara Joy Oluwatuyi-Akpan

4 **Inclusion and the Right to Education in Latin America and the Caribbean: Policies, Resources, and Good Practice in the COVID-19 Social and Educational Emergency** 49
Andres Paya Rico

5 **On the Cultivation of Autonomous Learning During Times of a Pandemic: Pedagogical Implications of Inclusive Online Education** 63
Naima Al-husban and Yusef Waghid

6 **It Takes a Village: Preparing Chinese Immigrant Families for Remote Learning of their Children with Disabilities** 81
Lusa Lo and Kathy Tsang

7 **Factors Influencing Five Foundation Phase Teachers' Teaching Experiences During COVID-19 in an Inclusive Suburban School** 97
Carin Stollz, Heather Nadia Phillips, and Janet Condy

8 **The Potential of Online Education: Beyond the Status Quo of Equity and Inclusion** 115
Meaghan Krazinski and Megan E. Cartier

9   Perspectives on Reconceptualizing and Recontextualizing
    Schools' Inclusive Culture for Students with Disabilities
    During the COVID-19 Pandemic... 131
    Efthymia Efthymiou

10 Inclusive Art Pedagogies for Refugee Children
    and Youth with Mental Health Disabilities
    During COVID-19: A Canadian Perspective 159
    Susan Barber

11 Supporting Students with Disabilities in Transition:
    Collaboration Between School Counselors
    and Special Educators 177
    Sara L. McDaniel, Zachary Pietrantoni, and Szu-Yu Chen

12 The Spirit of Volunteerism: Supporting Young Children
    of Medical Workers During the COVID-19 Pandemic
    in the United Arab Emirates 195
    Lawrence Meda

13 Collaborative Roles of Rural Stakeholders
    to Benefit Learners Within Inclusive Education 211
    Patrick Mweli and Ntombizandile Gcelu

14 Teaching in a Global Pandemic: Experiences
    of Five Educators Supporting Students with Disabilities
    in Inclusive Classrooms in the United States 225
    Adam Moore, Abigail Higgins, Carly Doulette, Kayla Hoff,
    and Simoneil Sarbh

15 Educators Coming Together to Empower Learners, Families,
    and Teachers in Developing Culturally Responsive/Sustaining
    Postsecondary Transition Plans During COVID-19 241
    Rebekka J. Jez, Keitha Osborne, and Clara Hauth

16 Understanding Life in Lockdown for Autistic Young
    People in Northern Ireland 263
    Gillian O'Hagan and Bronagh Byrne

17 Inclusive Educational Practices in Turkey
    During the Period of COVID-19 287
    Ismail Hakki Mirici

18 Inclusive Pedagogical Practices Amidst a Global Pandemic:
    Lessons Learnt from Across the Globe 301
    Jonathan Chitiyo and Lawrence Meda

List of Reviewers... 305

Index... 307

About the Editors

Dr. Lawrence Meda holds a PhD in Curriculum Studies. He is currently working as an Associate Professor and Director of Research at Sharjah Education Academy in the United Arab Emirates. He is a certified online instructor and very passionate about research. His main research interests are in Inclusive Education, Curriculum Studies, Educational Technology and Teacher Education. He has supervised Masters and Doctoral students and published in high impact accredited journals.

Jonathan Chitiyo holds a PhD in special education from Southern Illinois University Carbondale, USA. He is currently working as Associate Professor of Special Education and Director of Teacher Education at the University of Pittsburgh at Bradford, USA. His research interests include the implementation of different school-based practices, factors affecting the education of vulnerable children, and the development of special education systems in developing countries, especially in Africa.

Chapter 1
Introducing the Road to Inclusion During the COVID-19 Global Pandemic

Lawrence Meda and Jonathan Chitiyo

The global pandemic caused by the Coronavirus (COVID-19) affected the education sector world-wide. At the inception of the pandemic in 2020, many learning institutions across the globe were forced to close as a preventative measure to reduce and contain the spread of the deadly virus. However, teaching and learning did not stop as many institutions implemented emergency remote teaching. Many schools and tertiary institutions around the globe which predominantly relied on traditional face-to-face instruction had to go through a rough transition to online learning since they did not have ample time to prepare for virtual teaching (Ontong & Waghid, 2020; Ngwacho, 2020). Rapanta, Botturi, Goodyear, Guàrdia and Koole (2020, p. 923) concurred with the ill-preparedness of tertiary institutions for remote teaching and learning saying, "a particular challenge has been the urgent and unexpected request for previously face-to-face university courses to be taught online." The sudden change from regular face-to-face classes to online learning did not provide students, teachers, and parents enough time to prepare for a new instructional pedagogical method. This resulted in many school children wanting additional support to access and succeed in online learning during the time of the global pandemic. Students with exceptional learning needs bore the brunt of this tumultuous instructional transition.

The purpose of this edited book was to bring together social scientists, scholars and other school practitioners to present current and ongoing research focused on the pedagogical practices teachers, parents, and other educational stakeholders are using to meet the diverse learning needs of students during the time of COVID-19.

L. Meda (✉)
Sharjah Education Academy, University City, Sharjah, United Arab Emirates
e-mail: lmeda@sea.ac.ae

J. Chitiyo
University of Pittsburgh Bradford, Bradford, PA, USA
e-mail: chitiyoj@pitt.edu

© The Author(s), under exclusive license to Springer Nature Switzerland AG 2022
L. Meda, J. Chitiyo (eds.), *Inclusive Pedagogical Practices Amidst a Global Pandemic*, Inclusive Learning and Educational Equity 7,
https://doi.org/10.1007/978-3-031-10642-2_1

Chapters presented focused on different ways in which students' diverse learning needs were accommodated to ensure the success of inclusion during the time of a global pandemic.

The book consists of 16 chapters which report how inclusive education was realized in different contexts across the globe during the COVID-19 period. The chapters covered the following regions: Poland, Northern Ireland, United States of America (USA), South Africa, United Arab Emirates (UAE), Canada, Malawi, Jordan, Turkey, Latin America, and the Caribbean region. Each chapter made a significant contribution to the scientific knowledge around inclusive education. Chapters provided in-depth insights related to teaching children during the time of the pandemic. A glimpse of each of the chapters is presented below.

In Chap. 2, titled 'Students with disabilities in inclusive educational settings in Poland', Joanna Głodkowska, Barbara Marcinkowska, and Emilia Wojdyła addressed the issue of inclusive education and presented the results of a longitudinal study on the outcomes of educating students with disabilities (mild intellectual disabilities, autism, Asperger's Syndrome) in Polish public schools. It was found that schools created inclusive structures which provided a milestone of achievement in terms of supporting students with diverse learning needs during the global pandemic of COVID-19.

In Chap. 3, Louis Akpan and Omolara Oluwatuyi-Akpan in their chapter titled 'Inclusion of economically deprived secondary school children in virtual-based learning during COVID-19 in Malawi' explore the inclusive pedagogical practices implemented to accommodate the diverse learning needs of poor school children in Malawi. Findings of the study indicate that due to years of neglect and marginalisation of economically deprived rural school children, their inclusion in virtual-based learning was received with apprehension.

Chapter 4 is titled 'Inclusion and the right to education in Latin America and the Caribbean: Policies, resources, and good practice in the COVID-19 social and educational emergency'. In this chapter, Andres Paya Rico analyses various educational policies, good practice, and resources that countries in Latin America and the Caribbean region, in consultation with international institutions, have implemented. Results show the enormous collective effort being made by countries and international organizations to alleviate negative effects at a socio-educational level.

Chapter 5 is titled 'On the cultivation of autonomous learning during times of a pandemic: pedagogical implications of inclusive online education'. In this chapter, Naima Al-husban and Yusef Waghid focused on some pedagogical encounters among teachers and learners in selected secondary schools in Jordan during the time of the COVID-19 pandemic. It is argued that learning can be autonomous in the context of inclusive online pedagogical practices. The study concludes that learner autonomy can most appropriately be enhanced during inclusive online teaching and learning especially when teachers encourage and summon learners to learn independently, through engaging with reading and school texts.

Lusa Lo and Kathy Tsang presented their topic, 'It takes a village: preparing Chinese immigrant families for remote learning of their children with disabilities' in Chap. 6. This chapter reports on how a community-based parent support group in the

United States empowered and prepared Chinese immigrant families for supporting their children with disabilities during remote learning. The community-based parent support group offered technological and advocacy training that had a substantial influence on equipping families to support remote learning for their children with disabilities as well as advocate for the special education services and inclusive support their children required. The study concludes that community support plays an indispensable role towards empowering immigrant parents of children with disabilities to be successful in remote learning. When parents are equipped with the skills they need to help facilitate their child's learning, the ones who benefit are their children.

Chapter 7, written by Carin Stollz, Heather Phillips, and Janet Condy is titled 'Factors influencing five Foundation Phase teachers' teaching experiences during COVID-19 in an inclusive suburban school.' Results reveal that even though teachers experienced increased levels of fear of transmission of the virus, fear of curriculum not being covered, and fear of not being able to manage learners and keep them safe, they (teachers) did their best to ensure that teaching and learning was implemented successfully while ensuring that COVID-19 protocols were observed.

Chapter 8 is titled, 'The potential of online education: beyond the status quo of equity and inclusion.' In this chapter, Meaghan Krazinski and Megan Cartier explored issues of equity and inclusion during the global pandemic. Authors explore how stakeholders conceptualize and prioritize equitable and inclusive pedagogy and decisions when a school goes online. Authors found significant obstacles to equity, inclusion, and solidarity during the pandemic predominantly residing within racial injustices and harm that predate the pandemic and online learning.

In Chap. 9, Efthymia Efthymiou presents a study titled 'Perspectives on reconceptualizing and recontextualizing schools'inclusive culture for students with disabilities during the COVID-19 pandemic.' The study examines whether federal primary schools in the UAE respond flexibly and effectively to the needs of students with disabilities through an inclusive school culture. Results showed that school principals and teachers responded to the needs of society, embraced an inclusive vision, and engaged in inclusive practices aimed at enhancing the quality of sustainable inclusive schools. This study argues that efforts to create a 'School for all' and a more equitable response to diversity during the COVID-19 pandemic should not only aim at accommodating the heterogeneous needs of students with disabilities, but at considering a shift in underlying cultural values and beliefs.

In Chap. 10, titled 'Inclusive art pedagogies for refugee children and youth with mental health disabilities during COVID-19: A Canadian perspective', Susan Barber explores inclusion of forced immigrants. Teachers shared their effective COVID-19 teaching strategies which helped students find deeper meaning and new identities in the time of a global pandemic.

In Chap. 11, 'Supporting students with disabilities in transition: collaboration between school counselors and special educators', Sara McDaniel, Zachary Pietrantoni, and Szu-Yu Chen explore the responsibilities of school counsellors and special educators within Multi-Tiered Systems of Support (MTSS), and proposes a collaboration framework in which MTSS might be utilized to support the transitions of students with disabilities, including transitions related to the impact that COVID-19 has had on schools (i.e. service delivery models, changes in socialization patterns). Collaboration is presented as valuable in terms of supporting students with disabilities.

Lawrence Meda authored Chap. 12, titled 'The spirit of volunteerism: supporting young children of medical workers during the COVID-19 pandemic in the United Arab Emirates'. He examines the nature of learning support which was offered to young children of medical workers during the start of the COVID-19 pandemic in the UAE. A significant contribution that emerges from this study is a demystification of misleading thoughts that children in early childhood development cannot learn meaningfully online.

In Chap. 13, titled 'Collaborative roles of rural school managers to benefit learners within inclusive education', Patrick Mweli and Ntombizandile Gcelu examined how stakeholders in a South African context collaborated to help learners cope with learning in an inclusive environment. Hinged on the collaborative leadership theory, the chapter concludes that collaboration plays an indispensable role in achieving better education for rural school learners.

Chapter 14 was written by Adam Moore, Abigail Higgins, Carly Doulette, Kayla Hoff and Simoneil Sarbh and is titled 'Teaching in a global pandemic: experiences of five educators supporting students with disabilities in inclusive classrooms in the United States'. The study revealed three salient components to championing inclusive practices during the pandemic. These are focusing on social emotional well-being, ensuring academic access, and fostering family/caregiver partnerships.

Chapter 15, which is innovatively titled, 'Educators coming together to empower learners, families, and teachers in developing culturally responsive/sustaining postsecondary transition plans during COVID-19', was written by Rebekka J. Jez, Keitha Osborne, and Clara Hauth. The study focused on assessing teachers' knowledge and perspectives around culturally responsive/sustaining postsecondary transition and then training them using remote pedagogical practices. The multinational study recruited 21 primary and secondary teachers from Jamaica and the United States to participate in a pre-survey, workshop, and post-survey to explore how educators could empower learners and their families in developing culturally responsive/sustained postsecondary transition plans. The study showed that teachers gained comprehensive knowledge and skills about inclusive and culturally responsive/sustained transition practices, strategies, and resources. Teachers also established strong community relationships with families.

Chapter 16, titled 'Understanding life in lockdown for autistic young people in Northern Ireland' by Gillian O'Hagan and Bronagh Byrne, discusses the impacts of COVID-19 on children with autism. The study examines coping strategies developed by young people with autism during lockdown and makes recommendations for helping them manage in similar situations in the future.

Chapter 17 was written by Ismail Mirici and is titled 'Inclusive educational practices in Turkey during the period of COVID-19.' The study investigates how inclusive education was provided for students in Turkey. Results revealed that although inclusive pedagogical approaches were put in place, neither students nor parents and teachers were satisfied with emergency distance education in Turkey as it was not truly inclusive or effective.

Chapter 18 presents concluding remarks. It provides a succinct conclusion of the whole book and discusses lessons learnt from the contexts represented in the project. Recommendations are presented in this chapter and directions for future studies.

References

Ngwacho, A. G. (2020). COVID-19 pandemic impact on Kenyan education sector: Learner challenges and mitigations. *Journal of Research Innovation and Implication in Education, 4*(2), 128–139.

Ontong, K., & Waghid, Z. (2020). Towards cultivating a critical pedagogy of place: A response to teaching practices in higher education amidst COVID-19. In *L. Ramrathan, N. Ndimande-Hlongwa, N. Mkhize & J.a. smit (Eds,) re-thinking the humanities curriculum in the time of COVID-19* (pp. 56–73). CSSALL Publishers.

Rapanta, C., Botturi, L., Goodyear, P., Guàrdia, L., & Koole, M. (2020). Online university teaching during and after the COVID-19 crisis: Refocusing teacher presence and learning activity. *Postdigital Science and Education, 2*(2020), 923–945. https://doi.org/10.1007/s42438-020-00155-y

Dr. Lawrence Meda holds a PhD in Curriculum Studies. He is currently working as an Associate Professor and Director of Research at Sharjah Education Academy in the United Arab Emirates. He is a certified online instructor and very passionate about research. His main research interests are in Inclusive Education, Curriculum Studies, Educational Technology and Teacher Education. He has supervised Masters and Doctoral students and published in high impact accredited journals.

Dr. Jonathan Chitiyo holds a PhD in Special Education from Southern Illinois University Carbondale, USA. He is currently working as an Associate Professor of Special Education and Director of Teacher Education at the University of Pittsburgh at Bradford, USA. His research interests include the implementation of different school-based practices, factors affecting the education of vulnerable children, and the development of special education systems in developing countries, especially in Africa.

Chapter 2
Students with Disabilities in Inclusive Educational Settings in Poland

Joanna Głodkowska, Barbara Marcinkowska, and Emilia Wojdyła

Abstract According to Polish law, children with disabilities and youth who possess a special needs education certificate have the opportunity of learning in all types of schools (special, integration and public), depending on their individual developmental and educational needs and predispositions. This article addresses the issue of inclusive education and presents the results of a longitudinal study on the outcomes of educating students with disabilities (mild intellectual disabilities, autism, Asperger's Syndrome) in public schools. The objective of this study was to identify selected outcomes of implementing inclusive education in the Polish education system while taking into consideration the educational and general developmental achievements of students with disabilities graduating in primary schools. An evaluation of certain factors in the process of inclusive education in the educational centres covered in the study was also included. Several references to the pandemic situation were introduced into the structure of the theoretical framework of this project and the analysis of the research findings. The study was conducted in 30 primary schools throughout the 2019/2020 school year. In each of these schools, one student with disability in the graduation process was included by analysing his/her accomplishments in Grades 6, 7 and 8. The research results allow us to conclude that more progress is made in their social functioning compared to their acquired school skills and knowledge. School principals have undertaken activities aimed at building inclusive education at their educational centres. However, there are still various kinds of barriers, at times difficult or even impossible to overcome. Schools are creating inclusive structures; however, the attitude of the parents of other students and the local community, which is not always friendly, is an evident problem.

Keywords Inclusive education · Patterns of special didactics · Educational achievements · General developmental achievements · Disability

---

J. Głodkowska (✉) · B. Marcinkowska · E. Wojdyła
Maria Grzegorzewska University, Warsaw, Poland
e-mail: joanna@aps.edu.pl

© The Author(s), under exclusive license to Springer Nature Switzerland AG 2022
L. Meda, J. Chitiyo (eds.), *Inclusive Pedagogical Practices Amidst a Global Pandemic*, Inclusive Learning and Educational Equity 7,
https://doi.org/10.1007/978-3-031-10642-2_2

Introduction

The multifaceted exploration of the educational process of students with disabilities among their peers remains an inspiring area of interest and cognitively important in the work of Polish researchers. For more than 30 years, activities aimed at implementing inclusive education have included developing theoretical concepts, carrying out numerous studies, constructing systemic projects and adopting national legislation. In creating inclusive education in Poland, we implement and constantly monitor the effectiveness of changes made to improve the education system, which ensures high-quality education for all learners. In accordance with Polish educational law, children with disabilities and youth, on the basis of having a special needs education certificate, have the opportunity of being educated in all types of schools (special, integration or public), depending on their individual developmental and educational needs and predispositions. Efforts made to build inclusive schools as close as possible to the child's place of residence, have brought about many positive changes in education, particularly over the last decade. Systematic activities aimed at improving the education system are an important task of the government's educational policy, which also includes inclusive education as an essential element.

The studies conducted in this project took place in a specific period of time – the beginning stages and intensification of the coronavirus disease (COVID-19) pandemic. The first case was diagnosed in Poland on March 4th, 2020. Pursuant to the Regulation of the Minister of Health, the epidemic in Poland has been in effect since March 20th, 2020. At the same time, the Minister of Education issued a regulation stipulating solutions to be implemented during the temporary period of restrictions in the functioning of educational units in relation to preventing, counteracting and combating COVID-19 (Regulation of the Minister of National Education of March 20th, 2020). This regulation set out that principals were responsible for organizing the implementation of these tasks, including classes with the use of distance learning methods and techniques. Consequently, education has taken place in both hybrid and remote forms. Although the study included in this project was conducted throughout the 2019/2020 school year, and thus during the pandemic, the majority of longitudinal research into the students' achievements covered pre-pandemic periods (Grade 6, Grade 7 and the first semester of Grade 8). Perhaps unsurprisingly, the final semester, in which the pandemic emerged and intensified, had an impact on the achievements of Grade 8 students. Therefore, the research conducted in this project unexpectedly covered the pandemic period. However, documenting the link between the pandemic and students' achievements would require an in-depth comparative study. The findings of this research could be grounds for undertaking more in-depth analyses of the educational effects of the pandemic. Although the main objective of this study did not directly concern the pandemic situation in schools, several references to the pandemic were introduced into the structure of the theoretical framework and analyses of the research findings.

This chapter addresses the issue of inclusive education in Poland and presents the research results pertaining to the educational and general developmental achievements of students with disabilities attending public schools in their place of residence. It also offers the opinions of school principals on the factors determining the achievements of students with disabilities and their schools' readiness to create inclusive educational settings.

Inclusive Education in Poland – Patterns of Special Didactics as a Generalization and Explanation of an Attainable Educational Reality

Inclusive education is best expressed in implementing the idea of unity in diversity (Głodkowska, 2010, 2020a). At the school level, this idea, emphasising the value of differences between students, points towards planning such educational goals that enable building a coherent school environment that accepts otherness, nurtures peer bonds and reinforces tolerance (Głodkowska, 2020a, c).

Implementing inclusive education in public schools requires appropriate organizational, content-based, methodical preparation, including providing staff prepared to accept students with disabilities, eliminating physical barriers, and barriers in the social awareness of the school environment. It is also essential to honestly and thoroughly identify and diagnose the abilities, needs and limitations of students with disabilities and their family environment, and their peer environment in which the process of common education takes place. In accordance with governmental regulations, an individual educational and therapeutic program (IETP) is designed by a team of teachers and other specialists for every student with a special education certificate (Regulation of the Minister of National Education of August 28th, 2017).

The implementation and effectiveness of such programs are accessed systematically (Marcinkowska, 2012; Trochimiak & Gosk, 2012; Wielebski, 2018). Teachers evaluate the effectiveness of their activities intended for special needs students, which in turn allows them to determine whether a particular educational and developmental goal has been achieved.

At the Maria Grzegorzewska University, we undertake several academic, didactic and implementation tasks related to educating students who require special needs education. This has been the purpose of various projects conducted whose scope has been nationwide and has encompassed nearly every public school in Poland. For years, we have been conducting numerous research projects, publishing academic and methodological work, educating and training teachers and participating in legislative work. In this way, we have been engaged in creating inclusive education and widely promoting the idea of "a good school for all". Based on figures from recent years, it can be stated that the number of students with disabilities in the public school system has been gradually increasing, year by year. Data from the 2019/2020 school year indicates that 99,831 students (61.6% of the total number of students with disabilities in the education system) attended public schools (inclusive education) and integration centres (integrative education) (Educational Information System, Ministry of Education, as of September 30th, 2019).

For nearly a decade at the Maria Grzegorzewska University, we have frequently worked on defining, systemizing and interpreting special needs education. In this manner, we are in the process of developing an important academic field – special didactics. We search for sources of didactic studies in wider contexts by analysing, among others, inclusive social culture and considering issues "unity in diverse education". This research project is based on previously conducted theoretical studies on important didactic aspects in educating students with special needs (Głodkowska, 2017a, b, 2020a, b). In particular, the theoretical framework is determined by the construct of the patterns of special didactics.

These patterns are certain models that generalize the educational circumstances of students who require education accommodated to their needs and conditions and the special organization of the teaching-learning process. The following patterns of special didactics have been specified:

1. The right to equal access to education – ensuring that every child, able-bodied or with disability, with learning difficulties or particularly gifted, has equal rights to high-quality education.
2. Diversified education – the diversified needs and abilities of students are a determining factor in for creating good education for all.
3. Participative education – creating conditions for all students to belong to their social, class and peer community.
4. Diagnostic education – diagnosing the general and educational development of students as the foundation for constructing an appropriate education and therapeutic process.
5. Subjective education – nurturing relationships based on dialogue and a school culture and shaping students' independence and decision-making skills.
6. Education in an integrative space – building education contexts that take into account what unites and not only what causes division.
7. Harmonized education – creating conditions for cooperation between all those involved in education (able-bodied and students with disabilities, specialists and parents).
8. Professional education – educating special needs students by professionally trained specialists.
9. Liberating education – creating educational conditions for self-actualization and experiencing self-esteem.
10. Education with pedagogical optimism – the hope that every student can develop is the basic assumption of special needs education (Głodkowska, 2017a, 2020a).

It should be noted that the findings and reflections on the patterns of special didactics outline the complementary concept of recognizing, explaining and improving the educational process of students whose educational needs require special didactic accommodation and methodological solutions. With confidence in the purposefulness of using these patterns in new approaches, applications and reflections, further systematization and explanation of the realities of special education have been repeated. In 2020, two monographs were published (Special Didactics – on the horizon of meanings, concepts and educational practices and Special Didactics – from theoretical constructs to research models), in which the richness of special education was uncovered in theoretical and empirical findings and proposals for its practical application.

The research project presented in this chapter was built on the patterns of special didactics construct on the following grounds: (1) the study takes place in public schools with inclusive education programs in place (a reference to patterns: the right to equal access to education, education in an integrative space); (2) the study identifies the students' educational and developmental achievements (a reference to patterns: diversified education, diagnostic education, participative education, subjective education, liberating education); (3) the study evaluates the factors determining the students' school achievements (a reference to patterns: harmonized education, professional education, education with pedagogical optimism).

At the same time, we are aware that the theoretical background of this research, outlined by the patterns of special didactics, was unexpectedly penetrated by eighth-grade students and teachers' experience of the coronavirus pandemic. The research was conducted in the 2019/2020 school year, therefore during the early stages of the pandemic. The theoretical and empirical analyses gathered so far indicate that the pandemic situation has caused unexpected difficulties in the proper course of the learning process (Domagała-Zyśk, 2020; Ptaszek et al., 2020; Buchner et al., 2020; Winiarczyk & Warzocha, 2021; Pauluk, 2021). In these circumstances, a particular discrepancy appears between the individual subjective conditions of students and teachers and the external constraints in undertaking and performing school tasks. Students and teachers are experiencing a difficult situation. They are compelled to meet the requirements of implementing the curriculum in changed, restricted and unnatural conditions. At the same time, both teachers and students often find themselves unable to cope with these demands because they do not have the capacity or appropriate competencies. The difficult situation spurred on by the pandemic has affected students in general and students with disabilities in particular (Szustkowska, 2020). Kocejko (2021) illustrates this situation by referring to the concept of intersectionality. It describes the phenomenon of intersecting and a certain overlapping of various social categories, which leads to intensified discrimination against various groups and individuals. In the case of people with disabilities, pandemic-related inconveniences only add to the difficulties caused by their disabilities. This may reinforce their feelings of isolation or rejection.

Based on the theoretical framework of the patterns of special didactics, and in part considering the pandemic situation, this project undertook empirical analyses to answer the following question: how effective is educating students with disabilities attending public schools?

Methods

The objective of this research was to explore the selected effects of implementing inclusive education in the Polish education system, taking into account the educational and developmental achievements of students with disabilities. The study also included an evaluation of certain educational conditions of inclusive education in the educational centres covered in its scope.

The research problems were formulated in the following manner:

1. What are the educational and general developmental achievements of students with disabilities, who participate in inclusive education in public schools in their place of residence?
2. What is the opinion of public school principals on the conditions of the students with disabilities achievements and creating an inclusive school culture?

The diagnostic poll method was used in this study. The study used an original individual case analysis questionnaire to assess the students' educational (marks obtained in compulsory subjects with an exam) and general developmental (cognitive, motivational, emotional and social functioning, interests and skills) achievements. For the purposes of analysing the students' educational achievements, marks obtained in compulsory subjects with an exam (Polish, mathematics and English) from over a period of three years of learning (Grades 6, 7, 8) were taken into consideration. The students' educational achievements were evaluated according to a six-point scale – from 1 to 6, in which "6″ was the highest mark possible and "1″, the lowest. School principals were also interviewed. This article employs the information obtained from the interviews on assessing the significance of various factors in the achievements made by the students with disabilities participating in inclusive education. It also takes into account the principals' opinion on their school as an inclusive educational space.

The criterion for selecting the research sample was public primary schools with the largest number of students with a given type of disability. Data provided by the Educational Information System (SIO) indicated that the majority of students who participate in inclusive education have mild intellectual disabilities, autism or Asperger's syndrome (data from the Educational Information System, Ministry of National Education as of September 30th, 2019). A multi-stage scheme of selecting research samples was applied. At first, schools were selected randomly from the education units identified in the Educational Information System as meeting the basic criterion: a public primary school attended by students with intellectual disabilities, autism or Asperger's syndrome. Afterwards, a sixth-grade student who met the sample selection criterion was randomly chosen from each school.

The study was conducted in 30 elementary schools throughout the 2019/2020 school year. Primary schools with eighth-grade students meeting the sample selection criteria in the school year covered by the study were selected. The condition for participation was possessing a special needs education certificate resulting from one of the following disabilities: a mild intellectual disability, autism or Asperger's syndrome. Intellectual disability is seen as being at least about two standard deviations or greater below the population, which is approximately an IQ score of 70 or less (American Psychiatric Association, 2013). Core features of disorders of intellectual development are: (1) significant limitations in intellectual functioning, (2) significant limitations in adaptive behaviour functioning, (3) with onset during the developmental period. Individuals with mild ID are slower in all areas of conceptual development and social and daily living skills. These individuals can learn practical life skills, which allows them to function in ordinary life with minimal levels of support (American Psychiatric Association, 2013). To meet diagnostic criteria for Autism Spectrum Disorder (ASD) according to DSM-5 (American Psychiatric Association, 2013), a child have persistent deficits in each of three areas of social communication and interaction (deficits in social-emotional reciprocity; deficits in nonverbal communicative behaviors; deficits in developing, maintaining, and understand relationships) and at least two of four types of restricted, repetitive behaviors (stereotyped or repetitive motor movements; insistence on sameness, inflexible adherence to routines; highly restricted, fixated interests; hyper- or hyporeactivity to sensory).

One student with a disability in the process of completing primary education from each of the selected schools was covered by the study. Thus, the research sample consisted of 30 students from 30 schools. The schools participating in the study were found in the Mazowiecki voivodship, which according to ministerial data (source: Educational Information System, Ministry of National Education as of September 30th, 2019), constituted a representative region for making general conclusions. At the same time, municipalities in which the schools included in the study were located were selected after analysing the so-called 'G indicator'. Municipalities with the highest G indicator were chosen. This indicator sets out the basic income tax for every resident of a given municipality. Analysing this indicator in the context of a school's affluence and the various possibilities of working with students made it possible to assess its ability to provide learning conditions and care for students with disabilities. A local government unit's financial resources are significant for a school's qualitative development and its ability to organize education. The study also included 30 school principals for the purposes of understanding their opinions on the significance of various factors in the achievements of students with disabilities and their assessment of their schools in terms of an inclusive culture. The quantitative research method was applied. The obtained results of the study were analysed statistically. The IBM SPSS Statistics 26 program was used to conduct analyses of the basic descriptive statistics, one-way analysis of variance, the post-hoc (Šidák correction), Fisher's exact test and the Student's t-test for dependent samples.

In order to verify the differences in the assumed variables in the three years being compared, a one-way analysis of variance in the "within group" variation was conducted. The people taking part in the study were informed of the research's objective, character and subject matter. The participants (parents, teachers, principals) expressed consent to participating in the study, their anonymity was ensured, and the study was conducted in a friendly atmosphere. Parents expressed consent to their children's participation in the study. The study also included teachers and specialists who led classes with a randomly selected eighth-grade student. They filled out a questionnaire on the student's individual case. A total of 325 teachers and other specialists participated in the study. By means of filling in our questionnaires, principals expressed their opinions on inclusive education in their schools.

Results and Discussion

There are very few empirical studies that have been conducted in Poland on inclusive, integrative and special education. These forms of education take place in three types of schools: public, integration and special needs schools. It should be noted that identifying issues related to inclusive education in Polish academic research is concentrated on both the systemic solutions of institutional forms of educating special needs students (including those with disabilities) and assessing their success at school. It could be said that since the first integration educational centre in Poland was opened (1989), research on integration education has developed significantly, and this provides important cognitive information, evaluations and practical recommendations. It also contributed to the next step in developing the education system, i.e., implementing inclusive education in public schools. When discussing the results of this research project, we only refer to the empirical analysis of Polish researchers. We have made this decision because we believe that the issue of education, including inclusive education, results directly from the Polish legislative foundations of the education system and legal acts concerning the curriculum, student evaluations and preparing schools and teachers for implementing inclusive education.

This project's study was conducted in public schools in which inclusive education is in place. Therefore, with reference to this research project's previous theoretical grounds, the analyses may be considered at the systemic level or at least in the context of the following patterns of special didactics: equal access education and education in an integrative space.

In Polish academic literature, this field is presented to a large extent in studies comparing the various forms of special education. Theoretical analyses and empirical studies indicate that integration and inclusive education produce better outcomes than education in traditional school settings and special classes. The authors of academic work published to date have developed proposals for an inclusive education model (Głodkowska, 2010), considered inclusive education as an unfinished project (Szumski, 2014), compared the segregation and inclusive education systems (Kubicki, 2016), analysed aspects of integration in education (Dryżałowska, 2018) and have also reflected on the real possibilities of inclusive education (Bąbka & Nowicka, 2019) and creating a good school for all (Wojciechowska, 2020), and have considered constructivism and diversity pedagogy in the context of inclusion (Rzeźnicka-Krupa, 2020). It can be assumed that the more beneficial effects of learning in integration/inclusive educational settings are partially the result of changes that have taken place in the Polish education system since the end of the twentieth century. Changes in social awareness, largely due to a more intensive promotion of the idea of a good school for all, are also significant. This idea arises from normalizing trends and the more clearly understood truth that everyone has something to offer the world, and that disability is a normal social phenomenon (Głodkowska, 2020a).

In this chapter, the following research results were analysed and interpreted in terms of: (1) the educational achievements of students with disabilities, (2) their general developmental achievements, and (3) an assessment of certain factors determining the outcomes of these students' attendance in public schools and an evaluation of the implementation of an inclusive culture in school settings. We also made several references to the current pandemic situation in the analysis.

Educational Achievements The results of exploring educational achievements of students with disabilities can be related to this project's theoretical construct reflected in the following patterns of special didactics: diversified education and diagnostic education.

The analysis of the educational achievements covered the students' school final grades in subjects that conclude with an external exam. External exams were introduced in Poland several years ago (earlier in middle school and Grade 6). These examinations are conducted at the conclusion of every stage of education and are evaluated by external examiners employed by district examination commissions. Furthermore, in primary schools, an eighth-grade written exam is conducted in the following subjects: Polish language, mathematics and a foreign language.

This research project identified the dynamics of students with disabilities mastery of specific areas determined in the basic curriculum in comparison to two examination subjects: Polish language and mathematics (the third examination subject, a foreign language, was excluded).

Achievements in Polish Language In terms of mastering Polish language examination skills, the following statistically significant test result was found [$F(1.66; 41.60) = 18.57; p < 0.001; \eta^2 = 0.39$]. The effect size was very large. The post-hoc (Šidák correction) carried out indicated that all of the differences are statistically significant. Students in Grade 6 obtained the lowest grade in Polish language ($M = 2.24; SD = 0.74$). This result was significantly lower in comparison to Grade 7 ($M = 2.51; SD = 0.73; p = 0.002$) and Grade 8 ($M = 2.64; SD = 0.80; p < 0.001$). The difference between Grade 7 and Grade 8 marks was also statistically significant ($p < 0.012$) (Fig. 2.1).

While analysing the specific knowledge and skills in terms of the Polish language, it can be observed that the relatively highest average results were noted in the following categories: reception of expressions and using information contained in them (in the following grades: $M = 2.47; M = 2.7; M = 3.01$), recognizing the speaker's intention ($M = 2,50; M = 2,77; M = 2,93$), the ability to search for necessary information in literary/non-literary texts and making conclusions ($M = 2.50; M = 2.77; M = 2.93$). The relatively lowest results were found for:

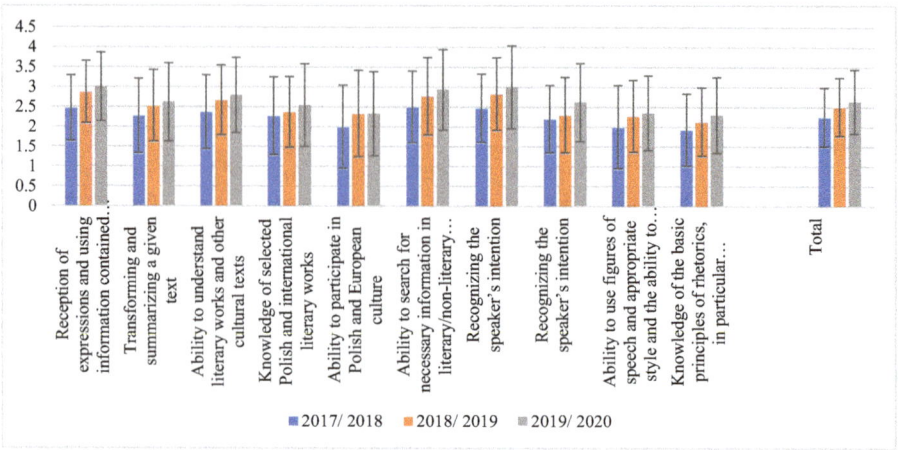

Fig. 2.1 Polish language examination results for the three years covered in the study. This chart presents the average value in the studied group (bars) and the standard deviation (hooks)

knowledge of the basic principles of rhetoric (M = 1.93; M = 2.3; M = 2.30), ability to participate in Polish and European culture (M = 2.00; M = 2.33; M = 2.33). The relatively greatest progress (comparing the average grades from Grade 6 compared to Grade 8) was noted in the following categories: recognizing the speaker's intention (a difference of 0.53 points), reception of expressions and using information contained in them (a difference of 0.53 points), ability to search for necessary information in literary/non-literary texts and ability to make conclusions (a difference of 0.42 points) (Fig. 2.1). In general, it can be concluded that the results in particular sections of the Polish language examination indicate low results in the participating students' ability to acquire school knowledge and skills. The analysed results did not exceed a satisfactory grade (3.0), and frequently oscillated between a satisfactory and acceptable (2.0) grade.

When referring the research findings on achievements made in Polish language classes to the pandemic situation, the difference in the overall results can be taken into consideration. A difference in the achievements made by students between Grade 6 (M = 2.24) and Grade 7 (M = 2.51) compared to Grade 7 (M = 2.51) and Grade 8 (M = 2.64) is evident. The greatest difference was in the first case (0.27) compared to the latter (0.14). Therefore, it can be assumed with some caution that certain circumstances (perhaps the pandemic situation) reduced the dynamic of acquiring school knowledge and skills in terms of Polish language classes. However, this claim requires further in-depth comparative analysis. It should be noted that the sudden and exceptionally severe situation forced attempts to implement new methods and generating new ideas for conveying knowledge to students. These attempts were not always effective. At the same time, direct communication was replaced by distant communication, which definitely proved to be less effective, causing difficulties and frequent misunderstandings (Piechowska & Romanowska, 2020). While conducting lessons remotely, teachers used online platforms, applications and messaging services. For the most part, they were not prepared for this situation and were forced to quickly improve their skills in order to meet the challenges (Jankowiak & Jaskulska, 2020).

Achievements in Mathematics Afterwards, the level of examination skills in terms of mathematics was analysed. A statistically significant result for this test was noted [F (1.36; 39.40) = 10.62; p = 0.001; η^2 = 0.27]. The effect size was large. The post-hoc tests indicated that all of the differences were statistically significant. The lowest level of examination skills in terms of mathematics was found in Grade 6 (M = 2.43; SD = 0.94) and was statistically significant in comparison to Grade 7 (M = 2.61; SD = 0.93; p = 0.024) and Grade 8 (M = 2.72; SD = 0.93; p = 0.003). The difference between the marks obtained by Grade 7 and 8 students was also statistically significant (p < 0.036) (Fig. 2.2).

The study revealed that the relatively highest average marks were found in terms of arithmetic fluency (M = 2.80; M = 3.00; M = 3.07), while the lowest results were noted in using and creating information (M = 2.50; M = 2.60; M = 2.83). It was also found that reasoning and argumentation skills fell in Grade 8 (M = 2.24) in comparison to Grade 7 (M = 2.33). The remaining skills improved slightly in comparison to the results of the three last grades of primary school. The relatively largest increase was noted in the following areas: using and interpreting representations (a difference of 0.34 points), and the lowest increase in arithmetic fluency (a difference of 0.27 points), despite the fact that the average mark is highest in this category. In general, it can be concluded that the educational achievements of the students with disabilities in mathematics range between acceptable and satisfactory marks with a predominance of the higher mark.

When referring the research findings on achievements made in mathematics to the pandemic situation, a comparison of the differences in the overall results was also made. However, in this case it can be claimed that student accomplishments

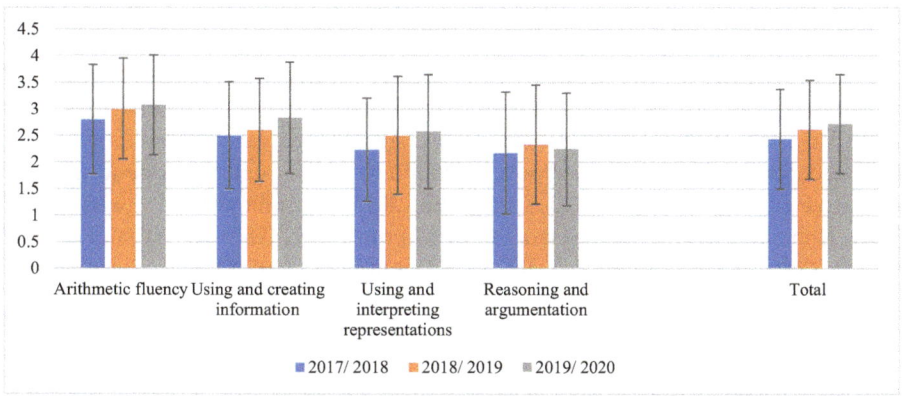

Fig. 2.2 Mathematics examination results for the three years covered in the study. This chart presents the average value in a studied group (bars) and the standard deviation (hooks)

between Grade 6 (M = 2.43) and Grade 7 (M = 2.51) in comparison to Grade 7 (M = 2.61) and Grade 8 (M = 2.72) did not show any significant differences.

It should be noted that there is a greater increase in the average level of Polish language skills (M = 2.25; M = 2.51; M = 2.64; the difference between Grade 6 and 8 amounted to 0.39 points) in comparison to mathematics (M = 2.43; M = 2.61; M = 2.72; with a difference of 0.29 points) (Fig. 2.1, Fig. 2.2). However, it can be stated that the overall marks in mathematics are higher in every grade. Within the scope of both subjects, there is an upward trend between the first (Grade 6) and second (Grade 7) school year included in the study and a slight increase in the final year of primary education (Grade 8). Therefore, these facts should play a significant diagnostic role in the methodological planning of teaching these subjects.

While summarizing the analysis of educational achievements, it can be concluded that student performance gradually increases over these 3 years of education. It should be noted that they are generally low school achievements ranging of 2–3 points out of 6. At the same time, it should be noted that the students included in the study represent the second school year after the 2017 education system was implemented and were affected by the major staffing problems in primary schools. It can also be assumed that staffing problems were not the only reason for these outcomes. The significant changes in the education system, including structural changes and introducing a new core curriculum, also had a major impact. It is worth emphasising that the 2017 education reforms in Poland were yet another change in the education system over the last 20 years. In 1999, junior high schools were created, and in 2017, they were liquidated after 18 years of functioning. Subsequent changes in the core curriculum were also introduced (in 1999, 2008, 2012 and 2017) (Sadowska, 2016). The lack of stability in the education system and curriculum changes have significantly changed the conditions and principles of teaching in Polish schools (Szymański, 2008; Zahorska, 2009; Bąbka, 2015; Szymański et al., 2016; Janiszewska-Nieścioruk, 2016). It can be noted that the students included in this study experienced constant changes (Dyduch & Trojańska, 2020). This instability creates problems for students, teachers and parents alike. Moreover, this situation has an even more negative impact on the students who require special needs education.

Polish literature on the subject covers research into the outcomes of teaching students with disabilities, particularly students with intellectual disability (Szumski, 2010; Buchnat, 2015). However, comparative studies have been carried out in special education and integration schools, although to a lesser extent in public schools (inclusive education) (Bąbka, 2015; Antonik, 2015; Bartnikowska & Ćwirynkało, 2016; Kubicki, 2016; Dryżałowska, 2018; Mikrut, 2019; Godawa, 2020). For this reason, the project presented in this article enriches a niche area of cognitive research.

At the same time, it should be pointed out that the research findings that have been published so far frequently have been conducted in relation to very young students, particularly those in the early childhood education period (Szumski, 2010; Buchnat, 2015). Meanwhile, including younger students with disabilities in public schools and classes is easier than including older students for several reasons. In this respect, educators mention more favourable conditions, including special preparation for early childhood education teachers, a greater familiarity of students, a more flexible education program, and smaller differences between students at this stage of development. It is also relatively easier for younger, able-bodied students to accept peers with disabilities. This situation is more difficult in higher grades due to the more significant differences between able-bodied students and students with disabilities. This also includes problems with self-esteem, accepting one's own disability, maturity problems and often lack of support in one's family environment. Therefore, this project, which explores the educational achievements of students from the last three years of primary school, addresses new issues in Polish research.

It should also be pointed out that this article presents the results of longitudinal research, a research method that is not used frequently in empirical reports. Cross-sectional studies dominate more frequently, which, despite its diagnostic value, limit the possibilities of interpreting and explaining the dynamics of the changes occurring and also prevent causal inferences.

School assessment, used as an indicator of the educational achievements of students with disabilities, provides important information about learning outcomes. As a value judgement of learning outcomes, such assessments should always be based on verifying possible differences between the student's expected and actual achievements. It is clear that in the case of students with disabilities, school progress reports play an essential role throughout the learning process. It could even be said that they are more significant than in the education process of able-bodied students (Kosakowski, 2003). The process of special education is enriched with an intervention effect on the students' developmental deviation. Therefore, when evaluating their knowledge and abilities, an important revalidation aspect of pedagogical measures is taken into account. This includes the students' individual abilities and limitations, their progress in the areas of instrumental processes (knowledge and skills) and directional processes (motivation, emotions), and also their developmental achievements resulting from pedagogical measures (including compensation, correction, improvement and strengthening processes). Evaluations fulfil a revalidation role as they give students feedback on meeting school expectations, and what is also important, such reports activate their so-called auto-revalidation (Kosakowski, 2003, p. 260). This process reinforces the students' subjectivity. It enables a gradual departure from external controls on the activity of students with disabilities in order to systematically provide them with an initiative to decide about their own development. It is essential to create such conditions for students so they will be able to experience the effort of overcoming barriers and gain awareness of their own weaknesses and inner resources. In this manner, they will acquire adequate and honest self-knowledge, perceive their own authentic cognitive and practical abilities, gain the ability to experience success, and deal with their own failures. These abilities are extremely important for people with disabilities, who are somehow destined to face failures, difficulties, limitations, and exclusion and stigmatization.

General Developmental Achievements The subject of analysis in this research project was also the students' level of functioning within their school environment.

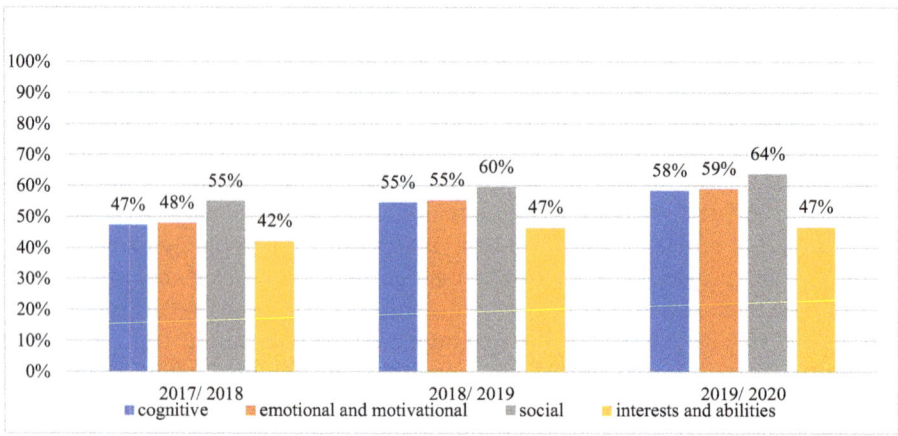

Fig. 2.3 The categories of the general development achievements of students with disabilities

The study also covered the following variables: the level of cognitive, emotional and motivational functioning, social development and areas of interests and abilities. Therefore, once again referring to the theoretical justification of this project, it is possible to clarify this situation in the context of the following patterns of special didactics: participative education, subjective education, and liberating education.

Cognitive Functioning This area was analysed in terms of the students' perceptiveness, observation skills, cause and effect thinking, the ability to absorb concepts, form opinions, judgements, evaluations and argumentation skills, and long-term memory skills, concentration, and ease of verbal interaction. A statistically significant result on the scale measuring the level of the students' cognitive functioning was also noted [$F (1.23; 35.69) = 34.22$; $p < 0.001$; $\eta^2 = 0.54$]. The observed effect size was significant. Post-hoc tests were conducted to determine which differences between the years were statistically significant and the dynamic of the changes. It turned out that all of the differences were statistically significant ($p < 0.001$). The lowest level of cognitive functioning was noted in Grade 6 ($M = 2.37$; $SD = 0.78$) and increased in Grade 7 ($M = 2.73$; $SD = 0.83$) and Grade 8 ($M = 2.92$; $SD = 0.80$) (Fig. 2.3).

Emotional and Motivational Functioning covered the following categories: cognitive interest, planning one's own work, striving to learn, active class participation, motivation to learn at school, controlling emotions. Within the area of emotional and motivational functioning, a statistically significant test result was also noted [$F (1,34; 38,83) = 23.53$; $p < 0.001$; $\eta^2 = 0.45$], with a very high effect size. The post-hoc tests indicated that all of the differences were statistically significant. The lowest level of emotional and motivational functioning was noted in Grade 6 ($M = 2.40$; $SD = 0.87$); however, it rose in Grade 7 ($M = 2.77$; $SD = 0.94$) and Grade 8 ($M = 2.95$; $SD = 0.92$). The difference between 2017/2018 and 2018/2019, and

2017/2018 and 2019/2020 was significant ($p < 0.001$), as was the case with the difference between the results for Grades 7 and 8 ($p < 0.005$) (Fig. 2.3).

Social Functioning was analysed in terms of active class participation, group work skills, establishing relationships with peers, social interaction skills, the engaged performance of additional instructions given by teachers, decision-making skills, the ability to cope in difficult situations, respecting social norms, a sense of responsibility, and observing classroom rules. In the next step, the level of social functioning was analysed. As was the case in previous areas, a statistically significant test result is evident [$F (1.27; 36.87) = 13.12; p < 0.001; \eta^2 = 0.31$]. The effect size was considerable. The conducted post-hoc tests revealed two statistically significant differences. The highest level of social functioning was observed in 2019/2020 ($M = 3.9; SD = 0.2$) and it was statistically significantly higher in comparison with 2018/2019 ($M = 2.98; SD = 0.73; p < 0.001$) and 2017/2018 ($M = 2.75; SD = 0.74; p = 0.001$). The difference between the results for Grade 7 and Grade 8 was close in terms of statistical significance ($p < 0.053$) (Fig. 2.3).

Interests and Abilities were identified in terms of showing interest, the need for achievement, participation in school competitions, achievements in school competitions, participation in external competitions, achievements in external competitions. Statistically significant test results were also noted in this area [$F (1.30; 37.72) = 6.98; p = 0.007; \eta^2 = 0.19$]. The effect size was significant. The conducted post-hoc revealed one statistically significant difference. A higher level of interests and abilities were noted in Grade 7 ($M = 2.33; SD = 0.94$) in comparison with the achievements made in Grade 6 ($M = 2.11; SD = 1.06; p = 0.002$). The difference between 2017/2018 and 2019/2020 ($M = 2.34; SD = 0.94$) was close in terms of statistical significance ($p = 0.054$). The difference between the results of the last two grades was not even close in terms of statistical significance (Fig. 2.3).

In order to comprehensively illustrate the students' functioning in the four developmental areas analysed, a percentage summary table with the maximum result in each category was presented (Fig. 2.3). It reveals that progress occurred in three of the four developmental areas in the group of students covered in the study. The results indicated that students complete primary school with relatively the highest achievements in the area of social development (64% of the maximum result). This fact should be seen as an important forecaster of the students' future. It can also be concluded that schools indeed accomplish one of the important goals of the rehabilitation process of people with disabilities, i.e., empowering and preparing them for future independent adult social functioning, fulfilling a specific type of social role and coping on the labour market. It is also worth noting that cognitive functioning is clearly stronger in these students (11% of the difference between Grade 8 and Grade 6), together with emotional and motivational functioning (11%). However, there is little progress in terms of these students' interests and abilities (5%) (Fig. 2.3). The research results obtained should be used in organizing experiences for students with disabilities, that would embrace their interests and abilities.

When looking at the results obtained in relation to the pandemic situation, it can be noted that in every category of general developmental achievements, the difference between the results attained by Grade 7 and Grade 8 students in comparison to the results attained by Grade 8 and Grade 7 students is relatively smaller. This tendency can also be noted in cognitive functioning (8% compared to 3%), emotional and motivational functioning (7% compared to 4%), social functioning (5% compared to 4%) and interests and skills (4% compared to 0%). With some caution, one may conclude that the pandemic situation reduced the dynamic of the students' overall developmental achievements. However, these findings require further in-depth comparative research.

It can be anticipated that in this unusual situation marked by the pandemic, all of the participants in the education process had no choice but to adapt to it by making attempts and choices and often by taking risks. For teachers, a major problem was their lack of knowledge and skills in remote teaching. On the one hand, this was associated with a feeling of incompetence in this area, while on the other hand, a feeling of possessing inadequate knowledge and experience in pandemic situations (Pyżalski, 2020; Buchner, et al., 2020).

Based on the information obtained, it can be assumed that the visible increase in the students' level of psychosocial development is the result of important conditions. These factors include designing an individual educational and therapeutic plan, teachers integrating revalidation activities, eliminating barriers and limitations preventing children and youth from functioning and fully participating in the life of their school and class (Bartnikowska & Ćwirynkało, 2016). In terms of general developmental achievements, the predominant view in Polish publications is that expanding the educational offer for students with disabilities is necessary and that educational opportunities in public and integration schools should be created for them (Rutkowski & Bidziński, 2018; Bąbka & Nowicka, 2019; Głodkowska, 2020a, b). Such educational conditions enable this group of students to develop mentally, socially and emotionally in a harmonious manner. Being educated with able-bodied peers gives them a sense of belonging to the school community (Głodkowska, 2013; Gajdzica, 2015) and the local community as well (Tersa, 2017). In terms of general developmental achievements, Polish researchers have identified, among others, peer relations and attitudes towards students with disabilities (Oszwa & Fedaczyńska, 2017; Fiedorczuk & Fiedorczuk, 2013, Gajdzica, 2015), the friendships made between integration school graduates (Lipińska-Lokś, 2015), satisfaction with peer relations and the status of students with disabilities in public school classes (Papuda-Dolińska, 2015).

Public schools in Relation to Students' Achievements and Inclusive school Culture In this research project, the issue of conditioning achievements of students with disabilities was addressed, or at least indicated, by focusing on essential factors. This aspect of the analysis directly refers to three of the patterns of special didactics: harmonized education, professional education, and education with pedagogical optimism.

The Factors of Students' school Achievements For this purpose, the opinions of school principals on implementing inclusive education at their educational centres were analysed.

It can be stated that principals highly assessed planning work with students based on a team analysis of their needs (80% of the respondents) as a factor having the greatest impact on the effectiveness and efficiency of educational work with students with disabilities. Another aspect that turned out to be very important was information about the students obtained by teachers from each other (70%). However, it is surprising that public school principals assessed the significance of teachers' professional skills relatively low. It turned out that school principals also ascribed lesser importance to more in-depth analysis by teachers of counselling centre records (27%), information obtained from students' parents (17%) and cooperation with counselling centres (10%). Principals provided a negative assessment of cooperation with schools/educational centres (0%), school facilities (0%), and systemically promoting the idea of inclusive education (3%), and changes in financing special education (10%) (Fig. 2.4).

When surveying the principals, this project did not take the pandemic factor into account, i.e., coping with difficult situations or the ability to adapt to new teaching conditions. However, most of the factors analysed could be interpreted in categories related to the pandemic. The various factors mentioned by the principals may be considered in this context, e.g., planning work with students based on a team analysis of their needs, or an exchange of information on students between teachers and their mutual cooperation. Throughout the pandemic situation, ensuring the optimal implementation of these conditions gives rise to many difficulties in terms of direct contact with students, teachers, specialists and teachers, observing students in their natural educational situations and reliably assessing the effectiveness of the teaching methods used. In the category of various difficulties, limitations, hindrances and barriers, other factors indicated by the principals may also be considered. Polish studies have also addressed the positive effect of the several months' experience with distant education. The surveyed principals stated that throughout the pandemic situation, it was possible to observe greater engagement on the part of teachers and their readiness to cooperate and efforts made to integrate the school environment (Gurba, 2020). At the same time, principals also perceived future opportunities after the pandemic situation. They mentioned beneficial effects linked to developing the skills of teachers and students in using digital tools, developing a didactic base of educational centres, and increasing teachers' creativity (Gurba, 2020).

Unfortunately, it must be noted that the school principals' recognition of the categories of inclusive space may appear less favourable. It turns out that principals of schools in which inclusive education has been implemented highly assess the following aspects: the school attempts to minimize all forms of discrimination (90%), staff and school administration cooperate with each other (87%), staff attempt to remove barriers in the educational process in all areas of school life (73%), everyone feels welcome (70%). These areas include: staff and parents'/guardians' cooperation with each other (50%), staff, school administration,

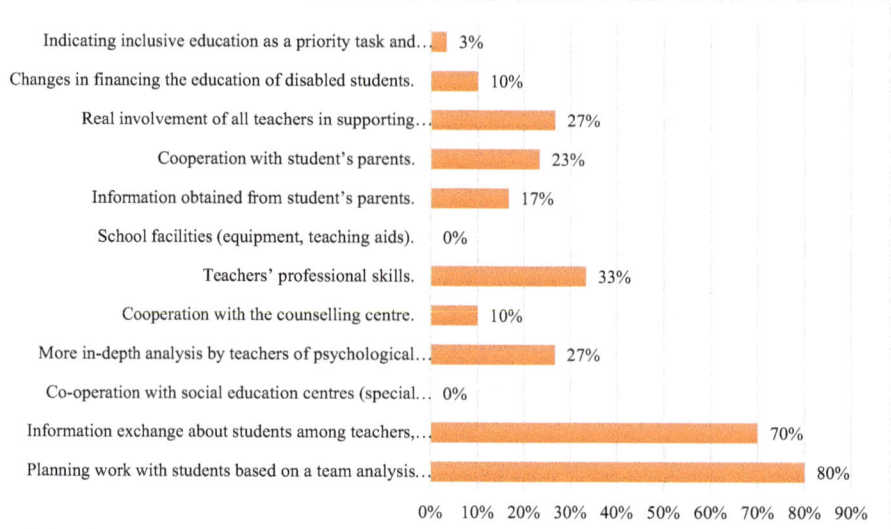

Fig. 2.4 An evaluation of the significance of certain factors in the school achievements of students with disabilities

teachers/guardians adhere to a common philosophy of inclusive education (40%), and high demands are placed on all students (50%) (Fig. 2.5).

Inclusive School Culture The analysis of the responses provided by the directors also provided valuable information on their assessment of inclusive education at their schools.

Polish literature on the subject has presented research conducted on the attitudes of public primary school teachers who work with children with special educational needs certificates (Kossewska, 2000; Kołodziejczyk, 2020; Nowak, 2020); and has portrayed public schools as a meeting place for teachers and special educators (Rutkowski & Bidziński, 2018). The results reveal the difficulties teachers experience when working with such students, particularly in the area of didactics. It was also noted that every third teacher expressed the view that special needs students lower their class's level of education. However, numerous class divisions, the lack of cooperation between public school and special needs teachers, the absence of individualized teaching, perceiving students with disabilities in terms of their limitations and excluding them from extracurricular activities (Parys, 2007) do not favour effective inclusive education. Research was also conducted into parents' attitudes and opinions regarding segregation, integration, and inclusion (Przybyszewska, 2014; Skibska, 2016; Myśliwczyk, 2016).

Teachers in Poland represent various views on inclusive education ranging from support and great scepticism depending on the type of school represented, their own experience and the type and degree of a student's disability. However, these views have changed over the years. The research revealed that over 80% of teachers

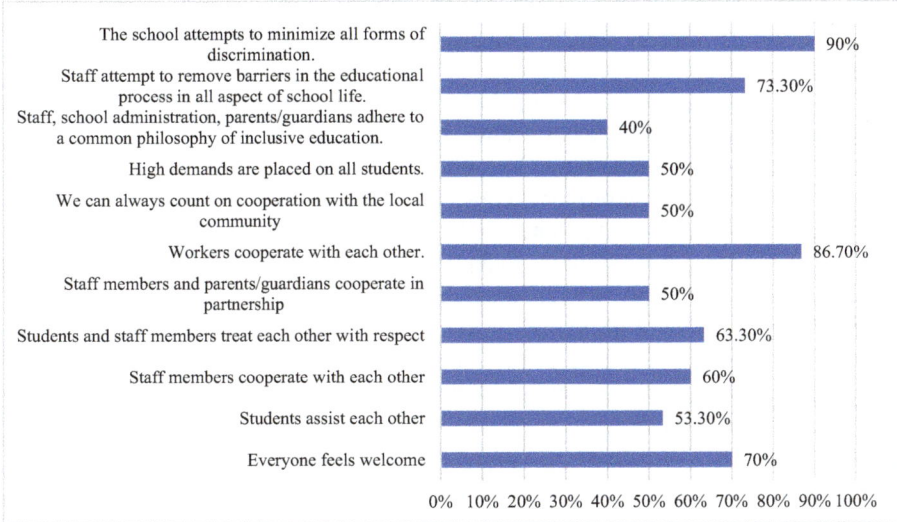

Fig. 2.5 Principals' assessment of inclusive culture at their schools

believe that public schools are not the best place for educating children with disabilities (Gajdzica, 2011). At the same time, other studies have indicated otherwise (Chrzanowska, 2019; Barańska & Sirak, 2015). Therefore, it is difficult to clearly determine what public school teachers think in terms of inclusive education, which is an essential element of shaping an inclusive social culture. It should be emphasised that the beliefs and values recognized at school form the foundation of an inclusive culture. Moreover, it is worth noting that researchers agree in terms of the fundamental thesis that claims: including students with disabilities in non-segregated education increases their chances of better social, professional and personal functioning. As a result, the efforts made by Polish academics and practitioners are directed towards strengthening the effectiveness of inclusive education. This tendency has been confirmed by statistics revealing that over the last two decades, the number of students with disabilities in public schools has multiplied.

Conclusion

As a result of the several actions taken, we have noted a series of beneficial changes in Poland's education system. At the individual level, these changes affect students with disabilities themselves, their peers and parents. At the institutional level, they concern the organization and functioning of particular schools and the entire education system. While summarizing this research project, we have formulated significant conclusions:

1. Students with disabilities' learning outcomes have gradually improved in the last three years of primary school; however, these achievements cannot be considered satisfactory
2. Educational achievements in terms of mathematics are relatively lower in comparison to Polish language knowledge and skills. However, in the scope of these two subjects, the average mark does not exceed a satisfactory grade.
3. Students graduate from primary school with the highest achievements in the area of social development. This outcome bears witness to the fact that rehabilitation aimed at making these students independent and preparing them to fulfil social roles, has been implemented successfully.
4. Unfortunately, school principals do not appreciate the important factors of the achievements of students with disabilities, including cooperation with schools/special education centres, school facilities and promoting the idea of inclusive education.
5. In the category of inclusive space, the principals assessed cooperation between teachers and parents and the need for adhering to a common philosophy of inclusive education as least important.

At the same time, it should be emphasised that this project's research was carried out for the most part in pre-pandemic conditions, with the exception of the second semester of Grade 8. Therefore, certain results were interpreted with some caution, suggesting that the pandemic situation could have contributed to a reduction in the dynamics of the students' general developmental and educational achievements. This affected their cognitive, emotional, motivational and social functioning, skills and interests, and their performance in Polish classes. As indicated, further in-depth research on the educational and developmental effects of the pandemic on educating students with disabilities is required.

It is important to build a school environment where acceptance and respect are inalienable values of being together and participating in the joint teaching–learning process. In a complex education system, everyone involved (students, parents, teachers, other specialists, the local community) must be convinced that differences give meaning to being together and are both a valuable educational and social quality. Social awareness of the fact that inclusive educational activities create an opportunity for improving the entire school's culture is vital in this respect. As a result, they are also an essential factor in changing social mentality.

References

American Psychiatric Association, D. S., & American Psychiatric Association. (2013). *Diagnostic and statistical manual of mental disorders: DSM-5* (Vol. 5). American Psychiatric Association.

Antonik, A. (2015). Edukacja włączająca i integracyjna. O pozornej tożsamości znaczeń. [Inclusive and integration education. On the apparent identity of meanings.]. *Ogrody Nauk i Sztuk [Gardens and Science and Arts]*, 5, 367–372.

Bąbka, J. (2015). Edukacja osób z niepełnosprawnością w systemie niesegregacyjnym–wykluczające czy dopełniające się formy kształcenia [The education of people with disabilities in non-segregated systems – Exclusive or complementary forms of education]. *Interdyscyplinarne Konteksty Pedagogiki Specjalnej [Interdisciplinary Contexts of Special Pedagogy], 11*, 9–34.

Bąbka, J., & Nowicka, A. (2019). Edukacja inkluzyjna, aby nie była iluzją [Inclusive education so that it wouldn't be an illusion]. *Niepełnosprawność. Dyskursy Pedagogiki Specjalnej [Disability. Discources of Special Education], 36*, 11–30.

Barańska, M., & Sirak, K. (2015). Poglądy osób związanych z oświatą na wspólne nauczanie dzieci o zróżnicowanych potrzebach edukacyjnych [Views of educational workers on integrated teaching of children of varying educational needs]. *Niepełnosprawność. Dyskursy Pedagogiki Specjalnej [Disability. Discources of Special Education]*, 128–142.

Bartnikowska, U., & Ćwirynkało, K. (2016). Wyznaczniki kształtujące sytuację ucznia z niepełnosprawnością w klasie ogólnodostępnej i integracyjnej–analiza dostępnych badań [The Determinants Shaping the Situation of Students with Disability in Public School and Integration Classes – an analysis of available studies]. *Interdyscyplinarne Konteksty Pedagogiki Specjalnej [Interdisciplinary Contexts of Special Pedagogy], 13*, 29–48.

Buchnat, M. (2015). *Formy organizacyjne kształcenia dziecka z lekką niepełnosprawnością intelektualną a jego kompetencje społeczne* [Organizational Forms of Educating Children with Mild Intellectual Disabilities and Their Social Skills]. Wydawnictwo Naukowe UAM.

Buchner, A., Majchrzak, M., & Wierzbicka, M. (2020). *Edukacja zdalna w czasie pandemii. Raport z badań* [Remote Education in the Pandemic Era. Research findings]. Centrum Cyfrowe, https://centrumcyfrowe.pl/edukacja-zdalna.

Chrzanowska, I. (2019). *Nauczyciele o szansach i barierach edukacji włączającej* [Teachers on the Opporunities and Barriers of Inclusive Education]. PWN.

Domagała-Zyśk, E. (2020). *Zdalne uczenie sie i nauczanie a specjalne potrzeby edukacyjne. Z doświadczeń pandemii COVID-19* [Remote Learning and Teaching and Special Needs Education. The COVID-19 Experience]. Wydawnictwo Episteme.

Dryżałowska, G. (2018). Wyobcowani w integracji a edukacja włączająca [Alienated in integration and inclusive education]. *Niepełnosprawność. Dyskursy Pedagogiki Specjalnej [Disability. Discources of Special Education], 29*, 28–42.

Dyduch, E., & Trojańska, M. (2020). Wsparcie ucznia z niepełnosprawnością w okresie zmian edukacyjnych [Support for student with disability in times of educational changes]. *Szkoła Specjalna [Special School], 81*, 99–107.

Fiedorczuk, J., & Fiedorczuk, I. (2013). System wartości młodzieży szkół integracyjnych [The Value System of the Youth in Integration Schools]. *Szkoła Specjalna [Special School], 1*, 17–25.

Gajdzica, Z. (ed.) (2011). *Uczeń z niepełnosprawnością w szkole ogólnodostępnej* [Students with Disabilities in the Education System]. Oficyna Wydawnicza Humanitas.

Gajdzica, Z. (2015). Uczeń z niepełnosprawnością w kilku odsłonach – o drogach i bezdrożach zaspakajanie potrzeb edukacyjnych w szkole ogólnodostępnej [Students with Various Disabilities – on the roads and wilderness of meeting educational needs in public schools]. *Przegląd Badań Edukacyjnych [Educational Studies Review], 20*(1), 161–170.

Głodkowska, J. (2010). Model kształcenia uczniów ze specjalnymi potrzebami edukacyjnymi – różnice nie mogą dzielić [A Model of Education for Students with Special Educational Needs – differences cannot divide]. In: *Podniesienie efektywności kształcenia uczniów ze specjalnymi potrzebami edukacyjnymi. Materiały szkoleniowe – część I* [Raising the Effectiveness of Education of Students with Special Educational Needs. Training materials – part 1] (pp. 10–41). Wydawnictwo MEN.

Głodkowska, J. (2013). Uczniowie ze specjalnymi potrzebami edukacyjnymi–integracja edukacyjna procesem złożonym i trudnym [Students with Special Educational Needs – educational integration is a difficult and complex process]. *Szkoła Specjalna [Special School], 1*, 5–16.

Głodkowska, J. (2017a). *Dydaktyka specjalna – od wzorca do interpretacji* [Special Education – from pattern to interpretation]. Wydawnictwo Naukowe PWN.

Głodkowska, J. (2017b). Dydaktyka specjalna– system znaczeń i relacji w projektowaniu dydaktyk specjalistycznych [Special Didactics – a system of meanings and relations in the design of specialized didactics]. In Głodkowska, J. (ed.) *Dydaktyka specjalna – od systematyki do projektowania dydaktyk specjalistycznych* [Special Didactics – From systematics to the design of specialized didactics] (pp. 61–75). Wydawnictwo Naukowe PWN.

Głodkowska, J. (2020a) (ed.). *Dydaktyka specjalna w horyzoncie znaczeń, koncepcji i praktyki pedagogicznej* [Special Didactics – on the horizon of meanings, concepts and educational practices]. Wydawnictwo Akademii Pedagogiki Specjalnej.

Głodkowska, J. (2020b) (ed.). *Dydaktyka specjalna – od konstruktów teoretycznych do modeli badawczych* [Special Didactics – from theoretical constructs to research models]. Wydawnictwo Akademii Pedagogiki Specjalnej.

Głodkowska, J. (2020c). A socially inclusive culture as a source of the model of educational changes from the perspective of teaching according to differences. In J. Głodkowska (Ed.), *Inclusive education. Unity in diversity* (pp. 15–38). Wydawnictwo Akademii Pedagogiki Specjalnej.

Godawa, J. (2020). Wokół integracji społecznej. Edukacja inkluzyjna i integracyjna w opiniach studentów pedagogiki specjalnej i pedagogiki rewalidacyjnej [On social integration. Inclusive and integration education in the opinion of students of special education and revalidation pedagogy]. *Niepełnosprawność–zagadnienia, problemy, rozwiązania [Disability–issues, problems and solutions], 1*(34), 24–37.

Gurba, K. (2020). Edukacja na odległość w czasie pandemii w ocenie dyrektorów szkół. W: *Wyzwania dla edukacji w sytuacji pandemii COVID-19*, s. 151.

Educational Information System, Ministry of Education, as of September 30th 2019, https://cie.gov.pl/sio/ (access: May 15th, 2021).

Rozporządzenie Ministra Edukacji Narodowej z dnia 28 sierpnia 2017 r. zmieniające rozporządzenie w sprawie warunków organizowania kształcenia, wychowania i opieki dla dzieci i młodzieży niepełnosprawnych, niedostosowanych społecznie i zagrożonych niedostosowaniem społecznym [The Regulation of the Minister of National Education of 28 August 2017 amending the Regulation on the conditions of organizing education and care for children and you who are disabled, socially maladjusted or at risk of social maladjustment]. Retrieved from: https://isap.sejm.gov.pl/isap.nsf/DocDetails.xsp?id=WDU20170001652.

Rozporządzenie Ministra Edukacji Narodowej z dnia 20 marca 2020 r. w sprawie szczególnych rozwiązań w okresie czasowego ograniczenia funkcjonowania jednostek systemu oświaty w związku z zapobieganiem, przeciwdziałaniem i zwalczaniem COVID-19 [The Regulation of the Minister of National Education of 20 March 2020 on the temporary limitation of the functioning of educational system units in connection with the prevention, prevention and combating of COVID-19. Retrieved from: https://prawo.cea-art.pl/COVID-19-szczegolne-rozwiazania/.

Janiszewska-Nieścioruk, Z. (2016). (Nie) dojrzałość proinkluzyjnych zmian w kształceniu osób z niepełnosprawnością [The (Im)maturity of pro-inclusive changes in educating people with disabilities]. *Niepełnosprawność [Disability], 22*(2016), 47–59.

Jankowiak, B., & Jaskulska, S. (2020). Dobrostan nauczycieli i nauczycielek a ich postawy wobec kształcenia na odległość w czasie pandemii COVID-19 [The Well-being of teachers and their attitudes towards distant education in the COVID-19 pandemic]. *Przegląd Pedagogiczny [Pedagogical Review], 1*, 219–232.

Kocejko, M. (2021). Sytuacja dzieci z niepełnosprawnościami w czasie pandemii COVID-19–analiza intersekcjonalna [The Situation of Children with Disabilities in the COVID-19 Pandemic – an intersectional analysis]. *Dziecko krzywdzone. Teoria, badania, praktyka [The Harmed Child. Theory, Research, Practice], 20*(2: Ochrona dzieci przed krzywdzeniem w czasie pandemii COVID-19 [Protecting Children Against Harm during the COVID-19 Pandemic]): 76–91.

Kołodziejczyk, R. (2020). Gotowość nauczycieli do pracy w systemie edukacji włączającej [The Readiness of Teachers to work in the Inclusive Education System]. *Roczniki Pedgogiczne [Annals of Pedagogies], 12*(3), 125–142.

Kosakowski, Cz. (2003). *Węzłowe problemy pedagogiki specjalnej* [Nodal Problems of Special Education]. Wydawnictwo Edukacyjne "Akapit".

Kossewska, J. (2000). *Uwarunkowania postaw. Nauczyciele i inne grupy zawodowe wobec integracji szkolnej dzieci niepełnosprawnych* [Conditioning attitudes. Teachers and other professional groups in relation to the school integration disabled children]. Wydawnictwo Naukowe Akademii Pedagogicznej.

Kubicki, P. (2016). Między włączaniem a segregacją–szkoły w Polsce wobec uczniów z niepełnosprawnościami [Between Inclusion and Segregation – Schools in Poland in Relation to Students with Disabilities]. *Niepełnosprawność. Dyskursy Pedagogiki Specjalnej [Disability. Discources of Special Education], 22*, 107–118.

Lipińska-Lokś, J. (2015). Koleżeństwo i przyjaźń w doświadczeniach osób z niepełnosprawnością [Companionship and Friendship in the Experience of People with Disabilities]. *Niepełnosprawność. Dyskursy Pedagogiki Specjalnej [Disability. Discources of Special Education], 20*, 57–69.

Marcinkowska, B. (2012). Indywidualne programy edukacyjno-terapeutyczne [Individual Educational and Therapeutic Programs]. In: J. Głodkowska (ed.) *Dydaktyka specjalna w przygotowaniu do kształcenia uczniów ze specjalnymi potrzebami edukacyjnymi* [Special Education in the Preparation for the Education of Students with Special Educational Needs] (pp. 224–234). Wydawnictwo Akademii Pedagogiki Specjalnej.

Mikrut, A. (2019). Edukacja integracyjna czy włączająca? [integration or inclusive education?] O prawie do edukacji w kontekście interpretacji terminologii Konwencji o Prawach Osób Niepełnosprawnych [On the rights to education in the context of interpreting terminology found in the convention on the rights of persons with disabilities]. *Niepełnosprawność-zagadnienia, problemy, rozwiązania [Disability – issues, problems, solutions], 4*(33), 77–94.

Myśliwczyk, I. (2016). Inkluzja edukacyjna na etapie przedszkola w rozumieniu rodziców dzieci niepełnosprawnych [Educational inclusion at the preschool stage in the understanding of the parents of disabled children]. *Problemy Wczesnej Edukacji [Issues in Early Education], 2*(33), 166–180.

Nowak, A. (2020). Edukacja włączająca w opiniach i ocenach nauczycieli–doniesienia z badań [Inclusive education in the opinions and assessments of teachers – Research reports]. *Roczniki Pedgogiczne [Annals of Pedagogies], 35*, 169–181.

Oszwa, U., & Fedaczyńska, M. (2017). Postawy uczniów kl. III szkoły podstawowej wobec rówieśników z niepełnosprawnością ruchową i słuchową [The attitudes of third grade students towards their physically disabled and hearing impaired peers]. *Lubelski Rocznik Pedagogiczny [Lublin Pedagogical Yearbook], XXXVI*(3), 187–206.

Papuda-Dolińska, B. (2015). Satysfakcja z kontaktów rówieśniczych a pozycja socjometryczna uczniów z niepełnosprawnością wzroku w klasach ogólnodostępnych i integracyjnych [Satisfaction with peer relationships and the Sociometric position of visually impaired students in public school and integration classes]. *Interdyscyplinarne Konteksty Pedagogiki Specjalnej [Interdisciplinary Contexts of Special Pedagogy], 11*, 55–74.

Parys, K. (2007). Problemy integracji szkolnej w badaniach empirycznych – przegląd materiałów pokonferencyjnych [The problems of integration school in empirical studies – review of post-conference materials]. In: Z. Janiszewska-Nieścioruk. (ed.). *Problemy edukacji integracyjnej dzieci i młodzieży z niepełnosprawnością intelektualną* [The problems of integration education for children and youth with intellectual disabilities] (pp. 233–278). Oficyna Wydawnicza "Impuls".

Pauluk, D. (2021). Pandemia COVID-19 i (nie) wykorzystany potencjał edukacyjny [The COVID-19 pandemic and (un)used educational potential]. *Horyzonty Wychowania [Educational Horizons], 20*(53), 39–48.

Piechowska, M., & Romanowska, S. (2020). Proces edukacji w cyfrowej przestrzeni według nauczycieli i rodziców uczniów w dobie pandemii COVID-19 [The Process of Education in Digital Space According to Teachers and Parents of Students in the COVID-19 Pandemic Era]. *Com. press, 3*(2).

Przybyszewska, D. (2014). Rodzice uczniów kształcących się w klasach integracyjnych – ich motywy i oczekiwania [Parents of students educated in Intergration classes – Their motives and expectations]. *Interdyscyplinarne Konteksty Pedagogiki Specjalnej [Interdisciplinary Contexts of Special Pedagogy], 6*, 49–68.

Ptaszek, G., Stunża, G. D., Pyżalski, J., Dębski, M., & Bigaj, M. (2020). *Edukacja zdalna: co stało się z uczniami, ich rodzicami i nauczycielami* [Remote Education: what happened to students, their parents and teachers]. Gdańskie Wydawnictwo Psychologiczne Sp. z oo.

Pyżalski, J. (2020). *Edukacja w czasach pandemii wirusa COVID-19. Z dystansem o tym, co robimy obecnie jako nauczyciele* [Education in the COVID-19 pandemic era. With distance concerning what we currently do as teachers]. EduAkcja.

Rutkowski, M., & Bidziński, K. (2018). Szkoła ogólnodostępna przestrzenią spotkania nauczycieli i pedagogów specjalnych – realizatorów idei edukacji włączającej [Public school as a meeting space for teachers and special needs teachers – The implementors of the idea of inclusive education]. *Niepełnosprawność. Dyskursy Pedagogiki Specjalnej [Disability. Discources of Special Education], 29*, 43–65.

Rzeźnicka-Krupa, J. (2020). Konstruktywizm i pedagogika różnorodności w kontekście edukacji włączającej [Constructivism and educational diversity in the context of inclusive education]. *Problemy Wczesnej Edukacji [Issues in Early Education], 51*(4), 153–166.

Sadowska, S. (2016). Polityka oświatowa w rozwiązywaniu kwesti kształcenia uczniów z niepełnosprawnościami (1989–2016) [The educational policy in terms of resolving issues of educating students with disabilities (1989–2016)]. *Niepełnosprawność. Dyskursy Pedagogiki Specjalnej [Disability. Discources of Special Education], 22*, 13–36.

Skibska, J. (2016). Wymiary spostrzegania integracji i edukacji włączającej przez rodziców dzieci w młodszym wieku szkolnym uczących się w klasach integracyjnych. Komunikat z badań. [Dimensions of the perception of inclusive education by parents of children at early school age studying in inclusive classes. The report from the study.]. *Niepełnosprawność. Dyskursy Pedagogiki Specjalnej [Disability. Discources of Special Education], 23*, 146–159.

Szumski, G. (2010). *Wokół edukacji włączającej. Efekty kształcenia uczniów z niepełnosprawnością intelektualną w stopniu lekkim w klasach specjalnych, integracyjnych i ogólnodostępnych* [Inclusive Education. The Effects of Educating Students with Mild Intellectual Disabilities in Special Needs, Integration and Public School Classes]. Wydawnictwo APS.

Szumski, G. (2014). Edukacja włączająca – niedokończony projekt [Inclusive education – And unfinished project]. *Ruch Pedagogiczny, 4*, 127–139.

Szustkowska, M. (2020). Zdalne nauczanie uczniów z niepełnosprawnością [The distance learning of students with disabilities. *Student niepełnosprawny. Szkice i rozprawy* [Disabled Student. Sketches and Thesis], 20(13): 93–99.

Szymański, M. J. (2008). *W poszukiwaniu drogi: szanse i problemy edukacji w Polsce* [In search of ways: The opportunities and problems of education in Poland]. Wydawnictwo Naukowe Akademii Pedagogicznej.

Szymański, M. J., Walasek-Jarosz, B., & Zbróg, Z. (2016). Zrozumieć szkołę dla (jej) zmiany [Understanding Schools for (Their) Change]. *Zrozumieć szkołę. Kontekst zmiany* [Understanding Schools. Contexts of Change] (pp. 7–21).

Tersa, K. (2017). Zakorzenienie jako istotny warunek integracji szkolnej. [Rootedness as an Essential Condition for Integration Schools]. *Interdyscyplinarne Konteksty Pedagogiki Specjalnej [Interdisciplinary Contexts of Special Pedagogy], 16*, 63–78.

Trochimiak, B., & Gosk, U. (2012). Diagnoza pedagogiczna uczniów ze specjalnymi potrzebami edukacyjnymi [The educational diagnosis of special needs students]. In: J. Głodkowska (ed.) *Dydaktyka specjalna w przygotowaniu do kształcenia uczniów ze specjalnymi potrzebami edukacyjnymi* [Special Education in the Preparation for the Education of Students with Special Educational Needs]. Wydawnictwo Akademii Pedagogiki Specjalnej.

Wielebski, M. (2018). Od orzeczenia o potrzebie kształcenia specjalnego do indywidualnego programu edukacyjno-terapeutycznego [From a special need education statement to an individual educational and therapeutic program]. *Interdyscyplinarne Konteksty Pedagogiki Specjalnej [Interdisciplinary Contexts of Special Pedagogy], 22*, 339–354.

Winiarczyk, A., & Warzocha, T. (2021, July). Edukacja zdalna w czasach pandemii COVID-19 [Distance Learning in the COVID-19 Pandemic]. In *Forum Oświatowe* [Educational forum] (Vol. 33, No. 1 (65), pp. 61– 76). University of Lower Silesia.

Wojciechowska, J. (2020). Edukacja włączająca – horyzonty myślenia i działania w "szkole dla wszystkich" [Inclusive Education – horizons of thought and action in a "school for all"]. *Rocznik Pedagogiczny* [Pedagogical yearbook], *43*: 183–195.

Zahorska, M. (2009). Sukcesy i porażki reformy edukacji [The successes and failures of educational reforms]. *Przegląd Socjologiczny [Sociology Review]*, *58*(3), 119–142.

Joanna Głodkowska is a professor of social sciences. Fifteen years she was the director of the Institute of Special Pedagogy, head of the Department of Interdisciplinary Disability Studies at the Maria Grzegorzewska University. Since 2005 to 2020, she was the editor-in-chief of the scientific journal *Man*–Disability–Society (Człowiek–Niepełnosprawność–Społeczeństwo). She is the creator of cyclical conferences (since 2003) titled PERSON. She is the author of many books, articles in the field of special pedagogy and Disability Studies. In her publications, she undertakes multidimensional recognition of the phenomenon of disability in the context of interdisciplinarity, and in the perspective of well-being, subjectivity and optimal functioning. Her theoretical and empirical analysis cover issues of education and rehabilitation, implementation of the idea of normalization, construction of the paradigm of supporting people with disabilities. She developed the concept of the authorship of their own lives in people with disabilities (AOL–PwD), and currently undertakes tests to verification of this construct and to create a measurement tool. Theoretically and empirically, she expanded the academic area of special didactics, developing the first textbook in Poland and four subsequent monographs in this field . Since 2015 she has been creating Interdisciplinary Disability Studies at the Maria Grzegorzewska University.

Barbara Marcinkowska is a special educator, a habilitated Ph.D. in the humanities in the discipline of pedagogy, professor at Maria Grzegorzewska University, head of the Department of Education and Rehabilitation of People with Intellectual Disabilities. Currently she is the Rector of the University and the Chairperson of the Conference of Rectors of Pedagogical Universities in Poland. Since 2020, she is the editor-in-chief of the scientific journal *Man*–Disability–Society (Człowiek–Niepełnosprawność–Społeczeństwo). Since 1991 she has been involved in research in the field of special education, in particular rehabilitation and education of people with moderate, severe and profound intellectual disabilities. Her research and publishing activities focus on the recognition of abilities and limitations of people with profound intellectual disabilities and people with multiple disabilities; communication competences of people with profound intellectual disabilities; and supporting teachers in fulfilling tasks resulting from the education of students with disabilities in integrated and mainstream institutions. She has coordinated projects related to teacher preparation for teaching children with special educational needs. She is the author of many scientific and popular studies, including a model of communicative competence of people with moderate, severe and profound intellectual disabilities.

Emilia Wojdyła is PhD in social sciences in the discipline of pedagogy, expert in inclusive education, speaker at many conferences and seminars devoted to inclusion in education and educating students with special educational needs. Co-author of the new concept of educating students with disabilities in mainstream schools adopted in 2010. Author / co-author of articles and studies on special educational needs of students, author of training programs. Associate of universities and teacher training institutions. Provider of trainings for teachers. Associate of non-governmental organizations dealing with disability issues. Author and implementer of projects co-financed by the European Union related to the individualization of work and social exclusion.

Chapter 3
Inclusion of Economically Deprived Secondary School Children in Virtual-Based Learning During COVID-19 in Malawi

Louis Okon Akpan and Omolara Joy Oluwatuyi-Akpan

Abstract Coronavirus disease (COVID-19) has brought untold hardship to the entire world. In recent times, people rarely move from one part of the world to the other. In the area of education, all institutions of learning in Malawi, which is the study focus, were closed. After much pressure from the stakeholders to reopen schools, the government announced the commencement of virtual-based learning for all children in the country. Based on the above, the study examined the inclusion of economically deprived secondary school children in virtual-based learning. Qualitative approach was adopted to tease the phenomenon under investigation. Furthermore, interpretive paradigm was used as a lens to have an in-depth understanding of the participants' narratives. Ten participants were purposively selected from the population. All ethical issues were adhered to. Narrative analysis was used to tell the story as reported verbatim by the participants. Findings indicated that due to years of neglect and marginalisation of economically deprived rural school children, their inclusion in virtual-based learning was received with apprehension. Additionally, these children were in the state of melancholy and anxiety due to the fact that the newly introduced technology was too complex to access.

Keywords Coronavirus disease (COVID-19) · Economically deprived secondary school children · Inclusion · Malawi · Virtual-based learning

---

L. O. Akpan (✉)
Department of Educational Foundations, National Open University of Nigeria, Abuja, Nigeria

O. J. Oluwatuyi-Akpan
School of Social Justice Education, University of KwaZulu-Natal,
Berea, Durban, South Africa

© The Author(s), under exclusive license to Springer Nature Switzerland AG 2022
L. Meda, J. Chitiyo (eds.), *Inclusive Pedagogical Practices Amidst a Global Pandemic*, Inclusive Learning and Educational Equity 7,
https://doi.org/10.1007/978-3-031-10642-2_3

Introduction

Coronavirus disease (COVID-19) has brought untold hardship to the entire world. In recent times, people rarely move from one part of the world to the other. In fact, there is a complete restriction of movement of people and goods around the world. Frankly speaking, economic, political, religious, educational and other social activities have been brought to a complete halt during the outbreak of the disease. In the area of education, which is the focus of this study, all institutions of learning the world over were closed, thereby sending billions of learners back home. UNESCO (2020) says that over 2.8 billion school children in the world were placed out of school as a result of the closure of schools. Furthermore, it was reported that half of the population of school children stated above were left on the streets (UNESCO, 2020). Miller and Blumstein (2020) added that because of the presence of school children on the streets, the world has witnessed a surge in criminal activities. The implication of this surge in criminal activities around the world is that various prisons around the world have witnessed an astronomical increase of inmates who were school children before the outbreak of the pandemic (Simpson & Butler, 2020).

In Malawi, which is the research site of this study, in March, 2020 the government directed the closure of all schools and universities for months as a precaution against COVID-19 spread. The closure of institutions of learning received a backlash from the generality of Malawians. They threatened to demonstrate on the streets if the central government does not reverse the order. The reason many Malawians advanced for closure of schools was because it promoted social vices. For instance, Kaponda (2020) says that within five months of schools closure, teenage pregnancies had increased by about twenty-two percent. Similarly, Kaponda (2020) went further to say that trafficking in minors, armed robbery and street violence were increased by thirty-eight percent. Additionally, a Non-Governmental Organisation (NGO) called Malawi Network Against Trafficking Organisation (M-NAT) in her report stated that the lockdown declared by government had empowered human traffickers to engage vulnerable children in their trade. Therefore, they mounted pressure on the government to direct the re-opening of all institutions of learning in the country. Based on this agitation, the Malawian president then, President Peter Mutharika, ordered the resumption of academic activities in all institutions of learning in the country. To ensure adherence to the COVID-19 protocols, there was a directive issued by the president that on resumption, all institutions of learning should be provided with toilet facilities, hand sanitisers and running water. It was also instructed that schools which are unable to provide these amenities should introduce virtual-based learning. In line with the presidential directive, virtual-based learning was introduced in some schools which were unable to provide those essential amenities. It was observed that schools that were unable to provide that COVID-19 safety protocols were located in rural areas and mostly dominated by economically deprived children. From all indications, this was the first time economically deprived children in rural schools received lesson virtually in Malawi. Big questions begging answers are: How did economically deprived school children in rural areas receive their inclusion in virtual-based learning? What challenges did economically deprived secondary school children face during virtual-based learning?

Purpose of the Study

In Malawi, the first wave of COVID-19 pandemic compelled all secondary school children to remain at home. However, on resumption of schools as directed by the president, virtual-based learning was introduced in rural schools that were dominated by economically deprived children. In light of the above, study investigated the inclusion of economically deprived secondary school children in virtual-based learning during the first wave of COVID-19 in Malawi.

Theoretical Framework Underpinning the Study

From all indications, the theoretical framework which anchored the study is called vulnerability theory developed by Martha Fineman. In this theory, Fineman (2005) says that vulnerability is essential to the human condition, and that the government has the responsibility to respond positively to that vulnerability by making sure that everyone has unlimited equal access to the societal institutions that allot resources (Fineman, 2019). In other words, it is Fineman's (2010) position that in order to meet its obligation to human vulnerability, the government must provide the same access to the societal bodies that allocate social goods such as healthcare, employment, and security. According to Kohn (2014, p.3), "the theory provides an alternative basis for defining the role of government and the justification for expansive social welfare policies." Actually, the theory afforded useful framework to understand social responsibility and the role that will be played by the government. In recent times, this theory has been gaining wide recognition among scholars, particularly in education. For instance, Knowles (2014) used vulnerability theory as a lens to transform knowledge frames, norms and knowledge concerning teaching and learning in the classroom. Similarly, Curtis (2014) applied the theory to examine the sense of emotional vulnerability felt by student nurses which leads to a disengagement from compassion. In light of the above, we believe it is appropriate to adopt vulnerability theory to investigate the inclusion of economically deprived secondary school children in virtual-based learning during COVID-19 in Malawi.

Literature Review

Who Are the Vulnerable Children?

COVID-19 offers an unprecedented challenge for children to learn. According to UNICEF (2020), over two billion children the world over had been affected by their inability to physically attend classes every day. Out of this number, only one third of the figures were able to virtually attend lessons at home, whereas others were left to seek for alternative sources of livelihood during the COVID-19 (UNICEF, 2020). For vulnerable Malawian school children in which this study is focused, there are several challenges they encountered when they study at home. Before we focus on these challenges, it is pertinent to explain who this vulnerable child is. Vulnerability is one of the concepts we confidently, but carelessly assume that we know the meaning. In fact, this concept means different thing to different people. For instance, New Oxford Dictionary (2020) looks at vulnerability from the context of susceptibility to something. From the community perspective, vulnerability means a child who lives on the streets or sexually exploited (Smart, 2003). In another vein, using Australian case to explain vulnerability of children, Hattie (2020, p.12) stated that "students who come from well-resourced families are far much better academically than those from lower resourced families." Here, it is absolutely wrong to treat all school children as vulnerable because those children who are particularly vulnerable do not get the support they needed. Therefore, it is proper to conclude that vulnerability is a dynamic characteristic of a particular child, in which it changes as the circumstances evolve (Te Riele, 2015). Also, it is widely acknowledged that vulnerability is associated with a diverse range of factors, in which time and space does not allow for adequate explanation. A Centre on Child Protection and Wellbeing in Indonesia which is popularly called PUSKAPA opined that vulnerability may be conceptualised as:

> a condition that is disproportionately experienced by children due to a lack of access as a result of poverty, remoteness, mobility limitations, lack of responsiveness of public services, and exclusion based on age, disabilities, and social identities such as gender, religion, ethnicity, and sexuality (PUSKAPA, 2019, p.14).

From the meanings given above, it is appropriate to say that one is vulnerable, when he/she is prone to attack, harm, exploitation, molestation and helplessness with no caregiver to look after him/her. Based on the above narrative and within the confines of the study, we look at a vulnerable child as an orphan following the parental death or shock which jeopardises his/her health and well-being. In fact, in this study Malawian school children were vulnerable because they were not able to have equal access to essential and adequate instructional aids before the outbreak of the first wave of the pandemic.

Challenges Faced by Vulnerable Children During COVID-19

In Malawi, vulnerable school children face a lot of challenges. For instance, many children's physical health has been compromised by COVID-19. Sutton (2020) held that the health of children with inherent issues such as AIDS and chronic cough worsened during the COVID-19 pandemic. COVID-19 does not affect children's health as severely as it does in adults. Roberts et al. (2019) aver that vulnerable children who rely solely on school feeding programme for nutrition for livelihood are made to go hungry and malnourished during the pandemic. Aside from hunger and malnourishment, World Bank (2020) asserted that school closure during the COVID-19 also affect deworming exercise in many low and middle-income countries in Africa.

In the area of digital inclusion, Thomas et al. (2019) opined that it is based on the ground that every person irrespective of who one is and the circumstances of his/her birth has access to, and use of, communication technologies. Non-acquisition of digital skills and access has a negative impact on learning (Chandra et al., 2020). Voorst and Jorgen (2015) asserted that vulnerable children experience serious challenges in online technology. From all indications, this is because of uneven digital landscapes which thwart children from low-income background, and the ones living in rural and deep informal settlements from accessing the Internet and related virtual spaces (Beltsazar, 2020). It is appropriate to say that online services come at a cost, which includes ownership of devices such as laptop or desktop, and airtime subscription to energise the Internet in which vulnerable children do not have financial muscles to purchase them. Again, most vulnerable children do not have the proficiency to access the virtual world productively due to its strangeness and complexity (Drane et al., 2020). In other words, due to the fact that virtual-based learning is a new innovation introduced as a result of COVID-19 pandemic, vulnerable children do not possess the necessary skills to manipulate it. This assertion was supported by Lestiyanawati and Widyantoro (2020) who aver that vulnerable children who were not from well-off family experienced difficulty in navigating Internet sites properly.

Research Methodology

The nature of the study under investigation and research questions developed which bordered on examination of the phenomenon in its natural setting necessitated the adoption of a qualitative research method. In fact, it is appropriate to say that a qualitative approach search for answers from the natural social context, instead of isolating the subject of research study (Aseery, 2020). Flick (2014) held that a qualitative method is multi-methods in focus which involve interpretive and naturalistic approaches to its subject matter. Furthermore, it is our intention to make sense from the narratives of economically deprived children from rural secondary schools.

Therefore, based on the above assertion, we adopted an interpretive paradigm. Rahman (2020) submitted that an interpretive paradigm has the ability to understand different people's voices, meanings and events.

Case Study Approach

The study is a case study in nature. According to Jabbarova (2020), case study is an empirical research method used to examine a contemporary phenomenon which focuses on the dynamics of the case within its real-life context. In this study, however, all the selected secondary schools and economically deprived rural children in Malawi now become our case. The choice of a 'case study' is to generate an in-depth and multi-faceted understanding, and also make sense of our participants' complex narratives which were used to contextualise our research findings.

Research Site

The site for the study is located in Nsanje, Malawi. Generally, Malawi is a small country in Southern Africa. Nsanje is in the southernmost district of Malawi. This district lies in the Lower Shire River Valley. Nsanje is one of the poorest districts in Malawi. Due to poverty, girl children are forced into early marriage by their parents (Omoeva & Hatch, 2020). In fact, our personal efforts to establish the number of secondary schools were fruitless due to poor recordkeeping by the Ministry of Education. However, our observation revealed that there were about twenty-two secondary schools in Nsanje district. Most of these schools are located in deep rural areas where there is absence of electricity, pipe borne water and good roads. Out of these twenty-two schools seen, we selected six secondary schools based on their proximity. For the sake of ethical issue adherence, we would not mention the actual names of the schools selected. Chikhungu et al. (2020) reported that the student-teacher ratio in secondary schools in Nsanje district stands at 42:1 in 2019.

Sampling Technique and Size

The sampling technique used for the study was purposive. According to Handayani et al. (2020), purposive sampling is a non-probability sample that is based on characteristics of a population. Drawing from Handayani et al. (2020) and within the context of Malawi, economically deprived children have little or no guidance, live in rural area with little or no social amenities, no hope of having a square meal in a day, do not have basic education materials while in school and always look unclean. It was based on these characteristics that we decided to use purposive sampling in the selection of our participants for the study. We chose economically deprived children in rural schools that were involved in virtual-based learning during COVID-19 pandemic. Campbell et al. (2020) held that in a qualitative approach, it is appropriate to have a small sample size in order to have an in-depth understanding and interpretation of participants' narratives. Based on the above, we selected twelve participants from six secondary schools in Malawi.

Ethical Issues and Instrument Administration

Since the study bordered on economically deprived secondary school children, therefore, the issue of ethics is paramount. First and foremost, we applied for permission from the Ministry of Education to conduct interviews with economically deprived secondary school children. In the letter, we stated that the confidentiality of our participants would be upheld. For confidentiality, the real names of the participants were replaced with pseudonyms such as Chiponda, Azibo, Catha, Kafele, Mapira and Mbizi. Others are Ndembo, Thandizo, Zondiwe, Lisimba, Malawa and Fukala. Furthermore, we also assured the officials in the Ministry that no harm shall befall any of the participants. We also stated that cameras would not be used so as to hide the identities of the participants. Similar letters were written to the principals of the schools and parents of the children who volunteered to take-part in the study. It gladdened our hearts to report that positive responses were received from the Ministry of Education, principals and the parents. Before the actual commencement of the interviews, we developed a Consent Form (CF) for the participants to endorse their willingness to take-part in the study.

Data Collection Instrument

In qualitative study, semi-structured interviews are often used (Whiting, 2008). As if this was not enough, DeJonckheere and Vaughn (2019) stated that the main purpose of using semi-structured interviews for data collection in a qualitative study is to gather information from key participants who have personal and undiluted experiences, attitudes, perceptions and beliefs related to the topic under investigation. Based on this assertion, a semi-structured interview which directly addressed the research questions stated earlier was designed. Moreover, it is appropriate to state that the instrument (eighteen interview questions) was used to elicit information from each participant.

As good researchers, we carried audio recorders and field notes to the field. Cremin et al. (2021) stated that though audio recorders and field notes are most economical in terms of time and money, they are very important because ideas and memories from the interviews are sustained for a long time. The interview with each participant was conducted after school hours to create room for participant's concentration. During the interview, we spent about two hours with each participant. Again, since we did not get any sponsor for the study, we tried to curtail our expenditure by spending only two weeks in the field. Furthermore, due to the fact that we delayed our participants from leaving for home after school hours with other students, we often made arrangements for a motorcycle to drop off each participant at home after the interview.

Since we used an audio recorder to elicit information from our participants, laptop was used to download the information. The downloaded information on the laptop was repeatedly listened to for clarity and understanding. We began the transcription of information into textual form. The entire transcription took us eight days to complete. After the transcription, we were compelled to meet the participants again to look at the information they volunteered to determine its exactness and accuracy. Aside from that, we did this trustworthiness for establishment of objectivity, reliability, dependability and conformability of the data (Easton et al., 2000; Stuckey, 2014). The transcribed data was further subjected to coding for the emergence of themes. We adopted coding because it enables us to acquire deep, comprehensive and thorough insights into our own data for the study (Saldaña, 2015; Younas et al., 2020). With the emergence of themes, narrative analysis was used to tell the story as reported verbatim by the participants.

Results and Discussion

In this section, we state beforehand that the discussion of findings follows immediately after data presentation. We did this in order to ensure that our audience religiously followed our argument on the subject under investigation.

Research Question 1 How did economically deprived school children in rural areas receive their inclusion in virtual-based learning?

Our Inclusion in Virtual-Based Learning Was Unexpected

From all indications, the outbreak of COVID-19 pandemic instead of being a 'curse' to economically deprived school children in rural areas of Malawi, became a blessing to them. One of the participants declared that it is a blessing because during this period new technological innovations have been integrated into the teaching and learning process. In fact, Mbizi reported that before the outbreak of the pandemic, she was very comfortable with the conventional face-to-face method of teaching. She went on to say that teachers and learners usually converged in the classroom for lessons using chalkboards as instructional material. However, she continued "in recent times, technology has been introduced into the teaching and learning process, and this was not expected, especially from us" (economically deprived rural school children, here, our words). Furthermore, Chiponda stated that he was surprised to receive a brand-new laptop from the government during COVID-19 for online learning. He continued that all his lessons are held virtually. He mentioned subjects in which he enjoyed learning online such as history, civil education, mathematics and English language. He, therefore, expressed his gratitude to the government for the good gesture it extended to all economically deprived rural school children in the country.

In a similar vein, Catha and Thandizo informed us that they did not expect the government to provide them with laptops for online learning during the pandemic. As interrogators, we were confused and disturbed over Catha and Thandizo's submission, we therefore asked them why they did not expect this good gesture from their government. In response, Thandizo declared:

> Since I was born, I have not received or enjoyed any social welfare from the government. Before now, the government concentrated the provision of social welfare in towns, and cities. Children whose parents are economically sound were the ones who benefited from them. In fact, when I collected the laptop during the outbreak of COVID-19 from the government, I was so surprised because I did not expect it (Interviewed alongside Thandizo, 2021).

Aside from Thandizo's view, Catha further informed us that the distribution of laptops to all economically deprived school children in rural areas was the best thing to ever happen to them. She wondered why the government should be so magnanimous during COVID-19 pandemic. Whereas before the outbreak of the pandemic, we were completely neglected and marginalised in the provision of instructional materials such as laptops and internet service. One of the interrogators therefore asked the participant whether internet service was also provided to them by the government during the pandemic. Catha responded:

> Yes, of course, we were provided with internet service for our laptops. Every Sunday, the government ensured that every child was given one hundred Kwacha worth of data for the week (interviewed alongside Catha, 2021).

Different narratives presented above indicated that economically deprived rural school children received their inclusion in virtual learning exercises by the Malawian government as unexpected. Participants' unexpectancy for their inclusion in the virtual learning process was based on the fact that before now (COVID-19 outbreak), they were usually subjected to all manners of marginalisation by the government. However, they were surprised to see the same government being generous enough to include them in virtual learning during the outbreak of the pandemic. From the interpretive point of view, it is obvious that the children knew that they were neglected and marginalised on the provision of social welfare. Moreover, they cannot receive any tangible amenities as citizens of Malawi from the central government based on their vulnerability. Therefore, their inclusion in virtual learning exercises during the economically strained period occasioned by COVID-19 was seen as unexpected and surprising. Though, through our extensive search in their literature, we discovered that there is little or no scholar to support or refute the findings. However, the World Bank Report (2020) held that the outbreak of COVID-19 has improved the less privileged children's accessibility to virtual learning in recent times, hence they are comfortable with the government for introducing this new technological innovation.

Inclusion In Virtual-Based Learning Was a Huge Shock

From the analysis, the inclusion of economically deprived rural school children in virtual-based learning in Malawi was a huge shock to the majority of our participants. Particularly, Ndembo, Lisimba and Fukala reported that since their births about 15, 17 and 18 years ago respectively, they had not felt the government's presence in their communities. They stated that most social amenities provided by the government were usually executed in the cities. Specifically, Lisimba indicated that before now, rural schools were neglected in the area of provision of relevant instructional materials. He cited his school as an example, where relatively old instructional materials such as chalkboards, bottle caps and counting sticks were used for teaching and learning. He therefore concluded that the provision of computers and other modern equipment to rural children for virtual learning during the COVID-19 is a huge shock to him. In contrast, Malawa reported that she did not see their inclusion in virtual-based learning as 'extraordinarily done' by the government. When asked what she meant, Malawa declared:

> Government's responsibility to its citizens is to provide them with all the necessary social amenities for their good habitation. Rather, what we see in Malawi is the reverse. Government provision of computer and internet services for their inclusion in virtual-based learning exercises during COVID-19 was aimed at scoring cheap political points in the eyes of international communities. Therefore, it is not a shock to me (interviewed alongside Malawa, 2021).

From all indications, Chiponda totally agreed with Malawa when he said that the government may want the World Health Organisation (WHO) and other international organisations to see her as a caring government whose citizens' welfare is of paramount importance to her. Further, Chiponda reported that the government's good gesture during this COVID-19 period might be as a result of billions of dollars COVID-19 palliative received from the international organisations therefore, they may want to justify her spending, hence their inclusion in virtual-based learning.

The excerpts explained the position held by participants that their inclusion in virtual-based learning by the Malawian government was a huge shock. The government attitude towards economically deprived rural school children before the pandemic was negative. In fact, the children were made to use absolute instructional materials during lessons. But with the outbreak of COVID-19, the situation appeared to change for the better. For the first time in history, rural children were incorporated into virtual learning, and it was shocking to the majority of Malawians. However, some of these children still believed that this good gesture by the government was executed to earn cheap political points and justified their huge spending of billions of dollars given by international organisations. In spite of this disdainful assertion, it was generally agreed that the inclusion of economically deprived rural school children in virtual learning was a shock because it was unanticipated by the government.

Research Question 2 What challenges did economically deprived secondary school children face during virtual-based learning?

Non-availability of Electricity

In Malawi, some participants made us understand that only 18% of the entire population has electricity and the remaining 82% are without power. One of the participants (Thandizo) said that the major challenge she faced during virtual learning on a daily basis was the issue of energising her digital device. She reported that she is from a deep rural village where electricity is non-existent. According to Thandizo, she had not seen electricity since she was born, therefore, to power her digital devices for virtual learning was out of context. Thandizo was interrogated on how she participated in virtual facilitation by her educator(s) when there was no electricity. In response, she declared; "Though I come from a low economic family, my father was able to buy a power generating set which supplies electricity to our house. I use this generator to power my laptop each time I want to connect to the Internet for virtual learning." In a similar vein, Azibo and Catha held that though there is no electricity in the village which made digital devices and internet connectivity impossible, their parents were able to acquire solar power which generates electricity to their homes. Azibo concluded thus; "it was this solar power we used in powering our system for virtual learning." Notwithstanding Thandizo's position, Mapira was of the view that though she used a generator set to power her home, it was very expensive to maintain. She narrated how her parents spent the sum of three hundred Kwacha which is almost seventeen dollars to buy petrol (fuel) to run the generator on a daily basis. She concluded by saying that the amount of money spent on fuel is high considering her low socio-economic background.

Findings actually indicated that all economically deprived rural school children who engaged in virtual-based learning faced electricity challenges. Some of the participants interviewed reported that they had not seen electricity in their villages since birth. Based on that, the possibility of powering their digital devices for virtual learning was completely out of reach. However, some of the participants who had the same electricity challenge were able to either acquire generating sets or solar power systems, though they complained of the high cost of petrol to run their power generating sets. Supporting this finding, Ivala (2013) said that lack of electricity in rural communities makes it difficult to join the virtual learning process. Similarly, Adarkwah (2021) asserted that the limited amount of electric supply for virtual learning exercise had compelled children to use affordable solutions such as solar power gadgets which are readily accessible in Africa.

Inability to Access Computer Service

Zondiwe's interrogation revealed that before the outbreak of COVID-19, she did not have computer skills at all and that all lessons in the class were traditionally taught. We (interviewers) were surprised with the use of the concept 'traditionally taught,' hence we asked what she referred to as 'traditionally taught.' Zondiwe responded thus; "What I mean by 'traditionally taught' is that our educators used old instructional materials such as chalkboard and chalk to teach in the class." She went further to say that assignments given to her were done manually and submitted in hard copies. Similarly, Azibo averred that he came in contact with digital devices such as laptops during COVID-19. According to Azibo, the first week the laptop was given to him, he was completely ignorant on how to operate it. On the basis of this ignorance, he missed some virtual facilitation which he considered very important. In sharp contrast, Catha and Kafele informed us that though they come from deep rural areas, they were not completely ignorant in the use of computers. They have a fair skill on the use of laptops. We, therefore, questioned them how they got the computer skills, Catha replied:

> Yes, I used to visit my uncle in the city (Lilongwe). In his house, he has bought laptops for his children in which I used the opportunity to learn simple computer programming. Frankly speaking, I have good knowledge and skills in computer application (interviewed alongside Catha, 2021).

In a similar vein, Kafele responded:

> I was familiar with word processing and other minor applications, because when I was in the city for two years, my aunt made me go for computer training for six months. Though the period for the training was short, I was able to learn basic computer applications (interviewed alongside Kafele, 2021).

Findings indicated that the majority of the participants lack basic computer application skills due to the rurality of the communities they come from. Zondiwe, Azibo, among others were so blunt to accept that they were novices in handling laptops, therefore, missing or joining the virtual facilitation late was very common. Though Catha and Kafele agreed that they had a fair knowledge in computer programming, it was not enough to guarantee effective virtual learning without assistance. From the above discourse, the obvious challenge was that economically deprived rural school children did not possess adequate levels of proficiency in technological skills for virtual-based learning. Thompson (2013) and Wang et al. (2014) had earlier affirmed that economically deprived learners did not have high levels of self-confidence to use a digital platform for virtual learning or did not have the basic computer skills for virtual-based learning. Apparently, that may be the reason why Perrotta (2013) submitted that those children who can selectively access and assess technology content, that is, to use technology critically are more likely to be those from more materially resourced families.

Conclusion

Apparently, the hitherto marginalised children in Malawi were subjected to all kinds of deprivation particularly in the area of education. However, the outbreak of COVID-19 had turned out to be a blessing in disguise in the sense that the government had introduced virtual classes for this group of children. However, the government's good gesture was received by economically deprived rural secondary school children with apprehension due to years of neglect and marginalisation. The inclusion of these children in virtual-based learning did not go without various challenges. In fact, due to the deep rurality where these children come from, electricity to power their digital devices such as laptops was a serious issue. Similarly, most of the children were in a state of melancholy and anxiety due to the fact that the newly introduced technology was too complex to access.

References

Adarkwah, M. A. (2021). "I'm not against online teaching, but what about us?" ICT in Ghana post COVID-19. *Education and Information Technologies, 26*(2), 1665–1685.

Aseery, A. Y. F. (2020). *A qualitative approach to explore teaching methods used to teach religious courses in Saudi Arabia*. Doctoral dissertation, Ohio University.

Beltsazar, K. (2020). *COVID-19 exposes vulnerabilities in our cyberspace*. DMRU-010. CSIS Commentaries. Center for Strategic and International Studies.

Campbell, S., Greenwood, M., Prior, S., Shearer, T., Walkem, K., Young, S., & Walker, K. (2020). Purposive sampling: Complex or simple? Research case examples. *Journal of Research in Nursing, 25*(8), 652–661.

Chandra, S., Chang, A., Day, L., Fazlullah, A., Liu, J., & McBride, L. (2020). *Closing the K–12 digital divide in the age of distance learning*. Common Sense Media, Boston Consulting Group.

Chikhungu, L., Kadzamira, E., Chiwaula, L., & Meke, E. (2020). Tackling girls dropping out of school in Malawi: Is improving household socio-economic status the solution? *International Journal of Educational Research, 103*, 101578.

Cremin, H., Aryoubi, H., Hajir, B., Kurian, N., & Salem, H. (2021). Post-abyssal ethics in education research in settings of conflict and crisis: Stories from the field. *British Educational Research Journal, 2*(1), 25–36.

Curtis, K. (2014). Learning the requirements for compassionate practice: Student vulnerability and courage. *Nursing Ethics, 21*(2), 210–223.

DeJonckheere, M., & Vaughn, L. M. (2019). Semi-structured interviewing in primary care research: A balance of relationship and rigour. *Medical and Community Health Journal, 7*(2), 41–55.

Drane, C. F., Vernon, L., & O'Shea, S. (2020). *Vulnerable learners in the age of COVID-19: A scoping review*. The Australian Educational Researcher. Retrieved from https://doi.org/10.1007/s13384-020-00409-5

Easton, K. L., McComish, J. F., & Greenberg, R. (2000). Avoiding common pitfalls in qualitative data collection and transcription. *Qualitative Health Research, 10*, 703–707.

Fineman, M. A. (2005). Gender and law: Feminist legal theory's role in new legal realism. *Wisconsin Language Review, 4*(2), 405–415.

Fineman, M. A. (2010). The vulnerable subject and the responsive stat. *Language Journal, 1*(2), 251–257.

Fineman, M. A. (2019). Vulnerability and social justice. *Valparaiso University Law Review, 53*(2), 341–370.

Flick, U. (2014). *An introduction to qualitative research* (5th ed.). Sage Publications Ltd..

Handayani, S., Youlia, L., Febriani, R. B., & Syafryadin, S. (2020). The use of digital literature in teaching reading narrative text. *Journal Of English Teaching, Applied Linguistics And Literatures (JETALL), 3*(2), 65–74.

Hattie, J. (2020). *The new normal of learning: Build Back Better*.

Ivala, E. (2013). ICEL2013-proceedings of the 8th international conference on e-learning: ICEL 2013. Academic Conferences Limited.

Jabbarova, A. (2020). The role of case study technology in teaching English classes. *Архив Научных Публикаций JSPI*, 1–4.

Kaponda, C. (2020). School re-openings in Malawi face challenges with a lack of financial support. *Africa at LSE, 1*(2), 25–38.

Knowles, C. (2014). Vulnerability: Self-study's contribution to social justice education. *Perspectives in Education, 32*(2), 89–101.

Kohn, N. A. (2014). Vulnerability theory and the role of government. *Yale Journal of Language & Feminism, 26*(1), 3–10.

Lestiyanawati, R., & Widyantoro, A. (2020). Strategies and problems faced by Indonesian teachers in conducting e-learning system during COVID-19 outbreak. *Journal of Culture, Literature, Linguistics and English Teaching, 2*(1), 71–82.

Miller, J. M., & Blumstein, A. (2020). Crime, justice and the COVID-19 pandemic: Towards a national research agenda. *American Journal of Criminal Justice, 45*(4), 515–524.

New Oxford dictionary. (2020). *English advanced dictionary*. Oxford University Press.

Omoeva, C., & Hatch, R. (2020). Teenaged, married, and out of school: Effects of early marriage and childbirth on school exit in Eastern Africa. *Prospects*, 1–26.

Perrotta, C. (2013). Do school-level factors influence the educational benefits of digital technology? A critical analysis of teachers' perceptions. *British Journal of Educational Technology, 44*(2), 314–327.

PUSKAPA. (2019). *Theory of change and program logic (internal document)*. PUSKAPA.

Rahman, M. S. (2020). *The advantages and disadvantages of using qualitative and quantitative approaches and methods in language "testing and assessment" research: A literature review*.

Roberts, M., Federico, S., & Sailesh, T. (Eds.). (2019). *Time to act: Realising Indonesia's urban potential*. World Bank.

Saldaña, J. (2015). *The coding manual for qualitative researchers*. Sage.

Simpson, P. L., & Butler, T. G. (2020). COVID-19, prison crowding, and release policies. *British Medical Journal, 369*, 1551.

Smart, R.A. (2003). The policies of orphans and vulnerable children: A framework for moving abroad. .

Stuckey, H. L. (2014). The first step in data analysis: Transcribing and managing qualitative research data. *Journal of Social Health and Diabetes, 2*(1), 6–15.

Sutton, T. (2020). *COVID-19 impacts: school shutdown*. Retrieved on from https://www.suttontrust.com/ourresearch/COVID-19-and-social-mobility-impact-brief/.

Te Riele, K. (2015). Conundrums for youth policy and practice. In K. Te Riele & R. Gorur (Eds.), *Interrogating conceptions of "vulnerable youth" in theory, policy and practical sense* (pp. 17–32). Sage.

Thomas, J., Barraket, J., Wilson, C. K., Rennie, E., Ewing, S., & MacDonald, T. (2019). *Measuring Australia's digital divide: The Australian digital inclusion index 2019*. RMIT University and Swinburne University of Technology, for Telstra.

Thompson, P. (2013). The digital natives as learners: Technology use patterns and approaches to learning. *Computers & Education, 65*, 12–33.

UNESCO (2020). *International day of education*: Learning for people, planet, prosperity and peace. UN Headquarters-Room IV. Retrieved from https://unesdoc.unesco.org/

UNICEF. (2020). *Internet of good things*. Retrieved from www.unicef.org/innovation/IoGT.

Voorst, R., & Jörgen, H. (2015). One risk replaces another: Floods, evictions and policies on Jakarta's Riverbanks. *Asian Journal of Social Science, 43*(6), 786–810.

Wang, S. K., Hsu, H. Y., Campbell, T., Coster, D., & Longhurst, M. (2014). An investigation of middle school science teachers and students use of technology inside and outside of classrooms: Considering whether digital natives are more technology savvy than their teachers. *Educational Technology Research and Development, 62*(6), 637–662.

Whiting, L. S. (2008). Semi-structured interviews: Guidance for novice researchers. *Nursing Stand, 22*(1), 35–40.

World Bank. (2020). *World bank education and COVID-19*. Retrieved from. https://www.worldbank.org/en/data/interactive.

World Bank Report. (2020). *Guidance note on remote learning and COVID-19*. Retrieved from http://documents.worldbank.org/curated/en/531681585957264427/pdf/.

Younas, M., Afzaal, M., Noor, U., Khalid, S., & Naqvi, S. (2020). Code switching in ESL teaching at university level in Pakistan. *English Language Teaching, 13*(8), 63–73.

Louis Okon Akpan is from the Niger Delta region of Nigeria. He is a seasoned scholar with five degrees in climatology, governance and leadership, and international and comparative education. His area of interests are international education, marginalised children's education and gender and sexuality studies. As a specialist in international and comparative education, he is widely travelled. Similarly, his numerous scholarly papers are in some renowned journals of the world. Aside from that, he attended both national and international conferences. A good hockey player and loves watching football.

Omolara Joy Oluwatuyi-Akpan is a young researcher from South West of Nigeria. She began her academic journey from Ambrose Alli University in Edo state, Nigeria. Currently, she is a doctoral student at University of KwaZulu-Natal, South Africa. Her area of research is in social justice education. She has attended both national and international conference. She likes watching films.

Chapter 4
Inclusion and the Right to Education in Latin America and the Caribbean: Policies, Resources, and Good Practice in the COVID-19 Social and Educational Emergency

Andres Paya Rico

Abstract The complex and fragile situation in which various policies have been implemented at the national and supranational levels to achieve inclusive quality education in the Latin American and Caribbean region has become even more complicated in the face of the sanitary, social, and educational emergency caused by COVID-19. The pandemic's impact on fragile education systems is devastating, as the closure of schools has consequences extending beyond pedagogy. The digital divide and difficulties in developing distance education have put various countries in the region to the test. With great effort and scarce resources, they are implementing a variety of solutions to compensate for this situation. This study analyses the various educational policies, good practice, and resources that the countries (Anguilla, Antigua and Barbuda, Argentina, Aruba, Bahamas, Barbados, Belize, Bolivia, Brazil, Chile, Colombia, Costa Rica, Cuba, Curaçao, Dominica, Ecuador, El Salvador, Grenada, Guatemala, British Virgin Islands, Guyana, Haiti, Honduras, Cayman Islands, Jamaica, Mexico, Montserrat, Nicaragua, Panama, Paraguay, Peru, Dominican Republic, Saint Martin, Saint Vincent and the Grenadines, Saint Lucia, Suriname, Trinidad and Tobago, Uruguay, and Venezuela) have implemented in consultation with international institutions. With the horizon of the 2030 Agenda SDGs, our study provides a global, holistic, and comprehensive view of the region, with a focus on key elements such as: distance learning, educational activities and curriculum, teachers, families, gender and education, external platforms, mental health and psychosocial support, among others. The study is based on the methodology of international comparative education, with qualitative analysis of national and

A. Paya Rico (✉)
University of Valencia, Valencia, Spain
e-mail: andres.paya@uv.es

© The Author(s), under exclusive license to Springer Nature Switzerland AG 2022
L. Meda, J. Chitiyo (eds.), *Inclusive Pedagogical Practices Amidst a Global Pandemic*, Inclusive Learning and Educational Equity 7,
https://doi.org/10.1007/978-3-031-10642-2_4

supranational educational policies. Primary results show the enormous collective effort being made by countries and international organizations to alleviate negative effects at a socio-educational level.

Keywords Latin America · Inclusive education · Educational policies · COVID-19

Introduction and Background

The complex, fragile situation in which various policies have been implemented at a national and supranational level to achieve inclusive quality education for all in the Latin American and Caribbean region (Payà, 2010, 2020, 2021) has become even more complicated in the face of the sanitary, social, and educational emergency caused by COVID-19. The pandemic's impact on fragile education systems is devastating, as the closure of schools has consequences extending beyond pedagogy. According to data from the Economic Commission for Latin America and the Caribbean, more than 160 million students in Latin America and the Caribbean had stopped having face-to-face classes in school by 2020 (ECLAC, 2020a). This region has taken the longest time to implement a return to school worldwide, representing nearly 60% of the children in the world who have lost a full school year due to the pandemic (Planeta Futuro, 2021). Specifically, and by April 2021, only 7 countries (Anguilla, Costa Rica, Dominica, Haiti, Nicaragua, Surinam, and Uruguay) had managed to fully reopen classrooms. Even before the pandemic began, the social situation in Latin America and the Caribbean region had deteriorated sharply due to rising poverty rates, persistent inequality, and growing social unrest. Considering this deteriorated context, the COVID-19 pandemic crisis is having a significantly negative impact on various social sectors, particularly within health, education, employment, and the evolution of poverty.

The two major challenges in the region were and are now, to a greater extent, quality and inequality (UNESCO, 2015; UNESCO OREALC, 2020a). Regarding the quality of education, the majority of students acquire insufficient competences in their learning achievements across all areas, including reading, writing, mathematics, and science. In terms of inequality, aspects such as access or permanence in the educational system are accentuated through large differences in marginalized groups (essentially migrants and indigenous or rural inhabitants) and in girls and adolescents.

As we can see within this difficult context, the consequences of the pandemic are devastating to this region. The interruption of face-to-face classes has also had a huge pedagogical (development of the curriculum, teaching-learning methodologies, and evaluation), social and community (early school dropout, vulnerability, and social and community uprooting), and health (poor diet, nutrition, and mental health problems) impact on the majority of students in Latin America and the Caribbean. The ever-widening digital divide (no internet access, no devices, or connectivity) and the difficulties in developing distance education have put the various countries in this region to the test. With great effort and scarce resources, policymakers from different countries are implementing various solutions to compensate for this situation, as we will look at in this chapter.

Methodology

Our study employs the methodology of international comparative education (description, interpretation, juxtaposition, and comparison), with a double analysis which is both quantitative and, fundamentally, qualitative of the national and supranational educational policies of inclusive quality education for all during the April 2020 to May 2021 COVID-19 pandemic. The sampling has been intentional and has been based on the availability of data and reports from the different countries on social and educational policies. The sample consists of official social and education policies of 39 countries in the Latin America and Caribbean region, including Anguilla, Antigua and Barbuda, Argentina, Aruba, Bahamas, Barbados, Belize, Bolivia, Brazil, Chile, Colombia, Costa Rica, Cuba, Curaçao, Dominica, Ecuador, El Salvador, Grenada, Guatemala, British Virgin Islands, Guyana, Haiti, Honduras, Cayman Islands, Jamaica, Mexico, Montserrat, Nicaragua, Panama, Paraguay, Peru, Dominican Republic, Saint Martin, Saint Vincent and the Grenadines, Saint Lucia, Suriname, Trinidad and Tobago, Uruguay, and Venezuela. This geopolitical, ethnic, cultural, and geographical region defined by the United Nations (United Nations, 2020) has an estimated population of more than 652 million people (World Bank, 2021). Data collection was based on best practices indicated by the reports, policies, studies, and documentation from the Ministries for Education in the represented countries, in addition to studies and documentation produced by international organizations, including the Information System on Educational Trends in Latin America (SITEAL) from the Institute for Educational Planning (Buenos Aires, Argentina), the Economic Commission for Latin America and the Caribbean (ECLAC), the Regional Bureau of Education for Latin America and the Caribbean (OREALC), the Latin American Laboratory for Assessment of the Quality of Education (LLECE) from UNESCO, the Organization of Ibero-American States (OEI), the Inter-American Development Bank (BID), and UNICEF (BID, 2020; ECLAC, 2019, 2020a, b; ECLAC/UNICEF, 2020; OECD, 2019; UNESCO, 2015, 2016, 2017; UNESCO/ECLAC, 2020; UNESCO/OREALC, 2020a, b, c; United Nations, 2020; UNICEF, 2020). For the qualitative analysis of the data contained in the reports, policies, studies, and documentation, MAXQDA 2020 software was used. After the relevant grouping, it resulted in six categories of analysis that constitute the core of the study: Continuity of Distance Learning and the Digital Divide; Teachers; Evaluations, Food, Health, and Psychosocial support; Vulnerable Groups; and Families and Home Schooling.

Results and Discussion

The educational responses to the situation caused by COVID-19 in such a heterogeneous region varied greatly both between and within countries, depending on the social and territorial context. School closures were the initial response for all countries excluding Nicaragua and were followed by emergency education policies in accordance with the capacities of each country, including the distribution of printed material to homes and the implementation of online platforms for distance learning. Media platforms, including mainly television and radio, were also used to broadcast classes, in addition to social networks, mobile messaging services, and the creation of specific educational materials for specific groups. Be that as it may, emergency education policies have come about more through the availability of resources than to what would be more pedagogically appropriate if the context and conditions had been favorable (UNESCO ORALC, 2020b). Thus, the different governments have intended to continue the school curriculum as it was designed before the pandemic, despite the fact that it was designed to be within face-to-face contexts and non-exceptional circumstances (BID, 2020). Although we are aware of the social, political, and economic difficulties involved and the barriers existing in the region, we agree with Huang, Liu, Tili, Yang and Wang (2020) that, in the current context, it would be more appropriate to move towards more flexible learning. Flexible learning would allow greater independence for students to choose what and how to learn, despite being partly utopian due to the precarious infrastructure available and the economic, social, and pedagogical conditions of most Latin American and Caribbean countries.

The following is a summary of the various policies and good practices analyzed in our study and developed in the region since the beginning of the pandemic, exemplifying, as far as possible, the heterogeneity of responses and educational situations in various thematic blocks.

Continuity of Distance Learning and the Digital Divide

Most of the countries had established ways of continuing distance studies in various formats. Specifically, 26 countries have implemented forms of online learning and 24 have established distance learning strategies in offline formats, including 22 countries that offer distance learning in both online and offline formats. Of these, four use exclusively online formats, and two are exclusively offline. Of the online distance learning formats, the most used is the availability of educational material and content on the web through the use of asynchronous virtual learning platforms (18 countries), and only 4 countries (Bahamas, Costa Rica, Ecuador, and Panama) have provided live classes. Additionally, and among offline forms of distance learning, 23 countries broadcast (exclusively or in combination with the use of learning platforms) educational programs via radio or television (UNESCO ECLAC, 2020).

Finally, faced with connectivity problems, in addition to sending printed pedagogical material to homes, several countries have used instant messaging applications (mainly WhatsApp), as a resource for schools and teachers to maintain linkages with students and their families (UNESCO OREALC, 2020c) and thus avoid students uprooting and dropping out from school. Some notable examples of these policies are:

- Digital teaching-learning platforms: Juana Manso Federal Plan and Seguimos Educando (We Keep on Educating) (Argentina); Conta praMim (Count on Me) and Tempo de Aprender (Time to Learn) (Brazil); Aprendo en línea (I Learn Online) (Chile); Estrategia Aprender Digital (Digital Learning Strategy) (Colombia); Aprendo en Casa (I Learn at Home) (Costa Rica); Mineduc Digital (Guatemala); Te Queremos Estudiando en Casa (We Want You Studying at Home), Proyecto de Aulas Virtuales (Virtual Classrooms Project) and Seduc-Emergencia (Seduc-Emergency) (Honduras); ESTER, Ayudinga and Educa Panamá (Educate Panama) (Panama); Tu Escuela en Casa (Your School at Home) (Paraguay); Aprendo en Casa (I Learn at Home) and Estrategia Formativa 360 (360 Training Strategy) (Peru); Plataforma Crea (Crea Platform), Plan Ceibal (Ceibal Plan) (Uruguay); and PR@TIC Plataforme numérique de ressources éducatives et d'apprentissage (Digital platform for educational and learning resources) (Haiti).
- Educational programs broadcasted on television or radio channels: Educa Chile (TV channel, Chile); Mi señal (TV channel, Colombia); Aventura Bikëtsö (Radio program, Costa Rica); Teleclases (Remote Learning on TV COVID-19, Cuba); A-Prender la tele (Switch the TV On and Learn) and Educa TV (TV and radio channel, Ecuador); educational tv and radio strip (El Salvador); Project on Suyapa Educational Radio (Honduras); Aprende en Casa (Learn at Home) (radio and TV, Mexico); Conéctate con la Estrella (Connect with the Star) (radio and TV, Panama); Cada Familia Una Escuela (A School in Each Family) (TV, Venezuela); and radio broadcasts of the Interactive Radio Instruction and NCN Radio (Guyana).
- Instant messaging for cell phones and social media channels: WhatsApp (Honduras; Peru) and YouTube video channels (Telebásica, Honduras; Cada Familia Una Escuela, Venezuela).
- Printed material: pedagogical guides (Ecuador); booklets for students with disabilities and bilingual Spanish-indigenous languages (Guatemala); printed notebooks (Honduras); and preschool and educational support guides (Panama).

Despite the efforts policymakers have made in recent years to improve internet connectivity and increase access to digital devices and skills training for teachers and students, the countries within Latin America and the Caribbean are unequally prepared to face the pandemic crisis and take advantage of the digitalization of education (Trucco & Palma, 2020). Considerable gaps in connectivity and access to the digital world persist in the region (ECLAC, 2019). Only 33% of secondary school students attend schools that have sufficient internet connections to develop interactive pedagogical activities (BID, 2020). These digital gaps are substantially different both between and within countries, and replicate other already existing social marginalization gaps including less access and use of the internet among girls, adolescents and women, inhabitants of rural areas and the indigenous population, and accessibility for people with disabilities (Galperin, 2016; UNESCO, 2017). These conditioning factors imply that digital learning continuity policies are not feasible for many households, communities, or regions, which subsequently increases the digital divide due to connectivity between rural and urban areas (not only internet access, but even lack of electricity supply); a lack of training in digital skills for teachers, families, and students; or the lack of quality or obsolescence of available computer equipment.

The lack of available resources means that, in countries such as Ecuador, 70% of students have connectivity difficulties, and only 16% of rural households have Internet. Meanwhile, in Bolivia, 93.2% of students have expressed the criticism that during the pandemic they have learned "nothing," "almost nothing," or "more or less" through e-learning initiatives (UNICEF, 2020). Accordingly, there exists a need to rethink and reevaluate policies on digitization that can be adapted and accompanied by alternatives for marginalized groups, in addition to providing technical support and equipment to make use easier. In this regard, several countries have implemented policies to increase infrastructure and connectivity, such as: Educación Conectada (Connected education) (Brazil); Conectividad para la Educación 2030 (Connectivity for Education 2030) (Chile); Campaña Conectando al Futuro (Connecting to the Future Campaign) (Ecuador), Estrategia Todos y Todas conectados (Everyone Connected Strategy) (Peru) or the donation of tablets in Argentina, Bahamas, Belize, Chile, Ecuador, Jamaica, Peru, and Suriname.

Teachers

The role of teachers has been shown to be key to the process of adapting to the pandemic situation and maintaining basic levels of inclusive education (Sánchez et al., 2020). Teachers have done, and are doing, their utmost to maintain linkages with students, which have proven to be irreplaceable and indispensable. As essential workers, teachers are additionally under great emotional stress while trying to maintain the role of personal and professional containment, withstanding the emotional and economic pressures generated by COVID-19 (Sánchez et al., 2020). The tasks they have to perform are twofold, including replanning and adapting educational processes such as methodology, curricular reorganization, design of materials, and so forth, in addition to ensuring conditions of material security for students and their families (distribution of food, health products, and school supplies). Educators have protested and claimed the need for extra training, claiming that the technology available in their centers is inadequate or insufficient to manage the educational situation resulting from the pandemic (OECD, 2019).

Data reveals that 63% of teachers in Chile consider that they are working "more" or "much more," 62% feel "worried," and 52% feel "anxious" (Elige Educar, 2020).

It should also be noted that in Latin America and the Caribbean, the teaching staff is mostly made up of women, with 95.5% in early childhood education, 78.2% in primary school, and 57.8% in high school (UIS, 2018). Accordingly, female teachers suffer intensified workdays that increase pressure and work-related stress, while either teaching work in the classroom or outside of it, with unpaid domestic and care work. This scenario makes it necessary to improve in at least five areas of work:

1. Training, advice, and resources for working with various distance education formats.
2. Support to maintain and extend methodological innovation and alternative forms of teaching, with an open curriculum and educational strategies for the acceleration and recovery of learning for the students most affected by the pandemic.
3. Safeguarding health and socio-emotional support through the development of competencies and skills.
4. Guaranteed job stability and contractual conditions.
5. Strengthening teacher networks through support spaces and joint curricular and pedagogical work (UNESCO ECLAC, 2020).

Various countries in the region have launched a number of teacher training programs to address these issues, through online courses or plans such as: Formación del Profesor Digital (Digital Teacher Training) (Bolivia), Mi Aula en Línea (My Online Classroom) (Ecuador), Todos a Aprender (Lets's All Learn), Plan Padrino (Godfather Plan) and Escuela de Liderazgo para Directivos Docentes (Leadership School for Teachers'Managers) (Colombia), healthcare courses (Uruguay), Bitácora Docente (Teacher's Logbook) and Aprendo en Línea Docente (I Learn Online for Teachers) (Chile), Caja de Herramientas para Docentes (Teacher's Toolbox) (Costa Rica), SOS Docente (SOS Teacher) (Guatemala) and On Line Resources for Teachers (Barbados).

Evaluations

Evaluations have also been modified by the pandemic, in addition to suspending or postponing participation in international or institutional evaluations. With respect to the former, distance education has strengthened the formative function of evaluation through the diagnosis and monitoring of individual student learning, making it possible to provide feedback and modify teaching strategies to make them more effective. In addition, formative assessment has also provided an opportunity for more independent work by students and which has resulted in a different school culture. Thus, most countries in the region have opted for flexible assessments (UNESCO OREALC, 2020c), using a variety of resources such as project-based learning (Argentina, Brazil, Chile, Colombia, Dominican Republic, Ecuador, El Salvador, Honduras, Panama, Paraguay, and Paraguay), portfolio assessment (Argentina, Bolivia, Colombia, Ecuador, Honduras, Mexico, Panama, and Uruguay), exams with continuous assessment (Argentina, Chile, Costa Rica, Honduras, and Paraguay) and, more unusually, final exams (Paraguay). Likewise, countries also had to choose different options for promoting students to the next school grade, with a heterogeneity of decisions ranging from automatic promotion of all students, promotion based on their annual performance, to a final evaluation, as had been done prior to the pandemic.

On the other hand, national and international evaluations of educational systems have also been affected. In the case of international assessments, some countries have postponed the dates (Argentina, Brazil, Chile, Colombia, Costa Rica, Dominican Republic, El Salvador, Panama, Paraguay, and Panama), modified formats (Peru), canceled evaluations (Mexico and Uruguay), and have generally applied greater flexibility and reservations when making decisions resulting from these assessments.

Food, Health, and Psychosocial Support

Some 85 million children in the region receive at least one basic meal of the day through school-feeding programs (WFP, 2016), and the COVID-19 pandemic has deprived many families of this opportunity (WFP, 2020). Scientific evidence demonstrates that child malnutrition directly affects school performance, decreases their ability to concentrate, increases absenteeism due to a greater propensity to illness, and in the long term, limits the cognitive development of students (Meléndez & Solano, 2017). Additionally, it has been shown that school feeding programs encourage regular class attendance and help ensure the completion of studies (WFP, 2016), demonstrating the pedagogical implications of proper nutrition, which go beyond physical and mental health. Faced with this pandemic-induced challenge, countries have developed policies to ensure that food reaches students' homes: Argentina Contra el Hambre (Argentina Against Hunger), Programa de Alimentación y Nutrición del Escolar y del Adolescente (Children and Adolescent Food and Nutrition Program, PANEA) and Huertas Estudiantiles (Student Vegetable Gardens) (Costa Rica), Programa de Alimentación Escolar (School Feeding Program) (Colombia), Canastas individuales Junaeb (Junaeb Individual Baskets) (Chile), Kit Saldremos Adelante (We Will Get Ahead Kit) (Guatemala), Operación Honduras Solidaria (Honduras Solidarity Operation), Panamá Solidario (Panama Solidarity), Canasta de emergencia alimentaria (Emergency Food Basket) (Uruguay, Haiti, and Jamaica), Mi almuerzo escolar en familia (My school Lunch With My Family) (Paraguay) and Comer es lo primero (Eating Comes First) (Dominican Republic). Other countries have opted to make economic transfers directly to families so that they can purchase food themselves (e.g., Bono Familia (Family Voucher) (Bolivia), Brazil, Bono Yo me Quedo en Casa (I Stay at Home Voucher) (Peru) and El Salvador.

In addition, the social isolation of the pandemic, an alteration to routines, and feelings of uncertainty, anxiety, stress, sensitivity, and greater vulnerability of emotional states, typical of confinement, have had a notable psychological impact on students, families, and teachers. Poverty also plays a role, in which economic precariousness favors the appearance of health problems, with overcrowded housing and added psychological pressures (ECLAC, 2020b) that have serious implications for mental health and increased exposure to situations of violence. Economic Commission for Latin America and the Caribbean and UNICEF (ECLAC/UNICEF, 2020) point out that 51.2% of children (more than 80 million children) living in urban areas in Latin America suffer some type of housing precariousness, preventing them from having an adequate space to study and rest, as well as having a detrimental impact on cognitive development and favors abusive situations. Thus, it is necessary to maintain their psychological, social, and emotional well-being to develop adaptation skills and emotional resilience, through socio-emotional learning with the necessary support and resources. In this sense, some countries have implemented various policies aimed towards emotional containment, self-care and socio-emotional well-being (Chile), psychosocial support plans for students, teachers, and families (Venezuela, Uruguay, and Dominica), education for socio-emotional care in natural, technological, and health disasters (Cuba), guides for the promotion of healthy habits and self-regulation of emotions (Bolivia), protocol for tele-assisted mental health, psychological, and psychiatric care (Ecuador), and online psychological assistance programs such as Aquí Estoy (Here I am) (Costa Rica).

Vulnerable Groups

The guarantee of inclusive and equitable education for all people determined by SDG 4 of the 2030 Agenda emphasizes the need to address all forms of exclusion and marginalization (Payà, 2021; UNESCO, 2016), making it necessary to focus extra efforts on the most disadvantaged, vulnerable groups or those at risk of exclusion, with the idea of "leaving no one behind." In the context of the COVID-19 pandemic, the mandate to prioritize these groups has become a priority to avoid further deepening of the conditions of inequality. In Latin America and the Caribbean, ethnic and racial disparities associated with historical and structural discrimination against the Afro-descendant and indigenous populations are highly marked, but we cannot forget that refugees, the displaced and migrants, people with disabilities, children and youth, or those with HIV and AIDS, among others, must also be prioritized within these inclusive policies, as they are at high risk of disengaging from education and dropping out of school. The promotion of gender equality deserves special attention in this regard, as one of the greatest risks faced by women and girls in pandemic contexts is violence (Fraser, 2020; United Nations Women, 2020), sexual abuse, and teenage pregnancy. In addition to the obvious physical and psychosocial impacts, there are also the immediate- and long-term implications that these situations have on the learning and well-being of girls and adolescents.

In an attempt to alleviate the adverse effects of the pandemic on these vulnerable groups, the various national governments in the region and international institutions have activated a series of policies including: care programs for students with disabilities (Guatemala and Peru), pedagogical guides and policies for indigenous students in native languages (Ecuador, Mexico, and Peru), guides for situations of domestic violence (Uruguay) or reports and resources for gender equality (UN Women, International Federation of Red Cross and Red Crescent Societies and PLAN INTERNATIONAL), among others. Special mention should be made of the work being done by the indigenous communities themselves to reinvent educational processes based on their circumstances, practices, and knowledge (Quezada, 2021). These initiatives have replaced suspended classroom classes with a combination of lessons in the field and at home, with intercultural bilingual education programs, curricula that include the "tequio" (an indigenous word meaning the collective work that everyone owes and performs for free for the benefit of the community itself) as a form of community work to meet collective needs, or intercultural community projects for social learning such as the "milpas para el buenvivir" (cornfields for good living), among other initiatives.

Families and Home Schooling

Finally, it is worth mentioning the role of families, who are the main players in their children's education and who, with the closure of classrooms and confinement, have also had to assume a teaching role with school training and support in curricular learning. Logically, the heterogeneity of the cultural level of the families and their pedagogical skills, as well as the temporal limitations due to working hours and spatial limitations due to home sizes, have also conditioned the responses they have been able to give to homeschooling in this context. To alleviate possible shortcomings, policies for training, accompaniment, counseling, and support to families have been activated, with the provision of pedagogical materials and other resources to assist families in assuming their new teaching roles. Some examples of these policies implemented in the region are: Aprendo en casa. Únete al reto (I learn at home. Join the challenge), tools to develop activities at home with children focused on continuing learning, strengthening the family bond, and taking care of physical and emotional health (UNICEF); Vamos a jugar (Let's Play) (Cuba), #Educarescuidar (#TeachingIsCaring) UNESCO Ecuador, Bolivia, Colombia, Ecuador, and Venezuela), #YoMeQuedoEnCasa y la pasamos bien (#IStayAtHome And We Have Fun) (UNICEF Peru), specific support and orientation guides for families (Antigua and Barbuda, Barbados, Bahamas, Belize, Bolivia, Chile, Colombia, El Salvador, Jamaica, Mexico, Panama, Peru and Saint Vincent, and the Grenadines) and Plan Cada Familia Una Escuela (A Schoon in each Family Plan) (Venezuela).

Conclusion

After what has been analyzed here, we see that during the pandemic and post-pandemic situation, education systems in Latin America and the Caribbean cannot limit themselves to continuing to facilitate access to school content. Instead, they must be concerned with maintaining their functions of social protection and educational inclusion through preserving existing linkages with students and families to avoid key issues such as school dropout and the increase in social inequalities, inequities, and exclusions (UNESCO OREALC, 2020b). This pandemic crisis has favored (or should favor) social resignification and a sense of global citizenship, but, above all, it has corroborated the need to rethink education in order to understand reality, and to coexist and act in times of uncertainty, making individual and collective decisions for a structural transformation of the region.

We agree with the Latin American Laboratory for Assessment of the Quality of Education (LLECE) that the challenges for inclusive education policies in the region are (UNESCO OREALC, 2020c):

- In the short term: to work on effective plans for a safe return to school and, in the meantime, to perfect distance or hybrid education formats.
- In the medium term: to design strategies to measure the impact of the crisis and implement effective measures to mitigate its effects, revising learning objectives and curricula, and prioritizing content and competencies, in addition to increasing efforts so that students who are lagging behind and are within the most vulnerable groups can make up for lost school time.
- In the long term: to rethink educational models for a more holistic understanding of education, in order to train citizens of the twenty-first century and create sustainable societies through more flexible and truly inclusive quality educational systems (Payà, 2020, 2021).

References

BID. (2020). *La educación en tiempos del coronavirus: los sistemas educativos de América Latina y el Caribe ante COVID-19*. Inter-American Development Bank.
ECLAC. (2019). *Panorama social de América Latina, 2018*. ECLAC.
ECLAC. (2020a). América Latina y el Caribe ante la pandemia del COVID-19. Efectos económicos y sociales. *Informe Especial COVID-19, 1*, 1–15.
ECLAC. (2020b). El desafío social en tiempos del COVID-19. *Informe Especial COVID-19, 3*, 1–22.
ECLAC/UNICEF. (2020). La ciudad y los derechos de niñas, niños y adolescentes. *Desafíos, 23*, Santiago, Chile, January 2020, 1–10.
Elige Educar. (2020). *Situación de docentes y educadores en contexto de pandemia: reporte de resultados 20 de mayo 2020*. Elige Educar.
Fraser, E. (2020). Impact of COVID-19 pandemic on violence against women and girls, *VAWG Helpdesk Research Report*, 284. Retrieved from https://www.sddirect.org.uk/media/1881/vawg-helpdesk-284-COVID-19-and-vawg.pdf

Galperin, H. (2016). The digital divide in Latin America: Evidence and policy recommendations from household surveys. *SSRN Journal,* 9–41. Retrieved from https://doi.org/10.2139/ssrn.2852942

Huang, R. H., Liu, D. J., Tili, A., Yang, JF., & Wang, HH. (2020). *Handbook on facilitating flexible learning during educational disruption. The Chinese Experience in maintaining undisrupted learning in COVID-19 outbreak.* Smart Learning Institute of Beijing Normal University; UNESCO.

Meléndez, L., & Solano, V. (2017). La desnutrición y el estrés van a la escuela: pobreza infantil y neurodesarrollo en América Latina. *Innovaciones Educativas, 27*(1), 55–70. Retrieved from https://doi.org/10.22458/ie.v19i27.1955

OECD. (2019). *Talis 2018 results (volume I): Teachers and school leaders as lifelong learners.* OECD.

Payà, A. (2010). Políticas de educación inclusiva en América Latina. Propuestas, realidades y retos de futuro. *Revista de Educación Inclusiva, 3*(2), 125–142.

Payà, A. (2020). Inclusive and special education policies in South America. In *Oxford research encyclopedia of education.* Oxford University Press. Retrieved from https://doi.org/10.1093/acrefore/9780190264093.013.1030

Payà, A. (2021). Construyendo una educación inclusiva en América Latina. El reto de la educación de calidad para todos/as. In Lázaro, LM & Ancheta, A. (Coord.) La educación en América Latina en la perspectiva 2030, : Tirant Humanidades, 290–310.

Planeta Futuro. (2021, March 25). *Un año sin pisar mi escuela.* El País.

Quezada, M. (2021, March 25). *Todo el pueblo educa a los niños.* El País.

Sánchez, M., Martínez, A. M., Torres, R., Agüero, M. M., Hernández, A. K., Benavides, M. A., Jaimes, C. A., & Rendón, V. J. (2020). Retos educativos durante la pandemia de COVID-19: una encuesta a profesores de la UNAM. *Revista Digital Universitaria, 21*(3), 1–23.

Trucco, D., & Palma, A. (2020). *Infancia y adolescencia en la era digital: un informe comparativo de los estudios de Kids Online de Brasil, Chile, Costa Rica y el Uruguay. Documentos de Proyectos.* ECLAC.

UIS. (2018). *Education: Percentage of female teachers by teaching level of education.* UNESCO Institute for Statistics.

UNESCO. (2015). *Informe de resultados TERCE (Tercer Estudio Regional Comparativo y Explicativo de Calidad de la Educación): factores asociados.* UNESCO.

UNESCO. (2016). *Educación 2030.* Declaración de Incheon y Marco de Acción para la realización del Objetivo de Desarrollo Sostenible 4. UNESCO.

UNESCO. (2017). *Sociedad digital: brechas y retos para la inclusión digital en América Latina y el Caribe.* Policy Papers UNESCO.

UNESCO ECLAC. (2020). *La educación en tiempos de la pandemia de COVID-19.* UNESCO ECLAC.

UNESCO OREALC. (2020a). *¿Qué se espera que aprendan los estudiantes de América Latina y el Caribe? Análisis curricular del Estudio Regional Comparativo y Explicativo (ERCE 2019).* UNESCO & UNICEF.

UNESCO OREALC. (2020b). Aportes para una respuesta educativa frente a la COVID-19 en América Latina. Documento de programa. : UNESCO.

UNESCO OREALC. (2020c). *Sistemas educativos de América Latina en respuesta a la COVID-19. Continuidad educativa y educación.* UNESCO.

UNICEF. (2020). *La continuidad educativa durante la pandemia. Encuesta de U-Report Bolivia escucha mi voz.* UNICEF Bolivia.

United Nations. (2020). *Geographical regions.* United Nations Statistics Division.

United Nations Women. (2020). *COVID-19 en América Latina y el Caribe: cómo incorporar a las mujeres a la igualdad de género en la gestión de la respuesta a la crisis.* Oficina Regional de ONU Mujeres para las Américas y el Caribe.

WFP. (2016). *Fortaleciendo las redes de protección social: apoyando los programas nacionales de alimentación en América Latina y el Caribe.* World Food Programme.

WFP. (2020). *Global monitoring of school meals during COVID-19 school closures*. World Food Programme.
World Bank. (2021). *Population, total. Latin America and Caribbean*. World Bank. Retrieved from https://data.worldbank.org/indicator/SP.POP.TOTL?locations=ZJ

Andres Paya Rico is an Associated Professor of Theory and History of Education, and Head of Department of Comparative Education and History of Education at the University of Valencia (Spain) (2014–2019). He is a course director of the Master's in Psychopedagogy at the University of Valencia (2019–present). He is a consultant professor in education at the Open University of Catalonia (UOC). He is a member of the Academic Board for the PhD Programme Pedagogical Sciences at the University of Bologna (Italy). Research stays and visiting professorships at: University of Macerata (Italy), University of Gent (Belgium), Autonomous University of the State of Morelos (Mexico), Pontifical Catholic University of Peru (Peru) and the Universidad Técnica Particular de Loja (Ecuador). Spokesman for the Steering Committee of the Sociedad Española de Historia de la Educación (SEDHE – Spanish History of Education Society). Has some 100 academic publications (10 books, 50 book chapters and 40 articles) on the topics of history of education, educational policy and comparative education. He has directed or participated in 25 competitive and innovative teaching projects, granted by European, national and regional institutions.

Chapter 5
On the Cultivation of Autonomous Learning During Times of a Pandemic: Pedagogical Implications of Inclusive Online Education

Naima Al-husban and Yusef Waghid

Abstract This study investigates secondary learners' challenges while reading texts during times of the COVID-19 pandemic. The argument proffered in this contribution is that learning can be autonomous in the context of inclusive online pedagogical practices. Qualitative methodology was employed, specifically having used a semi-structured interview technique to collect data. The sample of the study was purposefully selected, and it consisted of 11 EFL [English as a foreign language] learners and 11 EFL teachers. It was found that learners did not necessarily present reading stamina due to the expectation that teachers should constantly provide explanations, lacking confidence, and inadequately using time management. All these constraints highlighted the pedagogical barriers that learners had to overcome to motivate themselves to read critically with enough time to complete their pedagogical tasks of textual analysis, interpretation, and summaries. The main argument of this investigation is constituted in the cultivation of autonomous learning during the times of a pandemic. This means that the possibility of evoking the learners' capacities, whether these be either normal or those with disabilities, to read by themselves and to think for themselves. This can contribute towards enhancing their critical learning. Based on the finding, the effective way to prepare young learners, regardless of their ability, for the future with all its obstacles and complexities, is to teach them what it means to act with autonomy, that is, independence and self-directedness.

Keywords Autonomous learning · Pandemic · Reading comprehension · Inclusive online education

N. Al-husban (✉)
Arab Open University, Amman, Jordan
e-mail: n_husban@aou.edu.jo

Y. Waghid
Stellenbosch University, Stellenbosch, South Africa

Introduction

Plunging into the Challenge of Online Teaching-Learning

During the COVID-19 pandemic, many learners in the secondary stage have limited access to the internet or to technological devices that would enable them to participate productively in virtual classes. Most poignantly, they do not or cannot read independently. Therefore, they may appear demotivated, silent, and disengaged in these studies while schools are closed, despite the government having made online and distance teaching-learning mandatory for schools during the duration of the pandemic. In this unusual situation, who can guarantee that learning happens? Almost the entire world is affected by the pandemic and invariably universities, colleges, and schools are also challenged. By implication, educational institutions ought to find innovative ways to advance teaching-learning. Considering that more than 1.5 billion learners are affected by school closures in 165 countries, constituting 87% of the worlds' population of learners, devising technologically enhanced forms of online (virtual) teaching-learning seems to be a definitive response to the crisis (UNESCO, 2021).

It was a matter of a few months in which COVID-19 reshaped how education is conducted. Along with the spread of COVID-19, many countries have taken swift and decisive actions to encourage teaching-learning during the pandemic by adopting an "online home-schooling trend". The latter involves using interactive apps, platforms, TVs, and YouTube videos for teaching-learning. In this context, the United Nations Educational, Scientific, and Cultural Organization (UNESCO, 2021) exerted tremendous efforts to encourage the affected countries to respond appropriately to teaching-learning during the pandemic. Attuned to its fourth sustainable development goal that focuses on quality of education, UNESCO responded to the call that no one should be left behind. In this situation, UNESCO asked member states to make their educational systems resilient, open, and innovative by thinking of expanding open and distance teaching-learning. This is in line with the fourth sustainable development goal that focuses on quality of education, more specifically, inclusive pedagogical encounters, and how to reduce the gap created by COVID-19 in forcing students to stay at home and having online opportunities to attend to their learning in a remote fashion (Chabbott & Sinclair, 2020). In other words, online teaching-learning encounters are considered as sustainable when learners are included in pedagogical activities to ensure quality education. What makes pedagogical encounters inclusive is that sufficient opportunities are established for learners to engage with one another and with the ideas advanced by teachers.

The rationale for this contribution does not only emanate from a dire need to implement online teaching-learning. Rather, the point about this contribution is to ascertain as to whether online teaching-learning as a pedagogical practice can enhance a form of learning whereby learners in schools can become autonomous, that is, critical, independent, and self-directed. Focusing on some of the pedagogical encounters among teachers and learners in some secondary schools in Jordan during the time of the pandemic, the argument is proffered that learning can be autonomous if learners were taught to read, think, and critically interpret meanings for themselves without always having to be told what and how to conjure up meanings.

Background

In Defense of Autonomous Online Teaching-Learning

In Jordan and South Africa, the closure of educational institutions also manifested during the height of the COVID-19 pandemic. Although school closures affect people's daily activities and keep many learners at home, such unprecedented measures were necessary and must be maintained until the danger of the pandemic subsides. In both countries, online platforms for teaching-learning have been encouraged both by government and civil society. For example, Darsak, Microsoft Teams and Noorspace are learning management systems to unify the efforts of teachers in interacting and communicating with learners, providing learners the resources they need, sending assignments, and providing assessment feedback. These platforms target all grade levels in formal educational institutions. Additionally, schools in the private sector have their own platforms, and apps like Zoom, Microsoft Teams, and Google Classrooms have emerged as technological platforms in expediting teaching-learning. For instance, in Jordan the Ministry of Education launched an e-professional development programme to train teachers to use technology effectively to assist and engage with learners.

Despite the implementation of innovative platforms for teaching-learning, many challenges for learners ensued, especially about equitable access to online teaching-learning. The usage of online education seems to be limited in many disadvantaged communities, refugee camps, and rural places where there is no free internet, as well as the unaffordability of smartphones, tablets, or computers (Dreesen et al., 2020). By implication, several parents of school learners, especially mothers, who may be unable to teach their children using the resources either because of their limited access to these resources, or digital illiteracy, were challenged. Most of all, the daunting challenge encountered by many school learners in both countries seems to have been their lack of readiness and preparedness to engage in online education. Although some parents could at times monitor learning, explain curricular content through videos and questioning, not all of them have been prepared for such a drastic situation (Moriarty, 2020).

Teachers could use Zoom, Microsoft Teams, or any other app for some time to explain key aspects, and even try to simplify concepts concomitantly attempting to overcome any technical problems that would prevent the learners from continuing their pedagogical tasks. However, learners were always encouraged to learn by themselves and be able to read with comprehension. The point is that the cultivation of learner autonomy seems to have emerged strongly during the teaching-learning pedagogical processes during the pandemic in both countries. This claim about learner autonomy will be revisited later.

The twenty-first century, the century of technology, still needs learners who can read independently and comprehend texts in various disciplines with limited supervision. According to Burnett and Merchant (2019) the unprecedented adoption of mobile devices for communication has altered how individuals stay connected and communicate ideas and information. But, critical literacy is still necessary, especially as the world faces an unparalleled environmental crisis, financial instability, and an influx of refugees to foreign countries in many parts of the world, including Jordan and South Africa. Therefore, learners need to be confident in their skills of reading critically, understand messages accurately, and to make reasonable and intuitive judgments (Waghid, 2019). Additionally, they must have the chance to play their roles in shaping the world for their own sake, rather than waiting for others to improve it for them. The following is an example of this situation happening in 2020. Students in more than 165 countries are waiting for adults to solve the problem of education disruption due to the COVID-19 pandemic (d'Orville, 2020). To this end, independent reading could play a key role in facing this challenge if, during their learning at school, learners get used to reading texts with minimal supervision from their teachers, and teachers ask them to read texts at home, summarize them and present main ideas in the virtual classroom. The latter approach to learning can only happen if learner autonomy is encouraged in private and public schools. By learner autonomy, what is meant is that learners develop the intellectual and emotional capacities that not only include them in the process of learning, but also encourage them to adopt innovative ways of learning, and to act responsibly in and beyond their learning experiences (Waghid, 2019). The point is that learners are motivated to see pedagogical matters for themselves without having to be told to do so all of the time by teachers. In this way, learners would genuinely be included in pedagogical activities. Learners will have gained a sense of learner autonomy if their potential has been motivated to come to the fore in intellectual and intuitive ways (Waghid, 2019). That is, they can speak their minds without having to be told incessantly to do so. Put differently, their learner autonomy could inspire them to be critical (Chamberlain et al., 2020). And, through critical engagement within pedagogical encounters, learners could be included democratically because their voices would not be denied (Waghid, 2019). When they engage critically, they speak their minds and are allowed to contribute to the pedagogical conversations – that is, learners are democratically included because they have something to contribute to the encounter by broadening their cognitive and moral imaginations (Waghid, 2019).

Moreover, policy makers, teachers, and parents could exert all their efforts during school closures to ensure continuous learning by adopting distance teaching-learning. But learners would not benefit if they are not used to reading independently and cannot process any text in any subject without direct instruction by adults who cannot be available constantly in these critical times. This reveals the importance of developing learners' capacities and skills of independent (autonomous) reading. According to Sanden (2012) and Mahmood (2021), several studies confirm that providing elementary learners with opportunities to make choices in reading activities increases their motivation to participate. Similarly, when learners are motivated, they should be able to think and read for themselves and act with self-confidence and determination (Waghid, 2019). This is an important point as during the COVID-19 pandemic, many learners seemingly showed a reluctance to study or to read different subjects independently. With less direct teaching, many learners seemed to have been unmotivated to pursue self-directed (autonomous) learning. According to Sanden (2012), independent reading includes providing students with the opportunities to read tasks in various areas such as languages, history, science, and math, to work at their own paces, and to interact with the text without depending on teachers and parents to read for them. Independent reading is also important as it provides learners with the feeling of being responsible for their own learning and they are more likely to be involved in reading tasks even when not required to do so. Taylor et al. (2000) and Huang et al. (2014) posited that those learners who read more independently (autonomously), performed better than those who read less frequently, and learners who followed free reading activities did better on tests that required reading comprehension than their equivalents in traditional educational programmes.

Reutzel et al. (2010) purport that the instruction process should integrate independent reading as a valuable technique and that growth in literacy programmes should be one of the required outcomes of the education system in every country. No country could avoid a global problem like COVID-19. Similarly, Kelley and Clausen-Grace (2009) emphasized that learners who were highly engaged in independent reading demonstrated higher levels of reading achievement, and high skills of independent reading helped students to overcome obstacles such as low family income, less varied educational backgrounds, and poor conditions of learning due to natural disasters or other reasons. In turn, Allington (2014) suggested that independent reading increases the quality of learning experiences, reading proficiency, and academic success. To this end, it is necessary to start integrating independent reading activities early on in all subjects, for enjoyment and information. These activities should be performed under the supervision of teachers, who request learners to perform tasks based on their independent reading (Pilgreen, 2000). Regular exposure to such reading activities creates an intrinsic motivation to read and become involved in various reading activities, even some challenging ones, and to even extend the time allotted for reading. Furthermore, Horne (2014) investigated the effect of independent reading programmes which were incorporated in the traditional way of teaching. Horne (2014) found that students in the secondary stage developed a positive attitude towards reading topics and textbooks that they are interested in and as a result, they performed better in academic examinations.

This kind of autonomous reading is a priority in normal conditions. Some teachers identified a literacy crisis as one where there are many learners who lack reading comprehension skills and could not understand texts even in their mother tongue.

Some teachers could not consider love of reading as an academic goal, and it is known that teachers generally focus on teaching the content because there is a scheduled time to cover it, so their focus on teaching learners reading skills is not a priority. Learners seem to acquire similar attitudes towards reading and instead memorize the content that allows them to pass to the next grade level. This type of rote learning is incompatible with critical education in the twenty-first century, which emphasizes abilities such as critical thinking, communicative skills, life-long learning, and independent learning. However, in difficult times like the spread of COVID-19 in 2020 when schools were closed, parents could only guide learning but could not participate in teaching. In this way, independent reading, and self-directed learning become indispensable to pedagogy.

During the crisis, learners stayed at home all the time, so they needed the motivation to read, referred to as reading stamina. Reading stamina is the capacity to read for a sufficient time with attentiveness and without becoming distracted (Head et al., 2018). Reading independently could help learners develop this skill, which they need when they find themselves responsible for learning different subjects with minor direct instruction from their teachers. At the same time, English as foreign language (EFL) teachers could play an essential role in helping students become independent readers through designing certain reading comprehension activities that develop learners' reading stamina.

According to Jain et al. (2021), teachers encountered several challenges during the COVID-19 pandemic due to the closure of schools. They attribute these challenges to a shortage of pedagogical skills and inadequate digital literacy capacities, including the limited use of technology during the pre-stage of the pandemic. However, EFL teachers responded positively to several of the challenges related to learning. In Jordan, for example, some EFL teachers were criticized for extensively relying on technological applications which required substantive learner engagement. This criticism from some parents and learners, were often waged against self-directed learning on the basis that learners were summoned to read texts and perform tasks. According to Nugent et al. (2019), learners require a type of modeling in the use of comprehension strategies with a gradual release of the responsibility before they can use such strategies independently. In order to read comfortably, the same authors state that it is important to help students develop fluent reading, that is, providing students more opportunities for guided and independent reading. During the pandemic, teachers encouraged students to read with comprehension as part of their remote learning experiences in order to improve their reading comprehension. The focus on pedagogy seems to go against an abundant and uncritical reliance on technological applications which is often encouraged by educational authorities. The point is, using technology on its own does not always enhance learning unless the focus is also on pedagogical understanding.

The study has implications for international agencies like UNESCO on how to strategize education in the future, how to visualize education in a crisis, and the importance of developing skills over acquiring content, as well as identifying the training needs of teachers during an emergency. Moreover, this study offers implications to be considered for future research regarding reading practices in difficult times, disruption of education especially during the emergence of pandemics. Therefore, the study tried to answer the following research questions:

(i) How much time did learners spend on reading comprehension during the pandemic, and what factors contributed to their failing to submit their reading assignments?
(ii) What are the common reading comprehension practices and strategies teachers utilised during their classes?

Methods

This study employed a semi-structured interview technique to collect data during a two-month period, especially during the time teachers were teaching remotely and learners in public schools received ready-made lessons without communicating with their teachers. Of course, as constituent of their inclusive learning encounters, the idea behind the provision of predetermined learning opportunities, is that learners would critically engage with what they had been provided with. In no way, has the provision of predetermined learning opportunities been meant to ensure learner passivity.

Procedures of Conducting Interviews

The interview questions were developed based on reviewing literature related to reading comprehension, independent reading, learners' reading practices, and EFL teachers' reading comprehension strategies during online pedagogy. There is a dearth of literature regarding reading practices during the time of a crisis. Interview questions were formulated in such a way so that interviewees were encouraged to articulate what they read, how they read, the time they spent reading, the use of multiple online learning resources from different teachers, and the practices teachers used during the pandemic.

Data analysis relied on qualitative thematic analysis; To guarantee the validity of the results, the author and inter-rater reread all interviews, transcribed them using open coding to infer emergent categories, and evaluated them with reference to the literature implications, and requests of practitioners and researchers. Specifically, the questions having been reviewed by a jury of reviewers who suggested rewording some phrases to be understandable by the interviewees. Then, a pilot interview was conducted with a teacher and students from the sample. This interview schedule was repeated after ten days. After the authors had analyzed the data, there were no significant differences in the interviewees' responses with agreement having been reached to a large extent. Consequently, the authors found the reliability in the pilot interview to be acceptable for this study.

More specifically, the interview plan was as follows: Asking learners the question pertaining to how much time they spent on reading; posing the question, of how much time they spent on each reading activity examining which factors constrain learners' submission of assignments on time; and ascertaining from EFL teachers which common teaching strategies they used during the pandemic. These questions are mostly qualitative on the grounds that the authors wanted to construct rich data that corroborated teaching-learning experiences regarding remote learning.

Ethical Considerations

All interviews were conducted after having received interviewees' informed consent, and explained the participation in the study is voluntary. Teachers and learners' parents were informed of the aim of this study and approved the participation thereof. They were also informed that they could withdraw at any time and data would be constructed anonymously and treated confidentially. All interviews were conducted in the Arabic language and were manually recorded and transcribed to enable thematic coding.

Participants of the Study

The study being reported on now, examines how EFL teachers used remote teaching-learning to engage learners so that learners could read and learn more autonomously. The study comprises 22 in-depth, semi-structured interviews held with 11 EFL secondary learners and 11 EFL teachers at three public schools in Jarash (Jordan), 25 km from the capital, Amman. All learners remained at home during the emergence of the pandemic. Considering that it was forbidden to leave houses or to meet in groups at schools, all interviews were conducted via a mobile phone. Some interviews lasted 15 minutes whereas other tenth-grade learners of about 16 years of age required 20 minutes to complete the interviews at public schools. The demographic data of the interviewees (teachers) is provided in the following Table 5.1:

Results

An analysis of the interviewees' responses to the interview questions revealed two main themes:

- Students' responses focused on the overall time they spent while reading and the factors that constrained learners from doing and submitting assigned tasks on time.

Table 5.1 Demographic information of the study participants (EFL teachers)

Interviewees	Age	Years of experience	Gender	Stage of teaching	type of school
Teacher 1	35	3	Female	Primary	Public
Teacher 2	30	5	Female	Primary	Public
Teacher 3	33	1	Female	Primary	Public
Teacher 4	37	2	Female	Primary	Public
Teacher 5	40	2	Female	Primary	Public
Teacher 6	40	4	Female	Primary	Public
Teacher 7	34	4	Female	Primary	Public
Teacher 8	37	5	Female	Primary	Public
Teacher 9	40	6	Female	Primary	Public
Teacher 10	30	6	Female	Primary	Public
Teacher 11	33	4	Female	Primary	Public

- The reading comprehension strategies EFL teachers delivered in the remote teaching during the pandemic.

Interviewees' responses are presented and discussed in the following sections:

Learners' Duration of Reading in Relation to Activities

The first theme emanated from an analysis of the first two questions: How much time do you spend reading; and how much time do you spend on each reading activity? These questions pertain to learners' cognition during reading practices. Learners identified the reading activities they performed every day and the time they needed to carry them out. Eight out 11 of the respondents stated that they spent five hours weekly, two of 11 participants stated that they spend nine hours weekly, and one out of 11 participants said 14 hours weekly. This shows that there was such a variety in the duration of participation regarding reading. Learners expended less time on reading because of the difficulty of tasks or they were used to receiving specific instructions on how to perform tasks. Also, during remote learning, learners missed out on these instructions that hampered them from managing their learning appropriately.

Regarding the time allocated to reading activities or tasks, six out of 11 interviewees stated that they allotted an hour to perform tasks provided by their teachers in Microsoft Teams, the platform that the Ministry of Education in Jordan implemented to ensure the continuity of teaching-learning, and the rest of the time for electronic reading, especially posts on social media like Facebook, Twitter, and messages in WhatsApp. Three out of 11 interviewees stated that the types of assignments provided by teachers impacted learning. These assignments were structurally organized to involve learner participation which involved: engaged reading between one and two hours per day; focusing on content knowledge; and watching videos uploaded by teachers in performing the required tasks. These results led to the conclusion that learners did not value reading and wanted to read aspects of texts that assisted their successful completion of examinations or what is called knowledge-based reading. That is, they could not spend much time reading texts, summarize, record notes to understand them thoroughly and answer any question without direct instruction of teachers. Likewise, these findings revealed what research highlighted regarding sustaining learners' attention while reading for enough time or "reading stamina". The difference between good readers and bad readers is the difference in the amount of time spent on reading tasks. That is, reading instruction in the previous years was not up to the mark, and did not prepare learners to be independent and strategic autonomous readers.

Factors for Not Submitting the Assigned Reading Tasks on Time

The analysis of interviewees' responses revealed several reasons as to why learners were prevented from reading. Eight learners averred that "Online learning increased the reading tasks, and many assignments teachers sent without taking into consideration our psychological status … [thus becoming] demotivated to read [always eager to access] mobile [phones] and read messages and posts on social media regarding news of COVID-19". Additionally, a lack of confidence seemed to have been another factor that prevented learners from being attentive to the reading tasks. Some learners claimed that they lacked confidence in understanding what they read and retrieved what they had read. As remarked by a learner: "I need to read each sentence several times to be able to understand especially if they were not explained by the teacher, and there is no video about the reading topic. I feel frustrated as I did not feel I could achieve anything on the exams." Furthermore, many learners cited inefficient time management as an issue that prevented their diligence in reading. Some learners remarked: "I have 24 hours to do the reading in open-ended curfew during the pandemic, but I did not feel that I achieved any of them. I could not manage my time; I wasted time in playing, talking, and reading posts and news regarding the pandemic, and I paid little attention to reading". Learners revealed all these psychological barriers as they have encountered an unprecedented situation. They used to receive direct instruction form teachers with minimal space for self-directed learning. And expecting learners to do tasks without any guidance would invariably challenge their self-confidence to do the tasks independently.

Regarding EFL teachers' transformative practices during emergency online teaching-learning, the analysis of interviewees' responses revealed that there were some practices and strategies that were employed by EFL teachers during online teaching-learning to enhance learners' reading comprehension skills and to increase their time of reading. Nine teachers stated that they provided learners with recorded videos explaining the reading of texts and explaining meanings of new words in the mother tongue to facilitate understanding. One teacher asserted, "I could not meet my students in the fifth-grade face-to-face, and I noticed they did their homework badly, I think the best way to explain the reading texts in Arabic, and explain the main words, thereby they could answer questions correctly". Ten of the interviewees stated that they encouraged learners to summarize texts to make sure they (learners) understood the texts and were capable of articulating understanding in their own words. One teacher accentuated, "I think it is important to make sure students understand the text by asking them to paraphrase the text using their own words".

Seven of the interviewees confirmed their creation of a WhatsApp group, through which they could communicate with learners. These teachers sent texts in parts and asked questions, thus encouraging learners to speak via text messages about their understanding and comprehension of texts. A teacher stated, "I found the WhatsApp group with my tenth-grade a good way to communicate with my students and help them practice reading comprehension skills regularly, so they sent their answers and I sent them continuous feedback, and they could ask me questions about the texts or any other parts of the content. I also do competitions [such as] who are the best reader to motivate them to read and feel their reading has value and they are studying and not on holiday".

In addition, there are several ways in which teachers contributed to promoting learning. Having used short stories to discuss topics related to the themes in the prescribed textbooks was one of the common practices that almost all the interviewees employed. This practice was implemented by sending short stories to learners and asking them to summarize texts in their own language. As stated by a teacher, "using short stories is one of the favorite practices that students enjoy, especially using sections of stories to motivate students to wait for the next sections. I noticed the vocabulary items of my students became better, and they could answer inference questions". About two interviewees accentuated the importance of memorization in addition to the comprehension of texts: "If I wanted students to read a test and understand it, I ask students to memorize lists of words related to the reading texts". Similarly, three teachers claimed that "they used pictures to make the text easy to understand". Then, four teachers stated that it is necessary to cooperate with parents to make sure learners did the reading tasks they asked students to carry out and to use the technological platforms that provide students with extra reading comprehension activities. It appears that most teachers used strategies like games, mind maps, flipped instruction, puzzles, probing questions, and mind maps in their contact teaching. However, they found it challenging to implement through online pedagogy thus pointing to a deficiency in online teaching-learning. As remarked by a teacher: "I know several strategies to encourage my students to read effectively like flipped instruction and games, but I am afraid I could not employ them remotely".

Moreover, an interviewee (teacher) revealed that the most important point to help learners in reading and understanding texts, is teaching them how to read in a direct way by showing learners how to contemplate meanings of new words used in varying contexts, with the use of prediction, scanning, skimming, summations, and design activities based on games or puzzles. This teacher stated the following: "I usually record a video before the meeting using ZOOM and sent it to my eighth-graders to watch it then, I meet them; I try to save time by providing students with a model, I acted out the role of student by doing all the tasks I usually ask students to do, how to use clues before and after clues, how to predict the topic of the text, how to scan the text, how to skim, how to answer questions especially critical thinking questions, how to summarize the text, how to design mind maps that organize thoughts in the texts in the mind of students … I help students to read by telling them what to do, how to do, and when to do, and I found my students motivated and they did they tasks perfectly, and their level of reading is up to the mark". Even though this statement seems so innocuous, it also seemingly accentuates the problem of critical online teaching-learning. Although learners seem to have been invited and summoned to engage in learning, this teacher seems to equate critical reading of texts with teaching as always "telling" learners what to do. If this form of 'telling' persists, it could also undermine the possibility that autonomous learning will manifest. Critical teaching-learning cannot be primarily on teachers "telling" learners what to do, as this would prevent them (learners) from developing intelligence and speech. As a result, autonomous learning may be jeopardized.

Discussion

Theme one showed that there was a fluctuation in the time learners allotted to reading. Simultaneously, learners could not spend the necessary time to perform their tasks professionally. The results of the first theme are to some extent consistent with previous research done by Thomas et al. (2015) and St Clair-Thompson et al. (2018). There seems to be agreement with existing research that learners do not appear to value reading and preferred attending lectures. In lectures, teachers seem to be examination-oriented, so learners seemingly did not need to have read everything in each unit whereas in independent reading, or out-of-classroom reading, they needed to read intensely, understood the content, and summarized it with minimal assistance from teachers. This is a new experience that learners faced. Previously, all subject content was explained and clarified by teachers, and there seemingly was no need to read independently and read with comprehension with continuous assistance.

The responses of interviewees to the latter approach can be summarized as follows in the words of one learner, "I tried to read Arabic texts, math, and science, and this takes about an hour more or less, but I could not understand all what I read, I have some questions at the moment of reading, I could not focus more than an hour". The latter response corroborated that reading for enough time with "reading stamina" would enhance comprehension – a claim supported by McVeigh (2019) who posited that the difference between good readers and bad readers is the difference in the amount of time spent in reading. In this regard, the demand for reading with understanding and comprehension is evident. The research suggested that teachers did not teach reading comprehension but rather tested reading, so it was expected that students memorize what teachers explain (Al-Husban, 2019). Put differently, if reading does not entail an urgency for comprehension, learners would merely perpetuate learning by rote which seems to be detrimental to their education. Education not only requires learners who are articulate but also ones who can advance a critical understanding of pedagogical matters in an autonomous way (Waghid, 2019).

Results regarding the second part of the first theme showed that invariably, time management is inextricably linked to learner performance and achievement, and a lack thereof undermines learning (Nasrullah & Khan, 2015). In this context, learners required much more than just knowing how to organize their time. They seemed demotivated, apprehensive, and insecure to the extent that they wasted time and showed an unwillingness to be attentive to reading – a view corroborated by St Clair-Thompson et al. (2018). Inefficient time management could be perceived as a barrier to reading independently and doing reading tasks punctually with minor supervision from teachers. Learners were too used to an approach to learning that required them to attend schools and study by rote.

Teachers usually identified what was important for them to read, without learners having thought deeply about what they should have read. On the contrary, autonomous learning, partially triggered by the disruptive influence of COVID-19, pressured them into approaching the reading of texts differently. Learners were now expected to increase their reading time and to read the texts more systematically such as to analyze, summarize, and link new understandings of knowledge with their previous knowledge constructs. Of course, critical reading demands that learners understand, analyze, summarize, and make judgments about their analyses of texts. It seems as if the emergency approach to online teaching-learning may have bade them adopt an autonomous approach to reading and learning. Unless learners acquire more confidence and criticality in their analyses of reading texts concomitantly with more time allocated for reading, they could continue with indefensible practices such as rote learning that is not always desirable in the pursuit of understanding, clarity of meaning, and seeing things anew.

Whereas the results regarding Teachers' practices and strategies revealed that they were aware of the difficulties that their learners faced while being away from their school and face-to-face classes. They recognized learners' incapacity to read independently and doing their reading tasks confidently. Teachers seemed to have diligently used certain reading comprehension practices which they used to employ in the face-to-face classes but now through the support of technologically enhanced applications. Interestingly, teachers revealed they could employ some of them without any difficulties like asking questions, sending texts or stories, and asking them to summarize texts in their own language. Of course, the latter approach in reading comprehension online seems challenging for learners as they did not always respond adequately to an approach that required intense self-determination and confidence. So, they did not always get it right. But, at least, learners were afforded opportunities to think for themselves even though they might not have been successful at times. Yet, there was one teacher who showed the significance of cultivating independent learning through reading comprehension as supported in the seminal works of Head et al. (2018) and Al-Husban (2019). Like Head, et al. (2018) and Al-Husban (2019) this teacher recognized that proficiency in reading and comprehension can result in a critical understanding of texts, especially when learners are summoned to speak their minds. In other words, Despite the obstacles to critical thinking, one teacher had the opportunity to speed up reading exercises that elicited learners' ability to become more conscientious. And, when evocation among learners took place on the grounds of teachers having provoked them to think for themselves, it can be inferred that online teaching-learning encounters moved towards inclusive practices.

Conclusion

Teaching that leads to the unexpected and improbable seems to be endorsed by some learners. That is, learners do not always want to be told exactly what to do and what the required outcomes of learning should be. Suddenly having asked them to manage their own independent learning through reading and performing many pedagogical tasks with limited supervision, could be perceived as daunting. Yet, the possibility that they learnt autonomously was still there even during the presence of a pandemic. It seems as if learners felt included in the pedagogical activities on the grounds that they could offer their views on pedagogical matters. Speaking independently seems to be a condition for pedagogical inclusion. This means that when teachers create sufficient opportunities to engage learners critically in pedagogical encounters, the possibility is always there that they will equally participate and hence not be excluded from the pedagogical encounters. Elsewhere, it has been argued that democratic inclusion in pedagogical encounters depends on the urgency to listen to learners' voices as they come to speech (Waghid, 2019).

It is erroneous to think that learning will just happen when new technological approaches are used. However, what this study showed is that teaching-learning should be foregrounded in a different way as to ensure plausible pedagogical practices. If learners' capabilities or potentialities are evoked whereby, they can critically think for themselves, commit themselves to the reading and comprehension of texts, and manage their engagement time and opportunities with texts efficiently, the possibility is always there that their learning will be or become autonomous, that is, self-directed and independent. It is not that a teacher should always tell learners what to do, for that would constrain autonomous learning. When learners are challenged to read texts by themselves, analyze their understandings in justifiable ways, and commit to spending enough time with texts, the possibility that they could learn critically and independently will be highly likely. However, if teachers think that they should always tell learners what to do and learners themselves rely only on the voices of teachers, they could not appear to be interested in intellectual discourse, at least not in a critical way. This study has shown that online teaching-learning can enhance autonomous learning in the sense that teachers evoked the self-understandings of learners to articulate speech as a corroboration that they have learnt. Equally, when teachers summoned learners to think for themselves and not always having told them what to do, the possibility that learning could be autonomous remained highly likely.

The upshot of autonomous learning is that learners will invariably be included democratically within pedagogical encounters (Waghid, 2019). They would experience moments of profound openness when they are included, and opportunities are provided for them to have a voice in highly inclusive pedagogical environments. Finally, the research regarding autonomous learning which we have reported on, can be framed within the context of inclusive education: learners spoke independently about their learning encounters; learners engaged critically, and teachers cultivated pedagogical actions for critical and hence, democratic engagement. When human independence, criticality, and engagement are foregrounded in pedagogical actions, then possibility will always be there for such encounters to be inclusive.

Needless to say that, further research would benefit exploring the accurate time student spent reading different academic tasks, and other factors that exhibit reading habits. In addition to that, findings of the current study have important implications for policy makers in curricula and textbooks and professional development programs to take these notes into consideration. Curricula and textbooks agency should select the content that stimulate students' interest to read, and provide enough room for students to select their own reading to develop their reading stamina, with more focus on the twenty-first century skills, and these classifications of curricula and textbooks need a qualified teacher who could help and support students during face to face teaching and learning process or during online learning, and focus his/ her teaching in acquiring students skills rather than content to make student ready to any challenging situation in the future, because no one knows what the future will bring to this globe.

References

Al-Husban, N. (2019). EFL teachers' practices while teaching reading comprehension in Jordan: Teacher development implications. *Journal on English as a Foreign Language, 9*(2), 127–145.

Allington, R. L. (2014). How reading volume affects both reading fluency and reading achievement. *International Electronic Journal of Elementary Education, 7*(1), 13–26.

Burnett, C., & Merchant, G. (2019). Revisiting critical literacy in the digital age. *The Reading Teacher, 73*(3), 263–266.

Chabbott, C., & Sinclair, M. (2020). SDG 4 and the COVID-19 emergency: Textbooks, tutoring, and teachers. *Prospects, 49*(1), 51–57.

Chamberlain, L., Lacina, J., Bintz, W. P., Jimerson, J. B., Payne, K., & Zingale, R. (2020). Literacy in lockdown: Learning and teaching during COVID-19 school closures. *The Reading Teacher, 74*(3), 243–253.

d'Orville, H. (2020). COVID-19 causes unprecedented educational disruption: Is there a road towards a new normal? *Prospects, 49*, 11–15.

Dreesen, T., Akseer, S., Brossard, M., Dewan, P., Giraldo, J. P., Kamei, A., ... & Ortiz, J. S. (2020). *Promising practices for equitable remote learning: Emerging lessons from COVID-19 education responses in 127 countries*. https://www.unicef-irc.org/publications/pdf/IRB%20 2020-10.pdf

Head, C. N., Flores, M. M., & Shippen, M. E. (2018). Effects of direct instruction on reading comprehension for individuals with autism or developmental disabilities. *Education and training in autism and developmental disabilities, 53*(2), 176–191.

Horne, S. (2014). *The effectiveness of independent reading and self-selected texts on adolescent reading comprehension: A quantitative study*. Unpublished doctoral dissertation, Liberty University, Lynchburg, Virginia, the USA.

Huang, S., Capps, M., Blacklock, J., & Garza, M. (2014). Reading habits of college students in the United States. *Reading Psychology, 35*(5), 437–467.

Jain, S., Lall, M., & Singh, A. (2021). Teachers' voices on the impact of COVID-19 on school education: Are ed-tech companies really the panacea? *Contemporary Education Dialogue, 18*(1), 58–89.

Kelley, M. J., & Clausen-Grace, N. (2009). Facilitating engagement by differentiating independent reading. *The Reading Teacher, 63*(4), 313–318.

Mahmood, S. (2021). Instructional strategies for online teaching in COVID-19 pandemic. *Human Behavior and Emerging Technologies, 3*(1), 199–203.

McVeigh, F. (2019). Creating passionate readers through independent reading. Literacy leadership brief. . https://www.literacyworldwide.org/docs/default-source/where-we-stand/ila-creating-passionate-readers-through-independent-reading.pdf.

Moriarty, K. (2020). Collective impacts on a global education emergency: The power of network response. *Prospects, 49*(1), 81–85.

Nasrullah, S., & Khan, M. S. (2015). The impact of time management on the students' academic achievements. *Journal of Literature, Languages, and Linguistics, 11*(1), 66–71.

Nugent, M., Gannon, L., Mullan, Y., & O'Rourke, D. (2019). Effective interventions for struggling readers. In *A good practice guide for teachers* (pp. 1–47). National Educational Psychological Service.

Pilgreen, J. L. (2000). *The SSR handbook: How to organize and manage a sustained silent reading program*. Boynton/Cook Publishers.

Reutzel, D. R., Jones, C. D., & Newman, T. H. (2010). Scaffolded silent reading: Improving the practice of silent reading practice in classrooms. In E. H. Hiebert & D. R. Reutzel (Eds.), *Revisiting silent reading: New directions for teachers and researchers* (pp. 129–150). International Reading Association.

Sanden, S. (2012). Independent reading: Perspectives and practices of highly effective teachers. *The Reading Teacher, 66*(3), 222–231.

St Clair-Thompson, H., Graham, A., & Marsham, S. (2018). Exploring the reading practices of undergraduate students. *Education Inquiry, 9*(3), 284–298.

Taylor, B. M., Pressley, M. P., & Pearson, P. D. (2000). *Research-supported characteristics of teachers and schools that promote reading achievement*. National Education Association, Reading Matters Research Report.

Thomas, L., Hockings, C., Ottaway, J.,& Jones, R. (2015). *Independent learning: Student perspectives and experiences*. https://s3.eu-west-2.amazonaws.com/assets.creode.advancehe-document-manager/documents/hea/private/independent_learning_final_1568037336.pdf

UNESCO. (2021). *Supporting learning recovery one year into COVID-19, global education coalition in actions*. https://unesdoc.unesco.org/ark:/48223/pf0000376061

Waghid, Y. (2019). *Towards a philosophy of caring in higher education: Pedagogy and nuances of care*. Palgrave Macmillan.

Naima Al-husban received her Ph.D in Curriculum and Instruction from the University of Jordan in 2016. In 2001 she worked as an EFL teacher for ten years, and she has participated in projects in cooperation with the British Council about developing Syrian refugees' skills in English language as a foreign language and training EFL teachers in Jordan how to teach English language. She is currently an associate professor at Arab Open University. She is interested in issues of online teaching, blended learning, literacy instruction, refugee education, education in emergencies and she has some publications related to teaching English language as a foreign language, refugees education, and blended learning. She is also a member in the Editorial Review Board of Reading Teacher journal, and a reviewer in several journals in the field of instruction of EFL.

Yusef Waghid, a leading African philosopher of higher education, holds three doctorates in education, policy, and philosophy from the University of the Western Cape and Stellenbosch University in South Africa respectively. As a tenured professor since 2002 and distinguished professor (commenced in 2014) at Stellenbosch University he has been a prolific author with 401 publications to date of which 49 are academic books and edited collections. He promoted 32 PhD candidates to completion, and received the Association for the Development of Education in Africa's prestigious Education Research in Africa Award: Outstanding Mentor of Education Researchers (2015). His most notable scholarly contributions in the field of [African] philosophy of higher education feature in significant international scholarly books (one-year period) which include, Towards an Ubuntu University: African Higher Education Reimagined (2022, co-authored, Palgrave-MacMillan); Education, Crisis, and Philosophy: Ubuntu within Higher Education (Routledge, 2022); Democratic Education as Inclusion (co-authored, Lexington Publishers, 2021); Higher Teaching and Learning for Alternative Futures: A Renewed Focus on Critical Praxis (co-authored, Palgrave-MacMillan, 2021); and Academic Activism in Higher Education: A Living Philosophy for Social Justice (co-authored) (Springer, 2021). He is editor-in-chief of both Citizenship, Teaching and Learning (since 2018), and South African Journal of Higher Education (since 2005).

Chapter 6
It Takes a Village: Preparing Chinese Immigrant Families for Remote Learning of their Children with Disabilities

Lusa Lo and Kathy Tsang

Abstract Due to the COVID-19 pandemic, all United States PreK-12 students were forced to move from in-person to remote learning at the beginning of March 2020. Schools scrambled to identify ways to continue educating their students. Families, particularly those from low socioeconomic and diverse backgrounds, as well as those with students with disabilities, struggled to balance their work schedules with their children's remote class and service schedules, as well as ensuring that their children received the necessary instructional support and special education services. The purpose of this chapter is to share how one community-based parent support group in the United States empowered and prepared Chinese immigrant families for supporting their children with disabilities during remote learning. This community-based parent support group also offered technological and advocacy training that had a substantial influence on equipping these families to support remote learning for their children with disabilities as well as advocate for the special education services and inclusive support their children required. Recommendations on what schools can do to eliminate the barriers parents face are provided.

Keywords Parent engagement · Chinese immigrant families · Disabilities · Special education · Pandemic

Introduction

Existing research indicates that parent engagement is one of the crucial factors for school success and student achievement (Henderson & Mapp, 2002; Epstein et al., 2018). Studies have shown that when parents are involved in their children's lives

L. Lo (✉)
University of Massachusetts Boston, Boston, MA, USA

K. Tsang
Project Able, Boston, MA, USA

and academic careers, their children's academic achievement, behavior, and attitudes toward school are more likely to improve (Castro et al., 2015; Henderson & Mapp, 2002; Topor et al., 2010). Parent engagement is even more crucial in special education, since parents are the only ones who can make decisions and advocate for their children with disabilities about placement and special education services.

In the United States (U.S.), with the update of the Individuals with Disabilities Education Act in 2004, more mandates have been embedded in the regulation that require schools to engage parents in their children's special education process (Individuals with Disabilities Education Improvement Act, 2004). For instance, parents must be on their child's individualized education program (IEP) team, so parents and schools can work collaboratively to determine what services and placements are appropriate for students with disabilities. Parental consent must be obtained prior to any formal evaluation. Additionally, parents must be informed of the evaluation results within a specific timeframe. However, even with these mandates, not all parents are knowledgeable enough to take on the roles as decision makers and advocates for their children with disabilities, especially ones from low socioeconomic and culturally and/or linguistically diverse (CLD) backgrounds (Hirano et al., 2018; Kim et al., 2007). Furthermore, some schools may not always fully engage parents in the special education process (Lo & Bui, 2020).

Challenges CLD Students and Families Faced During Remote Learning

Due to the COVID-19 pandemic, each state in the U.S. has implemented the stay-at-home policy since March 2020. All schools were forced to close temporarily (Education Week, 2020). Schools had no choice but to move student learning from in-person to remote. This sudden change did not provide schools with sufficient time to plan and be prepared. Schools did not know how they could provide remote instruction effectively. Many teachers were also not technologically prepared to teach remotely (Adams, 2020; Newton, 2020). In order to ensure that some forms of remote learning could take place, schools scrambled to distribute instructional materials, such as textbooks, for students to take home.

While a computer and a stable internet connection are required to engage in remote learning, the National Telecommunications and Information Administration (2020) reported that 72% of families do not own a desktop computer and 53% of them do not own a laptop. Additionally, over seven million families do not have internet access at home (National Telecommunications and Information Administration, 2020). To address this, many schools attempted to loan any technological devices they had available, such as Chromebooks and iPads, and provided students with free internet connections for a limited time. However, as of December 2020, almost half of the largest school districts in the U.S. were still in the process of distributing devices to students and determining internet connectivity issues

(Richards et al., 2021). Additionally, many school districts had stopped offering free internet services to students after the summer of 2020 (Lo et al., in press). Many families, particularly those who live in rural areas, struggled to maintain a consistent internet connection (Dao, 2020; Maher, 2020). Some students were forced to attend remote classes in their schools' parking lots through their school Wi-Fi, since that was the only stable connection they could find (Jung, 2020).

During the COVID-19 pandemic, the necessity to engage families has become even more obvious and critical. Teachers required a lot of help from families, otherwise remote learning could not have taken place. Families, for example, were expected to be responsible for ensuring that their children attended remote classes on time. Families with young children would also be responsible for assisting their children in logging in online, understanding how to access online materials provided by teachers, and using any online applications that their teachers required (Villano, 2020). All of these required a lot of schedule coordination and preparation by families. However, not all families were available to help support their children at home. While non-essential businesses were ordered to be closed, parents who worked in essential businesses, such as hospitals, grocery stores, plumbing companies, and emergency construction and/or repair companies, were required to return to work. Low-income families had no choice but continued working, so that they could maintain their household income. When schools scheduled students' remote classes, they might not have considered family's work schedule. When families were unable to monitor and support them, many students ended up missing classes (Brody, 2020; Villano, 2020).

For families of students with disabilities, in addition to making sure that their children were included in their classes, they must ensure that they attended additional sessions scheduled by specialists, such as speech and language pathologists, physical therapists, and occupational therapists. While specialists attempted to be creative about delivering services to students with disabilities remotely, technology had its own limitations. These specialists must rely on parents to provide direct services at home (Wintersmith, 2020). Besides coordinating their children's remote class schedule, parents now suddenly became their children's special education service providers (Nelson, 2020). Furthermore, although IDEA (2004) requires schools to assess students with disabilities and review their placement and services annually, the Department of Education in many states had given schools waivers to delay testing due to the COVID-19 quarantine policy (U.S. Department of Education, 2021). Schools had difficulty determining their students' performance and how much they might have regressed during this period due to a lack of evaluation data.

During remote learning, teachers frequently used online applications such as Google Classroom, Seesaw, and many other Google applications such as Google Docs and Jamboard. Many school districts provided training to teachers, because not all of them were aware of and/or knew how to use these applications. However, such training was not available to parents which prevented them from facilitating their children's learning. When surveying 65 Vietnamese parents, 85% of them indicated that they lacked skills to provide technological support to their children with disabilities (Lo et al., in press). Additionally, when they were unable to stay at home to support their children's remote learning, due to work schedules, they relied on their children's grandparents or relatives, who also had limited to no technological skills (Lo et al., in press).

Community Support

When schools are unable to provide adequate support to families, families often look for help elsewhere. Community involvement is one of the essential types of family engagement and is crucial for many families (Epstein, et al., 2018). This is especially true for CLD families and those with children with disabilities (Lo, 2010, 2019). Currently, CLD students comprise over half of our U.S. student population and special education student population (U.S. Department of Education, 2019a, b). With the continued increase of foreign-born immigrants in the U.S., almost half of them spoke no to limited English (Batalova et al., 2021). With cultural and linguistic challenges, foreign-born parents struggle to support their children's education and often turn to their community for support.

In each state of the U.S., there is at least one Parent and Training Information Center to support families of students with disabilities (Center for Parent Information & Resources, 2021). Some states with a high percentage of diverse population, such as California, also have Community Parent Resource Centers which serve and support underserved families of children with disabilities, such as low-income families, families of children who are English learners, and parents with disabilities. Some of these centers also target serving specific ethnic subgroups, such as Chinese, Spanish, and Samoan. CLD families in states that do not have Community Parent Resource Centers often turn to smaller non-profit organizations and/or community-based parent support groups for support, since they are more likely to be familiar with their cultural and linguistic needs (Lo, 2019).

Having a child with a disability can be stressful for many families. CLD families often have additional stress, due to their cultural views of disability and limited resources to educate themselves about disability (Lamorey, 2002; Lynch & Hanson, 2004). Existing research about parent support groups consistently suggests that parents participating in these groups not only can connect with families who face similar challenges but could also receive psychological and emotional support from their fellow parent group members (Lo, 2010; Santelli et al., 2001). Furthermore, due to their limited English proficiency, CLD parents often encounter difficulties obtaining information and determining where to get resources. For instance, special education regulations and websites of community organizations and government agencies are often available in English only. Families who have limited to no English proficiency are unable to understand these materials. Often, families in community-based parent support groups can assist each other, since many of them have already gone through the special education process when helping their own children with disabilities (Lo, 2010). Therefore, the purpose of this chapter is to share how one community-based parent support group in the U.S. empowered and prepared

Chinese immigrant families to support their children with disabilities for remote learning and advocate for the special education services and inclusive support that they needed. This mixed-method study attempted to answer the following research questions:

1. How did the community-based parent support group impact Chinese immigrant parents' preparedness to support their children with disabilities for remote learning?
2. To what extent did the parent support group affect their ability to advocate for their children with disabilities for the needed special education services and support?

Methods

Overview of the Community-Based Parent Support Group

The participating community-based parent support group was founded in 2012 to support Chinese immigrant families of students with disabilities. At that time, it was the first and only parent support group for this ethnic subgroup in the community. The group grew from 10 to 78 parents. All parents had at least one PreK-12 child with a disability. Prior to the COVID-19 pandemic, this group met once a month at a community center for two hours. Childcare services and light dinners were provided. At the end of each year, participating parents were surveyed about what they would like to learn in the upcoming year. These topics were chosen to be the target of each monthly meeting. Guest speakers with specific expertise, such as applied behavioral specialists, were invited to speak with the group and share resources.

Since the advent of the pandemic, the group were unable to continue their face-to-face meetings and decided to meet online instead. An instant messaging system was also used to allow parents to raise questions/concerns and receive instant support from one another. Various types of support were provided to parents during this period. First, due to the limited technological skills of the parents, workshops related to improving and facilitating their child's online learning experiences were provided. Parents, for example, learned how to use various Google applications, such as Google Docs, which were widely used by teachers, as well as how to add extensions to their web browsers that could improve their child's remote learning experiences, such as using reader view to remove unnecessary images and content that could distract students when reading materials on the web. The use of reader view has been considered as effective in increasing readers' reading speed, since readers won't be disrupted by irrelevant content on the page (Li et al., 2019). Parents also learned how to use video conferencing applications, such as Zoom, and free apps to scan important documents such as IEPs and doctor's letters, so they could easily communicate with schools and share these documents with them. Second, advocacy training was provided, such as how to prepare for virtual IEP meetings, be involved in the process when their children with disabilities were about to exit high school, and to request for services that were stated on IEPs but were not provided. Third, parents were informed of helpful information and resources, such as virtual parent workshops and updated materials and guidance provided by the Department of Education. Fourth, parents were encouraged to engage their children with disabilities in art activities at home. The group provided art and recyclable materials and offered prizes to all participated families. Finally, the group coordinator conducted individualized and informal check-ins with the parents on a regular basis to assess their well-being and needs, so targeted assistance could be provided.

Participants

Purposive sampling is often used, when a specific group of participants can better inform researchers regarding a particular issue (Krathwohl, 2009). Since this study was designed to focus on the impact of the community-based parent support group on Chinese immigrant parents of students with disabilities in the U.S. during remote learning, purposive sampling is a suitable method to recruit participants for the study.

Among the 78 parent participants in the support group, 35 of them participated in the study. All parent participants were immigrants to the U.S and had at least one PreK-12 child with a disability. Most had a limited English language proficiency level and had educational levels of high school and below. See Table 6.1 for the demographics of the parent participants.

Data Collection and Analysis

Survey and interview data were collected in this mixed method study. Survey and interview questions were created and written in English first and then translated into Chinese by the first author. A professional translator checked the translation for accuracy. All instruments were piloted with three Chinese parents. No changes were required.

The online survey consisted of 15 questions which included both Likert scale questions (scale of 1 through 4, where 4 is the highest) and open-ended questions. For instance, "I am satisfied with the support provided by the parent support group" and "I am able to receive helpful information about advocating for my children with disabilities." Mean and standard deviation were derived for the Likert scale questions.

Due to the COVID-19 pandemic stay-at-home mandates, video conferences were chosen for the interviews. Interviews consisted of five guiding questions about their perceptions of the support they received from the parent group. For instance, "What was your first reaction when schools moved to remote learning at the beginning of the pandemic?" "How did the support group assist you, so you can support

Table 6.1 Demographics of the Parent Participants

Demographics	Number of participants
Gender	
Mother	30
Father	5
Education	
Not high school graduates	15
High school graduates in home country	12
Associate degree or diploma in home country	3
Bachelor's degree in the U.S.	3
Master's degree in the U.S.	2
Level of English language proficiency	
Non-English speaking	12
Limited English speaking	18
Fluent English speaking	5
Technological skills	
None (e.g., unable to turn on computer)	5
Minimal (e.g., search information on the web)	22
Moderate (e.g., navigate various technological applications)	6
Advanced (e.g., troubleshoot computer problems)	2
Types of their children/youth's disabilities	
Specific learning disability	10
Speech and language impairment	11
Emotional and behavioral disorder	20
Autism	10
Intellectual disability	8
Grade levels of their children/youth's disabilities	
Elementary school	15
Middle school	19
High school	25

your children during remote learning in the inclusive class?" The interview data were also used to further elaborate and triangulate the survey responses of parent participants. All parent participants chose to speak Chinese (Cantonese or Mandarin) during the interviews. All interviews were recorded, transcribed, and then translated into English. Parent participants were invited to review the translated transcripts for accuracy. No changes were required.

The constant comparative method, as described by Lincoln and Guba (1985), was used. The authors reviewed and categorized qualitative data into themes. Two independent reviewers with research experiences were asked to review the data independently and sort the data into categories. The interrater reliability was 95%. The authors met with the reviewers, reviewed the categories, and discussed the differences until consensus was found. Five themes emerged during the analysis. They were parent-to-parent support, technological skills, advocacy skills, student engagement, and unresolved barriers faced during remote learning.

Results

Parent-to-Parent Support

According to survey results, the community-based parent support group had made substantial impacts on preparing participating parents to support their children with disabilities' remote learning (M = 3.80; SD = 0.41). The data also suggested that participating parents were able to learn skills to advocate for their children with disabilities for special education services (M = 3.71; SD = 0.45). Seventy-one percent of the participating parents reported that they had received assistance and/or resources from their fellow parent members in the group. One parent of a 14-year-old youth with autism stated that,

> The parents in the group are very helpful. Many parents are more resourceful than me. They shared parent training opportunities and online resources. Whenever their district SPED PAC organized any parent training sessions, they shared them with the group. This has been very helpful, since my kid's district doesn't offer this kind of support to us.

Another parent of a second-grade child with specific learning disability stated,

> When school suddenly shut down, I didn't know what to do. My kids just kept watching TV and playing video games. I didn't know much. I also didn't have any educational materials at home to help them. Fortunately, one of the parents in the group lives close by us and shared some materials with me, so they could have something to do.

Technological Skills

During the pandemic, the parent group offered a variety of training to parents in the group. Survey data suggested that parents learned technological skills to help facilitate their children with disabilities during remote learning (M = 3.89; SD = 0.32). A parent of an eight-year-old child with specific learning disability and attention deficit hyperactivity disorder said,

> We do not have email accounts. I also have never heard of Google Doc. I didn't know what to do, when the teachers wanted my son to download/upload homework using Google Doc. I think the teacher might have shown him how to do that in class, but he didn't pay attention. When he asked me, I said, "How do I know?" Later, (one of the parents in the group) showed us how to use it. Now I can at least help him when needed. Besides teaching our kids, teachers should have also taught us, since our kids are at home now and would ask us for help.

Another parent of a 13-year-old son with emotional and behavioral disorder stated,

> I had so much trouble dealing with my son due to his behavior. He doesn't listen to me. He also keeps playing online video games. I was worried that he had too much screen time. I was also afraid that he would go to some bad sites that were not good for him. I shared this with (the group coordinator) who later taught me how to block certain sites on his computer and turn off Wi-Fi at home when needed.

Advocacy Skills

In addition to providing technological training, the group also offered advocacy training. In the surveys and interviews, the following topics were mentioned by the parent participants, but not limited to:

- Remote testing
- Transition planning
- Chapter 688 process for turning 22
- Attending remote IEP meetings
- Assistive technology needs
- Missing special education services or provided services were different from what was stated on IEP
- Issues with loaned school devices
- Compensatory services and recovery support

Parents reported that all these topics helped them learn how to advocate for their children, especially advocating for inclusive support and special education services ($M = 3.91$; $SD = 0.28$). During an interview, one parent of a child with 19-year-old daughter with autism reported that,

> I received a document from school stating that my daughter would be transitioning out of high school when she turned 22. I was asked to sign a document. I didn't even know what it was. The group organized a training about what the process was and shared materials with us about what we could do during this process and which government agencies could support her after leaving high school. This information should have been provided by the school. Fortunately, I learned that in the group.

Another parent of a 13-year-old son with multiple disabilities mentioned that the advocacy skills he had learned from the parent support group enabled him to advocate for the inclusive placement that was stated in the IEP,

> My daughter was supposed to be in an inclusive class during reading. However, during the remote time, the teacher put my son in a room with the TA. How was that inclusive? This was different from what's written on the IEP. I worked so hard to get him in the inclusive class, so I was worried that they changed it back. (The group coordinator) taught me that I could request a meeting with the school and share my concerns. With her help, I did that. After a while, the teacher put my son back in the main room and had the TA support him. There are still some challenges, but it's better than removing him from that setting.

Student Engagement

For many teachers, keeping students engaged during remote learning is a top priority. This is also true for the parents in this study. Because of their disabilities and learning on the online platform, many parents (85%) were concerned that their children with disabilities were not engaged in classes. Participating parents reported that the skills they had learned in the group allowed them to keep their children engaged during remote learning. One parent stated that her 15-year son with emotional and behavioral disorder often pretended to be in remote classes, but he was actually watching online videos during class. She said,

> I make sure that he logs into class on time every day. However, during synchronous classes, he didn't listen to the teacher. I found out that he was watching inappropriate videos on YouTube and other websites. The teacher didn't even know. Later I learned from (the group coordinator) how to block him from opening multiple browser tabs. Now he cannot do that anymore. When he is bored in class, he will walk away from the computer, since he cannot open another browser. Then his teacher can see that he is not engaged and will need to do something about it. It's better now.

Another parent of a 12-year-son with autism reported that,

> I don't know much English. When my son had to do homework, such as reading some online materials, and didn't know the meaning of some words, I didn't know how to help him. All I could tell him was to ask his teacher and classmates. Of course, he didn't. Recently, we learned how to add [Google] dictionary to the browser, so I showed him. Now he could find out meanings of words that he didn't know. We also learned to add [Google] translator to the browser, so I can understand what he was reading, if he asked me. This allows me to keep him engaged.

Unresolved Barriers Faced During Remote Learning

Although the participating parents received support and learned many skills from the group, they reported that schools did not always view them as school partners. They continued to face some challenges working with them. A father of two youths with autism reported,

> I know schools are also struggling during this time, but they are not making it easy for us. We have two kids with disabilities. Do you know how impossible it was for us to keep them stick with their class and service schedules? My wife and I cannot just quit our jobs and sit next to them every day. Their schools just told us their schedules and didn't even try to check with us. My parents watched them when we went to work and sometimes forgot about their class schedules, so my kids ended up missing a lot of classes. Their skills also keep regressing.

Another parent of a 20-year youth with cerebral palsy stated,

> Due to his disability, I have to attend all his lessons and therapy sessions with him. I can't understand a lot of English, so I couldn't understand what the teacher or the specialists said most of the time. Although they tried to show me, it's still very limited. When I couldn't understand them, those lessons became a waste of time. Schools know that I don't speak English. Why don't they automatically hire an interpreter during all his lessons?

Discussion and Recommendations to Schools

Almost everyone in the world is struggling because of the COVID-19 pandemic. In addition to battling issues about health, mental health, and employment, the closure of schools is one of the most influential changes to school personnel, students, and families. Student homes suddenly turn into their classrooms. Parents unexpectedly took on additional roles and responsibilities, such as being responsible for keeping track of their children's class and service schedule. Parents of children with disabilities have also taken on the role of being special education teachers and service providers for their children. Parents are concerned, not only about the loss of learning, but also about the loss of skills or opportunities to learn the skills that their children with disabilities lack (Alexander & Ross, 2020).

Studies from European countries indicate that families who have children with disabilities, especially autism, mental health, and intellectual disabilities, struggle the most (Fontanesi et al., 2020; Mazza et al., 2020). Families of students with disabilities in the U.S. are also feeling the effects. In a recent study by Neece et al. (2020), 77 predominantly Spanish speaking parents of preschool-aged children with developmental delays or autism were interviewed about the impact that COVID-19 had had on them. They found that parents struggled to keep their children engaged during school closure, noticed a reduction of special education services provided by the school, and lacked skills to support their children with disabilities. In another national survey about special education services during school closure, only 20% of the participating parents reported that their children received special education services that were stated on their IEPs, and 39% of them reported not receiving any support (ParentsTogether, 2020). The Chinese immigrant parents in this study also had the same experiences and faced similar challenges. During the first few months of the school closures, it was understandable that much of the schools' focus was to prepare their teachers for remote teaching and to ensure that technological devices were delivered to students. When a new school year started and remote teaching/learning continued, the parent participants in this study were still lost and did not know how to support their children with disabilities at home. Eighty-six percent of the parents in this study indicated that they had no to limited English language proficiency, and 77% of them had limited to no technological skills. Together with other factors, such as educational background, these parents had difficulty supporting their children's remote learning at home. It is obvious that remote learning could never take place and be implemented effectively without the support of parents at home.

With the limited support provided by the schools, the participating parents in this study had no choice but to turn to their community-based parent support group for assistance. With the help of the parent support group, parents were able to gain many necessary skills that could help their children. For example, they learned useful and effectives skills in the technological workshops provided by the group. They now knew how to provide some levels of technological support to their children with disabilities at home, help facilitate their remote learning, and keep them engaged. Additionally, the parents learned advocacy skills, so they could ensure that their children with disabilities received the support they needed, such as attending inclusive classes and receiving services from specialists. When services were not provided according to the IEPs, they learned to document them and were prepared to meet with the schools and discuss compensatory services and recovery support.

While support provided by the community-based parent support group had helped the parents tremendously, it still had its limitations. For instance, parents in the group reported that when they were expected to assist their children with severe disabilities during remote classes, due to their limited English proficiency, they were unable to understand the teachers or specialists. Interpreters were not provided in class sessions. Currently, over half of our U.S. special education student population are from CLD background, but most of our general education and special education teachers and specialists remain White and do not speak languages other than English (U.S. Department of Education, 2019a, b). There is an urgent need for school districts, especially those who have a large linguistically diverse student population, to have their own high quality and trained interpreters and translators. Furthermore, when parents are expected to help facilitate their children's learning, especially for those who have young children and children with severe disabilities, parent training is a must and should have been included in the school plan.

One of the main concerns of parents during the pandemic is that their children received limited or no special education services (Neece et al., 2020; ParentsTogether, 2020; The Education Trust, 2020). The parents in this study were no different. Many of them indicated that they understood that schools were also struggling during this time, so they were willing to wait until schools were ready. However, when a new school year began in September 2020, they noticed that services for their children with disabilities remained very limited. These parents did not know what to do and did not know how to reach school personnel. Often, the only ways parents could connect with school personnel was through emails. However, many of them did not own an email account and did not know how to write in English. All these barriers prevented them from communicating with schools. Most of the parents reported that two-way communication did not exist. They were often just notified of what schools wanted to do. Schools should consider communicating with families using their preferred mode of communication. Emails and texts should not be the only way. Additionally, besides informing families, soliciting family feedback is also crucial.

Conclusion

It is evident that community support has played an important role in empowering and engaging Chinese immigrant parents of children with disabilities in this study for remote learning and ensuring that their children receive inclusive education. Future research might want to explore two areas that were not addressed in the present study. First, although the parent participants did not mention their other needs during the pandemic, such as mental health support, this was informally shared with the researchers after the study. Future studies are needed to investigate if community-based parent support groups are equipped to offer this level of support. If so, how effective are they? Second, future studies could also investigate the impact of different types of community-based parent support groups (such as parent-run vs professional-run and English only vs non-English) on families of students with disabilities.

When parents are equipped with the skills they need to help facilitate their child's learning, the ones who benefit are their children. Effective two-way communications between schools and families are also essential for student success. True partnership requires schools to not only share important information with families, but also to seek feedback from them (National Alliance for Family Engagement, 2021). Such feedback can enable schools to determine the areas they need to improve. Due to budget constraints, school support is often limited. Partnering with the community can be an effective option.

References

Adams, C. (2020, April 17). *Coronavirus 'confusion': Teachers had little training for how to do online classes*. Retrieved from https://www.usatoday.com/story/news/education/2020/04/17/coronavirus-teachers-online-class-school-closures/2972529001/.

Alexander, C., & Ross, N. (2020, May 22). *'It's been hell': Parents struggle with distance learning for their kids with disabilities*. Retrieved from https://www.usatoday.com/story/news/education/2020/05/22/coronavirus-parents-distance-learning-woes-kids-disabilities/5227887002/

Batalova, J., Hanna, M., & Levesque, C. (2021). *Frequently requested statistics on immigrants and immigration in the United States*. Retrieved from https://www.migrationpolicy.org/article/frequently-requested-statistics-immigrants-and-immigration-united-states-2020#demographic-educational-linguistic.

Brody, L. (2020, May 1). *Struggling with remote learning, some families cut class*. Retrieved from https://www.wsj.com/articles/struggling-with-remote-learning-some-families-cut-class-11588334403

Castro, M., Exposito-Casas, E., Lopez-Martin, E., Lizasoain, L., Navarro-Asencio, E., & Gaviria, J. (2015). Parental involvement on student academic achievement: A meta-analysis. *Educational Research Review, 14*, 33–46.

Center for Parent Information & Resources. (2021). *Find your parent center*. Retrieved from https://www.parentcenterhub.org/find-your-center/

Dao, E. (2020, August 5). Remote learning creates issues for families without internet. Retrieved from https://www.kxly.com/remote-learning-creates-issues-for-families-without-internet/.

Education Week. (2020, July 1). *The coronavirus spring: The historic closing of U.S. schools (A Timeline)*. Retrieved from https://www.edweek.org/leadership/the-coronavirus-spring-the-historic-closing-of-u-s-schools-a-timeline/2020/07

Epstein, J., Sanders, M., Sheldon, S., Simon, B., Salinas, K., Jansorn, N., … Williams, K. (2018). *School, famiily, and community partnerships: Your handbook for action* (4th ed.).

Fontanesi, L., Marchetti, D., Mazza, C., DiGiandemenico, S., Roma, P., & Verrocchio, M. (2020). The effect of the COVID_19 lockdown on parents: A call to adopt urgent measures. *Psychological Trauma: Theory, Research, Practice, and Policy, 12*, S79–S81.

Henderson, A., & Mapp, K. (2002). *A new wave of evidence: The impact of school, family, and community connections on student achievement*. Southwest Educational Development Laboratory.

Hirano, K., Rowe, D., Lindstrom, L., & Chan, P. (2018). Systemic barriers to family involvement in transition planning for youth with disabilities: A qualitative metasynthesis. *Journal of Child and Family Studies, 27*, 3440–3456.

Individuals with Disabilities Education Improvement Act of 2004, 20 U.S.C. 1400 et seq. (2004).

Jung, C. (2020, May 8). *When your remote classroom is your car: How some rural students without broadband are connecting.* Retrieved from https://www.wbur.org/edify/2020/05/08/pandemic-learning-without-internet.

Kim, K., Lee, Y., & Morningstar, M. E. (2007). An unheard voice: Korean American parents' expectations, hopes, and experiences concerning their adolescent child's future. *Research and Practice for Persons with Severe Disabilities, 32*, 253–264.

Krathwohl, D. (2009). *Methods of educational and social science research: An integrated approach* (3rd ed.). Waveland.

Lamorey, S. (2002). The effects of culture on special education services: Evil eyes, prayer meetings, and IEPs. *Teaching Exceptional Children, 34*, 67–71.

Li, Q., Morris, M., Fourney, A., Larson, K., & Reinecke, K. (2019, May). *The impact of web browser reader views on reading speed and user experience.* Retrieved from https://doi-org.ezproxy.lib.umb.edu/10.1145/3290605

Lincoln, Y. S., & Guba, E. G. (1985). *Naturalistic inquiry*. Sage.

Lo, L. (2010). Perceived benefits experienced in support groups for Chinese families of children with disabilities. *Early Child Development and Care, 180*, 405–415.

Lo, L. (2019). Community involvement: What supports are available for diverse families of students with disabilities? In I. L. Lo & Y. Xu (Eds.), *Family, school, and community parnterships for families of individuals with disabilities* (pp. 29–39). Springer.

Lo, L., & Bui, O. (2020). Transition planning: Voices of Chinese and Vietnamese parents of youth with autism and intellectual disabilities. *Career Development and Transition for Exceptional Individuals, 43*, 89–100.

Lo, Y., Lo, L., Kourea, L., & Chang, W. (in press). How to meet the needs of students related to cultural and linguistic diversity. In B. Collins, No one told me I would have to teach like that! Guidelines for special education teachers working with remote students. Brookes Publishing.

Lynch, E., & Hanson, M. (2004). *Developing cross-cultural competence: A guide for working with children with their families* (3rd ed.). Paul H. Brookes.

Maher, K. (2020, September 13). *Remote schooling out of reach for many students in West Virginia without internet.* Retrieved from https://www.wsj.com/articles/remote-schooling-out-of-reach-for-many-students-in-west-virginia-without-internet-11599989401

Mazza, C., Ricci, E., Biondi, S., Colasanti, M., & Ferracuti, S. (2020). Nationwide survey of psychological distress among Italian people during the COVID-19 pandemic: Immediate psychological responsses and associated factors. *International Journal of Environmental Research and Public Health, 17*, 1–14.

National Alliance for Family Engagement. (2021). *Family engagement is about more than caring.* Retrieved from https://famengage.org/.

National Telecommunications and Information Admini. (2020). *Digial nation data explorer.* Retrieved from https://www.ntia.doc.gov/data/digital-nation-data-explorer#sel=internetUser&disp=map

Neece, C., McIntyre, L., & Fenning, R. (2020). Examing the impact of COVID-19 in ethnically diverse families with young children with intellectual and developmental disabilities. *Journal of Intellectual Disability Research, 64*, 739–749.

Nelson, A. (2020, September 29). *How COVID-19 has affected special education students.* Retrieved from https://now.tufts.edu/articles/how-COVID-19-has-affected-special-education-students

Newton, D. (2020, March 26). *Most teachers say they are 'not prepared' to teach online.* Retrieved from https://www.usatoday.com/story/news/education/2020/04/17/coronavirus-teachers-online-class-school-closures/2972529001/.

ParentsTogether. (2020, April 23). *ParentsTogether survey reveals remote learning is failing our most vulnerable students.* Retrieved from https://parentstogetheraction.org/2020/05/27/parentstogether-survey-reveals-remote-learning-is-failing-our-most-vulnerable-students-2/.

Richards, E., Aspegren , E., & Mansfield, E. (2021, February 4). *A year into the pandemic, thousands of students still can't get reliable WiFi for school: The digital divide remains worse than ever.* Retrieved from https://www.usatoday.com/story/news/education/2021/02/04/covid-online-school-broadband-internet-laptops/3930744001/

Santelli, B., Poyadue, F., & Young, J. (2001). *The parent to parent handbook: Connecting families of children with special needs.* Brookes Publishing.

The Education Trust. (2020, April). *Educational equity in crisis.* Retrieved from https://edtrustmain.s3.us-east-2.amazonaws.com/wp-content/uploads/sites/3/2017/11/24113810/ETW-K12-Parent-Poll-March-2020.pdf.

Topor, D., Keane, S., Shelton, T., & Calkins, S. (2010). Parent involvement and student academic performance: A multiple mediational analysis. *Journal of Prevention and Intervention in the Community, 38,* 183–197.

U.S. Department of Education. (2019a). *Status and trends in the education of racial and ethnic groups.* Retrieved from https://nces.ed.gov/programs/raceindicators/index.asp

U.S. Department of Education. (2019b, February). *Status and trends in the education of racial and ethnic groups.* Retrieved from https://nces.ed.gov/programs/raceindicators/index.asp

U.S. Department of Education. (2021, February 22). *U.S. department of education releases guidance to states on assessing student learning during the pandemic.* Retrieved from https://www.ed.gov/news/press-releases/us-department-education-releases-guidance-states-assessing-student-learning-during-pandemic

Villano, M. (2020, September 24). *Students with special needs face virtual learning challenges.* Retrieved from https://edition.cnn.com/2020/09/24/health/special-needs-students-online-learning-wellness/.

Wintersmith, S. (2020, May 19). *Specialists struggle to deliver special education services.* Retrieved from https://www.wgbh.org/news/education/2020/05/19/specialists-struggle-to-deliver-special-education-services.

Dr. Lusa Lo is an Associate Professor at University of Massachusetts Boston. Her research focuses on family-school-community partnerships and educational planning and practice for English learners with disabilities. Dr. Lo works closely with schools, communities, and government agencies to develop parent training programs and make policy changes nationally and internationally. She also collaborates with local organizations, such as the Multistate Association for Bilingual Education, and offers professional development to prepare administrators and educators for supporting students with disabilities and their families from culturally and linguistically diverse backgrounds.

Kathy Tsang is a family case worker at the Project Able which is one of the cultural/linguistic-specific family support centers funded by the Massachusetts Department of Developmental Disabilities. Project Able provides support to Vietnamese- and Chinese-speaking families of students with disabilities in the metro Boston area in Massachusetts. Ms. Tsang has extensive background working with students with disabilities and their families. She provides resources, support, and advocacy for Chinese-speaking families.

Chapter 7
Factors Influencing Five Foundation Phase Teachers' Teaching Experiences During COVID-19 in an Inclusive Suburban School

Carin Stollz, Heather Nadia Phillips, and Janet Condy

Abstract The role of teachers as agents of inclusion in education is inimitable at this time. While the more vulnerable students are already negatively affected, COVID-19 has created an environment where all learners are now being exposed to being socially vulnerable. The depersonalisation of classroom contexts and diminished interaction, hindered teachers from providing the necessary support and resources to satisfy the needs of all learners. This study explores the factors which influenced teachers' experiences in inclusive classrooms once they returned to school to do face-to-face teaching during COVID-19. A qualitative approach, using a case study design, allowed the researchers to gain an in-depth understanding of the teachers' classroom experiences during this time. Five teachers were purposively selected and semi-structured interviews were used to collect data. The results reveal that teachers experienced increased levels of fear: fear of transmission of the virus, fear of curriculum not being covered, fear of not being able to manage learners and keep them safe, resulting in them feeling pressured and overwhelmed. Brantmeier's (Pedagogy of vulnerability: Definitions, assumptions, and applications, pp 95–106) pedagogy of vulnerability approach allowed teachers to freely express their feelings of vulnerability as they struggled to adjust to new ways of teaching and learning. Greater collaboration with peers and expressing their feelings and fears made it easier to manage the challenges experienced. Recommendations included further development of teachers regarding alternative pedagogies to be used during crisis management as well as revisions of current policies to effect a smoother transition during pandemic times.

Keywords Curriculum delivery · Inclusivity · Collaboration · COVID-19 pandemic · Vulnerability · Rotational models · Foundation phase · Safety protocols

---

C. Stollz · H. N. Phillips (✉) · J. Condy
Cape Peninsula University of Technology, Cape Town, South Africa
e-mail: phillipsh@cput.ac.za

© The Author(s), under exclusive license to Springer Nature Switzerland AG 2022
L. Meda, J. Chitiyo (eds.), *Inclusive Pedagogical Practices Amidst a Global Pandemic*, Inclusive Learning and Educational Equity 7,
https://doi.org/10.1007/978-3-031-10642-2_7

Introduction

Teachers have a marked influence on student lives making a critical contribution to maintaining and supporting continuity of learning during the COVID-19 pandemic. Although the pandemic has had a great impact on all students, it has been especially taxing for students who are more vulnerable than others. South Africa's Department of Basic Education's (DBE) response to special needs and support services has been to convert ordinary schools to full-service schools where all learners can access education and training no matter what their individual needs are" (DBE, 2001). This means that learners from low socio-economic backgrounds, dysfunctional families, immigrants, refugees, special education needs and others have been merged into mainstream classrooms. These learners are at risk of falling even further behind, adding to the existing learning losses occurring during this time, losing the emotional and social support provided by the 'normal' school environment and their teachers. However, COVID-19 created an environment where all learners were now exposed to being socially vulnerable, greatly influencing teaching and learning contexts. The creation of such environments renders the teachers' role inimitable as agents of inclusion in education.

Teachers have proven to be the front-line workers in education during the unprecedented challenges evidenced by the COVID-19 pandemic. Globally, over 63 million teachers were affected as their day-to-day reality drastically changed. Education systems' weaknesses were emphasized and inequalities intensified as teachers across the world tried to, collectively, manage and create new classroom environments to ensure continued learning for all learners. With the role of teachers constantly evolving during this time and the pandemic recalibrating how teacher flexibility and resilience are meeting all learners' needs, new classroom environments have created feelings of uncertainty, fear and frustration among teachers (Mahaye, 2020).

The new safety protocols which included daily screening of learners, continued hand washing and sanitizing, ensuring all learners mask up and creating social distancing, were the new reality for teachers. These time-consuming adaptations to the pandemic classroom, in addition to embracing new pedagogies for teaching in inclusive classrooms where all protocols are adhered to, increased the existing challenges teachers faced on a daily basis.

There are various issues teachers need to be cognizant of during this pandemic which include: factors influencing curriculum delivery during COVID-19 and teachers' responsibility in ensuring safety and security of themselves and the learners during the outbreak (Western Cape Government, 2020). This study highlights how these influences affect teachers' classroom practice amidst the COVID-19 outbreak. Since research has not sufficiently specified the voices of teachers regarding challenges and day-to-day experiences in their classrooms during pandemic times, this study aims to give voice to teachers' experiences. We investigate through asking: Which factors influenced five Foundation Phase (FP) teachers' teaching experiences during COVID-19 in a suburban school?

In the South African context, the basic education system is divided into primary and secondary schools. The primary school is further divided into the Foundation phase (Grade 0 and Grades one to three), the Intermediate phase (Grades four to six) and the Senior phase (Grade seven). For the purpose of this research the teachers taught in the Foundation phase, comprising of learners from grades one to three, between the ages 6–9 years old.

Literature Review

The literature review discusses some of the factors, teachers experienced during the COVID-19 pandemic.

Fear Experienced By Teachers During the Pandemic

Presley (2021) states that the reopening of schools amidst the pandemic resulted in increased fear for teachers, since they were unaware of what was expected of them. Teaching is known to be complex, "a fundamentally unique and human task" and it is about interaction (Jones, 2017, p.1). However, the onset of the pandemic has depersonalized classroom contexts and diminished interaction, replacing the once 'safe' haven with increased stress and worry about both teacher and learner safety.

Teachers were forced to adjust to the new expectations required of them when they returned to work and had to adapt to a new way of teaching and learning which led to anxiety and teacher-burnout. The United Nations (UN) (2020) stated that the stress and anxiety caused by the onslaught of COVID-19 affected teachers in such a way that they were unable to give their best to all their learners. Teachers have increased levels of fear, since the disease is life threatening, leading them to stay absent from work or leave their jobs altogether.

Mertens et al. (2020) discuss the different fears teachers experienced during COVID-19 when face-to-face teaching resumed. In addition to fear of bodily harm and fear for learners, was the teachers' fear of the unknown. This fear of the unknown, according to Morales-Rodriquez (2021, p.1), stems from "a sense that the perceived information is not sufficient for coping with the situation at any point of processing or level of awareness". Furthermore, Morales-Rodriquez (2021, p.1) reports that the pandemic has activated increased fear which contributes to "growing levels of stress, anxiety, depression and post-traumatic stress".

The World Health Organisation (WHO) (2020) found that all children were more vulnerable and thus sought attachment and more care from their teachers. "Students are more than learners; they are small idiosyncratic people who want to be cared for, understood, liked by their peers, and engaged by instructional opportunities" (Jones, 2017, p. 1). Teaching is interaction and, therefore, teachers are fearful, fearful for their own personal safety and the well-being of their learners since the COVID-19 virus is an infectious disease (Owusu-Fordjour et al., 2020). This affected the management of the 'new' environment created by COVID-19.

How Teachers Manage the Changing Inclusive Classroom Environment During COVID-19

The landscape of education changed dramatically with the onset of the pandemic. The Department of Basic Education in South Africa (DBE, 2020a, b) designed different phased-in approaches to ensure teachers were able to manage their learners once they returned and were able to make the necessary adjustments to their classrooms to ensure the basic protocols for COVID-19, specifically social distancing, were met. The DBE (2020a, b) suggested a phased-in approach which consisted of different models which South African schools could implement according to their needs. The approaches are as set out in the following Table 7.1.

Regardless of which model the teachers chose, all the protocols remained the same. Teachers needed to ensure that there was social distancing in the classrooms, learners wore their protective masks correctly, temperatures were taken every morning and if it was higher than 38 degrees, learners were placed in an isolated room and had to avoid physical contact. Learners sanitize frequently since they come into contact with many surfaces and objects such as: desks, door handles, books, apparatus and ablution facilities (DBE, 2020a). Teachers spent a considerable amount of time enforcing these rules which meant less time spent on teaching and learning, and even less on intervention programmes for vulnerable learners. The new demands expected from teachers were time consuming and exhausting and affected curriculum delivery.

Table 7.1 Phasing-in approach models

Model	How learners are divided using this model	How does this model work?
Bi-weekly approach	Learners are divided into two groups. However, more groups can be created depending on the class size.	One group of learners attend school for one week and the second group of learners attend school the next week, alternating continuously.
Rotational approach according to days of the week		One group of learners will attend school for three days and the second group will attend school for two days. The following week learners will alternate.
Platoon system		The platoon system allows all learners to come to school on one day. The first group comes in the morning and the second group comes in the afternoon.

Factors Impacting Curriculum Delivery During COVID-19

Mahaye (2020) states that the delivery of the curriculum covers the learning experiences the child undertakes with the assistance of the teacher. However, the pandemic disruption has influenced curriculum coverage and the implementation thereof. On 6 July 2020, South Africa's DBE provided a 3-year curriculum recovery plan in the form of annual teaching plans (ATP) which is the basis of a trimmed curriculum for Grades R − 12. The ATPs were developed to help teachers recover the lost teaching time and guide teachers on how to assist all learners amidst the COVID-19 crisis. Hence, teachers were required to plan and prepare lessons, assessments and focus on teaching core content within the limited time (DBE, 2020a, b).

Since schools adopted the different rotational models, timetables had to be adjusted accordingly in order to meet the protocol requirements. The disadvantage of the rotational models was that all learners were not present in school every day leading to an additional loss in contact time. Learners, therefore, did not receive the full content curriculum as set out in the Curriculum and Assessment Policy Statement (CAPS). The DBE, therefore, designed the ATP's which were trimmed according to the time learners had left to complete the academic year (Hoadley, 2020). The DBE (2020a, b) emphasized that teachers should work collaboratively with their colleagues and do team-teaching in order for them to deal with the demands of the changing circumstances.

Adapting Pedagogies for Inclusive Classrooms Amidst the COVID-19 Pandemic

According to Jones and Kessler (2020), the COVID-19 intrusion affected the personal interaction shared between teachers and learners in the FP. Schools, especially teachers, provide learners with stability by ensuring that routine is followed and a safe haven is created within the classroom setting. Jones and Kessler (2020) emphasized that COVID-19 depersonalized that special connection between the teacher and the learner. Sharp et al., (2020) state that teachers were advised to avoid walking around the classroom and getting too close to the learners to mitigate the spread of the virus. Implementing these rules was challenging for teachers in the FP since Howard and Howard (2012) explain that learners in the FP enjoy physical contact with their teachers. Similarly, learners needed to refrain from using apparatus which enhances learning, especially for vulnerable learners. Teachers wearing masks while teaching, made it difficult for children to hear and see how the teacher formulates sounds and asks questions. The teacher might have to repeat herself more than once to make certain that all the learners hear and understand instructions (Phajane, 2014).

In FP classrooms, teachers adapt their teaching styles according to the learning styles and needs of their learners (Awla, 2014). Differentiated instruction, according to Webster (2014), is necessary to assist vulnerable learners in developing confidence promoting better learning. The new found confidence will be demonstrated to peers in group work, providing a greater sense of inclusion. However, during the COVID-19 pandemic, this was difficult as teachers had to find alternate ways to teach to accommodate the changing environment in which they found themselves. Various pedagogies are needed to ensure all the learners' needs are met in the classroom (Phajane, 2014), forcing teachers to resort to designing their own methods of teaching in order to reach the most marginalised (OECD, 2020:20). The COVID-19 rules and regulations hindered teachers from providing the necessary support and resources to satisfy the needs of all learners. In order to satisfy their own needs, teachers also require some measure of support with managing teaching and learning during COVID-19.

Teacher Collaboration

The current crisis has rendered teachers vulnerable and stressed. United Nations Educational Scientific Cultural Organisation (UNESCO) (2020) asserts that it is imperative that teachers embark on working in unison with one another with one goal in mind: to ensure that all children receive a quality education regardless of the challenges currently faced. Teachers' efforts and sacrifices amidst the pandemic do not go unnoticed since UNESCO (2020) emphasizes that teachers have done their utmost to make sure their learners received sufficient work during this time. Teachers relied on one another, drew on each other's professional knowledge and utilized one another as a resource to establish the learning needs of their learners. Hence, Reimers and Schleicher, (2020) concur that teachers need to collaborate with one another to ensure the execution of the curriculum is successful. Working together, sharing knowledge and experiences is essential during these uncertain times.

Theoretical Framework

Brantmeier's (2013) pedagogy of vulnerability informed this research. It highlights aspects that challenge teachers to embrace learning through communication, exchanging information, ideas and experiences amidst the adversities faced during the COVID-19 pandemic. The COVID-19 crisis we are currently facing has rendered teachers fearful, uncertain and anxious. Brantmeier's (2013) pedagogy of vulnerability approach allows the teachers to freely express their feelings of vulnerability which have been caused by the COVID-19 outbreak. Through this approach the teacher is able to admit that they are struggling to adjust to the new ways of teaching and learning and require support from others who are experiencing similar challenges (UN, 2020). Hence, the pedagogy of vulnerability provides opportunities for teachers to share their experiences of concern with one another, to co-learn and to exchange knowledge regarding the successful delivery of the curriculum (Brantmeier, 2013). Reimers and Schleicher (2020) allude to the fact that collaboration is essential amidst the pandemic. Engaging with neighbouring schools or colleagues who have adapted to the COVID-19 crisis afforded teachers the opportunity to ascertain which strategies were effective for them to implement to ensure the continuity of teaching and learning.

Kelly and Kelly (2020) argue that once teachers make admissions of their vulnerability, prospects for deeper learning occur. Deeper learning allows the teacher to acquire new knowledge, to be flexible and allow for transformative pedagogy to take place. A transformative pedagogy is an avenue that promotes social change through teacher interaction; self-disclosure and self-transformation (Brantmeier, 2013). When making admissions to vulnerability, teachers create a platform for deep learning, sharing and co-learning (Brantmeier, 2013). Teachers, one year after the pandemic struck, continue to experience fears of contracting the virus, which are impacting their efficacy in the classroom. Hence, Keet et al. (2009) suggest that pedagogies, like the pedagogy of vulnerability, aim to heal the trauma one experiences from pandemic crises. Reimers and Schleicher (2020) confirm that collaboration and communication during these difficult times aid in alleviating the stress and anxiety caused by the onslaught of the pandemic, thus heightening teacher efficacy in the classroom.

Methods

Research Design

A qualitative approach using an illustrative, group case study design was used for this study as it focused on acquiring an in-depth understanding of a small group of participants set in a real- world context (Yin, 2011). Creswell (2012) states that the qualitative approach aims to provide rich and meaningful information through observation of: behaviour, attitudes and feelings of teachers regarding the phenomenon under exploration. The illustrative case study design allowed the researchers to develop in-depth questions to gain an understanding of how different perspectives provided insight into the COVID-19 phenomenon and its impact on teaching and learning (Creswell, 2007). Crowe et al., (2011) state that "the group case study approach lends itself well to capturing information on more explanatory 'how', 'what' and 'why' questions, ... and allows comparisons to be made across several cases". In the case of this research, one researcher used the site where she is employed since easy access to the participants was of utmost importance as it allowed the researcher to get to know the 'cases' well and work co-operatively with each one.

Setting

The research was conducted at a full-service primary school in a suburban area in the Western Cape. Full-service schools are defined as "schools and colleges that will be equipped and supported to provide for the full range of learning needs among all our learners" (DBE, 2001, p. 22). The school is located in an advantaged socio-economic environment and is thus classified as a quintile 5 school. Schools are categorised into five quintiles based on their socio-economic status with quintile 5 being classified as a fee-paying and well-resourced school and quintile one being classified as a no fee paying, under-resourced school (Ogbonnaya & Awuah, 2019). However, the learners come from diverse backgrounds, many from low-socio-economic areas which border this suburb. The medium of instruction at this school is English with a learner teacher ratio of 35:1. There were eleven FP teachers in total at the school. The school was conveniently selected since it was the site where the main researcher was employed and was located in close proximity to the main researcher's home.

Participants

In order to gain an in-depth understanding of the phenomenon being investigated, five teachers were purposively selected using specific criteria. Etikan et al. (2016) state that purposive sampling focuses on candidates who share similar traits, qualities and experiences of the phenomenon under investigation. Hence, three Grade 1, one Grade 2 and one Grade 3 FP teachers were purposively chosen because they taught in the FP phase, were class teachers responsible for teaching only their own classes throughout the day and were part of the first group expected to teach face-to-face during COVID-19.

Procedure

Semi-structured interviews were conducted since they allowed the researchers to ask probing questions (Jamshed, 2014). The interviews between the researchers and the participants were audio recorded which allowed the researchers to retrieve explicit information from the five teachers. According to Alsaawi (2014) semi-structured interviews are time consuming and a lengthy process since it involves asking probing questions which increases the amount of time spent on the interview. Interviews were conducted at the school in the respondents' classrooms. They occurred after school when almost all learners had left the premises. Interviews lasted between one to one and a half hours each with no interruptions. Another limitation of the semi-structured interviews was that social distancing had to be kept between the researcher and the teachers which made communication difficult. We ensured at least two metres distance between the interviewer and interviewee. The researcher and the participants had to raise their voices to ensure they were heard over their face masks.

Interviews were transcribed verbatim to ensure accuracy and to avoid any bias. An inductive approach was used to validate the data since Thomas (2003) suggests that this method provides a sensible way to categorise information retrieved from participants. Thomas (2006, p. 242) discusses the strategy of the inductive approach as one which consists of five steps which include: "initial reading of text data, identification of specific text segments related to the objectives, labelling the segments of the text to create categories, reducing overlap and redundancy among the categories, and creating a model incorporating the most important categories". The inductive approach, according to Thomas (2003, p.1) "reflects frequently reported patterns used in qualitative data analysis". Using these five steps the researchers read and reread the data; manually identified data that was found to be relevant to the study and coded it; created the themes that emerged; with the final categories identified as: Fears experienced by the teachers; adaptation of classroom environment; adaptation of teaching style; curriculum delivery; and teacher collaboration.

Transcripts were handed back to the participants for member checking. Participants had to check accuracy of the information to ensure validity and reliability. According to Smith and Noble (2015) reliability resembles the consistency in the findings and enables the researcher to make comparisons between the differences and similarities derived from the views of the participants. Creswell and Miller (2000) argue that validity is based on the inferences made from the data. Hence, validity was determined by examining the data extensively to establish themes and categories related to the study.

Ethical Considerations

Ethical consent was obtained from all participants involved in the study including: the university where the one researcher was registered, Western Cape Education Department, the principal of the school and the five FP teachers. All research was conducted in an honest and truthful manner which guaranteed that judgements were based on facts and not a collection of personal opinions based on researcher bias (Resnik, 2015). Participants were informed of the purpose of the study and were notified that all information would remain confidential. Participants' names were kept anonymous and pseudonyms were used to protect participants' identity, for example: Teacher 1 (T1), Teacher 2 (T2). Participants were informed that they could withdraw from the research at any time.

Results and Discussions

The purpose of this study was to determine the factors that influenced five FP teachers teaching experiences during COVID-19. After inductive analysis five themes emerged: Fears experienced by the teachers; Adaptation of the inclusive classroom environment; Adapting pedagogies for inclusive classrooms; Curriculum delivery; and Teacher collaboration.

Fears Experienced by the Teachers

Teachers expressed feelings of fear and concern not only for the safety and security of themselves but for their learners, colleagues and loved ones.

T1: I have fear of contracting the virus and not knowing… where is this virus sitting.
T2: I'm actually very fearful of it [COVID-19 virus] especially because we come from different backgrounds…
T3: Yes, I had some fears… not necessarily fears but I had concerns about… how we would manage the learners and keeping them safe and keeping ourselves safe.

Although it was required of teachers to ensure that COVID-19 safety and security measures were adhered to (DBE, 2020a, b), teachers remained fearful of contracting the virus (Owusu- Fordjour et al., 2020). Dabrowsky (2020) argues that teachers, more than other frontline workers, are at greater risk of infection since there is no protective equipment for them. Added to this is the fact that many learners are asymptomatic and do not necessarily get tested, thus posing a great threat to the transmission of the virus from learner to teacher. However, the pedagogy of vulnerability promotes risk taking – when teachers are willing to risk sharing their fears, concerns and difficulties, they become more courageous (Brantmeier, 2013). Therefore, greater empathy for the realities teachers face each day during COVID-19 is needed and will motivate teachers during this pandemic time as well as reduce stress levels (Dabrowski, 2020).

Adaptation of the Inclusive Classroom Environment

Robinson and Rusznyak (2020) posit that the classroom setting is an integral part of teaching and learning. During the current pandemic classroom environments are characterised by the adherence to COVID-19 protocols. Of these protocols the most difficult to maintain was social distancing and constant sanitizing. The teachers remarked:

T1: I needed to make sure that the classroom is … rearranged … to give that social distance …

T4: … I had to make sure that there was social distancing … I placed them so that they won't be sitting next to one another …

T5: The learners' … were sitting one at a table … and the learners actually found it difficult to keep social distancing and away from their friends.

T2 mentioned that she had difficulty with the classroom arrangement since learners had to be reminded where they sat.

T2: I had to constantly remind the children where they are sitting … children come this day and they come that day… then I must try and find other places where they need to sit …

T1 and T5 indicated that the change in classroom environment affected the learners since they enjoy close interaction with the teacher and with one another. The "inclusion method of teaching challenges teachers to think about how their students learn" during this difficult time (Webster, 2014, p. 24).

T1: …These children are so impulsive they just tend to want to give you a… hug… or they come and touch you when they want your attention.

T5: They found it [social distancing] difficult because they use to being together with their peers … interacting with each other … they finding it difficult to adjust in this pandemic.

The WHO (2020) suggests that learners in the FP are young and vulnerable and constantly seek affection and comfort from their teachers. COVID-19 protocols include that all teachers, as far as possible, ensure social distancing between learners in order to minimise infection rates (Sharp et al., 2020). The challenge teachers experience with managing social distancing, amongst other protocols, results in new anxieties within the adapted classroom environment (Pressley, 2021).

It was the responsibility of the five teachers to ensure learners were sanitizing throughout the day. Three teachers mentioned that learners were sanitized upon arrival, before and after break time, before and after using the toilet and at the end of the school day. T3 mentioned that this adjustment affected her teaching time.

T3: We had to take sanitizing into consideration because in our daily routine it takes up a lot of our teaching time.

Carvalho et al. (2020) prioritises efforts to ensure a clean, disease free, safe environment for both teachers and learners. WHO recommends that the use of alcohol-based sanitizers, temperature checks and social distancing, when implemented well, are effective measures "to target the sources of disease transmission" (Carvalho et al. 2020, p. 10) assisting teachers with their responsibility to ensure a safe environment for all.

Adapting Pedagogies for Inclusive Classrooms During COVID-19

The change in classroom environment affected teachers' teaching styles since three teachers indicated that their group teaching was disrupted. In the FP, learners are grouped according to their learning abilities. The grouping of students according to their abilities is a form of support to vulnerable learners and creates a sense of belonging for them (Webster, 2014). Hence, group work is fundamentally important because teachers are able to focus on specific learning needs of the children (Logsdon, 2018). Teachers were forced to resort to whole class teaching and find alternate ways to educate the learners.

T1: Today I felt like I don't know what to do next because it's unnatural to teach like that… The children are there and I'm here and there's always that distance.

T2: Our children are not in groups at the moment so now… I can't really go around to all the children… What I do is I take them a lot to the board and then it's here that I can see if they do understand what I am doing.

T5: It [change in classroom environment] has affected … our group work on the mat … the groups will be less … we won't take ten [learners] we'll take five and we distance them.

The use of apparatus in the FP is paramount to teaching and learning. However, during COVID-19 learners were not allowed to share apparatus and stationery. Teachers were required to sanitize the equipment daily or make resources for each child individually since learners in FP need to manipulate concrete objects in order to grasp concepts taught (Logsdon, 2018). Teachers explain how difficult this task has become:

T1: If I use some of my apparatus… then I take the sanitizer… but I minimise it [using apparatus] because it's too much to clean… time consuming.

T4: … They need to manipulate their apparatus… so what we do is… we work on it… we sanitize it and we place it in the sun for the following day… It [sanitizing apparatus daily] can become a challenge… but we are adjusting to it…

Managing the use of apparatus became a tedious and time-consuming process for teachers. Sanitizing of apparatus became part of the daily routine, but had exhausting effects on the teacher, leading to teacher burnout and teachers not giving their best to the pedagogical processes (UN, 2020). At this point teachers experience vulnerability on an emotional level, yet with the disclosure of those feelings to their learners a potential exists to engage learners "in both caring for and about the issues" within the classroom environment (Brantmeier, 2013, p. 10), possibly mitigating teacher stress.

It became clear that there was collaboration and communication between two Grade 1 teachers who mentioned that they decided to remove their masks in order for their children to see the formulation of their mouths when teaching phonics.

T1: I needed to pull my mask a little bit down… because if you don't see my mouth, t, c and d sounds the same…

T4: It's quite difficult wearing the mask when doing phonics so we need to drop it a little bit so that they [the learners] can see the formulation of the letters and get the proper sound…

The medium to long term goals in 'Supporting teachers and education personnel during times of crisis' (UNESCO, 2020) states: "ensure that principals, teachers, and other education personnel are sensitized on the risk of future COVID-19 outbreaks and on key prevention measures." Teachers removing masks for the sake of the learners is not aligned with the global protocols for COVID 19 since it places others at risk. The pedagogy of vulnerability proposes that although teachers face challenges, they need to come together and find ways to ensure that teaching and learning continues successfully and safely (Reimers & Schleicher, 2020).

Curriculum Delivery

The DBE acknowledged that there were many gaps in the revised curriculum for face-to-face teaching which were not considered when the ATPs were designed. These include time management, content quantity, administration as well as assessment programmes (Mahaye, 2020). Teachers found the revised curriculum challenging. T1 remarked:

T1: …The revised curriculum I think they should've filtered [reduced] down more. They still expect too much in an uncertain situation… It is not practical because how many of these children benefit really because they not coming to school.

T3 claimed that the revised curriculum should have been work-shopped. Teachers should have been trained on how to use and integrate the ATP's.

T3: It's too much paperwork. I for one am frazzled by the amount of paperwork. … I think it should have been work-shopped with us… via … live stream it … I for one cannot make head or tails about what's going on there…

T4 and T5 stated that there is a gap in the children's learning since they missed out on term two's work due to the COVID-19 disruption. Hence, teachers tried to incorporate term two and term three's work into one term, with no talk of intervention. The teachers responded to the following question: What are your experiences regarding the revised curriculum we have?

T4: Very challenging because we have to teach certain things like … we cannot test them on since we didn't teach that.

T5: … It's a bit difficult because we had to catch up now with term two's work as well… the learners have a backlog …

The DBE (2020a, b) acknowledged that teachers will not be able to complete all the content in the ATP's and therefore suggested that teachers focus on the core content.

Hence, teachers needed to use their professional judgement and make decisions that were in the best interests of their learners (UN, 2020) regarding decisions around choosing core content that learners could cope with as well as assessment.

Teacher Collaboration

Since the COVID-19 pandemic was new to everyone, teachers relied on each other's experiences, shared ideas and knowledge on how to make teaching and learning easier. This close collaboration between teachers is aligned with Keet et al., (2009) statement that anxieties and fears experienced from a traumatic event can be overcome when there is engagement, communication, motivation and encouragement shared amongst one another.

T2: … We communicated daily with each other and that made it easier knowing that everybody is experiencing the same things.

T4: We exchanged ideas and we actually pulled each other along the way … we encouraged each other with positive ideas and how to deal with things …

Teachers communicated with each other on a daily basis and this made their task of teaching and learning easier.

T2: We [Grade 2 teachers] didn't really have an understanding of which way forward but when we found out about what other schools were doing in our area, we said let's try this method … let's try to incorporate the teaching in this way and that helped us with our collaboration in the grade.

These findings concur with Brantmeier's (2013) pedagogy of vulnerability theory which suggests that when you admit to your vulnerabilities, you allow yourself to learn from knowledgeable others. T2 mentioned that she found how other schools adapted to their teaching experiences amidst the COVID-19 pandemic which helped her move forward.

Conclusion

The study revealed that there were many factors that affected the five FP teachers teaching experiences during the COVID-19 pandemic. The teachers remained fearful of contracting the COVID-19 virus and feared for the safety and security of themselves, their learners, their colleagues and their loved ones. Despite these factors, teachers were doing their best to ensure that the teaching and learning was executed successfully while ensuring that the COVID-19 protocols, stipulated in the DBE guidelines for maintaining hygiene, were followed.

Teachers rearranged their classrooms and ensured that learners were sitting individually and away from one another. However, this resulted in teachers changing their teaching styles to accommodate the social distancing. Teachers resorted to whole class teaching since they were no longer able to teach using group work. This did not augur well for learners, especially the more vulnerable. Learners were not allowed to share apparatus and equipment which made teaching and learning difficult since FP learners were dependent on the use of concrete objects in order to grasp and understand concepts taught.

Teachers experienced challenges with the execution of the ATPs. There were many factors the DBE did not consider when the ATPs were designed which include time management, content quantity, administration as well as assessment programmes. Despite these factors, teachers were expected to teach to their full capacity and ensure that the curriculum was covered within the specified time-frame. Teachers felt overwhelmed with the pressure that was being placed on them and were concerned about how they were going to ensure curriculum coverage was maximized. Teachers explained that learners were struggling to adapt to the new change and elicited feelings of insecurity which have negatively affected interactions and engagement during class instruction.

Although teachers found it difficult to adapt to the changes of the COVID-19 pandemic, they were able to endure these challenges because they were supported by their colleagues. The challenges became easier to manage once teachers expressed their feelings of fear and concern with one another. The teachers communicated with each other on a daily basis, shared teaching ideas and experiences and were able to self-disclose in times of difficulty, co-learn from more knowledgeable others, thus making their teaching experience manageable.

It is important to realise that relationships and emotions matter. While the pedagogy of vulnerability invites vulnerability through self-disclosure, admitting you do not know, taking risks and being human, it is also an act of courage. A theory relevant during the pandemic when fear and uncertainty are the order of the day. The pedagogy of vulnerability is necessary in a context where a climate of trust is needed, where vulnerable learners and teachers need to be empowered and where strong communities of practice reign, resulting in deeper learning (Brantmeier, 2013).

Recommendations

Workshops for teachers are recommended in order for them to share their teaching experiences and the teaching methods they have adapted to include all learners during the COVID19 pandemic. It is suggested that the DBE revise the ATP policy document through consultation with teachers and educational leaders to address the issue of sufficient curriculum coverage so that it is aligned to the time learners are physically in school. It is also recommended that further research is conducted on a broader audience which can include urban and rural primary school teachers' teaching experiences in inclusive classroom settings during COVID-19.

References

Alsaawi, A. (2014). A critical review of qualitative interviews. *European Journal of Business and Social Sciences, 3*(4), 149–156.

Awla, H. A. (2014). Learning styles and their relation to teaching styles. *International Journal of Language and Linguistics, 2*(3), 241–245.

Brantmeier, E.J. (2013). *Pedagogy of vulnerability: Definitions, assumptions, and applications*. Re-envisioning Higher Education: Embodied Pathways to Wisdom and Social Transformation, (pp. 95–106).

Carvalho, S., Rossiter, J., Angrist, N., Hares, S., & Silverman, R. (2020). *Planning for school reopening and recovery after COVID-19: An evidence kit for policymakers*. Centre for Global Development. Retrieved from - https://www.cgdev.org/sites/default/files/planning-school-reopening-and-recovery-after-COVID-19.pdf.

Creswell, J. W. (2007). *Qualitative inquiry & research design: Choosing among five approaches*. Sage Publications.

Creswell, J. W. (2012). *Educational research: Planning, conducting, and evaluating quantitative and qualitative research* (4th ed.). Pearson.

Creswell, J. W., & Miller, D. L. (2000). Determining validity in qualitative inquiry. *Theory Into Practice, 39*(3), 124–130.

Crowe, S., Creswell, K., Robertson, A., Huby, G., Avery, A., & Sheik, A. (2011). The case study approach. *BMC Medical Research Methodology, 11*, 100. https://doi.org/10.1186/1471-2288-11-100

Dabrowsky, A. (2020). Teacher wellbeing during a pandemic: Surviving or thriving? *Social Education Research, 2*(1), 35–40. https://doi.org/10.37256/ser.212021588

Department of Basic Education. (2020a). *DBE guidelines for schools on maintaining hygiene during COVID-19 pandemic*. Pretoria.

Department of Basic Education. (2020b). *Teacher guidelines for implementing revised annual teaching plans (ATP's)*. Pretoria.

Etikan, I., Musa, S. A., & Alkassim, R. S. (2016). Comparison of convenience sampling and purposive sampling. *American Journal of Theoretical and Applied Statistics, 5*(1), 1–4.

Hoadley, U. (2020). Schools in the time of COVID-19: Impacts of the pandemic on curriculum. *RESEP Non-Economic Working Paper,* Stellenbosch University.

Howard, P., & Howard, J. (2012). Pandemic and pedagogy: Elementary school teachers' experience of H1N1 influenza in the classroom. *Phenomenology & Practice, 6*(1), 18–35.

Jamshed, S. (2014). Qualitative research method-interviewing and observation. *Journal of Basic and Clinical Pharmacy, 5*(4), 87–88. Retrieved from -http://www.ncbi.nlm.nih.gov/pmc/articles/PMC4194943/ [9 July 2020]

Jones, A. (2017). *Relational knowing and responsive instruction* (Unpublished Doctoral Dissertation). University of Illinois at Urbana-Champaign.

Jones, A. L., & Kessler, M. A. (2020). Teachers' emotion and identity work during a pandemic. *Frontiers in Education, 5*(1–9). https://doi.org/10.3389/feduc.2020.583775. [15 November 2020].

Keet, A., Zinn, D., & Porteus, K. (2009). Mutual vulnerability: A key principle in a humanising pedagogy in post-conflict societies. *Perspectives in Education, 27*(2), 109–119.

Kelly, U., & Kelly, R. (2020). Questions and dilemmas for a pedagogy of vulnerability. *Pedagogy of Vulnerability*, 177–202.

Logsdon, A. (2018). *Can ability grouping in school help your child?* http://www.verywellfamily.com/what-is-abilty-grouping-2161808 [6 July 2020].

Mahaye, N.E. (2020). The impact of COVID-19 pandemic on education: *Navigating forward the pedagogy of blended learning*, (pp. 1–13).

Mertens, G., Gerritsen, L., Duijndam, S., Salemink, E., & Engelhard, I. M. (2020). Fear of the coronavirus (COVID-19): Predictors in an online study conducted in march 2020. *Journal of Anxiety Disorders, 74*, 1–8.

Morales-Rodríguez, F. M. (2021). Fear, stress, resilience and coping strategies during COVID-19 in Spanish University Students. *Sustainability, 13*(11), 5824. https://doi.org/10.3390/su13115824

Ogbonnaya, U. I., & Awuah, F. K. (2019). Quintile ranking of schools in South Africa and learners' achievement in probability. *Statistics Education Research Journal, 18*(1), 106–119.

Owusu-Fordjour, C., Koomson, C. K., & Hanson, D. (2020). The impact of COVID-19 on learning- the perspective of the Ghanaian student. *European Journal of Education Studies, 7*(3), 88–101.

Phajane, M. H. (2014). Introducing beginning reading using phonics approach. *Mediterranean Journal of Social Sciences, 5*(10), 477–477.

Pressley, T. (2021). Factors contributing to teacher burnout during COVID-19. *Educational Researcher, 50*(5), 325–327.

Reimers, F.M., & Schleicher, A. (2020). A framework to guide an education response to the COVID-19 Pandemic of 2020. *OECD*, 1–40.

Resnik, D.B. (2015). *What is ethics in research & why is it important?* Retrieved from - http://www.niehs.nih.gov/research/resources/bioethics/whatis/index.cfm.

Robinson, M., & Rusznyak, L. (2020). Learning to teach without school-based experience: Conundrums and possibilities in a South African context. *Journal of Education for Teaching, 46*(4), 517–527.

Sharp, C., Nelson. J., Lucas, M., Julius, J., McCrone, T., & Sims, D. (2020). *Schools' responses to COVID-19: The challenges facing schools and pupils in September 2020*. National Foundation for Educational Research.

Smith, J., & Noble, H. (2015). *Issues of validity and reliability in qualitative research.* Retrieved from - http://ebn.bmj.com/content/18/2/34 [10 July 2020].

Thomas, R. (2003). A general inductive approach for qualitative data analysis. *American Journal of Evaluation, 27*(2), 1–11.

Thomas, D. R. (2006). A general inductive approach for analyzing qualitative evaluation data. *American Journal of Evaluation, 27*(2), 237–246.

UNESCO. (2020). *UNESCO COVID-19 education response*: Supporting teachers and education personnel: 2020. Retrieved from https://unesdoc.unesco.org/ark:/48223/pf0000373338

United Nations. (2020). *Policy brief: Education during COVID-19 and Beyond.* Retrieved from - https://www.un.org/development/desa/dspd/2020/04/social-impact-of-COVID-19).

Webster, T. (2014). The inclusive classroom. *BU Journal of Graduate Studies in Education, 6*(2), 23–26.

Western Cape Government, (2020). *WCED preparations for the return of learners to schools are progressing well.* [Online]. Retrieved from https://wcedonline.westerncape.gov.za/news/wced-preparations-return-learners-schoos-are-progressing-well

World Health Organization, *Coronavirus disease.* (2019). *(COVID-19). Situation report–72* Geneva: World Health Organization.

Yin, R. K. (2011). *Qualitative research from start to finish.* LondonThe Guilford press.

Carin Stollz is an educator, employed by the Western Cape Education Department (WCED). She works at Lotus River Primary school and has been teaching for 8 years. She will be starting a new post as a Head of Department at Merrydale Primary in 2021. Carin completed her studies at the Cape Peninsula University of Technology. She graduated with her Bachelor's degree in 2013 and with her Honours degree in 2019. She majored in Inclusive Education. Carin enjoys communicating with others, sharing best practices and continues to be a life-long learner.

Doctor Heather Nadia Phillips is a Post-Doctoral Research Fellow who worked in the Literacy Development Research Unit at CPUT. 2021 marks 41 years of teaching experience for her: having held positions of deputy principal and principal at a primary school as well as lecturer in the

Education Faculty of CPUT. She graduated with a doctoral degree in 2013. Her research expertise falls within Teacher Education focusing on Quality, Professional Development, Pedagogy and Literacy. Her core duties include publishing research articles; teaching and supervising B Ed Honours in Inclusive Education and Academic Literacy, and supervising Masters' and Doctoral students.

Professor Janet Condy was the Director of the Literacy Development Research Unit at CPUT. She has been teaching for the past 41 years. She taught for 19 years in mainstream schools and one Special School in Rondebosch and since then she has been developing teachers at the Education Faculty of CPUT. She graduated with her Doctoral degree in 2006 and in 2019 was inaugurated as a Full Professor. Her teaching and research focus has been primarily on Literacy, including Inclusive Education, Digital Storytelling, and Philosophy for Children. She has published over 60 articles, supervised 3 Doctoral students and 13 Masters students.

Chapter 8
The Potential of Online Education: Beyond the Status Quo of Equity and Inclusion

Meaghan Krazinski and Megan E. Cartier

Abstract Pandemic online schooling exacerbated inequities in education. Using Critical Discourse Analysis, the authors examine the growing pains of one school district as it grapples with issues of equity and inclusion during the pandemic. The authors explore how stakeholders conceptualize and prioritize equitable and inclusive pedagogy and decisions when a school goes online. This paper explores how discourse furthers or undermines equitable and inclusive educational ecologies; revealing the challenges of students, teachers, community members, and district leaders. This study analyzes three letters and 18 public comments from board meetings spanning May 2020–May 2021. The authors find significant obstacles to equity, inclusion, and solidarity during the pandemic predominantly residing within racial injustices and harm that predate the pandemic and online learning.

Keywords Critical discourse analysis · DisCrit · Equity · Inclusion · Online learning · Pandemic learning

Introduction

Equity and inclusion circulate within global educational discourse, often without unified definitions. Increasing reliance on technology places emphasis on inclusive and equitable online spaces, but without critical consensus and definitions needed for their creation. Much focus is placed on digital applications and the daily struggles of caregivers; or conversely, liability-driven federal guidelines. This study is an inquiry into these tensions and absences in the context of the United States and one

M. Krazinski (✉) · M. E. Cartier
The College of Saint Rose, Albany, NY, USA
e-mail: mkrazins@syr.edu

© The Author(s), under exclusive license to Springer Nature Switzerland AG 2022
L. Meda, J. Chitiyo (eds.), *Inclusive Pedagogical Practices Amidst a Global Pandemic*, Inclusive Learning and Educational Equity 7,
https://doi.org/10.1007/978-3-031-10642-2_8

school district in Upstate New York. Morrison (2019) wrote that stressed and ornate absences are intentional (p. 173); claiming problem-solving in education requires dialogues, not monologues (pp. 72–73). The discourse of stakeholders, board members, and administrators are powerful drivers of ideological underpinnings of pedagogy and priorities in a school district, and therefore a necessary unit of analysis. The pandemic reveals that boundaries within the classroom are fluidly permeable. What does it take to foster inclusive and equitable spaces when school goes online? Cultures of district spaces need attention as we seek to establish equity and inclusion in online spaces. Stakeholders hold potent knowledge of how in/equity and inclusion or exclusion operate in their community. Yet, analysis often overlooks this level of discourse, instead focusing on individual classrooms or on broader national discourse. As a result, opportunities for analysis that foster the solidarity required for inclusive and equitable classroom ecologies are lost (Annamma & Morrison, 2018).

Of post-COVID inequities, critical technologist Selwyn asks us to pause, take stock of "what's new," asking, "How might things be otherwise?" (Selwyn & Jandrić, 2020). Prior to COVID, board meetings were held at inconvenient times, and minutes were only available in offices upon request, making public spaces less accessible for stakeholder discussions. This study analyzes new discourse data from the critical level of school operations to understand how discourse supports or undermines equitable and inclusive pedagogies. The authors inquire, is this shift perpetuating inequities? And if so, as Selwyn asks, can it be otherwise? The following research question guides this study: What understandings are needed to reconceptualize best practices for inclusion and equity in a post-pandemic era?

Literature Review

Equity has to had contested meanings (For a complete review, see Laff, 2021), and inclusion is also a negotiated definition (Kamei & Harriott, 2021). As relating to disability, inclusion evokes historical place-based definitions, rooted in federal guidelines and marked by a lack of imagination (Love & Horn, 2019; Naraian, 2020; Ortiz et al., 2020). Universal Design for Learning (UdL) is often suggested as a framework for equity and inclusion that embraces all forms of learning, including online learning. Before the pandemic, education stakeholders acknowledged online learning as having the potential to advance achievement for students with disabilities via personalized and adaptive learning (Basham et al., 2020). Some literature focused on material access (Russ & Hamidi, 2021); instructional moves, or teacher experiences (Lambert & Schuck, 2021; Parmigiani et al., 2020). Still, others focus on caregiver roles (Aguilera & Nightengale-Lee, 2020) or affective domains and self-regulation (Chiu, 2021). Discourses of equity around mental health abound in the media (Stringer, 2020); however, the peer-reviewed literature on this seems lacking, despite increased focus on social-emotional learning (SEL) materials.

While the pandemic version of online learning brought unforeseen challenges, root causes of inequity and exclusion preceded the pandemic (Basham et al., 2020; Cutrara, 2021).

Some compartmentalize barriers to equity as separate from the social moment, but one cannot separate pandemic online learning from the historical and social context. Following the police killing of Breonna Taylor, Ahmaud Arbery, George Floyd, and many others, the Black Lives Matter movement remained the focus of many students and educators while transitioning to online learning. Educators grounded in social justice pedagogy noticed online learning's potential to be a vehicle for centering discourse of social justice, equity, and inclusion (Cutrara, 2021; Nasr, 2021). There appeared to be a deconstruction, an opening where online learning conversations against a backdrop of racial reckoning positioned education and pedagogy for reimagining. However, as conversations turned to logistics, schedules, and technology hardware, there was a "return to the rigidity of teaching and learning structures that do not invite radical possibilities" (Cutrara, 2021, p. 16).

Conceptual and Theoretical Framing

This study is grounded in DisCrit classroom ecologies (Annamma & Morrison, 2018), a framework built on Disability Studies Critical Race Theory (DisCrit), Culturally-Sustaining Pedagogy (Paris & Alim, 2014), transnational feminisms, and DuBois Gift Theory. DisCrit argues that race and disability are socially and mutually co-constructed and that movements towards equity and inclusion in education are generally characterized by the interest convergence of the white middle class, rather than those at the nexus of racism and ableism (Annamma et al., 2013), and DisCrit classroom ecologies "refuses deficit-oriented master narratives about learning and behavior of multiply-marginalized Students of Color that animate dysfunctional classroom ecologies" (Annamma & Morrison, 2018, p. 73). Additionally, this framework implies equity and inclusion beyond spatiality in its use of "ecology." Pandemic online learning revealed classrooms are part of a permeable ecology, blurring home, community, classroom, and district. District ecologies are a macrocosm of the classroom ecology, and district ideologies directly impact classroom pedagogies, especially in pandemic remote learning. In the subsequent analysis, online district spaces act as a discursive classroom ecology; therefore, the authors employ DisCrit Classroom Ecologies as a theoretical framework. The tenets of DisCrit Classroom Ecologies include DisCrit Resistance, DisCrit Curriculum, DisCrit Pedagogies, and DisCrit Solidarities (Annamma & Morrison, 2018). The authors employ critical technology theory as a secondary lens, rejecting techno-idealism, as technology abstracts away from interrogative modes that otherwise grapple with material accountability (Papendieck, 2018; Selwyn & Jandrić, 2020). The negotiated and contested aspects of Discourse around equity and inclusion, as well as productive analysis of absences as tensions, are bound up in these theories.

Methods

Critical Discourse Analysis

The authors use critical discourse analysis (CDA) (Gee, 2011) to examine definitions and ideologies of equity and inclusion in online district spaces. CDA addresses how discourse upholds and reveals power (Haddix & National Council of Teachers of English, 2016). The role of tensions, the gap between micro and macro levels of society, and ingroup/outgroup construction are central to CDA, which makes it suited for understanding how stakeholders constructed inclusion and equity during the pandemic (Khan et al., 2019, p. 115). The authors used Mullet's (2018) seven stages for CDA to sequence the analysis of this study.

The forthcoming analysis focuses on thematic tensions, interdiscursivity, "little d discourse" embedded within "big D discourse," describing how discourse signifies identity and a larger social fabric or power relations (Gee, 2011, p. 178). To examine tensions of power means attending to Morrison's ornate absences (2019) as intentional rhetorical moves. CDA refers to this as symptomatic reading (Voithofer & Foley, 2007). Mullet's (2018) study also informs the authors' thematic analysis. The analysis began with open coding, then thematic coding and reflective memos, followed by consolidating codes, and then relating them to the research questions and theoretical framework. Finally, the authors identify and discuss eight overarching themes in the results section.

Data Sources: Sample

Sampling began by searching for keywords of "inclusion" and "equity," along with "online learning," and "students with disabilities" from districts across the United States from March 2020–May 2021. We then narrowed our searches to five districts of varying demographics to compile the data, including board meeting documents, reopening plans, and other official district correspondence, newspapers, and other media reports. The criteria the authors established was that the district be explicitly addressing issues of equity and inclusion during the pandemic, and the presence of adequate contextual information and a robust amount of publicly available texts and data to provide validity to the analysis.

This study focuses on a mid-sized urban school district in upstate New York with a demographic of 10,000 students. During the pandemic, the school district was searching for a new superintendent, navigating possible budget cuts, and dealing with allegations of financial mismanagement and lack of transparency. While the contexts and actors are situated, many districts considered for this study navigated similar terrain and transitions, thus adding to the study's validity. The contexts and backgrounds of the texts, including social, cultural, and historical contexts, genres of authors, and other media, are explored (Mullet, 2018, p. 123). The final unit of analysis was three letters and 18 informal public comments retrieved from board meeting comments. The authors selected these data based on their relevance to issues of equity, inclusion, and the tenets of DisCrit. Topics retained included disability, race, accountability, instruction, pedagogy, teachers, solidarity, educational resources, online learning, parents, and community.

Researcher Positionality and Ethical Considerations

The researchers' positionality, as two former white public school special education teachers, is based on their recognition that school ecologies can enact harmful ideological positions that directly impact classroom ecologies, and that the teaching profession has historically been dominated by white women who are often complicit in perpetuating harm to students of color. They understand the ways that the field of Special Education itself may uphold exclusion, and how paternalism and its cousin martyrdom are used to deprofessionalize teachers, undermining resistance and solidarity from within. The authors connect to this study by acknowledging the harm that teachers can perpetuate and their roles in upholding status quo measures while they were teachers. They seek to use their privilege and research to reveal places where power and status quo are concentrated and upheld, presenting significant barriers to teachers and schools in embracing DisCrit pedagogies and including students in equitable learning.

The data used are public, so there are no ethical issues with consent or archiving. However, the authors considered that information becomes "more public" as it is posted online. To address this, the authors used ethnographically-based situated methods for digital environments (Patterson, 2018). The online spaces were treated as relational and situated, incorporating memos and discussing our interactions within the texts to consider ethical uses of public data. Ultimately, the authors decided to anonymize the information based on the aims of the study.

Results

Transparency: "I Don't Understand Why This Is Happening"

Much of the stakeholder discourse stemmed from expressing the inadequacy of virtual schools. Secondary students without specific support needs were fully virtual, as was the case in many districts during the pandemic. Stakeholders spoke about pandemic education with a combination of urgency and tragedy. Some expressed inevitable resignation: "dare I say fail, to provide a basic and sound education" (Union leader), while others framed the pandemic as catalyst, "…we don't have time for that" (community activist). The crisis was interpreted rhetorically to emphasize the importance of addressing specific issues of equity and inclusion. Many noted the lack of answers around instruction and funding. A National Association for the Advancement of Colored People (NAACP) representative even stated, "We would like answers." A letter from educators of color stated, "those responsible for dismantling these paradigms benefit from inequity." These statements show that public perception held that the school was negligent; abandoning them in their time of need and refusing solidarity. Demands for adequate explanations and echoes of mistrust abounded. One student remarked, "I don't understand why this is happening," describing the school as "molding from the inside out." Another stakeholder commented, "…in my mother's home, as a single mother, she, if we had a loaf of bread or half a loaf of bread, everybody ate." The authors likened this statement to a feeling of senseless suffering; if only motivated stakeholders could receive all the information and tools to support student learning and flourishing.

The Community

Community is frequently mentioned around topics of equity and inclusion during the pandemic. DisCrit pedagogy reminds us of valuing the communities of students of color (Annamma & Morrison, 2018). While many uttered "community," the authors note the word gets taken up in a plurality of ways. "Community" was sometimes synonymous with community members of color, speaking to how the term can generate solidarity, or conversely, entrench color-evasiveness (Annamma et al., 2017). Some speakers identified as "community members," but this was a rhetorical device to distance one's identity from the district while demanding accountability. One member used a parallel structure to emphasize this duality, "so you do better; as a community, we'll do better." Others called out this tendency to disown problem-solving; "but don't leave it all on community activists." The authors believe these statements indicate a desire to do better, but there is also a clear recognition that the work is meant to be shared among all and not just by some. Stakeholders repeatedly requested collaboration with community agencies to meet the need for carework, enrichment, and success, as well as solutions to the needs exacerbated by the pandemic. Community was used as a device to create paradoxical figured worlds of agency or powerlessness, and resource or liability. The community was also an underutilized source of pedagogical support ("where the community can come together and try to push forward education"). This was a world where solidarity was strength ("we might as well get to work ourselves"). Conversely, sometimes the discourse constructed the community as a liability: "the possible community issues, substance abuse, pregnancy, and delinquency." These comments engaged Discourses of White Saviorism, revealing a perception that allocation of resources is justified through deficit notions and devaluing the community.

Adaptive Systems: "Education Systems Are a Living Entity"

Some spoke about the purpose of school, and many demanded a more dynamic structure. A letter from educators of color described education systems as "a living entity...they adapt and evolve to meet the needs [of students]." This statement echoes their desire for a flexible and visionary approach to pedagogy. The letter criticizes the district for not thinking creatively enough or displaying adequate leadership to confront the challenges of pandemic education. Stakeholders used figurative language to compel the district to meet the needs of all students more effectively, linking to Discourses of Equity and Inclusion. Some used idiomatic language to illustrate the need for rapid problem solving, demands for a more iterative approach to education ("I'm not here for the blame game," and "we have to think outside the box"). These approaches run counter to liability-driven constraints underpinning school definitions of inclusion, such as class ratios and certification requirements.

Stakeholders and staff expressed frustration with unmet remote student needs, noting that solutions were available and present, yet untapped ("it's time to be creative and approve these alternative learning opportunities"). The authors note how these conversations recognize classrooms as an ecology, not restricted by walls, but constructed by ideologies and people. Many expressed an energetic willingness to help if it meant more students could access a dynamic variety of pedagogies. However, there remained a palpable frustration that they were not included in the problem-solving, given adequate information, or delegated responsibilities. "No one's coming to save us," said one community activist, attempting to galvanize solidarity towards creative solutions. Some envisioned more fluid experiential learning classrooms and internships beyond the classroom walls ("Put them outside"). The authors note how these beliefs connect to a recognition that arts and physical education are important and the discourse that acknowledged community agencies as a source of pedagogical knowledge and support. The analysis reveals a new consciousness of the conception of school, its boundaries, how to allocate resources, and who drives the discourse of allocation. Stakeholders used this more adaptive, dynamic, and democratically engaged school vision to exercise agency at meetings towards equity and inclusion. Still, they showed frustration that the district discourse clung to the mechanisms of pre-pandemic learning.

Online Learning: "It Cannot Be a Cookie-Cutter Package"

The data revealed that online pedagogy was woefully inadequate. Many linked their frustrations specifically to missing supplementary experiences and supplies that would support a virtual experience, citing aspects of education that sustain holistic and social-emotional student needs. One teacher described the arts as "critical" to trauma-informed instruction, arguing that the teachers need time and resources to overhaul the curriculum and design distance learning. "It cannot be a cookie-cutter package that is purchased and disseminated," he wrote, using an alliterative idiom to trivialize the implementation of a packaged curriculum without criticality. This corrects a common myth about pandemic pedagogy and online instruction and critiques the tendency of technoidealism. Instead, this calls to invest in teachers as valuable creative experts. Likewise, DisCrit pedagogies design "expansive learning opportunities and multiple forms and points of assessment such that...teachers, can critically reflect upon and improve their practice with attention to justice" (Annamma & Morrison, 2018, p. 75). Assuming teachers create online learning modules with a template stifles opportunities for affirming design, critical reflection, and justice. This teacher's sentiments reflect the reality that the conceptualization of virtual learning is not wholly separate from in-person learning. Student needs do not dissolve when students go online. Students need access to materials and support, and materials either need to be translated into online versions or reinvented to meet at-home learning needs. Teachers cannot fulfill all elements with a bundled package, especially when students face teacher absence during the implementation of such. Contrary to popular notions, online learning requires increased customization and teacher presence in order to adapt the curriculum to local situated knowledge and resources.

Missing in Engagement, Action, and Expression

Most access concerns centered on whether online learning could provide multiple modes of engagement, action, and expression, implying that online learning tools have favored the representational domain. One stakeholder wondered, "Will there be a way for questions to be asked," "...to be kept anonymous?" recognizing that in-person communication modes cannot automatically map onto online classrooms and that students receive impromptu in-person support built on relationships. Asking a question is often a spontaneous and embodied act that does not take place in passive modes. For instance, one student remarked, "I got lazy at the end...I couldn't ask my teacher questions." The authors find this statement especially poignant when considering the needs of all stakeholders—including students. Additionally, teachers monitor independent work and make instructional decisions based on body language and interactions. However, this often becomes impossible online.

Stakeholders expressed concerns about digital inclusion ("What about Wi-Fi?"), as well as a lack of proper training around learning management systems. The teachers' roles were largely ignored in much of this discussion, which focused on specific student needs created by the online format. Some expressed a lack of understanding of what teachers were doing during pandemic schooling, unaware of the pedagogical burden of pandemic teaching. One stakeholder noted that the district needed to provide instruction to caregivers, "Have you even thought about teaching the parents...you expect them to have the responsibility?" Statements like this reveal the district's initial oversight in helping parents and teachers to work together in solidarity towards educating students. School-to-home communication is a critical aspect of inclusive and equitable pedagogy. During this time, teachers became more responsible for working alongside these ecologies beyond their classroom, but without efficient and accessible systems in place to coordinate caregiver support feasibly and adequately. DisCrit solidarity is predicated on "quality classroom relationships" (Annamma & Morrison, 2018, p. 76), extending to the caregivers, especially during online learning. Discourse analysis across multiple documents revealed a dearth of instructional and home-to-school communication systems to foster the building of this solidarity, instead often lending itself to pitting home and school against one another. Implications include disability accommodations where the implementation language may be contingent upon in-person settings, speaking to the decision to allow certain students to attend in-person, since online learning may make some accommodations impossible and render the district out of compliance.

"Working Toward Equity"

The authors note how the district's recent equity initiatives were on the chopping block due to anticipated pandemic budget cuts. However, several staff members penned a letter in which they tied the history of racism to the current lived experiences of staff of color. Staff members used Discourses of Solidarity to resist tools of white supremacy, which sought to isolate staff of color. The letter preemptively names this strategy while refuting tendencies to essentialize experiences of teachers of color then:

> We ALL know Black and brown people haven't had the same experience; however, the signatures below clearly rule out coincidence or happenstance. In the recent past, when an individual of color would speak out about some of these issues, another person of color would be cherry-picked to provide a counter-narrative.

This statement connects equity to accountability, not allowing the district to merely perform optics of repair and then resume status quo. It reflects definitions of equity that require relationship, change, and sharing power. Additionally, it refutes notions of people of color as a monolith. Not all stakeholders shared this degree of understanding, even while advocating for equity. One stakeholder acknowledged the district "historically failed students of color" but added "students of the same type," implying that identities of students of color are all the same. DisCrit pedagogies assert that practitioners are committed to understanding the multiple-marginalizations that disabled students of color face without essentializing (Annamma & Morrison, 2018, p. 76). In both discourses, disability is not an identified factor. Notably, equity and racism were named in the letter from educators of color, whereas in most other instances, stakeholders named equity but without connecting it to racism or harm. While this letter named racism and gave specific examples, most others only used the term equity; and some constrained it to academics in a way that reified deficit assumptions and upheld transactional perspectives of education (i.e., "concerns from supervision to learning equity").

The letter not only names specific harms, "Staff members unwantedly touching the hair and bodies of staff of color," but uses a powerful analogy to connect individual responsibility to be accountable for privileges maintained by systemic racism, "Racism is a blazing fire. Your proximity to whiteness determines if you're incinerated or enjoy the warmth provided by the flames." Fire, like power, can be deadly or sustaining, and is endemic to the social realm. Here, the writers name proximity to whiteness as a location that sustains itself only by oppression. Suppose equity does indeed require relationships and a sharing of power. In that case, the authors believe this fire analogy demonstrates the need for transparency of relationships and specifically, investment in whiteness, so that all members of a community share in the work and have an equitable stake in dismantling systemic racism.

Disability and Inclusion as Absences

When the data explicitly mentioned disability, it was in ways that implied legalistic tensions and liability-driven decisions and injustices. These remarks were never the main concern of the text; and always situated as an aside, evidence of overall district negligence. A representative for the NAACP made accountability requests in parenthesis, "I am adding: parents have shared with us, students with special needs are being blocked from in-person attending because of lack of staff?" This is a violation of rights, but it is mentioned as a footnote. Another stakeholder, the only one to use the word "disabled," signs his statement as a member of a second amendment rights group, "property owner and concerned citizen." This evokes Discourses of Whiteness as a historical landowning class while also evoking Rights-Based Disability Discourse ("lack of Americans with Disabilities Act issues"). He speaks of academic achievement in attainment terms ("start graduating above the perennial abysmal 57%!"), connecting to texts of education as production and property. Interestingly, this is the only explicit mention of disability. It is connected to legislation and rights-based language, property, gun laws, citizenship, and grammatical markers from Discourses of Whiteness. While both examples are shaped by very different contexts, identities, and interdiscursive elements, they both situate disability as an aside, speaking to stigmas around disability and the relegation of disability advocacy to the private realm, depriving students with disabilities of solidarity.

DisCrit classroom pedagogies recognize the intersection of disability with race and other marginalized identities; as a "cohesive political identity with a lineage of material inequities and resistance" (Annamma & Morrison, 2018, p. 75). However, equity, inclusion, and disability were often not used in tandem, and certainly in a way that furthers solidarity of multiple marginalized students. "Inclusion" was in the title of the official equity plan, yet the term seemed to be a matter not explicitly present in discursive spaces, instead being implied or absent. Inclusion was mentioned far less than equity, indicating that equity is a resource-based predecessor to inclusion, or that when a dominant group represents conductors of harm and trauma, inclusion in systems that maintain these structures is not desirable. Inclusion was mentioned by a stakeholder noting that "Minoritized, not minority, but minoritized communities have been disproportionately impacted negatively, and now when it's time where we're trying to recover... are not included." These anchor conceptions of inclusion predicated on the pre-existing status and access to a presence in a decision-making space. The authors point to the use of inclusion often mentioned in conjunction with religious holidays. Notably, groups use inclusion when they want to be part of a process or in a shared space. In contrast, groups use equity to secure safe access to materials, name harm, and discuss racism, despite the terms appearing together in official district plans and broader pedagogical Discourse. The authors indicate these nuanced interpretations of equity and inclusion speak to how equity ties to Discourses of Racial Reckoning. Conversely, inclusion was used sparingly, mainly by those with white privilege and for specific events.

Not all stakeholders who evoked pedagogical injustices of students with disabilities positioned them as excluded. Conversely, one educator referred to prioritization of the "most vulnerable" but to argue that those who did not qualify for certain supports were excluded from the school experience. This discourse was tied to valuing socialization and traditional school rituals yet couched in ominous language to emphasize that these students had not developed socially since being at home ("pandemic isolation has consequences, especially when...developing collective voice"). Surprisingly, this indicates that stakeholders view students without disabilities as not being given a chance to develop solidarity and being excluded from the ritual of schooling. These discourses positioned students with disabilities as more included than students without disabilities, saying that Inclusion Discourse is tied to spatiality.

Getting Back to the Norm: Rituals, Carework, and Supervision

Pedagogy is not just academics but also about highly undervalued carework. Whilst many acknowledged the need for a teacher's presence and individual connection during online learning, this was often presented transactionally; as students who "need supervision" provided by any untrained adult. The authors note how this shows a lack of awareness of pedagogy more broadly and elides the many invisible ways teachers support students. Stakeholders remarked that teachers were "working hard" but never constructed the teachers as having valued pedagogical expertise. Some pitted the parents against the teachers, claiming, "The responsibility is on our parents more than our teachers." Despite this discourse, many teachers were reporting working longer hours than ever before. Some stakeholders took up the idea that if teachers were not physically present in the building, they were not working: "why are they still getting paid?" The authors believe this discourse connects to a Paternalistic Discourse which inherently distrusts teachers. Distrust often characterizes teachers as opportunists who lack professionalism and calls into question their dedication and expertise, unless given performative evidence of martyrdom. Many of these Discourses situate themselves in roots of carework perceived as domestic, gendered, and under-compensated labor without skills and expertise to be relegated to the private realm.

The Discourse marked teacher presence not only as providing instruction but also childcare, socialization, and the hallmarks of the traditional school. Some spoke about the social rituals of school as being fundamental to development, asserting that social development suffered without being able to gather in a building. One educator requested "ceremonial incentives" for the graduating class. This educator took up a Pandemic Discourse, speaking about efforts to get back to "the norm" as a service to children where in-person learning defines "Normal." Interestingly, discourse did not situate the suffering in learning loss, like so much global Discourse, but instead focused on deprivation from social milestones. The authors point out that the construction of online schooling is in opposition to traditional educational achievement rituals, and that it provides an opportunity to break free from toxic norms. Notably, the letter from educators of color specifically named parts of conceptions of "the norm" as unacceptable and undesirable as they are riddled with toxic complacency around racism "we can no longer afford to be complacent, in the norm." This shows that definitions and desirability of getting back to "the norm" were not necessarily a common vision.

Conclusion

This study shows that stakeholders felt online learning was inequitable during the pandemic and were frustrated with being excluded from problem-solving. Underutilization of resources and lack of coordination with the community became missed opportunities to enrich online pedagogy. Additionally, the study reveals a lack of support for teachers to produce high-quality inclusive and equitable online pedagogy, as well as an acknowledgment of their critical role. Overall, there is a demand for more creative, iterative, and adaptive school models and concerns about educational technology's functionality in multiple modes of action, engagement, and expression. Implications of these findings indicate that teachers and school districts are in need of a DisCrit curriculum and pedagogies that are rooted in building upon the identities and gifts of multiply-marginalized students, as well as provides relational and flexible options for more authentic assessment (Annamma & Morrison, 2018, p. 75). Given these changes, the curriculum and pedagogical approach would not be a contrived set of lessons based on compliance and supervision, but one designed by the very educators who teach the students and travel through and across various spaces as it acknowledges the students' identities.

This study revealed that despite "equity and inclusion" appearing in tandem on official district materials, they do not hold reciprocal discursive meanings. Inclusion was tied to spatiality and decision-making, while equity held ties to resources and access. Indirect references to students with disabilities in disparate ways indicate disability is a matter for the legal and private realms, at times intermingling with Discourses of Whiteness. Additionally, constructing in-person schooling as an important social ritual, more than a means of accessing the curriculum, indicated mixed perceptions of the inclusion of students with disabilities. The identities of disabled students of color are not considered in the dominant framing of problems. DisCrit resists asking students to compartmentalize a particular identity to meet an educational need (Annamma et al., 2013). A DisCrit resistance lens would actively engage in this discourse by relentlessly recentering students of color with disabilities as a starting point for inclusion and equity work (Annamma & Morrison, 2018).

The authors saw evidence that stakeholders pushed for equity and inclusion, but with varying levels of agreement, and some with deficit notions of students of color. Data revealed barriers to equity and inclusion, exacerbated by the pandemic and technological challenges, were products of historically entrenched racism. Analysis of discourses reflected how attempts at working towards solidarity in equitable online pedagogies could not bypass the past harm connected to systemic racism. Moreover, the analysis demonstrates that the compartmentalization of needs runs counter to establishing solidarity. DisCrit classroom ecologies is an effective framework for analyzing barriers to equity and inclusion and building understanding and solidarity toward justice, implying that DisCrit classroom ecologies is a particularly productive lens for driving participatory action research with school personnel around equity and inclusion, particularly during times of change or transition. Future research and endeavors on this topic should also include the perspectives of the many related service professionals working with educators in the field. Additionally, this study did not include analysis of livestreamed meetings, or a comparative analysis across multiple districts, which would yield a larger data set to inform and contextualize the findings.

References

Aguliera, E., & Nightengale-Lee, B. (2020). Emergency remote teaching across urban and rural contexts: Perspectives on educational equity. *Information and Learning Sciences*. https://doi.org/10.1108/ILS-04-2020-0100

Annamma, S., & Morrison, D. (2018). DisCrit classroom ecology: Using praxis to dismantle dysfunctional education ecologies. *Teaching and Teacher Education, 73*, 70–80.

Annamma, S. A., Connor, D., & Ferri, B. (2013). Dis/ability critical race studies (DisCrit): Theorizing at the intersections of race and dis/ability. *Race Ethnicity and Education, 16*(1), 1–31.

Annamma, S. A., Jackson, D. D., & Morrison, D. (2017). Conceptualizing color-evasiveness: Using dis/ability critical race theory to expand a color-blind racial ideology in education and society. *Race Ethnicity and Education, 20*(2), 147–162.

Basham, J. D., Blackorby, J., & Marino, M. T. (2020). Opportunity in crisis: The role of universal design for learning in educational redesign. *Learning Disabilities, 18*(1), 71–91.

Chiu, T. K. F. (2021). Student engagement in K-12 online learning amid COVID-19: A qualitative approach from a self-determination theory perspective. *Interactive Learning Environments*. https://doi.org/10.1080/10494820.2021.1926289

Cutrara, S. (2021). Beyond pandemic pedagogy: Thoughts on deconstruction, structure, and justice post-pandemic. *The Councilor: A Journal of the Social Studies, 82*(1), 1.

Gee, J. P. (2011). *How to do discourse analysis: A toolkit*. Routledge.

Haddix, M., & National Council of Teachers of English. (2016). *Cultivating racial and linguistic diversity in literacy teacher education: Teachers like me*. Routledge. Retrieved from https://rb.gy/usejwv

Kamei, A., & Harriott, W. (2021). Social emotional learning in virtual settings: Intervention strategies. *International Electronic Journal of Elementary Education, 13*(3) Retrieved from https://www.iejee.com/index.php/IEJEE/article/view/1487

Khan, M. H., Adnan, H. M., Kaur, S., Khuhro, R. A., Asghar, R., & Jabeen, S. (2019). Muslims' representation in Donald Trump's Anti-Muslim-Islam statement: A critical discourse analysis. *Religions, 10*(2), 115. https://doi.org/10.3390/rel10020115

Laff, J. R. (2021). *Sensemaking of education equity and equity policy: A case study of vice principal discourse*. University of Portland.

Lambert, R., & Schuck, R. (2021). "The wall now between us": Teaching math to students with disabilities during the COVID spring of 2020. *The Asia-Pacific Education Researcher, 30*(3), 289–298. https://doi.org/10.1007/s40299-021-00568-8

Love, H. R., & Horn, E. (2019). Definition, context, quality: Current issues in research examining high-quality inclusive education. *Topics in Early Childhood Special Education, 40*(4), 204–216. https://doi.org/10.1177/0271121419846342

Morrison, T. (2019). *The source of self-regard: Selected essays, speeches, and meditations* (5th ed.). Alfred A. Knopf.

Mullet, D. R. (2018). A general critical discourse analysis framework for educational research. *Journal of Advanced Academics, 29*(2), 116–142.

Naraian, S. (2020). What can "inclusion" mean in the post-human era? *Journal of Disability Studies in Education, 1*, 1–21. https://doi.org/10.1163/25888803-bja10001

Nasr, N. (2021). Heeding the call for social justice: How a CPED Ed.D. Program illuminates the instructional intersection between COVID-19 and the black lives matter movement. *Impacting Education: Journal on Transforming Professional Practice, 6*(2), 39–42. https://doi.org/10.5195/ie.2021.153

Ortiz, K., Rice, M., McKeown, T., & Tonks, D. (2020). Special issue: Inclusion in online learning environments. *Journal of Online Learning Research, 6*(3), 171–176.

Papendieck, A. (2018). Technology for equity and social justice in education: A critical issue overview. *Texas Education Review*. https://doi.org/10.15781/T2891278V

Paris, D., & Alim, H. S. (2014). What are we seeking to sustain through culturally sustaining pedagogy? A loving critique forward. *Harvard Educational Review, 84*(1), 85–100.

Parmigiani, D., Benigno, V., Giusto, M., Silvaggio, C., & Sperandio, S. (2020). E-inclusion: Online special education in Italy during the Covid-19 pandemic. *Technology, Pedagogy and Education, 1–14*. https://doi.org/10.1080/1475939X.2020.1856714

Patterson, A. N. (2018). YouTube generated video clips as qualitative research data: One researcher's reflections on the process. *Qualitative Inquiry, 24*(10), 759–767.

Russ, S., & Hamidi, F. (2021). Online learning accessibility during the COVID-19 pandemic. *Ljubljana, Slovenia: Association for Computing Machinery*. https://doi.org/10.1145/3430263.3452445

Selwyn, N., & Jandrić, P. (2020). Postdigital living in the age of Covid-19: Unsettling what we see as possible. *Postdigital Science and Education, 2*(3), 989–1005. https://doi.org/10.1007/s42438-020-00166-9

Stringer, H. (2020, October 13). *Zoom school's mental health toll on kids*. Retrieved July 5, 2021, from https://www.apa.org/news/apa/2020/online-learning-mental-health

Voithofer, R., & Foley, A. (2007). Digital dissonances: Structuring absences in national discourses on equity and educational technologies. *Equity & Excellence in Education*. https://doi.org/10.1080/10665680601088515

Meaghan Krazinski is a doctoral student in Special Education at Syracuse University and a former Special Education Teacher. She possesses a master's degree in Inclusive Secondary Special Education and is in the process of obtaining advanced certificates in both Disability Studies and Women's and Gender Studies. Her interests include inclusive education, disability studies, women's and gender studies, arts and arts-based research methods, neurodivergence, and trauma studies.

Megan E. Cartier worked as a high school special education teacher for 12 years in central Kentucky before coming to Syracuse University where she is now a doctoral candidate in Special Education. She has earned a certificate of advanced study in Disability Studies. Megan's research interests include inclusive education, the continuity of special education services for children of military service members, Universal Design for Learning, inclusive higher education for individuals with intellectual and developmental disabilities, and post-inclusive higher education outcomes for individuals who participate in and/or complete a post-secondary inclusive education program. She is now an assistant professor at the College of Saint Rose in Albany, NY.

Chapter 9
Perspectives on Reconceptualizing and Recontextualizing Schools' Inclusive Culture for Students with Disabilities During the COVID-19 Pandemic

Efthymia Efthymiou

Abstract This study examines whether federal primary schools in the United Arab Emirates (UAE) respond flexibly and effectively to the needs of students with disabilities through an inclusive school culture. School culture can support or undermine developments in education and influence education policies and practices, either positively or negatively. Principals and teachers determine the qualities of inclusive environments, and they need to reconceptualize their roles and responsibilities in terms of their professional knowledge, attitudes, disposition, and preparedness to implement child-centered and inclusive methodologies to accommodate children's diverse needs during the pandemic. This study argues that efforts to create a 'School for All' and a more equitable response to diversity during the COVID-19 pandemic should not only aim at accommodating the heterogeneous needs of students with disabilities but at considering a shift in the underlying cultural values and beliefs. School culture is affected by macro level social changes, reflected in micro level pedagogical practices, and learning processes. The research findings, based on qualitative and quantitative analyses of two survey questionnaires and of secondary data (e.g., 21 school policies; 35 school reports, 3 educational laws) showed that the 107 principals and the 105 teachers responded to the needs of society, embraced an inclusive vision, and engaged in inclusive practices aimed at sustainable inclusive schools. However, in this endeavor they encountered a plethora of challenges.

Keywords Inclusion · COVID-19 · School culture · Disability · Teachers · Principals

E. Efthymiou (✉)
Zayed University, Abu Dhabi, United Arab Emirates
e-mail: Efthymia.efthymiou@zu.ac.ae

Introduction

On March 22, 2020, all the primary and secondary schools in the United Arab Emirates (UAE) were closed in response to the global spread of the COVID-19 outbreak, which caused major disruptions in education, and further aggravated the challenges for students with disabilities (UNESCO, 2020) affecting their mental and physical well-being (Cerdan Chiscano, 2021; Kim & Rose, 2020). These children were 'left behind' as they experienced digital exclusion; absence of appropriate assistive equipment; and teachers' unpreparedness for teaching remotely. Growing evidence shows that students with disabilities have been significantly less engaged in remote learning (Flack et al., 2020).

A condition for the successful integration of new technologies in schools is the training of teachers and their active participation in the reorganization and implementation of educational programs. Past research has shown that innovations that have not given teachers the opportunity to participate in all stages of their implementation have failed (Clarke, 2007; Deglau & O'Sullivan, 2006). The educational transformation of implementing inclusive education has not been satisfactory. Several factors relating to undifferentiated curricula, large number of students, the educational material, material infrastructure of schools, and conventional educational methods have remained the same without the necessary reforms. The goal of recontextualizing and redefining inclusive education is a commendable social effort that requires rigorous scientific educational programming. According to Banathy (1991), a school is an open social system that interacts with constantly changing multiple environments and coordinates with many other systems. For a school to be able to cope with the uncertainty and ambiguity of constant societal changes, while maintaining the ability to co-evolve with the environment, it needs to develop into organizational learning systems that adjust to changes and redesigns its policies and educational frameworks. Schools need to recognize that the continuing explosion of knowledge requires specialization, differentiation, integration, and generalization, to turn information into organizational knowledge. In this context, teachers', and principals' contributions to the ever-widening understanding of barriers to inclusive education are central (Huang et al., 2020), as its implementation is predicated on their practices, beliefs, and attitudes (Mngo & Mngo, 2018). The study aims to answer the following research questions: (1) How is inclusive education practiced at the micro level of primary schools in the UAE and from various perspectives (e.g., teachers, principals) during the pandemic? (2) Which success factors and obstacles influence the implementation of inclusive education in primary schools in the UAE during the pandemic? and (3) To what degree do schools' distance learning practices reflect an inclusive school culture?

Background

An inclusive school culture aims at a more general change in sociocultural becoming, where the school needs to shift to the social model of disability. School leaders play a crucial role in promoting inclusive cultures within a sustainable school system by being flexible, transmitting an inclusive vision and laying the groundwork for continuous improvement. Hoy and Miskel (2008, p. 177) consider that "culture is a system of common orientation that keeps the members of the organization together and give them a distinct identity." The social environment of a school, its internal structure, and the actions of principals can affect its organizational culture, strengthening its values and standards. Culture is influenced by the perceptions and values of each member of the organization, and by their behaviors, thoughts, and tendencies, depending on how strong a school culture is. Moreover, school culture exerts a significant impact on a school's efficiency. Teachers take initiatives, use a variety of materials, teaching methodologies, and encourage students' progress by recognizing, and praising their efforts. This contributes to the achievement of the goals of a school. Effective school cultures are developed through common values, norms, and behavior patterns (Rudasill et al., 2018), where the goals of each teacher are identical to the general objectives of the school organization, with positive effects on students. The principal transmits common beliefs, values, and behaviors to school members, when teachers are encouraged to work together and learn from their experiences, and when promoting training and cooperation between teachers and external community agents.

According to Mitchell (2015), the basic responsibilities of a school leader for the development of a culture of inclusion in the school, include the creation and promotion of the vision for inclusion which is reflected in all their actions, e.g., in their conversations with parents, teachers, social agents, official school correspondence; the recognition and encouragement of school personnel who strive for the success of inclusion; the acquisition of resources for procurement; the construction or maintenance of infrastructure, supervisory material; the differentiation of curricula to meet the needs of students with Special Education Needs and Disorders (SEND); realistic goal setting; and the evaluation of the progressive course of all students. Black and Simon (2014) point out additional practices for principals, entailing the integration of democratic practices; broad organizational reforms; disseminating a vision to change the habits and practices of a school; digital citizenship; support of general education teachers by specialists, to harmonize practices with the purposes of inclusion; integrating inclusive values into teachers'values; cooperating with parents, and creating a culture of individual and organizational learning. As Schein (1985) aptly observes, "culture is created by the actions of leaders." According to Booth and Ainscow (2002), culture is the basis of the development of inclusive practices because it creates a community that inspires security, acceptance, and cooperation. Additionally, for teachers to collectively create an effective and inclusive school culture, the parameters of culture, politics; and practice need to be considered. An inclusive culture embraces the acceptance and integration of all school members. Principles and values lead to decisions about politics and practice in the classroom (Darling-Hammond et al., 2020).

According to the systemic approach, a school is a social system of high complexity consisting of intertwined microsystems, e.g., students, classes, general and special education teachers, which interact with each other; and mesosystems, including the local and wider community (Wenger, 1998). A school functions through the interactions of its macrosystems, mesosystems and microsystems which affect the setting of goals, decision-making, and problem-solving. By contrast, in a closed system, with rigid and limited permeability of its boundaries, microsystems are led into disorganization, affecting the mesosystems, going against the goals of the school, which then malfunctions. Given that the network of relationships between the education systems is important for their effectiveness and continuous improvement, recording and clarifying these relationships, is a priority. While a macrosystem, e.g., the state, includes innovative ideas and goals for the implementation of inclusive education processes, obscurities and conflicts might be found at the meso and microsystems. As a result, entropy is caused, as the school system ceases to be flexible and is unable to cope with changes and experiences the lowest responsiveness to a crisis. Sergiovanni and Starratt (2007) proposed changes in structural and in behavioral norms. But for changes to be permanent, they should be achieved at both levels.

Methods

Research Approach, Design, and Paradigm

The qualitative secondary data on UAE legislative and policy framework documents, as well as the quantitative responses of First Cycle principals and teachers to two survey questionnaires, were analyzed using a mixed methods approach. The mixed method approach explored the research phenomenon in a holistic way, reducing the disadvantages associated with the use of quantitative or qualitative methods alone and allowing generalizable results to be generated (Creswell & Poth, 2016). In addition, the mixed methodology enhances triangulation, which increases the validity and reliability of the results (Moon, 2019).

Research Design

The design model was cross-sectional. A review of the secondary sources of inclusive policies, disability laws, and school reports (e.g., 21 school policies; 35 school reports, 3 educational laws) was conducted to conceptualize and contextualize inclusive education practices. The cross-sectional design informed of any correlations that might exist between school cultural norms and the implementation of inclusion in primary schools (Nketsia, 2017). The research questions ask: (1) How is inclusive education practiced at the micro level of primary schools in the UAE and from various perspectives (e.g., teachers, principals) during the pandemic? (2) Which success factors and obstacles influence the implementation of inclusive education in primary schools in the UAE during the pandemic? and 3. To what degree do schools' distance learning practices reflect an inclusive school culture?

Context of the Study

Inclusive Education in the UAE was embraced in 2006 as a national policy (Elhoweris & Efthymiou, 2020). The percentage of people with disabilities in the UAE is close to 8–10% of the population (Bradshaw et al., 2004). According to Weber and City (2012), the first special education classroom was established in 1979 and special needs teacher training started at the same time at the United Arab Emirates University (Alahbabi, 2009). The UAE Federal law No. 29 of 2006, Articles 12 and 15, states that "the country assures equivalent education chances for the Person with Special Needs in all educational establishments…who shall be in the regular classes or in special classes" offering the option of inclusive education (Gaad, 2011, p. 4). Due to this foundation, most special needs students in the UAE are educated in separate classrooms or institutions. The law provides a framework for inclusion in the classrooms and encourages it; however, it is not clear that law 29 of 2006 requires schools to accommodate students with SEND. Some parents and general education teachers claim that children with SEND can be best accommodated in separate facilities as many parents believe that the general education system has not enough qualified special education teachers to meet the needs of these children. Alahbabi's (2009) survey of UAE teachers found that support for Inclusive Education was significantly higher among special needs education teachers than among general education teachers. Alghazo and Gaad's (2004) survey of UAE teachers found that most general education teachers had negative attitudes towards inclusion for students with SEND in the regular classroom.

The UAE has made noteworthy progress concerning legislation and policies for Inclusive Education and is developing positive practices in collaboration with governmental and non-governmental education providers. However, it seems that the normative beliefs of the traditional medical deficit model approach to special education still inform the development of inclusive educational systems. The primary and secondary legislation is being implemented, and the structure for enforcing the laws is still being developed. Federal Laws 2006 ("UAE Federal Law," 2006) and 2009 ("UAE Federal Law," 2009) and Dubai Law No 2/Concerning Protection of the Rights of Persons with Disabilities in the Emirate of Dubai ("Dubai Law No 2," 2014), the 'School for All' initiative of 2010, 'My Community…A city for everyone' initiative of 2013, and The National Policy for Empowering People of Determination (2017), constitute the policy framework for Inclusive Education. These laws reflect international best practices and align with the UAE's ratification of Art.24 of 2006 United Nations' Convention on the Rights of Persons with Disabilities-CRPD (Schulze, 2010) regarding their rights to Inclusive Education. Dubai's Inclusive Education Policy Framework of 2017 adds to the Inclusive Education policy and reinforces the government's commitment to achieving Inclusive Education provision in mainstream education, health and rehabilitation, employment, universal accessibility, and social protection for people with disabilities.

The UAE Vision 2021 considers education a core value, including aspirations for citizenship, a spirit of entrepreneurship, enhanced educational attainment, and a knowledge-based economy enhanced by innovation, research, science, and technology. The development of these objectives requires a world-class education system, responsive to national needs and aligned to international standards. In 2014, the UAE National Agenda for promoting the UAE Vision 2021 targeted central areas in education related to students, teachers, and school leaders. According to the Agenda, highly-quality teachers are a key focus for a world-class education system. The 2018–2019 inspection key findings by the Dubai School Inspection Bureau indicated a 5% increase of admissions from 2020 as 71% of private schools provide a good or better quality of provision for students of determination. However, it was reported that children with disabilities, i.e., those who need one to one support tend to be rejected. The problem is that schools do not yet provide sufficient specialized training to teachers and are deficient in teaching support staff (Rizvi, 2021).

The Dubai Inclusive Education Policy Framework (p. 53) states that inclusive education is "…the progressive development of attitudes, behaviours, systems and beliefs that enable inclusive education to become a norm that underpins school culture and is reflected in the everyday life of the school community." The stated objectives of the 2009 Abu Dhabi Education Council Policy on Special Educational Needs (UAE Federal Law 14/2009/ In Respect of the Rights of People with Special Needs), stress that special needs are not considered obstacles for students to enroll in any government or private education institution, providing equal chances in education, continuous teaching in the regular classes or in special classes; and provision of a curriculum in sign language or Braille. This is further supported by the Ministry of Education document 'School for All": General rules for the Provision of Special Education Programs and Services.

Many schools in the UAE currently have children with SEND, but so far, not many teachers have taken part in training or educational programs to utilize the strategies and services for these children in general education classrooms. At present, despite the tremendous need, there might be few institutional arrangements or training programs for teachers in the UAE to prepare them for implementing Inclusive Education. Teacher training in the UAE is a growing concern as the demand for educating learners with SEND within regular classrooms continuously increases. The result is that more students with SEND are included in regular classes, bringing additional changes and demands upon teachers. The perceived needs of teachers who are required to accommodate varied student needs must be addressed as these may cause problems related to implementation, and high levels of anxiety (Engelbrecht et al., 2001). While research (Alborno & Gaad, 2014; Alborno, 2013) justifies the need for highly qualified teachers, it comes at a time when inclusive education teaching has increasingly become a challenging and stressful matter in society amid the pandemic. Inadequate teacher training suggests that there is a gap between inclusive education policy initiatives and the actual implementation of inclusive teaching. Furthermore, inclusion is still an optional topic in pre-service teacher training courses.

Participants

The research sample consists of First Cycle school teachers and principals (i.e., Grades 1–4; 6–9 years old) working in public general education schools either as general or special education teachers. Convenience sampling was selected, based on the availability of the participants, and meeting the requirements for answering the research questions (Moser & Korstjens, 2018). The teachers and principals were informed by email about the study and asked for their consent. The principals in each of the participating schools were the main contacts who distributed information about the study to the participating teachers.

The study utilized two survey questionnaires, which were administered to the participating principals and teachers, respectively. Both questionnaires were sent electronically to 190 public primary schools across the country. The response rate was high as the survey questionnaires were answered by 107 principals and by 105 teachers, from 107 primary schools. Specifically, 82 female (78.1%) and 23 male teachers (21.9%), and 107 female principals (100%) participated in the survey questionnaires. The demographic information of the principals and the teachers are shown in Tables 9.1 and 9.2, respectively.

The distribution of the sample in terms of age (Table 1) shows that most of the principals are at the age of 51 and above. Specifically, 69 principals out of 107 in total (64.5% of the sample), belong to this age group, while 35 principals (32.7%) are between 41 and 50 years old. Lastly, only 3 teachers (2.8%) are up to 40 years old. Most of the principals (97.2%) are over 41 years old. Furthermore, of the 107 principals, who hold a basic degree, 33 principals (31%) of the total sample have a second degree, 58 principals (54.2%) are postgraduate holders, and 16 principals (15%) earned a doctorate degree. Regarding the principals' years of teaching experience, it was found that 15 principals (14%) have 10 to 20 years of service; 55 principals (51.4%) have 21–30 years of service, while 37 principals (34.6%) have more than 30 years of service. Moreover, 55 (51.4%) of the 107 principals have 0 to 5 years of service in this role; 32 (30%) have 6 to 10 years of service, while only 20 (18.7%) have more than 10 years of service. Additionally, for the years of service in

Table 9.1 Demographics-principals (N = 107)

Age	Education	Teaching experience	Service as principals	Service in current school	Training in inclusive education during the pandemic
40 years (3)[a]	Bachelor's degree (107)	10–20 years (15)	0–5 years (55)	Up to 2 years (31)	1–200 h (48)
41–50 (35)	Second degree (33)	21–30 (55)	6–10 (32)	3–5 (70)	201–400 (22)
51+ (69)	Master's degree (58)	30+ (37)	11+ (20)	6+ (6)	401+ (7)
	Doctorate degree (16)				

[a]Number in bracket = number of participants

Table 9.2 Demographics-teachers ($N = 105$)

Age	Education	Teaching area	Teaching experience	Service in current school	Training in inclusive education during the pandemic	No training in inclusive education during the pandemic
Up to 30 years (40)[a]	Bachelor's degree (105)	General education (85)	10–20 years (40)	Up to 2 years (24)	1–200 h (65 gen. ed. teachers) 13 special ed. teachers)	33 general education teachers
31–40 (25)	Second degree (37)	Special education (20)	21–30 (55)	3–5 (45)	201–400 (0)	7 special education teachers
41–50 (17)	Master's degree (63)		30+ (10)	6+ (36)	401+ (0)	
50+ (23)	Doctorate degree (5)					

[a]Number in bracket = number of participants

the current school it is indicated that 31 principals (29%) serve the current school for up to 2 years; 70 (65.4%) for 3–5 years, while only 6 (5.61%) principals serve their school for 6 years and above. From the 107 principals, 77 (72%) attended some training sessions in inclusive education during the pandemic, while only 30 principals (28%) mentioned that they have not received any kind of training in inclusive education during that time. Particularly, 48 (62.3%) out of the 77 principals attended 1–200 h of training, 22 (28.6%) attended 201–400 h, while only 7 principals (9.1%) had 401 h of training and above. Table 2 demonstrates the demographic data of the teachers, who participated in the study.

Out of the 105 teachers, who participated in the study, 82 were women (78.1%), while 23 were men (21.9%) (Table 2). Indicatively, 40 teachers (38%) were up to 30 years old; 25 teachers (23.8%) were between 31 and 40 years old; 17 (16.2%) were between 41 and 50 years old, while 23 teachers (21.9%) were over 50 years old. Regarding the teachers' academic qualifications beyond the basic academic degree (105); 37 (35.2%) hold a second degree; 63 (60%) hold a Master's degree, while only 5 (4.8%) hold a doctorate degree. Regarding the teachers' teaching area, 85 (81%) out of 105 were general education teachers, whereas 20 (19%) of them were special education teachers. In terms of the teachers' years of teaching experience, it was found that 40 teachers (38.1%) have 10–20 years of experience; 55 teachers (52.4%) have 21–30 years of service, while only 10 teachers (9.5%) have more than 30 years of service. Additionally, for the years of service in the current school, it was found that 24 teachers (22.8%) serve the current school for up to 2 years; 45 (42.8%) for 3–5 years, while 36 (34.3%) teachers serve their school for 6 years and above. From the 105 teachers, 65 general education teachers (72%) and 13 special education teachers (28%) attended 1–200 h of training in inclusive education during the pandemic, while 33 general education teachers and 7 special education teachers mentioned that they have not received any kind of training in inclusive education during that time.

Data Collection Instruments

The researcher created the two survey questionnaires after conducting an extensive literature review on inclusive education and school culture, and the survey questionnaire method was chosen due to the large number of participants. Likert scale survey questionnaires are considered a reliable quantitative method because they take place in the respondents' natural environment while also providing an insight into reality by recording the views of a large sample (Creswell, 2011). The questionnaire has the advantage of maintaining the respondents' anonymity, which allows them to respond to questions in an unbiased manner at their own pace and time. The survey questionnaires were piloted by five teachers and two principals to examine the questions and provide feedback. Both survey questionnaires use the Likert scale. The survey questionnaires start with a cover letter stating the purpose of the research and the ethical dimensions of participation.

Questionnaire Structure

The survey questionnaires given to the principals and to the teachers are divided into four thematic sections (Table 9.3).

The first section of the teachers' and of the principals' survey questionnaires includes questions on personal information, such as gender, age, studies, educational background, and previous service as a principal/teacher, and current service at the specific school. The second part is related to the first research question (RQ1) "How is inclusive education practiced at the micro level of primary schools in the UAE and from various perspectives (e.g., teachers, principals) during the pandemic?". More specifically, it examines the teachers'and the principals' views on inclusive learning practices in response to school closures. Their views are expressed

Table 9.3 Questionnaire structure

Section	Theme
Section 1	1-Demographics.
Section 2	2-Inclusive learning practices during COVID-19.
Section 3	3-Factors that impact the implementation of inclusive education during COVID-19.
Section 4	4-Distance learning practices and inclusive school culture.

through the five-point Likert scale, with a scale starting with 1 = Agree, 2 = Strongly agree, 3 = Neither agree nor disagree, 4 = Disagree, 5 = Strongly disagree. The third part is based on the second research question (RQ2) "Which success factors and obstacles influence the implementation of inclusive education in primary schools in the UAE during the pandemic?" and is divided into 5 sections. In more detail, using the Likert scale, with a scale starting from 1 = Agree, 2 = Strongly agree, 3 = Neither agree nor disagree, 4 = Disagree, 5 = Strongly disagree, the teachers and the principals express their views on success factors and obstacles that influenced the implementation of inclusive education with reference to (1) their training and preparation; (2) the school culture; (3) the students' needs (5) and the community. Finally, the fourth part is based on the third research question (RQ3) "To what degree do schools' distance learning practices reflect an inclusive school culture?" where the teachers and the principals are called upon to specify the degree to which distance learning practices reflected an inclusive school culture.

Analytically, the teachers' questionnaire included 8 demographic questions, 27 closed questions, and 1 open-ended question. The principals' questionnaire included 9 demographic questions, 29 closed questions, and one open-ended question regarding listing the obstacles to practicing inclusive education during the pandemic. The open-ended questions in both survey questionnaires were thematically analyzed. Both survey questionnaires were completed online through Google Forms from March to May 2020. Additionally, educational laws and policies as well as school reports about the schools'vision, mission, and practices that were available online in English language, were used as secondary data (e.g., 21 school policies; 35 school reports, 3 educational laws), which were thematically analyzed. These documents were selected based on their usefulness and depth of information in answering the study questions.

Validity and Reliability of the Study

The survey questionnaires were created after the best methodology and research instruments were chosen in relation to the research questions to ensure validity. The survey questionnaires were designed according to the research questions. A good level of readability of the questionnaire was ensured, and clear instructions and questions were formulated. Piloting, which was carried out by 5 teachers and 2 principals, helped to further refine the phrasing used in two items in the teachers' survey and one item in the principals' survey questionnaire, enhancing their concision and clarity. The analysis of the data was performed with descriptive statistics. Triangulation was ensured by employing a mixed methods approach and by survey questionnaires administered to different participants from several different schools across the country. The credibility of the study was enhanced by the anonymity of the teachers allowing them to express honest answers and by selecting an appropriate sample to answer the research questions.

Data Analysis

Descriptive Statistics and Correlation Tests

We utilized descriptive statistics to describe the data of the survey questionnaires. The statistical analysis of the data was performed with the SPSS v.19 after coding the variables. Through descriptive statistical analysis, the frequencies of the demographics and professional status and qualifications of the teachers and of the principals were calculated. Furthermore, a correlation test was performed on whether teacher training during the pandemic is related to the degree to which teachers believe that according to teacher survey questionnaire questions 'Q2-have confidence in teaching children with special educational needs during the COVID-19 pandemic.' and 'Q3- have been properly trained to meet the special educational needs of students during the pandemic.' The non-parametric Mann-Whitney U correlation test was performed, with a level of statistical significance $\alpha = 0.05$ (5%).

Coding and Thematic Analysis of the Open-Ended Survey Questionnaire Question and of the Secondary Data

Coding and thematic analysis was used to process the secondary data (e.g., 21 school policies; 35 school reports, 3 educational laws) and the data from the open-ended questions in both survey questionnaires where repetitive patterns of meaning were identified and themed in relation to the research questions (Herzog et al., 2019). These codes were clustered into key themes.

Ethical Considerations

Ethical considerations have been addressed and the guidelines set out by British Educational Research Association (BERA) and Zayed University Research Ethics Committee policies. Information about the aims, purposes and outcomes of the research were provided to the participants using an information sheet and code of conduct. Data gathering activities involving schools were carried out only with the agreement of the principal, or an authorized representative and after adequate notice had been given.

Additionally, in terms of confidentiality and withdrawal of data; no pressure was placed on the individuals or the institutions to participate in the research activities and having consented to participate, participants retained the right to withdraw from the study at any time without need to give a reason, and to have their data withdrawn. If participants became concerned about the sensitivity of some of their comments, they were provided with a period of one week after providing any data, in which to contact the PI/Co-I and ask for any comments they felt were too sensitive to be removed from the database. The Principal Investigator was responsible for ensuring the continued anonymity of respondents along the length of the project and beyond. The study's data were gathered openly and fairly, and records of research activity were made according to standard professional practices. Information was protected with appropriate levels of security and confidentiality and was stored at the University and only accessed by the researcher. All data stored on databases were anonymized, with care being taken to comply with the Data Protection Act of 1998 (Woulds, 2004). Furthermore, the research was carried out at mutually convenient times and negotiated in a way that minimize disruption to learning and teaching. The views of those involved in the research were respected and members of the research team were alert to cultural, religious, race, gender, age, and other relevant differences amongst participants when planning, conducting, reporting, and disseminating any findings.

Results

Teachers' Survey Questionnaire Questions-Descriptive Statistics

Survey Questionnaire Questions Related to RQ1-Teachers' Views on Inclusive Learning Practices in Response to School Closures & RQ3-Distance Learning Practices and Inclusive School Culture

Q1-Are you familiar with the term Inclusion or Inclusive Education? was answered positively by 61 out of 105 teachers (58.1%), while 44 teachers answered negatively (41.9%) (Table 9.4).

In Q2-I have confidence in my ability to teach children with special educational needs during the COVID-19 pandemic was answered by 105 teachers. Most teachers (57) answered "Strongly agree" (54,3%), while 48 teachers "Strongly disagree" (45,7%).

104 out of 105 teachers answered Q3- I have been appropriately trained to meet the special educational needs of students during the pandemic. More specifically, most teachers (56) "Strongly agree" (53.8%), while 48 "Strongly disagree" (46,1%).

Q4- I have attended some training webinars on inclusive education during the pandemic. Teachers (87) answered " Neither agree nor disagree," to "Strongly agree" (82.9%), while the remaining 18 answered "Disagree" to "Strongly disagree" (17.14%).

Table 9.4 Q1. Are you familiar with the term Inclusion or Inclusive Education?

Valid			Frequency	Percent	Valid percent	Cumulative percent
Valid	No		44	41.9	41.9	41.9
	Yes		61	58.1	58.1	100.0
	Total		105	100.0	100.0	

In Q10-I believe that inclusive education has a positive effect on the academic performance of children with special educational needs during the pandemic, 101 out of the 105 teachers answered. Most teachers (42) stated "Agree" to "Strongly agree" (41.6%), 36 " Neither disagree nor agreed " (35.6%), while 23 teachers stated that "Disagree" to "Strongly disagreed" (22.8%).

Q12-I believe that my school is doing the best to promote the social development of children with special educational needs during the pandemic, was answered by 78 out of 105 teachers. The teachers (33) stated " Neither disagree nor agreed" (42.3%), 26 responses ranged from "Disagree" to "Strongly disagree" (33.3%), while 19 ranged from "Agree" to "Strongly agree" (24.4%).

In Q21-Teachers regularly seek ideas from seminars, colleagues, and conferences on online teaching, 28 teachers answered, " Neither agree nor disagree" (26.6%), 33 responses ranged from "Disagree" to "Strongly disagree" (31.4%), while 44 teachers' responses ranged from "Agree" to "Strongly agree" (41.9%).

In Q22-The school mission provides a clear sense of direction for teachers in relation to teaching during the pandemic, 36 teachers' answers ranged from "I agree" to "I strongly agree" (34.3%), 28 "Neither disagreed nor agreed" (26.6%), while 41 "Disagreed" to "Strongly disagreed" (39%).

Q23-Teachers are encouraged to share ideas on how to teach online during the pandemic, was answered by 102 out of 105 teachers. Most teachers (81) "Agreed" to "Strongly agreed" (79.4%), 15 teachers "Neither disagreed nor agreed" (14.7%), while only 6 teachers "Disagreed" to "Strongly disagreed" (5.9%).

In Q24-The principal encourages online learning in informal virtual learning environments (e.g., in museums, zoos, neighborhood parks, etc.) during the pandemic, 102 out of 105 teachers answered. 63 "Agreed" to "Strongly agreed" (61.7%), 14 teachers "Neither disagreed nor agreed" (13.7%), while 25 "Disagreed" to "Strongly disagreed" (24.5%).

RQ2-Success Factors and Obstacles in the Implementation of Inclusive education during the Pandemic

Q5-I believe that inclusive education helps to address the difficulties faced by children with special educational needs, was answered by all 105 teachers. The teachers (103) answered "Agree" to "Strongly Agree" (98.1%), while only 2 teachers answered, " Neither agree nor disagree" (1.91%).

In Q6-I believe that training on inclusive education issues affects classroom management for students with special educational needs, the teachers (54) answered "Agree" to "Strongly agree" (51.4%), 29 answered " Neither agree nor disagree " (27.6%), while 22 teachers answered "Disagree" to "Strongly disagree" (21%).

In Q7-Students with educational needs have equal educational opportunities with other children in the school community, the teachers' (75) responses ranged from "Agree" to "Strongly agree" (71.4%), 25 answered " Neither agree nor disagree " (23.8%), while the remaining 5 responses ranged from "Disagree" to "Strongly disagree "(4.8%).

In Q8-There is updating and involvement of parents for the social support of children with special educational needs, the teachers (38) answered " Neither agree nor disagree " (36.2%), 35 responses ranged from "Disagree" to "Strongly disagree" (33.3%), while 32 teachers' responses ranged from "Agree" to "Strongly agree" (30.5%).

In Q9-The principal plays an active role in shaping an inclusive climate for students with special educational needs daily, most teachers (50) answers ranged from "Disagree" to "Strongly disagree" (47.6%), while 39 " Neither disagreed nor agreed " (37.1%), and 16 responded "Agree" to "Strongly agree" (15.3%).

In Q11-I believe that inclusive education has a positive effect on the academic performance of children without special educational needs, 103 out of 105 teachers answered. More specifically, 50 teachers "Agreed" (48.5%), 44 said "Disagreed" (42.7%), while 9 teachers "Neither disagreed nor agreed" (8.7%).

Q13-I believe that my school is doing the best to promote the social development of children without special educational needs, was answered by 102 out of 105 teachers. Most teachers (81) "Agreed" to "Strongly agreed" (79.4%), 19 teachers "Neither disagreed nor agreed" (18.6%), while only 2 teachers "Disagreed" to "Strongly disagreed" (2%).

Q14-The principal cultivates a culture of inclusion in the school, was answered by 79 out of the 105 teachers. 31 teachers "Agreed" to "Strongly agreed" (39.2%), 22 teachers "Neither disagreed nor agreed" (27.8%), 17 teachers (21.5%) "Disagreed", and 9 teachers (11.4%) "Strongly disagreed".

In Q15-The principal encourages the active participation and cooperation of all those involved in the learning process for joint decision-making, 32 teachers' responses ranged from "Disagree" to "Strongly disagree" (30.5%), 35 " Neither disagreed nor agreed" (33.3%), while 38 teachers' responses ranged from "Agree" to "Strongly agree" (36.2%).

In Q16-The culture of the school I serve inspires and supports the inclusion of all children, 24 teachers answered, "I agree" to "I strongly agree" (22.9%), 68 "Neither disagreed nor agreed" (64.8%), while 13 teachers answered "Disagree" to "I strongly disagree" (12.3%).

In Q17-There is substantial collaboration with other specialists (e.g., school counselor, school psychologist, speech therapist, etc.) who help to include children with special educational needs, 61 teachers' answers ranged from "I agree" to "I strongly agree" (58.1%), 30 "Neither disagreed nor agreed" (28.6%), while 14 "Disagreed" to "Strongly disagreed" (13.3%).

In Q18-Teachers have opportunities for dialogue and planning across grades and subjects, 52 teachers' answers ranged from "I agree" to "I strongly agree" (49.5%), 12 "Neither disagreed nor agreed" (11.4%), while 41 "Disagreed" to "Strongly disagreed" (39%).

In Q19-The school principal trusts the professional judgments of teachers, 39 teachers' answers ranged from "I agree" to "I strongly agree" (37.1%), 20 "Neither disagreed nor agreed" (19%), while 46 "Disagreed" to "Strongly disagreed" (43.8%).

In Q20-Teachers trust each other, 68 teachers' answers ranged from "I agree" to "I strongly agree" (64.7%), 19 "Neither disagreed nor agreed" (18.1%), while 18 "Disagreed" to "Strongly disagreed" (17.1%).

In Q25-Parents trust teachers' professional judgments, 46 teachers' answers ranged from "I agree" to "I strongly agree" (43.8%), 21 "Neither disagreed nor agreed" (20%), while 38 "Disagreed" to "Strongly disagreed" (36.2%).

In Q26-Leaders in our school facilitate teachers working together, 42 teachers' answers ranged from "I agree" to "I strongly agree" (40%), 34 "Neither disagreed nor agreed" (32.4%), while 29 "Disagreed" to "Strongly disagreed" (27.6%).

Correlation Tests

A correlation test checked whether teacher training during the pandemic is related to the degree to which teachers believe that according to teacher survey questionnaire questions 'Q2-have confidence in teaching children with special educational needs during the COVID-19 pandemic.' and 'Q3- have been properly trained to meet the special educational needs of students during the pandemic.' The non-parametric Mann-Whitney U correlation test was performed, with a level of statistical significance $\alpha = 0.05$ (5%). The Mann-Whitney U test generated the two following tables: Table 9.5 records Mean, Mean Rank and Sum of Ranks of variables for those who attended training and those who did not attend. Table 9.6

Table 9.5 Ranking statistics – Attending training I have been appropriately trained to meet the needs of SEND students during the pandemic

I have attended some training webinars on inclusive education during the pandemic.		N	Mean	Mean Rank	Sum of Ranks
I have confidence in my abilities to teach children with SEND during the pandemic.	No	48	2.81	39.80	1910.50
	Yes	57	3.56	64.11	3654.50
	Total	105	3.22		
I have been appropriately trained to meet the needs of SEND students during the pandemic.	No	48	2.08	36.99	1775.50
	Yes	56	3.25	65.79	3684.50
	Total	104	2.71		

Table 9.6 Mann-Whitney U test results

	I have confidence in my abilities to teach children with SEND during the pandemic	I have been appropriately trained to meet the needs of SEND students during the pandemic.
Mann-Whitney U	734,500	599,500
Wilcoxon W	1910,500	1775,500
Z	−4350	−5010
Asymp. Sig. (2-tailed)	000	000

[a]Grouping Variable: I have attended some training webinars on inclusive education during the pandemic

presents the results of the Mann - Whitney U test, which showed that there is a statistically significant difference, and therefore a correlation, of the relative training attendance with the degree to which teachers believe that: i) they have confidence in their abilities to teach children with SEND during the pandemic (Q2) (U (48.57) = 734,500, p = 0.000 < 0.05) and ii) have been appropriately trained to meet the needs of SEND students during the pandemic (Q3) (U (48, 56) = 599,500, p = 0.000 < 0.05). It was found that the extent to which teachers believe they have confidence in their abilities to teach SEND students and have been trained to meet their needs is related to their attendance at relevant training, with those who were trained to a greater extent having more confidence in their abilities to teach SEND students and have been trained to meet their needs (mean = 3.56 and mean = 3.25, respectively) than those who were not trained (mean = 2.81 and mean = 2.08, respectively).

Principals' Survey Questionnaire Questions-Descriptive Statistics

Survey questionnaire questions related to RQ1-Principals' views on inclusive learning practices in response to school closures during the pandemic & RQ3-Distance learning practices and inclusive school culture.

Q1. The principal ensures learning opportunities for all students at the school during COVID-19 pandemic. Most principals, with a percentage of 55.1% agreed, 36.4% neither agreed nor disagreed and only 8.4% disagreed with the statement.

Q2. The school administration ensures that good inclusive practices are incorporated into the school curriculum by all schoolteachers during the pandemic. 69.2% of the principals strongly agreed, 13.1 agreed, 12, 1 neither agreed nor disagreed, 4.7% disagreed and only 0.9% strongly disagreed.

Q9. The principal regularly participates in training and seminars on promoting online inclusive education. 52.3% of the principals stated that they strongly disagreed, while 47.7% disagreed.

Q17. The principal schedules training sessions according to the needs of teachers during the pandemic. 30.7% of the principals strongly agreed, 38.3% agreed, 31% neither agreed nor disagreed.

Q19. The administration encourages the modification of the curriculum to adapt it to the needs of students during the pandemic. 52.3% strongly agreed, 35.5% agreed while only 12.1% neither agreed nor disagreed.

Q20. The principal encourages the implementation of innovations in school reality during the pandemic. 73.8% of the principals strongly agreed, while 26.2% agreed.

Q21. The principal encourages joint decision-making in the design, implementation, and evaluation of individualized education programs during the pandemic. Most principals with 63.6% strongly agreed, while 36.4% agreed.

Q22. The administration ensures the appropriate upgrade of school equipment (e.g., assistive technology, textbooks, modern audio-visual materials, etc.) during the pandemic. 79.4% strongly agreed, 17.8% agreed and only 2.8% neither agreed nor disagreed.

Q23. The principal encourages online learning in informal virtual learning environments (e.g., in museums, zoos, neighborhood parks, etc.) during the pandemic. 31% strongly agreed, 19% agreed, while 50% neither agreed nor disagreed.

Q26. The principal creates a climate of trust and cooperation between the school and the parents/guardians during the pandemic. 62.9% strongly agreed, while 37.1% agreed.

Q27. The principal encourages the active participation of parents in the education of students during the pandemic. 55.1% of the principals strongly agreed, 28% agreed, while 16.8% neither agreed nor disagreed.

Q28. The school administration promotes cooperation between the school with services related to special education (e.g., special education counselor, medical centers) during the pandemic. 54.2% of the principals strongly agreed, while 45.8% agreed.

Q29. The administration interacts with the local government to jointly organize inclusive actions during the pandemic. 44.1% strongly agreed, 32.1% agreed and 23.8% neither agreed nor disagreed.

RQ2. Success factors and obstacles in the implementation of inclusive education during the pandemic.

Q3. The school administration makes decisions based on the values of equality and democracy. Almost half of the participants with a percentage of 49.5% strongly agreed, 33.6% agreed, 15.9% neither agreed nor disagreed, and only 0.9% disagreed.

Q4. The school administration makes decisions based on respect and acceptance of diversity. More than half of the principals, 58.9% agreed, 38.3% disagreed and only 2.8% neither agreed nor disagreed.

Q5. The administration cultivates a sense of shared responsibility among all members of the school community. Most principals, 75.7% strongly agreed, 12.1% agreed, 11.2% disagreed and only 0.9% neither agreed nor disagreed.

Q6. The principal prepares the teachers at school, so that in the future they can take over the administration of the school. Most principals, 62.6% strongly agreed, 27.1% strongly disagreed, 8.4% neither agreed nor disagreed and only 1.9% disagreed.

Q7. The country's education policy has as a priority the promotion of inclusive education for the formation of a sustainable culture in schools. Most principals with a percentage of 43.9% strongly agreed while 21.5% disagreed, 30.8% neither agreed nor disagreed and only 3.7% agreed.

Q8. The government provides the appropriate opportunities for continuing education of principals in matters of inclusive readiness.

Q10. The existing educational structures fully support the principal on issues of inclusion. Most principals, 71% strongly disagreed, 21.5% disagreed, while only 7.5% neither agreed nor disagreed.

Q11. The principal is constantly informed about the legislative developments in Special Education. 69.2% strongly agreed, while 30.8% stated that they agreed.

Q12. The principal promotes a common vision for the inclusion of all students. Most principals 78.5% strongly agreed while 21.5% agreed.

Q13. The principal cultivates a culture of inclusion in the school. 73.8% of the principals stated that they strongly agreed while 36.4% that they agreed.

Q14. The principal encourages the active participation and cooperation of all those involved in the learning process for joint decision-making. 63.6% of the respondents stated that they strongly agreed while 36.4% agreed.

Q15. The school administration encourages communication and information sharing among the members of the school community. 52.3% of the respondents strongly agreed while 47.7% agreed.

Q16. The principal cultivates high expectations for the personal and professional development of teachers. Most of the principals, 61.7% strongly agreed, while 38.3% agreed.

Q18. The administration encourages cooperation among teachers at school. 75.7% strongly agreed while 24.3% agreed.

Q24. School administration encourages the enrollment of students with special educational needs in the general school. Most principals with 71% strongly agreed, while 29% agreed.

Q25. The principal monitors and gets informed about the identification of marginalized students through communication with teachers. 71% strongly agreed, while 37.4% agreed.

Open-Ended Question and Secondary Data Coding and Thematic Analysis

The open-ended survey questionnaire question 'Are there any obstacles that you face in your efforts to promote Inclusive Education during the COVID-19 pandemic?' relates to RQ2 'Which success factors and obstacles influence the implementation of inclusive education in primary schools in the UAE during the pandemic?' based on the principals' and the teachers' responses on the obstacles to practicing inclusive education during the COVID-19 crisis. The question was answered by 55 of 105 teachers and by 44 of 107 principals. The creation of the code table was based on the analysis of the open-ended question and of the secondary data (e.g., 21 school policies; 35 school reports, 3 educational laws). The frequency of the codes after the analysis of the secondary data responds to RQ1 'How is inclusive education practiced at the micro level of primary schools in the UAE and from various perspectives (e.g., teachers, principals) during the pandemic?'. The frequency of the codes was measured considering how many times a code was encountered in the participants' answers and in the pertinent documents (Table 9.7).

Table 9.7 Codes and thematic categories (total)

RQ2. Obstacles that hinder the implementation of inclusive education during COVID-19 based on the open-ended survey question	Frequencies
Lack of teachers' knowledge and skills	81
Lack of teachers' training	74
Lack of equipment at home for students with SEND	62
Lack of parents' technical knowledge in supporting students with SEND at home	57
Minor socialization for students with SEND	53
Cost of facilities at home for online learning	46
Curriculum does not consider students' learning disabilities	43
Lack of cooperation between teachers and parents	33
Lack of specialized teaching staff	33
Difficulty in planning differentiating lessons	21
Connectivity issues	15
RQ1. Inclusive education practices in primary schools in the UAE based on the secondary data (e.g., school reports; educational policies & laws)	
Teacher training & skills in inclusion	35
Government support with legislative initiatives	13
Exchange of good practices with other schools	22
Training of principals	30
Teacher attitudes & practices towards diversity	27
Technology integration into teaching	25
Communication of schools with the community	16
Creation of a positive collaborative atmosphere	22
Parents & teachers working together	20

Discussion

The findings are discussed in terms of how inclusive education was implemented in primary schools in the UAE during the pandemic at the micro level and from various perspectives (e.g., teachers, principals); success factors and obstacles that influenced the implementation of inclusive education in primary schools in the UAE during the pandemic; and the degree to which schools'distance learning practices reflected an inclusive school culture.

RQ1. Inclusive education was practiced at the micro level of primary schools in the UAE and from various perspectives (e.g., teachers, principals) during the pandemic.

From the perspectives of the school principals, the research revealed that inclusive education was practiced during the pandemic in ways that enabled them to adopt the basic principles of sustainable leadership and take targeted action to shape the coveted sustainable leadership culture in school communities. Most principals agreed that they had taken measures to ensure that all students have increased learning opportunities to access the curriculum. They made decisions on creating a new learning environment aligned with universal values, such as equality, democracy, respect, and acceptance of diversity (Peterlin et al., 2015). They cultivated a sense of shared responsibility among all members of the school community; according to Hargreaves and Fink (2012), the distribution of leadership and the development of shared responsibility among teachers, students, and parents, are essential for education to be realized in a new context. Principals encouraged teachers to adjust to the new circumstances created by the pandemic to achieve this goal. However, they felt that teachers were not adequately prepared to teach students with sensory and motor impairments remotely, stressing the need for systemic improvements.

Although the promotion of inclusive education is an urgent need in the age of the pandemic, most of the principals agreed that the formal education policies seem to prioritize a sustainable school culture, but that the existing support structures do not fully support principals' and teachers' efforts to promote an inclusive culture. It seems that the gap between the adopted policies and the practices implemented, impede any efforts to achieve schools' inclusive visions. This problem also seems to have an impact on the training of principals, as training meetings and seminars in inclusive and digitized education during the pandemic were scarce. Ainscow and Sandill (2010) emphasize that school leaders should be trained in the basic principles of inclusive education to follow up on developments that constantly reflect upon their practices (Hagevik et al., 2012). Moreover, all the principals agreed that their role is primarily to promote a common vision for providing students with equal learning opportunities; continuous development of educational programs, and of teachers'skills and abilities, and continuous progress and improvement in learning (Alger, 2008). They believe that the vision and culture of inclusion should be distinguished by sustainable values of solidarity, justice, meritocracy, trust, honesty, and collaboration (Naraian & Schlessinger, 2017). According to Hargreaves and Fink (2003) these values from a community that is based on security, acceptance, and cooperation and seeks the intersection of good ideas and successful practices.

Regarding teachers' inclusive practices, most of the principals believe that they should raise teachers'awareness of social justice concerns through their own examples and cultivate high expectations of teachers' personal and professional development. In addition, they were positive about curricular modifications, emphasizing that the students who managed to cope with the closure of schools and similar disruptions were those who had mastered the mechanisms of learning, had access to digital media, and had a supportive environment at school and at home. The ones who were 'left behind' were students with SEND, who did not have the right digital tools, nor the ability to use them and received less support from teachers and at home, highlighting that the pandemic has dramatically reinforced the shortcomings and imperfections of education systems. The principals highlighted the need for an inclusive curriculum, characterized by personalization and student-centered orientation (Luciak & Biewer, 2011). They believe in teachers' cooperation and exchange of ideas that promote interaction, the reflection and transmission of experiences and knowledge and joint decision-making in the design, implementation, and evaluation of individualized educational programs. Furthermore, the principals agreed with the implementation of innovations in schools, as they view inclusive education as synonymous with openness, and advancement.

RQ2. Success factors and obstacles that influence the implementation of inclusive education in primary schools in the UAE during the pandemic.

They emphasized that attendance at school is an important social enterprise and a social experience when discussing the barriers to effective implementation of inclusive education. Therefore, the longer the students do not attend school, the less contact they have with their teachers, and the more their well-being is affected. Additional impediments included the lack of time and the fragmentary implementation of policy interventions without a vision for the future. When the education system is resilient, and there are front-line skills, effective educational leadership can handle teaching issues (Köpfer & Óskarsdóttir, 2019). But when schools function in a bureaucratic way, they end up with very long closures where many children are 'left behind', casting a shadow over the economy and society. International pressure emerging from goals and strategies in inclusive education and despite the great commitment of schools to adopt the inclusive educational vision highlighted by policy documents, such as the Dubai Inclusive Education Policy Framework (2017), there is the need to re-contextualize these goals at the macro, meso and micro levels, as according to the principals' experiences, the lack of resources and untrained personnel are challenges to quality education for all children.

RQ3. The degree that schools' distance learning practices reflected an inclusive school culture.

According to the principals, becoming more inclusive is about efficiency and productivity. They agreed that the extent to which schools' distance learning practices reflect an inclusive school culture depends on collective effectiveness, which is enhanced by the experiences and self-confidence of the school members. A key factor in the effectiveness of school culture is the principal's actions, that transmit common beliefs, values, and attitudes. The positive culture of a school accepts changes, which is not an easy task and requires systematic effort and input from all school members. The principals mentioned that during the pandemic, the biggest loss in distance learning concerned the children of kindergarten and primary schools, because at these ages, there are no alternatives. The principals agreed that they implemented a participatory leadership style as they promoted the active involvement of teachers in making decisions on remote teaching practices, developing their greatest possible commitment to achieving the goals of the school. In terms of the teachers' training, most of the principals agreed that the contribution of each teacher is essential to the school, in supporting new dynamics and collaborative initiatives (Padilla-Carmona et al., 2020).

From the teachers' perspectives, the research revealed that the ways inclusive education was practiced during the pandemic involved changes in attitude, teaching and assessment methods, curricula, learning environments, and teaching styles (Babane, 2002). The teachers agreed that they suddenly found themselves outside the lively interactive environment of a classroom, in which they guided their students, shared their problems, and reassured them of any concerns caused by the current reality. Similarly, the teachers felt that their students lost physical contact with the true socializing environment of the classroom, became estranged from their classmates, and became indifferent to digital technology. They agreed that their training in remote learning practices was insufficient as it was more theoretical than practical, but their care and love for children enabled them to communicate meaningfully with their students, to transmit knowledge, to keep their interest undiminished, and not to waste valuable time. The importance of training on teachers' positive attitudes towards inclusion has been discussed in the literature (Efthymiou & Kington, 2017; Saloviita, 2020). The teachers agreed that those who had been properly trained to teach students remotely with SEND, expressed more positive attitudes to teaching students, than did those who had no training during the pandemic. According to the trained teachers, hundreds of hours of online training took place that empowered them to face the challenges dynamically and to create student-centered environments, with collaborative activities that embedded critical and creative thinking. Moreover, the teachers considered distance education as an opportunity to develop skills, digital citizenship and create alternative practices and pedagogical approaches with flexibility and adaptability. Furthermore, the general education teachers over 50 years old agreed that even if their training was insufficient, their years of experience enabled them to be more flexible in practicing remote learning. Finally, all the teachers believe that there was solidarity and mutual support among trained and untrained colleagues in supporting distance learning (Sætra, 2021).

Overall, the teachers agreed that during the pandemic, the failures to practice inclusive education had an impact on students with SEND's participation and access to learning opportunities. These challenges included increased teaching workload and poor infrastructure (Bozkurt et al., 2020); limited collaboration between special and general education teachers in curricular modifications and accommodations; resistance of most general education teachers to breaking out of rooted stereotypes in conventional education; anxiety about students' level of responsiveness to the new learning conditions (Fawaz & Samaha, 2021) and technical difficulties; exposure to students' families through videos; students' absenteeism from the educational process; course of the curriculum; and efficiency of distance learning process.

Most of the teachers agreed that the principals played an active role in practicing inclusion. However, the teachers preferred principals to be more flexible, open to new ideas and innovations, with a vision of shaping an inclusive school culture that will not be constrained by the narrowness of the school context (Day & Sammons, 2016). The special education teachers believed that they need to be able to carry out individualized teaching, inform and sensitize the general context around the needs of each child to integrate smoothly in online learning (Lindacher, 2020). They value inclusion and agree that self-education enables them to act responsibly towards teaching students with SEND.

Conclusion

Changes towards a more inclusive school culture encompasses a 'transformative view of inclusion, in which diversity is seen as making a positive contribution to the creation of responsive educational settings' (Ainscow et al., 2006, p. 15). Societies need to promote inclusive education, while constant changes take place in the sociopolitical, economic, and educational contexts with the formation of a new normalcy. In this new challenge, school leaders and teachers are called upon to implement education policies with flexibility and innovative thinking. School leaders could create a vision for a sustainable school culture that promotes inclusion, redesigns educational reality, inspires all members of the educational community and makes radical changes (Gous et al., 2014; McLeskey & Waldron, 2015). School leaders need to embrace the principles of sustainable development reflecting on universal values and principles, e.g., prosperity, equality, democracy, and respect for individual rights, to strengthen the performance of those involved in the education process (Avery & Bergsteiner, 2011). The development of shared responsibility and joint decision-making are required in a recontextualized school culture (Hargreaves & Fink, 2012). A key prerequisite is for sustainable school leaders to listen to the needs of the school personnel and to select appropriate strategies and practices aimed at establishing a vision, a culture, and practical, social education inclusion (Muijs et al., 2010).

The existence of a strong school culture shows that there are common values and behavioral norms in the organization and is linked to school's efficiency and productivity. In addition, policymakers, universities, schools, NGOs, and parents must all commit to the principle of inclusion to implement promising inclusive education practices in schools and communities (Tan, 2021). The most frequently identified challenges to successful inclusive education according to the literature (Eide & Ingstad, 2011; Eleweke & Rodda, 2002; Johnstone & Chapman, 2009; Rose, 2010; Schuelka, 2018) are: lack of policy and legal support; inadequate school resources and facilities; inadequate specialized school staff; insufficient teacher training in inclusive methods; passive pedagogical systems; inflexible curriculum; unsupportive school and leadership; and socio-cultural attitudes about schools and special needs.

Based on the principals' and the teachers' views on the obstacles to remote inclusive education practices, it is proposed the systematic training of principals and teachers in recontextualized practices of inclusive education; the training programs to acquire a more experiential and practical character; establishing a meritocratic system to support the progress of children in the school community with specialized staff, logistical equipment, and easy accessibility; reconceptualizing existing inclusive school cultures, for promoting communication, cooperation and trust between members of school community.

Although in 2006 the United Nations called on states to provide inclusive education at all levels (Article 24) (UNHCR, 2006, p. 13), achieving this goal is a continuing challenge in terms of education policy, legislation, funding, and implementation.

There is a need to redefine the theoretical framework by focusing on the structure of the educational systems and the different ways that respond to the diversity of their students. There needs to be a reconceptualization and recontextualization of the UAE educational system in terms of the values and goals of inclusive education initiating an educational reform, which will not just rely on good intentions and humanitarian ideals but will implement new programs for inclusion to become a reality.

Inclusion concerns all those who participate in and have active roles in the education system. Making inclusive education a reality is a never-ending process. It is essential to examine inclusive education practices and policies that have been implemented realistically and meaningfully in developed countries, as developing countries struggle with inequality, insufficient resources, and education systems that are largely out of step with modern values (Walker et al., 2019). Creating a new perspective within a school organization, by activating the prospects for innovation, creativity, alternative attitudes, and perceptions, and planning response to challenges might require more research on leadership models that could redefine schools effectively. Principals as transformational leaders can have a profound impact on school culture (Alger, 2008). Teacher commitment is also essential.

References

Ainscow, M., & Sandill, A. (2010). Developing inclusive education systems: The role of organisational cultures and leadership. *International Journal of Education, 14*, 401–416.
Ainscow, M., Booth, T., & Dyson, A. (2006). *Improving schools, developing inclusion*. Routledge.
Alahbabi, A. (2009). K-12 special and general education teacher's attitudes toward the inclusion of students with special needs in general education classes in the United Arab Emirates (UAE). *International Journal of Special Education, 24*(2), 42–54.
Alborno, N. E. (2013). *The journey into inclusive education: a case study of three Emirati government primary schools* (Doctoral dissertation, The British University in Dubai (BUiD)).
Alborno, N. E., & Gaad, E. (2014). Index for inclusion': A framework for school review in the United Arab Emirates. *British Journal of Special Education, 41*(3), 231–248.
Alger, G. (2008). Transformational leadership practices of teacher leaders. *Academic Leadership: The Online Journal, 6*(2), 19.
Alghazo, E. M., & Naggar Gaad, E. E. (2004). General education teachers in the United Arab Emirates and their acceptance of the inclusion of students with disabilities. *British Journal of Special Education, 31*(2), 94–99.
Avery, G. C., & Bergsteiner, H. (2011). Sustainable leadership practices for enhancing business resilience and performance. *Strategy & Leadership, 39*(3), 5–15.
Babane, C. V. (2002). *Children experience of epilepsy: A case study*. Master of Education with specialisation in school guidance and counselling. University of South Africa.
Banathy, B. H. (1991). *Systems design of education: A journey to create the future*. Educational Technology.
Black, W. R., & Simon, M. D. (2014). Leadership for all students: Planning for more inclusive school practices. *International Journal of Educational Leadership Preparation, 9*(2), 153–172.
Booth, T., & Ainscow, M. (2002). *Index for inclusion: Developing learning and participation in schools*. Centre for Studies on Inclusive Education.

Bozkurt, A., Jung, I., Xiao, J., Vladimirschi, V., Schuwer, R., Egorov, G., ... Rodes, V. (2020). A global outlook to the interruption of education due to COVID-19 pandemic: Navigating in a time of uncertainty and crisis. *Asian Journal of Distance Education, 15*(1), 1–126.

Bradshaw, K., Tennant, L., & Lydiatt, S. (2004). Special education in the United Arab Emirates: Anxieties, attitudes and aspirations. *International Journal of Special Education, 19*(1), 49–55.

Cerdan Chiscano, M. (2021). Giving a voice to students with disabilities to design library experiences: An ethnographic study. *Societies, 11*(2), 61.

Clarke, D. (2007). Ten key principles from research for the professional development of mathematics teachers. In G. C. Leder & H. Forgasz (Eds.), *Stepping dtones for the 21st century: Australasian mathematics education research* (pp. 27–39). Brill Sense.

Creswell, J. W. (2011). Controversies in mixed methods research. *The Sage Handbook of Qualitative Research, 4*, 269–284.

Creswell, J. W., & Poth, C. N. (2016). *Qualitative inquiry and research design: Choosing among five approaches*. Sage publications.

Darling-Hammond, L., Flook, L., Cook-Harvey, C., Barron, B., & Osher, D. (2020). Implications for educational practice of the science of learning and development. *Applied Developmental Science, 24*(2), 97–140.

Day, C., & Sammons, P. (2016). *Successful school leadership. Education development trust*. Reading Berkshire, England RG1 4RU.

Deglau, D., & O'Sullivan, M. (2006). The effects of a long-term professional development program on the beliefs and practices of experienced teachers. *Journal of Teaching in Physical Education, 25*(4), 379–396.

Dubai Law No 2. (2014). *Concerning protection of the rights of persons with disabilities in the Emirate of Dubai*. Retrieved from https://www.cda.gov.ae/ar/aboutus/Documents/Concerning%20Protection%20of%20the%20Rights%20of%20Persons%20with%20Disabilities%20in%20the%20Emirate%20of%20Dubai%20-%20Law%202%20-%202014%20-%20EN.pdf

Efthymiou, E., & Kington, A. (2017). The development of inclusive learning relationships in mainstream settings: A multimodal perspective. *Cogent Education, 4*(1), 1304015.

Eide, A. H., & Ingstad, B. (2011). Some concluding thoughts: The way ahead. In *Disability and poverty: A global challenge* (pp. 225–231). Bristol University Press.

Eleweke, C. J., & Rodda, M. (2002). The challenge of enhancing inclusive education in developing countries. *International Journal of Inclusive Education, 6*(2), 113–126.

Elhoweris, H., & Efthymiou, E. (2020). Inclusive and special education in the Middle East. *Oxford Research Encyclopedia of Education*. https://doi.org/10.1093/acrefore/9780190264093.013.1219

Engelbrecht, P., Swart, E., & Eloff, I. (2001). Stress and coping skills of teachers with a learner with Down's syndrome in inclusive classrooms. *South African Journal of Education, 21*(4), 256–259.

Fawaz, M., & Samaha, A. (2021, January). E-learning: Depression, anxiety, and stress symptomatology among Lebanese university students during COVID-19 quarantine. *Nursing Forum, 56*(1), 52–57.

Flack, C. B., Walker, L., Bickerstaff, A., & Margetts, C. (2020). *Socioeconomic disparities in Australian schooling during the COVID-19 pandemic*. Pivot Professional Learning.

Gaad, E. (2011). *Inclusive education in the Middle East*. Routledge.

Gous, J. G., Eloff, I., & Moen, M. C. (2014). How inclusive education is understood by principals of independent schools. *International Journal of Inclusive Education, 18*(5), 535–552.

Hagevik, R., Aydeniz, M., & Rowell, C. G. (2012). Using action research in middle level teacher education to evaluate and deepen reflective practice. *Teaching and Teacher Education, 28*(5), 675–668.

Hargreaves, A., & Fink, D. (2003). Sustaining leadership. *Phi Delta Kappan, 84*(9), 693–700.

Hargreaves, A., & Fink, D. (2012). *Sustainable leadership* (Vol. 6). Wiley.

Herzog, C., Handke, C., & Hitters, E. (2019). Analyzing talk and text II: Thematic analysis. In H. Van den Bulck, M. Puppis, K. Donders, & L. Van Audenhove (Eds.), *The Palgrave handbook of methods for media policy research* (pp. 385–401). Palgrave Macmillan.

Hoy, W. K., & Miskel, C. G. (2008). School effectiveness. In *Educational administration: Theory, research, and practice* (pp. 299–308). McGraw-Hill.

Huang, R., Liu, D., Tlili, A., Knyazeva, S., Chang, T. W., Zhang, X., … Holotescu, C. (2020). *Guidance on open educational practices during school closures: Utilizing OER under COVID-19 pandemic in line with UNESCO OER recommendation*. Smart Learning Institute of Beijing Normal University.

Johnstone, C. J., & Chapman, D. W. (2009). Contributions and constraints to the implementation of inclusive education in Lesotho. *International Journal of Disability, Development and Education, 56*(2), 131–148.

Kim, J., & Rose, P. (2020). The threat of COVID-19 on Ethiopia's recent gains in pre-primary education. *The UKFIET Blog*.

Köpfer, A., & Óskarsdóttir, E. (2019). Analysing support in inclusive education systems–a comparison of inclusive school development in Iceland and Canada since the 1980s focusing on policy and in-school support. *International Journal of Inclusive Education, 23*(7–8), 876–890.

Lindacher, T. (2020). Perceptions of regular and special education teachers of their own and their co-teacher's instructional responsibilities in inclusive education: A case study. *Improving Schools, 23*(2), 140–158.

Luciak, M., & Biewer, G. (2011). Equity and inclusive education in Austria: A comparative analysis. In A. Artiles, E. Kozleski, & F. Waitoller (Eds.), *Inclusive education: Examining equity of five continents* (pp. 17–44). Harvard Education Press.

McLeskey, J., & Waldron, N. L. (2015). Effective leadership makes schools truly inclusive. *Phi Delta Kappan, 96*(5), 68–73.

Mitchell, D. (2015). Inclusive education is a multi-faceted concept. *Center for Educational Policy Studies Journal, 5*(1), 9–30.

Mngo, Z. Y., & Mngo, A. Y. (2018). Teachers' perceptions of inclusion in a pilot inclusive education program: Implications for instructional leadership. *Education Research International, 2018*, 1–13.

Moon, M. D. (2019). Triangulation: A method to increase validity, reliability, and legitimation in clinical research. *Journal of Emergency Nursing, 45*(1), 103–105.

Moser, A., & Korstjens, I. (2018). Series: Practical guidance to qualitative research. Part 3: Sampling, data collection and analysis. *European Journal of General Practice, 24*(1), 9–18.

Muijs, D., Ainscow, M., Dyson, A., Raffo, C., Goldrick, S., Kerr, K., … Miles, S. (2010). Leading under pressure: Leadership for social inclusion. *School Leadership and Management, 30*(2), 143–157.

Naraian, S., & Schlessinger, S. (2017). When theory meets the "reality of reality": Reviewing the sufficiency of the social model of disability as a foundation for teacher preparation for inclusive education. *Teacher Education Quarterly, 44*(1), 81–100.

Nketsia, W. (2017). A cross-sectional study of pre-service teachers' views about disability and attitudes towards inclusive education. *International Journal of Research Studies in Education, 6*, 53–68.

Padilla-Carmona, M. T., Martínez-García, I., & Herrera-Pastor, D. (2020). Just facilitating access or dealing with diversity? Non-traditional students' demands at a Spanish university. *European journal for Research on the Education and Learning of Adults, 11*(2), 219–233.

Peterlin, J., Pearse, N., & Dimovski, V. (2015). Strategic decision making for organizational sustainability: The implications of servant leadership and sustainable leadership approaches. *Economic and Business Review, 17*(3), 273–290.

Rizvi, A. (2021). Thousands more children with disabilities being taught in Dubai schools, report finds. *The National*. Retrieved from https://www.thenational.ae/uae/education/thousands-more-children-with-disabilities-being-taught-in-dubai-schools-report-finds-1.866495

Rose, R. C. (2010). *Confronting obstacles to inclusion*. Routledge.

Rudasill, K. M., Snyder, K. E., Levinson, H., & Adelson, J. L. (2018). Systems view of school climate: A theoretical framework for research. *Educational Psychology Review, 30*(1), 35–60.

Sætra, L. J. (2021). *Individualized education plans during the COVID-19 school lockdown in Norway. A quantitative study on teachers' self-reported success of online teaching* (Master's thesis).

Saloviita, T. (2020). Teacher attitudes towards the inclusion of students with support needs. *Journal of Research in Special Educational Needs, 20*(1), 64–73.

Schein, E. H. (1985). Defining organizational culture. *Classics of Organization Theory, 3*(1), 490–502.

Schuelka, M. J. (2018). *Implementing inclusive education*. Retrieved from https://opendocs.ids.ac.uk/opendocs/bitstream/handle/20.500.12413/14230/374_Implementing_Inclusive_Education.pdf?sequence=1&isAllowed=y

Schulze, M. (2010). *Understanding the UN Convention on the rights of persons with disabilities: A handbook on the human rights of persons with disabilities*. Retrieved from http://www.hiproweb.org/uploads/tx_hidrtdocs/HICRPDManual2010.pdf

Sergiovanni, T., & Starratt, R. (2007). *Supervision: A redefinition*. McGraw-Hill Humanities/Social Sciences/Languages.

Tan, Q. (2021). *Barriers to inclusive education in Chinese primary schools: Culture, policy, and practice*. Routledge.

The National Policy for Empowering People of Determination. (2017). Retrieved from https://u.ae/en/about-the-uae/strategies-initiatives-and-awards/federal-governments-strategies-and-plans/the-national-policy-for-empowering-people-with-special-needs

UAE Federal Law 14/2009. (2009). *Concerning the rights of people with disabilities*. Retrieved from https://u.ae/en/information-and-services/social-affairs/people-of-determination/rehabilitation-of-people-with-special-needs

UAE Federal law No. 29 of 2006. (2006). *In respect of the rights of people with special needs*. Retrieved from https://www.un.org/development/desa/disabilities/wpcontent/uploads/sites/15/2019/11/United-Arab-Emirates_The-Rights-of-People-with-Special-Needs.pdf

UNESCO (2020). *COVID-19 educational disruption and response*. Retrieved from https://en.unesco.org/covid19/educationresponse

UNHCR. (2006). *Policy on age, gender and diversity*. Retrieved from https://www.unhcr.org/60db21c14.pdf

Walker, J., Pearce, C., Boe, K., & Lawson, M. (2019). *The power of education to fight inequality: How increasing educational equality and quality is crucial to fighting economic and gender inequality*. Oxfam.

Weber, A. S., & City, E. (2012). Inclusive education in the gulf cooperation council. *Journal of Educational and Instructional Studies in the World, 2*(2), 85–97.

Wenger, E. (1998). Communities of practice: Learning as a social system. *Systems Thinker, 9*(5), 2–3.

Woulds, J. (2004). *A practical guide to the data protection act*. Constitution Unit.

Efthymia Efthymiou is an Assistant Professor of Education, at the College of Interdisciplinary Studies, at Zayed University, in the United Arab Emirates (UAE). Her research focuses on inclusive education, classroom discourse, Special Educational Needs & Disorders (SEND), and educational environments, which are conducive to supporting inclusive class teaching from the point of view of stakeholders, particularly SEND children, and how far the physical as well as psychological environments contribute to positioning and attitudes. She has worked in several qualitative research projects.

Chapter 10
Inclusive Art Pedagogies for Refugee Children and Youth with Mental Health Disabilities During COVID-19: A Canadian Perspective

Susan Barber

Abstract New refugee students to Greater Vancouver, Canada, who have been exposed to violence and war are in danger of remaining "stuck" in traumatic memories and unable to lead productive lives if they do not receive treatment, yet stigma towards mental illness prevents many from seeking help. Education offers crucial opportunities to feel safe, recover trust in others, and participate in school activities; however, COVID-19 has upended schooling and some refugees are suffering declines in mental health. Drawing on surveys with 16 educators, including in-depth interviews with three art teachers, this study examines effective COVID-19 teaching strategies, beginning with forming strong relationships, arranging one-to-one meetings, and playing games. Some employ art to allow refugee students to express symbolically difficult pre/migration experiences, which has the potential for generating deeper meanings in events and new identities. This chapter investigates the value of art pedagogies in particular, not only in facilitating trauma processing, but also linking art-making to improved language learning, literacy, creative and critical thinking, and other academic skills; also, Mertins's disability theory confronts the meaning of inclusion for those previously labelled as defective, preferring to understand them as "just different". Although ethics is still an obstacle, one recommendation is for school districts to provide educators with professional development starting with trauma-informed school programs before moving into activities that bring therapeutic benefits through engaging with the arts.

Keywords Refugee students · Teachers · Trauma · Art pedagogies · COVID-19

S. Barber (✉)
Simon Fraser University, Burnaby, BC, Canada
e-mail: susan_barber@sfu.ca

Introduction

Globally, there are 84 million forcibly displaced persons, half of whom are children (UNHCR, 2021). Among Syrian refugees, 50% experience emotional disorders, including depression, anxiety, and posttraumatic stress disorder (PTSD) due to exposure to war, violence, and the despair of losing family members. The sudden arrival of 40,000 Syrian refugees in Canada in 2015 overwhelmed teachers, necessitating the immediate implementation of trauma-informed classrooms without adequate training or explanation of the causes of refugee students' behavior from education officials (Levi, 2019). While progress is being made, school counselors are still overburdened; the few therapists who are available are spread across multiple schools, and some refugees are unable to overcome the stigma associated with mental illness. The danger for refugee children and youth not receiving treatment is the possibility of remaining "stuck" in traumatic memories and unable to lead productive lives. Education offers crucial opportunities to feel safe in the classroom, to begin trusting teachers, participate in social and academic activities, and achieve a sense of belonging (Barber, 2021). Before COVID-19, collaborations between teachers, school counsellors and art therapists yielded remarkable non-verbal opportunities for refugee students to begin a Canadian education, despite lacking English language skills or having no native literacy, also called "preliteracy" (Barber & Ramsay, 2020). The continuation of COVID-19 has demonstrated an essential need for newly arriving refugee students to find inclusive learning activities that not only engage, but also retain them.

COVID-19 has reformed the mode of instruction worldwide. The majority of classrooms were forced to transform from a traditional face-to-face approach to a socially distanced virtual approach, or hybrid version of the two. As of March 2022, the COVID-19 situation appeared more optimistic, but has not ended, and teachers must be equipped with the skills and knowledge to ensure each student continues their education, no matter the delivery method. Vulnerable refugee students can continue to learn holistically and develop personal strengths through adaptable inclusive art pedagogies. The following chapter will showcase how art is a universal language (Eisner, 2002) which allows refugee students with mental health disabilities to share parts of their lives with peers, process trauma, and imagine a more hopeful future. Findings from a case study in Greater Vancouver schools in British Columbia, Canada, will detail teacher experiences in the last 20 months, followed by recommendations for inclusive art pedagogies that maintain an ethos of inclusion to further a sense of belonging through engagement, healing, and transformation.

Background

Pre-COVID-19: Teachers' Best Practices for Refugees

Before COVID-19 up-rooted traditional education, teachers in Canada were being encouraged to adopt a pedagogy tied to trauma-informed schools. Previously, methods were aligned with the goal of acculturation which occurs as a process for all newcomers through feeling safe in school, having a daily routine, developing the trust of adults, and experiencing inclusion through participation (Berry, 2005; Custodio & O'Loughlin, 2017). Trauma-informed schools, however, require much more of educators, namely to:

- Share an understanding of how trauma impacts learning and why a school-wide approach is needed for creating a trauma-sensitive school,
- Support all students to feel safe—physically, socially, emotionally and academically,
- Address students' needs in holistic ways, taking into account their relationships, self-regulation, academic competence, and physical and emotional well-being,
- Explicitly connect students to the school community,
- Embrace teamwork with a sense of a shared responsibility for every student,
- Anticipate and adapt to the ever-changing needs of students and the surrounding community (Cole et al., 2013, pp. 11–12).

Schools are ideal locations to implement programs such as the Attachment, Regulation and Competency (ARC) model (The National Child Traumatic Stress Network, 2012), mainly because most teachers already have skills in place to prioritize their relationships with students and look beyond emotions to see underlying causes. These approaches aim to raise awareness about what may be happening with refugee students, how to choose appropriate responses to unregulated behavior, and what factors may cause re-traumatization (Substance Abuse and Mental Health Services Administration [SAMHSA] 2014). Once teachers are better able to comprehend complex reasons for student behavior, students may feel supported and apply themselves more in learning (Jacobson, 2021).

Although professional development programs are slowly reaching districts that enroll refugee students, the goal in acquiring trauma-informed strategies is to nurture a sense of belonging which is key to integration in the school as well as society. Although definitions vary, a student's sense of belonging is related to school attachment. If a student accepts school rules, teachers' expectations, academic learning, and comprehends the value of education, they are more prone to embrace a positive attitude towards school, leading to an array of advantages, including improved self-confidence, social skills, motivation, self-efficacy, and achievement, while reducing depression, anxiety, and other social-emotional issues (Kia-Keating & Ellis, 2007). For these reasons, the importance of the social environment in the classroom cannot be underestimated (Block et al., 2014).

During COVID-19

When schools went fully online from March to early June 2020, there were immediate practical concerns, mostly due to equity issues, such as a lack of technology, internet access, and food security. Although 98.8% of Canadians have devices with WIFI (Frenette et al., 2020) teachers determined that 58% of low-income student refugees were often sharing one mobile phone among multiple family members (Frenette et al., 2020) while others had no private space within the home to attend their online classes. The schools hastened to solicit laptops from the community to donate to student refugees. Families who relied on school meal programs asked for regular access to food to be maintained. Since schools were closed, teachers and support staff drove food supplies to the homes of refugee families.

Despite teachers' determination to eliminate barriers to education, many student refugees were not attending online class sessions, similar to other families with low income. Financial setbacks from unemployment, fear of leaving home, and dealing with mental health issues were the main reasons. Student refugees in particular require daily immersion in English to advance their language skills and bond with peers. When student refugees did attend online classes, teachers began to notice an overall decline in mental health. Without support from a multicultural worker to translate or assist, student refugees found the academic work inaccessible and difficult, and attendance slowly dwindled.

In May 2020, the British Columbia Ministry of Education accepted that academic goals for the school year would have to be set aside, and the emphasis shifted to maintaining relationships and advancing social and emotional learning. Gradually, teachers began to provide more support to student refugees through small group sessions on Zoom and then in socially-distanced classrooms. This paved the way for other marginalized students to join online classes, which increased attendance. Teachers played number games, read books aloud, showed nature videos, and acquired entertaining educational software programs for students. Although small group instruction continued until the end of the school year, some teachers were concerned about the possibility of refugees' return to isolation and lack of progress over the summer of 2020.

The Value of Art in Trauma and Learning

For decades, researchers have shown a direct relationship between art and improved literacy and language development for all students (Anderson, 2015; Field, 2016). Art develops creative and critical thinking, problem solving and reasoning through its ability to stimulate cognition and brain development through weighing artistic decisions, such as improvisation in drama, when the direction of the story may change (Sousa, 2017). Art is complex, and students have the potential to advance listening skills, respond to constructive criticism, and communicate more effectively overall (Anderson, 2015; Sousa, 2017). The practice of arts-based education boosts positive emotional development, deep thinking, better concentration, increased self-awareness, self-expression, and self-efficacy (Field, 2016). The arts engage both the left (rational) side with the right (creative) side of the brain, allowing the cognitive to work in tandem with the affective for more holistic learning (Berry & Loughlin, 2015).

While some online and socially-distanced activities encouraged student refugees to join inclusive learning, these activities were not directly addressing trauma and other mental health issues. A psychiatric definition of trauma is when "a victim is rendered helpless by an overwhelming force … traumatic events overwhelm the ordinary systems of care that give people a sense of control, connection and meaning" (Herman, 1997, p. 33). Trauma occurs when a person becomes "stuck" in "hyper-arousal" (on high alert, overreacting, frequent nightmares, easily triggered) or "hypo-arousal" (numb, isolated, depressed). Van der Kolk (2014) describes it as getting fixed in time and being lashed to the terrifying event(s). Being "scared speechless" blocks the brain's ability to form a narrative that would move the memory from the amygdala where emotions are joined to memory with fight, flight or freeze responses, to the more rational prefrontal cortex where the person can get some cognitive distance from the memory and reflect on their responses.

Before verbal communication, sounds are created, bodies move through space and scribbled images representing objects or stories are drawn (Dieterich-Hartwell & Koch, 2017). Gadamer (2003) believed that preverbal art induces an exalted or transcendental state of mind, even transporting us to earlier points in our lives, and permitting us to re-live past memories. Gadamer's thoughts support how visual art, music, dance and movement all precede verbal language and can assist in retrieving personal past narratives. The arts "speak" through a symbolic language that seeks to access "unacknowledged feelings and [provide] a means of integrating them creatively into the personality, enabling therapeutic change to take place" (Dieterich-Hartwell & Koch, 2017, p. 3).

Creative or expressive arts make the implicit explicit and what is unconscious becomes conscious (Adnams Jones, 2018). If a person can capture preverbal understanding in metaphor or symbol, the oral-visual interior of the person can be externalized, and the images become forms of self-expression in areas where language was silenced, allowing the possibility of therapeutic transformation of the self (Provencal & Gabora, 2007). The main objective is to evoke a healing narrative: the person is now able to tell their story, share their history through images and present an identity, as well as start to envision a new, blended future identity. Art can help bring painful memories to the surface, unblocking and releasing unique expressions of self. Finding meaning in tragic events is possible when articulated through a new voice. Thus, the creative arts are in the present, while building bridges to the past and to alternative ways of knowing and seeing the self in the future (Dieterich-Hartwell & Koch, 2017). Art is a safe, slow and healthy means of releasing psychic energy and transformation arises from catharsis (Adnams Jones, 2018).

Teachers are not trained to be art therapists nor should they do any kind of therapy with students, ethically speaking (Kalmanowitz & Potash, 2010), but teachers can still learn much about the power and potential of art to heal and transform students with past trauma. Many teachers have been introduced to creative or expressive art therapies in Greater Vancouver, Canada, and have witnessed the changes in the students.

Evidence-Based Creative/Expressive Arts Programs

Harvey (1989) first published his discovery in, "Creating Arts Therapies in the Classroom: A Study of Cognitive, Emotional, and Motivational Changes," on how therapy could successfully unite the cognitive aspect of creativity and the therapeutic aspect of behavioral and personality change. By integrating thought and feeling, expressive arts therapies were effective at altering social/emotional behavior, leading to academic improvement. Since then, schools have collaborated with art therapists to apply interventions that offer multiple benefits to all students.

Not too long ago, however, many art therapists felt a sense of ambivalence towards research (Gilroy, 2006), tracing back to the ancient debate between art and science. "Traditional" research was often characterized as in opposition to the practices of art and human interaction, something scientific and reductive, and, likely to be inauthentic to the art therapy process. Even today, meta-studies conducted to evaluate the effectiveness of art programs through standardizing criteria across studies are still hampered by the possible differentiation in delivery and adjustments for different kinds of participants, in different countries and cultures. For example, Beauregard et al. (2017) reviewed 19 scientific articles referring to eight different international classroom programs in order to evaluate the effects on children's mental health and confirm evidence-based practices. Overall, the results indicated that programs containing a major component of creative expression can be beneficial to children. Most studies reported clear improvements in hope, coping, resiliency, prosocial behaviors, self-esteem, impairment, emotional and behavioral problems, making meaning, and PTSD scores; however, several studies also recounted no major change in prosocial behaviors, self-esteem, emotional and behavioral problems, PTSD, coping, and resiliency in adolescent boys.

Similarly, in Van Lith's (2016) study, 30 articles on art therapy had comparable results. To bring art research more in line with empirical evidence and separate itself from anecdotal evidence, Van Lith suggested further criteria for arts researchers: provide more details of methods to ensure transferability of practice, add practitioner critiques of the therapy used, and embed participants' voices in the study to address questions related to expectations and the perceived goals of art therapy.

Gilroy (2006) reminds us of the "lack of fit" when superimposing art therapy research onto a scientific framework with the following statement:

> …the validity of all case-study research is internal, true only within the context of the particular case; the findings cannot be generalized to other populations and settings and so lack external validity. Nonetheless case studies describing work with people from the same population, with similar problems and using the same clinical approach contribute to the

cumulative evidence base of the discipline and form the bedrock of all forms of clinical research. (p. 9)

What is essential to keep in mind is that the effects of the programs were beneficial to students' mental health. The peripheral, more elusive benefits to classroom-based interventions of which students may be unaware include having interventions delivered within the classroom where there is no stigma of receiving "treatment" since students are creating art with their classmates. One of the ways younger children defeat trauma is through play (St. Thomas & Johnson, 2007), by acting out troubling life events and re-enacting emotional trials they have endured to locate the key to healing. The opportunity for memories to arise unbidden enters child play through humor, artistic expression and social interactions. What occurs may be a reconnection of fragmented stories, sometimes with a change of details, or a reconstructed understanding that provides deeper, transformative meaning from the worst experiences (St. Thomas & Johnson, 2007). Children intuitively gravitate to the expressive arts and play—or act out—what they are reliving, even what they may find "unspeakable" (Malchiodi, 2015). Play has the potential to make children generally happier, yet they may not notice the change.

For the reasons stated above, I set out to investigate how refugee students coped with disrupted learning during COVID-19, specifically the reduced opportunities for English language learning, socio-emotional development, peer interactions, and trauma processing in local schools.

Research questions, therefore, are centered on the following:

1. What are the main barriers to inclusion in refugees' education during COVID-19?
2. Do teachers feel art has a significant role to play in advancing refugees' holistic development, such as feeling safe, becoming more trusting, having a greater sense of belonging, and improving overall mental health?
3. How might schools navigate ethical issues around making art in schools in order for refugees to receive therapeutic benefits as well as greater educational benefits?

The following section outlines two useful lenses for examining ways of understanding these vulnerable members of the school population.

Theoretical Framework

The research questions in this study focused on how Canadian teachers ensure inclusion for traumatized refugee students during COVID-19. I was especially interested in learning how arts-based pedagogies might fill the gap in online learning when teachers struggled to advance all students' academic learning, often prevented by weak attendance or lack of computing technology.

Data collected are viewed through an approach that endeavors to understand transformation, and, specifically, what pedagogical tools might be required to lift students above their circumstances. A transformative framework may provide a better fit for marginalized subjects when other theories do not go far enough (Creswell & Poth, 2018). Refugees experience "intersectionality", or being impacted by numerous factors, including a lack of English language skills, preliteracy, PTSD, and underemployed or dysfunctional parents with their own health problems who are unable to support their children's educational needs. Mertins's (2003) transformative framework provides an alternate way of understanding marginalized individuals or groups, and endorses taking action to support them, often by considering equity and more socially just solutions. The purpose of knowledge construction is to improve society and raise the status of vulnerable people by instilling a hopeful, positive, and resilient view of the future. This qualitative research approach often involves reforming policy and effecting change in both the lives of participants and the institutions that affect them, usually through allowing participants a voice to express their needs.

Transformation dovetails well with disability theory, also advanced by Mertins (2009). It questions the meaning of inclusion in schools and unites educators and the parents of the disabled child to ensure inclusive decision-making. Distancing itself from the medical model that views disability as illness and avoiding its labels of "defect", this theory is likely to conceptualize disability as being due to, not intrinsic characteristics, but rather, environmental causes, and understanding disability as simply a difference. Transformation and disability theory for considering inclusion of refugee pupils with mental health problems, therefore, underpin the study.

Methodology

Over the course of 14 months, a mixed method chronological approach was used to investigate the research questions. Former Master of Education students who worked with refugee students and/or students with disabilities, were invited to participate, and a few did snowball recruitment within their school districts, particularly to enlist school counsellors. Each participant met the criteria of having more than eight years' teaching experience, with art teachers having 18+ years of experience each. All participants ($n = 16$) consented to filling in a semi-structured questionnaire and two agreed to be interviewed twice in more depth. The following is the breakdown:

- In the first questionnaire, ten educators (five teachers, three school counsellors and two vice principals) from three Greater Vancouver school districts consented to sharing ideas from the early COVID-19 stage (initial lockdown and online classes in April 2020). All questionnaires were intentionally designed chronologically to jog teachers' memories of the sudden nature of the lockdown, to capture the immediate priorities and to recall how educators, students and parents responded. Questions elicited comments on how different students

- experienced the lockdown in vastly different ways, based on the initial concerns they voiced.
- In the second questionnaire, four educators (three teachers and one vice principal) responded to questions about what was working well during COVID-19, characteristics of marginalized students and what had been learned at the end of the school year (June 2021). This second questionnaire directed educators to discuss how classes gradually achieved some stability and accepted limitations. While some schools reduced expectations for academic achievement, teachers realized mental health aspects of school could still be advanced through students maintaining social relationships and staying connected. Art was one subject deemed to play an important role for inclusion, especially for refugees.
- The third questionnaire targeted three highly experienced art teachers and encouraged them to share their pedagogies related to teaching refugee students (also June 2021). One was an elementary teacher (Gareth); another, a secondary school Art teacher (Shirley); and last, a special needs teacher who had earned a doctoral degree in Arts Education and had also been both a primary and secondary school teacher (Laura). To better understand what was happening through art, this last questionnaire targeted specifically what needs refugees were having met in art class that may not have been available in other subject areas or activities. For example, teachers were asked to reflect on whether art was able to offer greater social connection, language learning and communication, but in different ways.

The responses correspond to the COVID-19 period, which ran from April 2020 to June 2021. All teachers were asked how and why they incorporate art activities into their classrooms, with Art teachers being asked to provide additional information about their pedagogies. Due to COVID-19 restrictions, all questionnaires were sent via email, and interviews were conducted by phone. In the latter case, transcripts were read back to the participants to ensure accuracy. Questionnaires were deemed most suitable for the study because participants could reflect on their answers and speak from their situated viewpoints. Originally, refugee voices were to be included in the study to gain insights about making art, but this was impossible. Ethically, vulnerable minor populations are often deemed to be at risk of psychological harm when participating in research, and, meeting with a translator in the schools was blocked due to COVID-19 precautions.

To protect the identities of participants and schools, all data were anonymized and pseudonyms were assigned. Data were analyzed by date, school (elementary vs. secondary) and teachers' interest in art practices. After sorting through general patterns in teacher attitudes and COVID-19 experiences, an inductive approach proved useful for coding and generating themes (Saldana, 2009). I was especially alert to similarities in how teachers viewed refugee students' needs during COVID-19 and the reasons behind pedagogical choices. Categories were generated to organize the findings.

I begin with educators' experiences dealing with the immediate challenges that refugees and schools faced during the early lockdown phase.

Results

The Local Context

Before COVID-19, all participant teachers with refugees in their classrooms regularly used art as an inclusive means of support to advance preverbal/preliterate communication skills, to connect with peers and manage self-regulation. Art was regarded as a calming influence, which was critical during a refugee's initial disorientation upon arrival. Many teachers had expressive arts therapists enter their classrooms, observed their activities, and felt this had a significant impact on their refugee students.

Gareth, a grade 4 (ages 8–9) elementary school teacher, said, "Expressive arts gave some of my students the opportunity to connect with someone in the class and process some of their emotions and worries."

Shirley, a secondary school Art teacher, agreed. "They were able to engage with one another and make bonds".

An educator in both elementary, secondary and post-secondary, Laura described adolescents' responses. "Arts are non-threatening, particularly if it is their day-to-day interest like popular music/dance. Expanding definitions of art, like fashion and textiles, photography as artefact, and video for social justice issues, can support their cultural identity and reinterpretation of self in the classroom and new community cultures".

Difficult Beginnings

Then, like most teachers around the world, educators on the west coast of Canada were caught off guard by the mandatory shift to online learning in March 2020.

An urban secondary school administrator captured the frantic nature of the change. "Students had no time; they had to empty their lockers that day. Many refugee parents were concerned about food security and asked if the school could continue providing fruit and vegetables and the government's food program at the school. They didn't grasp that the school was closing. Administrators organized educational assistants and other volunteers to drive to refugee families' homes and deliver food hampers."

Almost immediately, the next issue became access to technology. One rural elementary teacher identified attendance as the biggest problem. "Low-income students are attending sporadically and there is the stress of bringing them up to speed. We were only online for one month and only six families came online." But another teacher reported the remarkable generosity of the community's donations. "Of our approximate 900 students, we gave out almost 200 laptops to support online learning".

Another phenomenon previously unknown to teachers was described by an administrator. "Some refugee students sleep until 2 pm—they can only get on a single mobile phone late at night that is shared among the family."

Hailey, a special needs teacher, reported, "Our concerns are not academic right now. The number one concern is social well-being. 'Classes' is a loose term. I'm just checking in. We have a laugh; I assess their state and give diverse opportunities for academics. Some are engaging, others not".

Franz, a teacher who supports students with disabilities, said, "We had multiple students contract COVID, one of which ended up in the hospital for a week. This has been incredibly stressful for everyone in our school. Early on, students with physical disabilities were the group most impacted, because their ability to participate online was limited in most circumstances. Then the Indigenous student population was severely impacted. Students coming from families who are living below the poverty line also experienced major struggles as parents lost jobs… Finally, {for} students with existing mental health conditions, {COVID} only amplified their struggles."

Fortunately, online classes only lasted only a few weeks and a socially-distanced hybrid model filled in till the end of the school year in June 2020.

Teachers Identifying Effective Practices

Teachers were able to evaluate their own performance and compare their experiences with other educators to see what could be improved during the summer break. When the new school year began in socially-distanced schools, Gareth reflected on the differences with refugee students. "I think the toughest part at the beginning {April 2020} was maintaining relationships with students (online), while later with new students in September 2020, it was building new relationships, being able to assess their needs and provide effective support in their learning. What worked well? Definitely reaching out to them one-on-one, having individual times when we could talk and work on activities together. Also providing group games and learning activities that didn't need a lot of language decoding went a long way to helping refugee students feel connected. We played games like Pictionary and 20 questions or What's in the Bag? My {refugee} students felt like they could participate and not have to worry about typing or speaking and making mistakes.

Shirley, a secondary school Art teacher, said "Both distance and blended was hard for refugees. Art requires hands-on and a one-on-one approach. Making art from home is a struggle. What was good was when later we were allowed more face-to-face days. We could have conversations, and I could give lots of examples and do art demonstrations. In terms of building relationships, nothing worked particularly well. It's a class that requires being there".

The Main Benefits of Art for Refugee Students

In observing their students making art, teachers described what they had noticed. Gareth said, "Art is a language that they can often communicate with when they don't know how to say how they feel or how to express themselves. Many of my refugee students feel successful when they have the opportunity to make something that is meaningful to them".

Shirley stated that, "Some engage thoroughly, others do not".

Laura believed that, "If the initial participation is from a place of meaning or knowledge or purpose, curiosity takes over and tension around language and classroom culture eases. There is an aspect of enjoyment and playfulness that naturally accepts new language as form of communicating that seems more like an embodied interplay."

Conflicts in the Field

While none of these teachers know one another and are not teaching at the same schools, many of their responses resonate with theorists' concerns discussed above. The biggest sticking point seems to emerge around the idea of probing into refugees' prior lives and soliciting stories from their pre-migration or migration stages, depending on the educator's prior training.

When asked, "Have you noticed them create art related to their homes, migration experiences, or express personal feelings?", Gareth stated, "Sometimes. If they feel like they are ready to show me their experiences. We usually have some trust built up first.

Shirley said, "I create projects that are personal/yes".

Laura added, "For younger students, visual arts begin with pleasant images from memory or from the current environment. If given contexts that make sense to them, like introduction of a storyline, there are openings for sharing past events, family, and emotions. Older students could segue to more emotive subjects through interests like hit songs, music from their country, images in videos or movies, or finding correlations with familiar published writing or lyrics in their language with English language expressions".

As a follow up question, each teacher was asked, "Every child is different, but do your refugee students sometimes open up and talk about the art they make, explaining what it is about or assigning meaning to it?

Gareth replied, "Rarely. I think some things are very personal to them, and maybe they aren't sure what they are even feeling themselves."

Shirley said, "It is required in my program".

And Laura explained, "Yes. If there is a sibling, a friend from the same culture, or a staff member from the same culture or language, verbal explaining begins sooner than when they learn the vocabulary on their own and then are ready to share with a trusted adult".

This raised more questions about how well refugee students understood what was going on around them, such as why they were required to wash their hands, not touch things that were not theirs, and maintain a safe distance, even on the playground. Even if they don't speak much English, refugee students could sense danger or a stressful situation. What was it about making art that was appealing?

Gareth described, "I feel it helps them feel connected to others and helps them build understanding of the world around them. Many of my refugee students will draw the things that they are learning the words for. It seems to begin there and then blossom. Sometimes students are also resistant though. They get frustrated or avoid the activity because they don't want to look like they don't know what they want to say, or don't feel comfortable opening up yet".

Shirley also sees the practical side of the class. "It is an art room. Many are placed here due to learning issues, but many repeat the class because it is a place where they have success".

Laura said, "Initially, I offer individual time with the most familiar art forms, so I start with music and visual arts including photography and video. Then, the students choose and I encourage trying new interpretations through other complementary art forms like drawing flowers for a group who are creating with found items. At first, if this is their interest or usual way of expression, there is a comfort level. If this is an unusual venue, I would try another arts experience, for example, switching drawing or painting with sculpture, video, collage… As soon as possible, I offer shared experiences, either students working together or sharing results for further collaboration which they enjoy".

I followed up with Laura, and asked if she felt these art activities were therapeutic and if there is a clear benefit of the arts for refugees. She responded, "Yes! All arts are therapeutic for everyone and I am careful to be inclusive with students who have different vulnerabilities and learning styles and model acceptance so that everyone experiences and expresses in their own ways but collaborating and taking new risks together are fun and support language goals.

Art Pedagogies

The last question was what advice these three teachers might have for preservice teachers.

Gareth shared, "I would say that art is probably the first area where a refugee student will be able to feel successful and be able to express themselves in a way that is non-threatening. They can't say the wrong words or mispronounce something. And with our understanding that children often work through their feelings through the things they draw, it is a very valuable activity to help refugee students feel as though they are safe and that they belong in the class.

Shirley summed it up. "{Art} is very beneficial and a critical means of expression."

Laura offered her view. "First, we all learn a lot about ourselves as we express in 'artful' and sometimes 'riskful' venues. If the environment is trusting and accepting, collaborative arts interpretations and re-interpretations create openings for developing literacy, language, empathy, and belonging, but the whole school must work together so leadership has to be strong, clear, and committed. If teachers and staff work towards any and all opportunities to integrate lesson planning and arts related projects with strong communication, staff will collaborate to include all students through passages of expression, learning, and belonging in ways that are safe but progressively challenging. Along the way, we learn a great deal about ourselves as educators and we learn how best to support students from traumatic pasts with ongoing emotional and mental health concerns."

All 16 teachers in a multiple-choice question identified key objectives for September 2021: "Building a strong sense of belonging, creating a safe classroom and encouraging relationships". Looking ahead, participants mostly believe that trust must be earned, and it also takes time to develop these key objectives, but once they are in place, they will create the conditions for refugees to open up to making the kind of art that has the potential to release emotions in an unforced, natural and healthy way.

Discussion

Refugee children and youth arrive in Canada bearing multiple burdens on their young shoulders, with school being their best chance of finding new identities and belonging that will lead them on to a more promising path into life. No one could have predicted that once in Canada, COVID-19 would turn their world upside down again, with the risk of worsening their mental health. The danger for refugee students who do not receive treatment is the increased chance of living with trauma throughout their lives.

Mertins (2003) has described transformation as a framework for capturing the struggles of marginalized people who desperately need a boost. Actively using knowledge from this study's findings to improve society, might improve individuals' mental health, especially in terms of resilience and hope for the future. Most school programs or refugee student interventions do not go far enough, are short term, or they only focus on one part of a refugee's life. In this study, several educators reported that once refugees expressed their needs, in this case, food or laptops, the response was quick; it was a clear example of schools committed to holistic care. Also, astute teachers recognized that their refugee students could be included in activities, like games that did not require a high level of English. Further, spending one-to-one time was effective in maintaining relationships, while simultaneously making progress in language acquisition, critical thinking, trust, feeling safe, and belonging. Despite being disadvantaged in many ways, refugees were exposed to social justice efforts aimed at balancing inequities and allowing them to reposition themselves as learners and build on their strengths.

Mertens's (2009) disability theory confronts the meaning of inclusion and difference in schools. When considering refugees' exposure to trauma in extreme environments, we now know many can heal, given the proper interventions. As a comparison to the possibility of contracting Covid-19 and its long-term effects, students may notice feelings of increased anxiety and depression, but these may be stronger in those who have pre-existing psychological conditions (Malboeuf-Hurtubise et al., 2021). In the long run, these mental health issues may impede academic achievement and school perseverance in some refugee students, and educators should be aware of the dangers of a deficit mindset.

Above all else, teachers in this study have clearly identified that art is a universal language (Eisner, 2002), especially for those who are preliterate, mostly due to art permitting them to communicate "pre-verbally" through metaphor and symbols (Gadamer, 2003) that nudge traumatic memories to the surface where they can be revisited slowly and gently in a therapeutic way that may lead to reduced disability, healing and even transformation.

Questions around ethics, however, remain unresolved. While teachers are not therapists, there is a dearth of qualified expressive arts therapists in British Columbian schools. Not surprisingly, a major conflict exists within the field between the possible harm of untrained teachers encouraging student engagement with art and sharing their artwork ("responsibility to the profession"), as compared to the harm of withholding development through art, both academically and emotionally ("responsibility to the clients''), which seems over-blown to many (Maat & Espinola, 2016). When educators are teaching art, they are following their usual art practices, exploring art forms, and allowing students to experience art making. The findings in this project reveal that teachers themselves are keenly aware of their relationships with their refugee students, who can either choose to embrace emotional content or avoid all personal material. Some art ethicists have stated that as long as teachers do not attempt to interpret artwork, are multiculturally-sensitive, and understand which paints or materials are toxic (Maat & Espinola, 2016), there is no real harm that may occur, or at least no more than could occur with non-refugee students.

This study fills a gap in the literature by examining the significance of art, both in processing trauma and continuing to advance language skills, overall literacy, creative and critical thinking, beginning communication with peers, and strengthening relationships, among many other benefits. No matter how long COVID-19 remains with us, understanding the enduring value of art, especially in its potential for transformation, is indispensable for creating inclusive, bright futures for our vulnerable students.

Conclusion

The limitations of this study stem from some participants not using art intentionally, being unfamiliar or unaware of what the expressive arts program does, or showing weak interest in art in general, as well as those not having refugee students in their classrooms during COVID-19. Additionally, most teachers indicated they were bordering on burnout at the end of the 2021 school year, which may have influenced their responses. However, I feel very privileged to have recruited three extraordinary and experienced teachers who not only implement the arts but are knowledgeable and think deeply about the processes behind it.

Recommendations that follow from this study involve school districts initiating professional development programs in art pedagogies aimed at all students, by first requiring training in trauma-informed school-wide strategies. To achieve this, leadership, access to resources and services, collaboration with families, academic instruction, and non-academic strategies are essential (Cole et al., 2013). In this way, school policy would be able to negotiate the ethical requirements necessary for teachers, administrators, and staff to understand refugees' particular challenges and to learn how to avoid re-traumatization. This might mitigate therapists' ethical concerns while inserting boundaries of practice and allow teachers to access the knowledge and skills required to enable the therapeutic benefits of engaging in art. Of course, this would necessitate research into what that professional development would entail.

In the end, the results of this study strongly indicate that the therapeutic value of the arts support refugee students in improving their mental health as well as academic learning. Clearly, art has significant, multiple roles to play for refugee students in these uncertain times.

References

Adnams Jones, S. (2018). *Art-making with refugees and survivors: Creative and transformative responses to trauma after natural disasters, war and other crises*. Jessica Kingsley Publishers.

Anderson, A. (2015). Understanding how and why arts integration engages learners. In A. Anderson (Ed.), *Arts integration and special education: An inclusive theory for action for student engagement*. Routledge.

Barber, S. (2021). Achieving holistic care for refugees: The experiences of educators and other stakeholders in Surrey and greater Vancouver. *British Educational Research Journal, 47*(4), 959–983. https://doi.org/10.1002/berj.3730

Barber, S., & Ramsay. (2020, September). Literally speechless? Refugees to Canada overcome preliteracy and learn to communicate through a literacy of the heart. *English 4–11*. Retrieved from https://englishassociation.ac.uk/wp-content/uploads/2019/07/Barber-and-Ramsay-Sept-2020-1.pdf

Beauregard, C., Papazian-Zohrabian, G., & Rousseau, C. (2017). Making sense of collective identity and trauma through drawing: The case study of a Palestinian refugee student. *Intercultural Education, 28*(2), 113–130. https://doi.org/10.1080/14675986.2017.1294851

Berry, J. W. (2005). Acculturation: Living successfully in two cultures. *International Journal of Intercultural Relations, 29*, 697–712. https://doi.org/10.1016/j.ijintrel.2005.07.013

Berry, K. A., & Loughlin, S. M. (2015). Cognitive and affective engagement, arts integration and students with disabilities. In A. Anderson (Ed.), *Arts integration and special education: An inclusive theory for action for student engagement* (pp. 46–58). Routledge.

Block, K., Cross, S., Riggs, E., & Gibbs, L. (2014). Supporting schools to create an inclusive environment for refugee students. *International Journal of Inclusive Education, 18*(2), 1337–1355. https://doi.org/10.1080/13603116.2014.899636

Cole, S. F., Eisner, A., Gregory, M., & Ristuccia, J. (2013). *Helping traumatized children learn: Creating and advocating for trauma-sensitive schools*. Massachusetts Advocates for Children. Retrieved from https://traumasensitiveschools.org/wp-content/uploads/2013/11/HTCL-Vol-2-Creating-and-Advocating-for-TSS.pdf

Creswell, J. W., & Poth, C. N. (2018). *Qualitative inquiry & research design: Choosing among five approaches* (4th ed.). Sage.

Custodio, B. K., & O'Loughlin, J. B. (2017). Unique issues of refugee children. In B. K. Custodio & J. B. O'Loughlin (Eds.), *Students with interrupted formal education: Bridging where they are and what they need* (pp. 41–68). Corwin. https://doi.org/10.4135/9781506359694.n3

Dieterich-Hartwell, R., & Koch, S. C. (2017). Creative therapies as temporary home for refugees: Insights from literature and practice. *Behavioral Sciences, 7*(69), 1–11. https://doi.org/10.3390/bs7040069

Eisner, E. (2002). *The arts and the creation of mind*. Yale University Press.

Field, M. (2016). Empowering students in the trauma-informed classroom through expressive arts therapy. *In Education, 22*(2), 55–71.

Frenette, M., Frank, K., & Deng, Z. (2020, April 20). *School closures and the online preparedness of children during the COVID-19 pandemic*. Catalogue no. 11–626-X no.103. Statistics Canada. Retrieved from https://www150.statcan.gc.ca/n1/pub/45-28-0001/2020001/article/00001-eng.htm

Gadamer, H. G. (2003). *Truth and method* (2nd ed.), (J. Weinsheimer, & D. G. Marshall, Trans.). The Continuum International Publishing Group.

Gilroy, A. (2006). *Art therapy research and evidence-based practice*. Sage.

Harvey, S. (1989). Creating arts therapies in the classroom: A study of cognitive, emotional, and motivational changes. *American Journal of Dance Therapy, 11*(2), 85–99.

Herman, J. L. (1997). *Trauma and recovery: The aftermath of violence—From domestic abuse to political terror*. Basic Books.

Jacobson, M. R. (2021). An exploratory analysis of the necessity and utility of trauma-informed practices in education. *Preventing School Failure: An Alternative Education for Children and Youth, 65*(2), 124–134.

Kalmanowitz, D., & Potash, J. S. (2010). Ethical considerations in the global teaching and promotion of art therapy to non-art therapists. *Arts in Psychotherapy, 37*(1), 20–26.

Kia-Keating, M., & Ellis, B. H. (2007). Belonging and connection to schools in resettlement: Young refugees, school belonging and psychosocial adjustment. *Clinical Child Psychology and Psychiatry, 12*(1), 29–43. https://doi.org/10.1177/1359104507071052

Levi, T. K. (2019). Preparing pre-service teachers to support children with refugee experiences. *Alberta Journal of Educational Research, 65*(4), 285–304.

Maat, M. B., & Espinola, M. (2016). Ethics in art therapy. In D. E. Gussak & M. L. Rosal (Eds.), *The Wiley handbook of art therapy* (pp. 814–821). Wiley.

Malboeuf-Hurtubise, C., Leger-Goodes, T., Mageau, G. E., Taylor, G., Herba, C. M., Chadi, N., & Lefrançois, D. (2021). Online art therapy in elementary schools during COVID-19: Results from a randomized cluster pilot and feasibility study and impact on mental health. *Child and Adolescent Psychiatry of Mental Health, 15*(15), 1–11. https://doi.org/10.1186/s13034-021-00367-5

Malchiodi, C. (2015). *Creative interventions with traumatized children* (2nd ed.). Guilford Press.

Mertens, D. M. (2003). Mixed methods and the politics of human research: The transformative-emancipatory perspective. In A. Tahakkori & C. Teddlie (Eds.), *Handbook of mixed methods in social & behavioural research* (pp. 135–164). Sage.

Mertens, D. M. (2009). *Transformative research and evaluation*. Guildford Press.

Provencal, A., & Gabora, L. (2007). A compelling overview of art therapy techniques and outcomes. *Psychology of Aesthetics, Creativity and the Arts, 1*(4), 255–256.

Saldana, J. (2009). *The coding manual for qualitative researchers*. Sage Publications Ltd.

Substance Abuse and Mental Health Services Administration (SAMHSA). (2014). *SAMHSA's concept of trauma and guidance for a trauma-informed approach.* HHS Publication No. (SMA) 14-4884. SAMHSA.

Sousa, D. A. (2017). *How the arts develop the young brain.* AASA. Retrieved from http://www.aasa.org/SchoolAdministratorArticle.aspx?id=7378

St. Thomas, B., & Johnson, P. (2007). *Empowering children through art and expression.* Jessica Kinsley.

The National Child Traumatic Stress Network (NCTSN). (2012). *ARC: Attachment, self-regulation, and competency: A comprehensive framework for intervention with complexly traumatized youth.* Retrieved from https://www.nctsn.org/resources/arc-attachment-self-regulation-and-competency-framework-intervention-complexly-traumatized

United Nations High Commission on Refugees (UNHCR). (2021, November 10). *Refugee data finder.* Retrieved from https://www.unhcr.org/refugee-statistics/

Van der Kolk, B. A. (2014). *The body keeps the score: Brain, mind, and body in the healing of trauma.* Penguin.

Van Lith, T. (2016). Art therapy in mental health: A systematic review of approaches and practices. *The Arts in Psychotherapy, 47,* 9–22. https://doi.org/10.1016/j.aip.2015.09.003

Susan Barber is a Senior Lecturer in Education at Simon Fraser University, and a counseling psychologist in Vancouver, British Columbia, Canada. Her research interests include the intersection of arts education, creative writing and learning through stories, counseling psychology and refugee education.

Chapter 11
Supporting Students with Disabilities in Transition: Collaboration Between School Counselors and Special Educators

Sara L. McDaniel, Zachary Pietrantoni, and Szu-Yu Chen

Abstract School-based practitioners are prepared to support students' academic, behavioral, emotional, and social needs, but they have historically done so through independent, rather than collaborative, efforts. In the midst of the worldwide COVID-19 pandemic, collaboration of school counselors and special educators could augment and enrich the development, implementation, and evaluation of instructional and support services. This review explores the responsibilities of school counselors and special educators within Multi-Tiered Systems of Support (MTSS), and proposes a collaboration framework in which MTSS might be utilized to support the transitions of students with disabilities, including transitions related to the impact that COVID-19 has had on schools (i.e. service delivery models, changes in socialization patterns). Examples of collaboration among school counselors and special educators, along with discussion of the implications that this collaboration might have on transitions of students with disabilities moving forward, are included.

Keywords Collaboration in schools · School counselors · Special education teachers · Special education · Transitions · COVID-19 in schools · Multi-Tiered Systems of Support · MTSS · Mental health

S. L. McDaniel (✉)
California State University, East Bay, Hayward, CA, USA
e-mail: sara.mcdaniel@csueastbay.edu

Z. Pietrantoni
Florida International University, Miami, Florida, USA
e-mail: zpietran@fiu.edu

S.-Y. Chen
Palo Alto University, Palo Alto, CA, USA
e-mail: dchen@paloaltou.edu

© The Author(s), under exclusive license to Springer Nature Switzerland AG 2022
L. Meda, J. Chitiyo (eds.), *Inclusive Pedagogical Practices Amidst a Global Pandemic*, Inclusive Learning and Educational Equity 7,
https://doi.org/10.1007/978-3-031-10642-2_11

Introduction

The COVID-19 global pandemic has caused considerable challenges for students and their families around the world. Transitioning from in-person instruction to distance learning was one of the many challenges that students and their families experienced when many states across the United States of America (U.S.A.) went into lockdown in March of 2020. Access to technology, stable internet connectivity, and adequate training in distance learning and support services were a few of the factors impacting student learning during the 2020–2021 school year. Frederick et al. (2020) suggested that these challenges were amplified for students with disabilities as many schools lacked resources and consistency in providing appropriate accommodations and support during distance learning.

The National Center for Education Statistics (NCES, 2021) reports that 7.3 million students received special education services under Individuals with Disabilities Education Improvement Act (IDEA) in the 2019–2020 school year. This equates to around 14% of the total population of students served in public schools in the U.S.A (NCES, 2021). Of the 7.3 million students receiving special education services, one third (33%) of those students were categorized as having specific learning disabilities (NCES, 2021). The transition to distance learning profoundly impacted students' access to services and the delivery of appropriate academic and social-emotional supports and accommodations to ensure their success.

Supporting students with disabilities is a formal responsibility for many school-based personnel. Special education teachers and school counselors are prepared to meet the academic needs (IDEA XE "Individuals with Disabilities Education Act (IDEA)", 2004) and the social-emotional needs of students with disabilities (American School Counselor Association; ASCA, 2019) respectively. Creating a collaborative working relationship between special education teachers and school counselors is essential as students transition back to face-to-face instruction in the 2021–2022 school year. Collaboration in schools is a process by which stakeholders (e.g., school-based practitioners, including special education teachers and school counselors) from various backgrounds and experiences exchange ideas, strategies, and solutions to achieve a common goal (Griffiths et al., 2021). Griffiths et al. (2021) noted that "…the complexity of school systems makes it particularly difficult for school professions to solve problems independently" (p. 60).

School counselors and special education teachers work within robust Multi-Tiered Systems of Support (MTSS) to meet the needs of diverse learners served in comprehensive schools (March & Mathur, 2020; Sink & Ockerman, 2016). Yet, they have historically done so through independent rather than collaborative efforts despite the natural intersection of responsibilities that exists in their roles (Frye-Myers, 2005; Hall, 2015; Johnson et al., 2020). This can be problematic as both practitioners offer invaluable knowledge and skills that could directly benefit students with disabilities. Moreover, the collaboration of school counselors and special education teachers could augment and enrich the development, implementation, and evaluation of instructional and support services.

Collaboration

Collaboration in schools is a process by which stakeholders (e.g., school-based practitioners, including special education teachers and school counselors) from various backgrounds and experiences exchange ideas, strategies, and solutions to achieve a common goal (Griffiths et al., 2021). Griffiths et al. (2021) noted that "…the complexity of school systems makes it particularly difficult for school professions to solve problems independently" (p. 60). School counselors and special education teachers work within robust MTSS to meet the needs of diverse learners served in comprehensive schools (March & Mathur, 2020; Sink & Ockerman, 2016). Yet, they have historically done so through independent rather than collaborative efforts despite the natural intersection of responsibilities that exists in their roles (Frye-Myers, 2005; Hall, 2015; Johnson et al., 2020). This can be problematic as both practitioners offer invaluable knowledge and skills that could directly benefit students with disabilities. Moreover, the collaboration of school counselors and special education teachers could augment and enrich the development, implementation, and evaluation of instructional and support services.

Herein, the purpose of this chapter is to explore how school counselors and special education teachers in the U.S.A. might collaboratively utilize MTSS to support students with disabilities in their transition back to in-person instruction.

Multi-Tiered System of Support (MTSS)

MTSS is implemented in many school settings throughout the U.S.A. to systematically support students with academic and behavioral struggles (Wexler, 2018). MTSS integrates data-driven decision-making into tiered systems of support (Sink & Ockerman, 2016). These systems of support include Response to Intervention (RTI) (National Center on Response to Intervention XE "Response to Intervention (RTI)" , 2010) and Positive Behavioral Interventions and Supports (PBIS) (Horner et al., 2010). Sink and Ockerman (2016) noted that RTI uses tiered instruction and intervention support to benefit the academic development of all students. PBIS embraces social-emotional interventions to enrich the academic, emotional, and behavioral development of all students (Chitiyo & May, 2018). Combining these systems of support allows multiple stakeholders to identify at-promise students and provide appropriate instruction and interventions that enhance their academic, college and career, and social-emotional development (ASCA, 2018).

Tiered Levels of Intervention

MTSS is a three-tiered framework that targets a variety of services and supports based on the intensity of concerns. Generally, Tier 1 is the primary tier, which contains the entire group of students in the general education classroom. In Tier 1, teachers provide universal instruction and schools monitor students' progress. Students who need additional support may be moved to Tier 2 supports. Students in Tier 2 still attend classes with the rest of the students. However, they receive more targeted support through small group interventions. Finally, students who do not make adequate progress in Tiers 1 or 2 may move to Tier 3. Students in Tier 3 may still spend time in the general education classroom. However, they may spend more time receiving intensive individualized support through small group work or individual lessons. It is noteworthy to mention that Tier 3 is not synonymous with special education. Students without disabilities can receive Tier 3 interventions, while not all students with disabilities require Tier 3 level support.

Interestingly, there is no uniform approach to MTSS globally, or even within the U.S.A. Guided by data-driven decision-making and student-centered approaches, it is imperative for MTSS teams to consider student development, the school's learning environment, and the associated needs related to students' disabilities when making educational and clinical recommendations and decisions. Collaboration among multiple stakeholders, such as caregivers, community providers, and professionals (e.g., teachers, school counselors, and psychologists) can assist in developing well-integrated systems of instruction and interventions and further provide a better opportunity for students with disabilities to succeed in home and school settings (ASCA, 2019; Sink, 2016; Wexler, 2018).

School counselors, who receive specialized training in addressing academic achievement, career readiness, and social-emotional learning, play a particularly pivotal role in the MTSS team. Collaborative efforts between school counselors and special education teachers are critical for MTSS teams to effectively identify and assess the needs of students with disabilities and then connect and implement comprehensive resources and interventions to support those needs (Goodman-Scott & Carlisle, 2015).

MTSS for School Counselors

The application of MTSS aligns with the school counselor's role in supporting student development and success in the academic, college/career, and social/emotional domains. Given that MTSS is primarily focused on academic achievement and behavior, schools are recommended to add the college/career readiness domain to their MTSS program and create a comprehensive school wide Multi-Tiered, Multi-Domain System of Supports (MTMDSS; Hatch, 2018). Within the MTMDSS framework, school counselors use a data-driven approach to analyze the aforementioned domains and utilize their coordination, collaboration, and advocacy skills to identify at-promise students who could benefit from additional support.

School Counselor Tier 1 Supports

Following the three-tiered framework, school counselors provide Tier 1 support for all students, including students with disabilities through a universal school counseling curriculum to address standards-aligned with academic, college/career, and social-emotional development. Tier 1 services are intended to be developmental, preventative, and proactive in design and comprehensive in scope. School counselors facilitate direct classroom instruction that reflects ASCA's standards and competency. Moreover, school counselors utilize individual student planning to prepare students for college/career readiness. School counselors also use school wide programs and activities, such as national awareness weeks and parent education workshops, to support the school counseling core curriculum (Hatch, 2018).

School Counselor Tier 2 Supports

Tier 2 is designed to focus on students who are facing barriers in learning and academic achievement or who need additional support. School counselors first use data-based decision making to identify indicators which put students at-risk (e.g., attendance rates, behavioral referrals, course failure, etc.) of not meeting academic achievement expectations. After identifying at-promise students, school counselors provide targeted data-driven interventions through short-term individual or small group counseling and referrals to on- and off-campus resources and interventions. School counselors actively monitor students' progress and collaborate with the MTSS team in this stage (Hatch, 2018).

School Counselor Tier 3 Supports

Tier 3 services are for students experiencing emergency and crisis response events (e.g., parental divorce, grief/loss, etc.) or needs that were left unresolved after Tier 2 supports were put in place. School counselors conduct risk assessments and provide individualized student interventions, such as individual crisis counseling and short-term solution-focused counseling. Ongoing collaboration among MTSS team members and caregivers are critical until the crisis is resolved. If unresolved, school counselors identify and make referrals to appropriate long-term, responsive services, such as community-based counseling (Hatch, 2018).

MTSS for Special Educators

Although MTSS is not a special education initiative, it aims to support all students, including students with disabilities. Statistics show that 95% of students with disabilities spend part of their time in general education while 65% receive the majority of their instruction in general education (Center on Multi-Tiered System of Support, n.d.). MTSS can also serve as screening for all students by monitoring student progress and responses to the delivery of tiered interventions as a basis for determining comprehensive evaluation for special education eligibility (Turse & Albrecht, 2015).

When individualized education programs (IEPs) are well implemented within a school wide MTSS, students with disabilities can receive Tier 3 intensive intervention through evidence-based individualization while ensuring access to aligned Tier 1 and Tier 2 interventions in other domains of identified needs (Center on Multi-Tiered System of Support, n.d.). As a result, special education teachers should play an integral role in the design and delivery of the MTSS. Additionally, given their aim to provide students with high quality and inclusive learning, special educators should extend responsibility and opportunity to co-plan and co-design instruction with general education teachers (Rodriguez & Novak, n.d.).

Often, students with disabilities receive specially designed instruction in special education classrooms when standard instruction in general classrooms does not meet their unique learning needs. However, this approach has been criticized because students lose instructional time in classrooms (Leach & Helf, 2016). Therefore, a co-teaching approach has also been recommended. In this model, general and special education teachers work together to deliver instruction so that students with disabilities can optimize their learning through receiving differentiated instruction within a general education environment (Leach & Helf, 2016). Although general education teachers specialize in the subject matter, special education teachers have expertise in delivering specially designed, evidence-based instruction to enhance students' learning. Special education teachers can therefore assist in incorporating special education services at each tier so that general and special education objectives, instruction, and support are aligned and embedded within MTSS.

It is evident that special education teachers are an integral part of creating and delivering an inclusive learning environment. Moreover, school counselors can utilize their knowledge and skills in assessing and advocating for students' social-emotional needs and college/career readiness to contribute to an equitable and inclusive learning environment. Thus, to implement a comprehensive MTSS, school counselors and special education teachers can collaborate to bridge the gap between general and special education instruction. Working collaboratively will create joint opportunities for all stakeholders to examine instructional design and strategies to improve equitable and inclusive learning environments for students with disabilities.

Transitions for Students with Disabilities

Students experience countless transitions throughout their school careers. These experiences, which range from small daily transitions between activities to monumental transitions between schools or life stages, can be tough for any student but often pose an even greater challenge for students with disabilities (Aldosirya et al., 2021). Students with disabilities may require a longer adjustment period when learning new school routines when compared to their peers with no disabilities (Hebron, 2017; Knesting et al., 2008). Challenges associated with students' disabilities can impact their readiness to access and engage in new educational settings, requiring school teams to provide additional support to help these students make smooth transitions and adapt to their new activity or environment (Knesting et al., 2008). Neal et al. (2016) reported that transitions can lead to negative outcomes for students with disabilities, including a decline in academic performance, higher levels of depression and/or anxiety, behavioral challenges, and lower self-esteem.

Transitions During the COVID-19 Pandemic

The COVID-19 pandemic has caused many obstacles for students and special education teachers, including interruptions to instruction, administering initial and re-evaluations of students with disabilities under the confines of the timelines required by IDEA (2004), and appropriately evaluating students' eligibility for special education services (National Center for Learning Disabilities, 2020). The wide-sweeping school closures designed to prevent community transmission of the virus, schools around the global were forced to adjust their instruction and service delivery to a distance learning format. The disruption of routines, lack of consistency, and massive changes in environment left many students with disabilities in a state of limbo, unable to translate the specialized instructional, behavioral, and social support that they received during in-person school to the home learning environment.

It is likely that the physical, academic, social, and emotional impact of COVID-19 on students with disabilities will continue to be discovered for years to come, but for now, the available data seem to indicate that these students faced immense challenges due to COVID-19. Consequently, in the U.S.A., concerns were quickly raised related to meeting the instructional support needs of students with disabilities served under IDEA (2004) during school closures. In response, the U.S.A. Department of Education released guidance for school districts to adapt IEP processes and services for a time of virtual learning (U.S. Department of Education, 2020). Despite this guidance, it is clear that the ongoing COVID-19 pandemic has left students with disabilities in a complicated and challenging situation.

It has been suggested that COVID-19 associated mental health risks will disproportionately affect children and adolescents who are already disadvantaged and marginalized (Fegert et al., 2020). This includes students with disabilities, who are already more likely to experience mental health challenges than their peers with no disabilities. Hughes et al. (2013) reported that students with disabilities are more likely to experience anxiety, be victims of bullying, and experience poor academic and socio-emotional outcomes after a period of transition. There is emerging evidence that school closures and the move to online instruction related to the COVID-19 pandemic could result in further increasing trauma and anxiety for students with disabilities (Fegert et al., 2020).

Additionally, the transition back to in-person instruction may be more challenging for students with disabilities as research predicts a significant learning loss for these students due to the extended period of distance learning with limited instructional and intervention supports (Kuhfeld & Tarasawa, 2020; Pier et al., 2021). A meta-analysis conducted by Gilmour et al. (2018) found that the reading academic performance of students with disabilities on average is three grade levels below students without disabilities. The researcher's results reflect the reading performance of students with disabilities prior to the pandemic (Gilmour et al., 2018). However, Kuhfeld and Tarasawa (2020) suggested that loss of learning will be a challenge for all students transitioning back from distance learning. Therefore, due to a lack of consistency and cohesion in accommodations and supports during distance learning (Frederick et al., 2020) and the estimated loss of learning for all students during distance learning (Kuhfeld & Tarasawa, 2020), students with disabilities might experience a greater loss of learning gains due to the lack of appropriate accommodations during distance learning and subsequently might experience more challenges than for students with no disabilities.

These challenges could result in more assessment of risk, tiered systems of instruction and intervention, and increased support needs for students with disabilities upon returning to in-person instruction. Griffiths et al. (2021) noted that multidisciplinary collaboration is essential to ensuring that all students experience positive academic and social-emotional outcomes. Special education teachers and school counselors can help to support these students during the transition back to in-person instruction by working together within the MTSS framework to specifically address and assist with the challenges that transitions like this can pose for students with disabilities.

Following the MTSS framework, school counselors and special education teachers should continue to monitor students' academic performance as well as social-emotional and behavioral development and modify instructions or intensify interventions if the interventions are not meeting student learning objectives. MTSS teams may consider allocating additional resources and support for students with disabilities who need intensive academic, social-emotional, and mental health intervention at Tier 2 and 3 (National Center for Learning Disabilities, 2020). The MTSS collaboration between special education teachers and school counselors is even more critical in the time of transition between virtual learning and the return to in-person schooling for students with disabilities.

Special Educator Teachers Supporting Transitions

Most special education teachers work frequently to support student transitions, as this is a well-documented area of challenge for many students with disabilities (Bannerjee & Horn, 2012). Typically, an IEP is designed to support students with disabilities who struggle with transitions by documenting the services provided by their special education teacher, which typically align with MTSS supports. Intervention support for transitions depends largely on (a) the type of transition and (b) the specific transition-related challenges. Additionally, it is required by IDEA (2004) that students' IEPs, by the time they turn 16, include an Individualized Transition Plan (ITP) outlining specific goals and services to prepare them for adulthood and post-school life. Special education teachers play an intricate part in developing the ITP to address minor and major transitions that students with disabilities might experience; however, this process has not traditionally been an area of collaborative support for students. Generally, special education teachers support transitions specific to their classroom through classroom procedures, strategies, and interventions.

According to Bannerjee and Horn (2012), some categories of commonly used, research-based interventions for supporting daily in-school transitions include (a) environmental supports, (b) material adaptation to promote independence, (c) using child preferences, (d) adult supports, (e) peer supports, and (f) invisible supports. Additionally, Test et al. (2009) found that many secondary transition practices, including evidence-based practices, research-based practices, and promising practices are predictors of positive post-school outcomes for students with disabilities. This body of literature is useful in helping to forecast how the impacts of COVID-19 might be addressed by special education teachers in supporting students with disabilities who transition back to in-person instruction. Furthermore, collaboration with school counselors can help to ensure that students with disabilities receive the academic, college/career, and social-emotional support necessary to help them during this transition.

School Counselors Supporting Transitions

School counselors have not traditionally been tasked specifically with supporting the transitions of students with disabilities. However, their unique vantage point within the school environment and their extended training in meeting the academic, college/career, and socio-emotional readiness needs of all students allows them to understand the broad implications of being able to successfully transition between activities and amongst environments. These supports could fit within the suggestions made by Hatch (2018) related to the structured supports that school counselors can provide within a MTSS framework. Supporting students with disabilities as they transition back to in-person learning should be designed and implemented collaboratively between school counselors and special educators within the MTSS intervention structure. Table 11.1 provides examples of the responsibilities of both school counselors and special education teachers within the MTSS framework, with particular attention paid to the types of support they might provide related to students' transitions.

Table 11.1 Examples of MTSS transition supports for students with disabilities

MTSS Tier	School counselor	Special education teacher
1	School counselor curriculum on mental health prevention (e.g., anxiety, self-regulation, etc.)	Individualized check-in and assessment of student well-being
	School personnel training about mental health risk factors/warning signs (e.g., anxiety, distress, etc.)	Class-wide instruction (e.g., academic content, self-regulation, self-monitoring, and executive functioning skills)
	Parent education training on mental health (e.g., anxiety, distress, etc.)	Parent support and strategies for addressing transition-related challenges at home
2	Group counseling about academic performance and mental health needs (e.g., self-regulation, anxiety, etc.)	Supplemental support for at-promise students requiring additional academic and/or mental health support (e.g., small groups, additional interventions)
	Consultation with school personnel about progress monitoring for student outcomes	Individualized student progress monitoring
	Support group for parents of children with disabilities who experience transitional challenges (e.g., anxiety, loss of learning, etc.)	Individualized parent support about student progress at school and home
3	Crisis response for students with disabilities who experience immediate mental health concerns (e.g., risk assessment, self-harm assessment, etc.)	Programs for students requiring intensive, individualized interventions and support to make progress (IEP serves as the outline for implementation of services for students receiving special education services)
	Parent consultation on support strategies for monitoring risk factors for their child who experienced immediate mental health concerns	Collaborate with IEP team members (i.e., parents, general education teachers, other school-based practitioners) to implement the additional support
	School personnel consultation on support strategies child transition back into the classroom after experiencing immediate mental health concerns	Referring students experiencing mental health-related challenges to appropriate resource

Collaboration to Support Transitions

School counselors and special education teachers can work collaboratively to coordinate services that will directly benefit students with disabilities who experience transitional challenges to produce successful transitions (Aldosirya et al., 2021). Although special education teachers may regularly enlist the support of their general education colleagues in supporting students in transitions, there is limited research on the collaboration process between school counselors and special educators in supporting students with disabilities.

One transition area for collaboration between school counselors and special education teachers to collaborate to support students with disabilities is working together to improve the communication between schools and families (Rodriguez et al., 2017). Family engagement is linked to positive transition outcomes and student achievement (Test et al., 2009). Given the varied challenges that students with disabilities might experience during this time (e.g., academic, behavioral, socioemotional, etc.), it would be beneficial to have an interdisciplinary team working together on this collaboration. An effective strategy for communicating information relevant to major transitions is holding orientations and school visits (Carter et al., 2014). These orientations and visits allow students with disabilities to become acquainted (or, for some, reacquainted) with school environments and have been shown to reduce anxiety and fear and foster relationships at the new school (Aldosirya et al., 2021).

Another distinct area for collaboration between school counselors and special educators is coordinating small groups for students with disabilities to discuss their fears, expectations, and perceptions about their transition (Swank & Anthony, 2016). These groups could help students with disabilities gain support in acquiring independence, confidence, organizational skills, friendship skills, and study skills that can help these students adjust effectively to "new" school environments (Rodriguez et al., 2017). Konrad et al. (2008) suggested integrating all of these skills into the curriculum, which would be a natural place for school counselors and special educators to collaborate on and implement Tier 1 and Tier 2 interventions to support these transition-related competencies.

A third area for collaboration is for school counselors and special education teachers to help students with disabilities gain meaningful relationships at school and develop a sense of belonging (Aldosirya et al., 2021). Feeling disconnected from the school and a lack of involvement can negatively affect students' experiences when transitioning to a new setting; a critical consideration since, throughout the COVID-19 pandemic, many students have been disconnected from, and uninvolved with, their schools (Aldosirya et al., 2021). Special education teachers and school counselors should collaborate on ways to foster peer acceptance and engage in meaningful connections with peers to help students adjust to a new environment and increase their satisfaction. Peer-mediated strategies such as peer networks (Carter et al., 2014) are research-based strategies for improving social skills and peer relationships of students with disabilities, and could be collaboratively implemented as a Tier 2 intervention by special education teachers and school counselors (Aldosirya et al., 2021).

Overall, students with disabilities have much to gain from the collaboration between special education teachers and school counselors in supporting their transition back to in-person school environments, academically, socio-emotionally, and behaviorally. See Table 11.2 for additional examples of how school counselors and special education teachers might collaborate within the three tiers of the MTSS system to support students with disabilities.

Table 11.2 Collaboration between school counselors and special education teachers

MTSS Tier	Examples of collaboration between school counselors and special education teachers on MTSS
1	Collaborate on class wide mental health supports (e.g., special education teacher leading a focused lesson while school counselor conducts universal screening on students).
	Co-facilitate professional development session related to identification of students' mental-health needs (e.g., school counselors share mental health risk factors, special education teachers share needs of students with disabilities related to transitions and mental health).
	Co-create resources for school personnel and families, particularly related to mental health needs and what to expect and how to support in times of transition.
	Coordinate communication with families to bridge the gap between home and school for students with disabilities.
2	Identify and refer students who require additional support in various transition-related challenges.
	Schedule regular meetings for school counseling and special education teams to collaborate on problem solving, decision making, goal-setting, and treatment evaluation.
	Co-monitor student progress data.
	Co-create groups in which students can meet to address challenges related to their academic progress or mental health needs.
	Identify, disseminate, and connect families to community resources for children with disabilities who experience transitional challenges (e.g., anxiety, loss of learning, etc.). If none exist, consider partnering with community resources to create support groups for families at the school site.
3	Collaborate on inclusion of mental health-related interventions into IEPs of students with disabilities who require additional support.
	Co-design school-wide crisis support for students with disabilities in the event of a mental health crisis.
	Educate team members on the specifics of intervention support and why these are necessary.
	Co-facilitate individualized sessions with families of students receiving Tier 3 support.

Discussion

Although educators are facing an immense challenge placed upon them by COVID-19, the challenge that many students with disabilities experience related to transitions are not exclusively unique to the pandemic. Navigating schools and school systems requires a great number of transitions over the course of individual school days, years, and lifetimes. There are also additional situations in which students with disabilities might require support specifically related to transitioning back to a school environment. In these instances, the same strategies and recommendations for collaboratively supporting students with disabilities during the COVID-19 pandemic might also apply. These situations include, but are not limited to, school closures due to (a) other unforeseen circumstances such as natural disaster, staff shortages, labor union negotiations/strikes; (b) extended school absences for children with medical complexity; (c) mental health challenges resulting in inpatient treatment; and (d) the transition to or from homeschooling.

Recommendations

The strategies proposed in this chapter may be considered for other school-based transitions as well, in addition to collaboratively supporting students with disabilities in transitioning back to an in-person learning environment after being out of school for an extended period of time. Approaching MTSS in a collaborative manner might help schools to increase data-driven decision-making with a focus on addressing inequities that students with disabilities may experience during times of transition. School counselors and special education teachers might also collaborate with general education teachers to identify instructional accommodations and support services that promote an inclusive learning environment for all students. A comprehensive and collaborative MTSS structure will reduce barriers that impede development during times of transition for students with disabilities.

Students navigate many transitions throughout their school days, including between subjects, between self-contained to inclusive classroom settings, between physical classroom spaces, between teachers, and between academic and non-academic focused spaces (i.e. classroom to cafeteria). There are also additional transitions to consider, such as those between school and the home environment, between grade levels, between schools (i.e. elementary to middle school), moving schools for other purpose (i.e. family move, placement, disciplinary), and the transition to postsecondary life. The potential gains that could be made for students with disabilities if school counselors and special educators can effectively collaborate to create an MTSS structure to support students transitioning back to on-campus schooling, as well as this wide array of additional transitions that are always present for students, are massive.

Successful transitions are associated with increased self-esteem and confidence, continuity of curriculum, development of new friendships, reduced parental concern, renewed interest in school and school work, and more (Evangelou et al., 2008). These positive outcomes are goals that special educators and school counselors alike have for students with disabilities, and their collaboration around student transitions might lead to more than just reestablishing the status quo in schools in a post-pandemic academic landscape; it could change the way that transitions of all varieties are collaboratively supported in schools.

Conclusion

Challenges caused by the global COVID-19 pandemic have presented immense challenges for children and their families around the world. For many students with disabilities, these challenges have been multiplied, with interruptions to their special education services, limited access to assistive technology, and limited resources further impacting their education during periods of distance learning (Frederick et al., 2020). This chapter set out to explore how school counselors and special education teachers in the U.S.A. could collaborate within MTSS to co-design and co-deliver robust support systems for students with disabilities in their transition back to in-person instruction. Ultimately, this vision of a comprehensive and collaborative MTSS structure has the potential to reduce barriers and support student resilience during times of transition for students with disabilities—both pandemic-related and otherwise. It is the hope of the authors that school-based practitioners consider the positive impact that effective and intentional collaboration amongst personnel within MTSS might have on students with disabiltiies, and that this MTSS collaboration is made a priority in school planning for a post-pandemic world.

References

Aldosirya, N., Alharbi, A. A., & Alrusaiyes, R. (2021). Practices to prepare students with disabilities for the transition to new educational settings. *Children and Youth Services Review, 120*, 1–7.

American School Counselor Association. (2018). *The school counselor and multitiered system of supports*. American School Counselor Association. Retrieved from https://www.schoolcounselor.org/Standards-Positions/Position-Statements/ASCA-Position-Statements/The-School-Counselor-and-Multitiered-System-of-Sup

American School Counselor Association. (2019). *The ASCA National Model* (4th edition). Author.

Bannerjee, R., & Horn, E. (2012). Supporting classroom transitions between daily routines: Strategies and tips. *Young Exceptional Children, 16*(2), 3–14.

Carter, E. W., Brock, M. E., & Trainor, A. A. (2014). Transition assessment and planning for youth with severe intellectual and developmental disabilities. *The Journal of Special Education, 47*(4), 245–255.

Center on Multi-Tiered System of Support. (n.d.). *Special Education*. American Institutions for Research. Retrieved from https://mtss4success.org/special-topics/special-education

Chitiyo, J., & May, M. E. (2018). Factors predicting sustainability of the schoolwide positive behavior intervention support model. *Preventing School Failure: Alternative Education for Children and Youth, 62*(2), 94–104. https://doi.org/10.1080/1045988X.2017.1385446

Evangelou, M., Taggart, B., Sylva, K., Melhuish, E., Sammons, P., & Siraj-Blatchford, I. (2008). *What makes a successful transition from primary to secondary school?* Department for Children Schools and Families.

Fegert, J. M., Vitiello, B., Plener, P. L., & Clemens, V. (2020). Challenges and burden of the Coronavirus 2019 (COVID-19) pandemic for child and adolescent mental health: a narrative review to highlight clinical and research needs in the acute phase and the long return to normality. *Child and Adolescent Psychiatry and Mental Health, 14*(20), 1–11.

Frederick, J. K., Raabe, G. R., Rogers, V. R., & Pizzica, J. (2020). Advocacy, collaboration, and intervention: A model of distance special education support services amid COVID-19. *Behavior Analysis in Practice, 13*, 748–756. https://doi.org/10.1007/s40617-020-00476-1

Frye-Myers, H. N. (2005). How elementary school counselors meet the needs of students with disabilities. *Professional School Counseling, 8*(5), 442–450. https://www.jstor.org/stable/42732487

Gilmour, A. F., Fuchs, D., & Wehby, J. H. (2018). Are students with disabilities accessing the curriculum? A meta-analysis of the reading achievement gap between students with and without disabilities. *Exceptional Children, 85*(3), 329–346. https://doi.org/10.1177/0014402918795830

Goodman-Scott, E., & Carlisle, R. (2015). School counselors' roles in creating and implementing social stories to serve students with autism spectrum disorder. *Professional School Counseling, 18*, 158–168. https://doi.org/10.5330/2156-759X-18.1.158

Griffiths, A., Alsip, J., Hart, S. R., Round, R. L., & Brady, J. (2021). Together we can do so much: A systemic review and conceptual framework of collaboration in schools. *Canadian Journal of School Psychology, 36*(1), 59–85. https://doi.org/10.1177/0829573520915368

Hall, J. G. (2015). The school counselor and special education: Aligning training with practice. *The Professional Counselor, 5*(2), 217–224. https://doi.org/10.1524/jgh.5.2.217

Hatch, T. (2018). *Multi-tiered, multi-domain system of supports*. Retrieved from https://www.hatchingresults.com/blog/2017/3/multi-tiered-multi-domain-system-of-supports-by-trish-hatch-phd

Hebron, J. (2017). The transition from primary to secondary school for students with autism spectrum conditions. In *Supporting Social Inclusion for Students with Autism Spectrum Disorders* (pp. 102–117). Routledge.

Horner, R. H., Sugai, G., & Anderson, C. M. (2010). Examining the evidence base for school-wide positive behavior support. *Focus on Exceptional Children, 42*(8), 1–14.

Hughes, L. A., Banks, P., & Terras, M. M. (2013). Secondary school transition for children with special educational needs: A literature review. *Support for Learning, 28*(1), 24–34.

Individuals with Disabilities Education Improvement Act of 2004, Public Law 108-446. (2004). Retrieved from https://ies.ed.gov/ncser/pdf/pl108-446.pdf

Johnson, K. F., Belcher, T. W., Zimmerman, B., & Franklin, J. (2020). Interprofessional partnerships involving school counsellors for children with special needs: A broad based systemic review using the PRISMA framework. *Support for Learning, 35*(1), 43–67. https://doi.org/10.1111/1467-9604.12285

Knesting, K., Hokanson, C., & Waldron, N. (2008). Settling in: Facilitating the transition to an inclusive middle school for students with mild disabilities. *International Journal of Disability, Development and Education, 55*(3), 265–276.

Konrad, M., Walker, A. R., Fowler, C. H., Test, D. W., & Wood, W. M. (2008). A model for aligning self-determination and general curriculum standards. *Teaching Exceptional Children, 40*(3), 53–64.

Kuhfeld, M., & Tarasawa, B. (2020). *The COVID-19 slide: What summer learning loss can tell us about the potential impact of school closures on student academic achievement*. NWEA. Retrieved from https://files.eric.ed.gov/fulltext/ED609141.pdf

Leach, D., & Helf, S. (2016). Revisiting the regular education initiative: Multi-tiered systems of support can strengthen the connection between general and special education. *Journal of the American Academy of Special Education Professionals*, 116–124.

March, R. J., & Mathur, S. R. (2020). Mental health in schools: An overview of multi-tiered systems of support. *Intervention in School and Clinic, 56*(2), 67–73. https://doi.org/10.1177/1053451220914896

National Center for Education Statistics. (2021). *Preprimary, elementary, and secondary education*. National Center for Education Statistics. Retrieved from https://nces.ed.gov/programs/coe/indicator/cgg

National Center for Learning Disabilities. (2020, November). *Navigating special education evaluations for specific learning disabilities (SLD) amid the COVID-19 pandemic*. Retrieved from https://www.ncld.org/wp-content/uploads/2020/11/Navigating-Special-Education-Evaluations-for-Specific-Learning-Disabilities-SLD-Amid-the-COVID-19-Pandemic.pdf

National Center on Response to Intervention. (2010). *What is Response to Intervention (RTI)*. U.S. Department of Education, Office of Special Education Programs, National Center on Response to Intervention. Retrieved from https://files.eric.ed.gov/fulltext/ED526859.pdf

Neal, S., Rice, F., Ng-Knight, T., Riglin, L., & Frederickson, N. (2016). Exploring the longitudinal association between interventions to support the transition to secondary school and child anxiety. *Journal of Adolescence, 50*, 31–43.

Pier, L., Hough, H. J., Christian, M., Bookman, N., Wilkenfeld, B., & Miller, R. (2021 January, 25). *COVID-19 and the educational equity crisis: Evidence on learning loss from the CORE Data Collaborative [Commentary]*. Policy Analysis for California Education. Retrieved from https://edpolicyinca.org/newsroom/covid-19-and-educational-equity-crisis

Rodriguez, H., & Novak, K. (n.d.). *MTSS and Special Education*. Department of Elementary & Secondary Education. Retrieved from https://ocde.us/MTSS/Documents/MTSS%20Special%20Education%20Insert%20(1).pdf

Rodriguez, C. D., Cumming, T. M., & Strnadova, I. (2017). Current practices in schooling transitions of students with developmental disabilities. *International Journal of Educational Research, 83*, 1–19.

Sink, C. (2016). Incorporating a multi-tiered system of supports into school counselor preparation. *The Professional Counselor, 6*(3), 203–219. http://tpcjournal.nbcc.org/wp-content/uploads/2016/09/Pages203-219-Sink.pdf

Sink, C. A., & Ockerman, M. S. (2016). School counselors and multi-tiered system of supports: Cultivating systemic change and equitable outcomes. *The Professional Counselor, 6*(3).

Swank, J., & Anthony, C. (2016). Counseling with older children. In S. Smith-Adcock & C. Tucker (Eds.), *Counseling children and adolescents: Connecting theory, development, and diversity* (pp. 9–11). Sage.

Test, D. W., Mazzotti, V. L., Mustian, A. L., Fowler, C. H., Kortering, L., & Kohler, P. (2009). Evidence-based secondary transition predictors for improving postschool outcomes for students with disabilities. *Career Development for Exceptional Individuals, 32*, 160–181.

Turse, K. A., & Albrecht, S. F. (2015). The ABCs of RTI: An introduction to the building blocks of response to intervention. *Preventing School Failure, 59*(2), 83–89.

U.S. Department of Education. (2020, March 21). *Supplemental fact sheet addressing the risk of COVID-19 in preschool, elementary and secondary schools while serving children with disabilities*. Retrieved from https://www2.ed.gov/about/offices/list/ocr/frontpage/faq/rr/policyguidance/Supple%20Fact%20Sheet%203.21.20%20FINAL.pdf

Wexler, D. (2018). School-based multi-tiered systems of support (MTSS): An introduction to MTSS for neuropsychologists. *Applied Neuropsychology: Child, 7*(4), 1–11. https://doi.org/10.1080/21622965.2017.1331848

Dr. Sara L. McDaniel is an Assistant Professor of Special Education at California State University, East Bay who works to prepare highly qualified special educators. A former high school special education teacher, Dr. McDaniel has contributed to numerous projects in the area of secondary transition. Her other research interests include interventions to support TK-22 students with high-incidence disabilities in inclusive settings, autism spectrum disorder, college and career readiness, and effective collaboration amongst school-based practitioners.

Zachary Pietrantoni is an Assistant Professor in the school counseling program at Florida International University. He teaches and supervises school counseling trainees. Zachary is committed to ensuring equitable and inclusive educational practices in K-12 settings. He is active in publishing and presenting research related to school counselor training and development. He also serves on the editorial boards for the Journal of School Counseling, Preventing School Failure: Alternative Education for Children and Youth, and International Journal of Psychotherapy. Zachary began his career as an elementary school counselor, where he worked collaboratively to implement multi-tiered systems of support to ensure equitable and inclusive education for all students.

Dr. Szu-Yu Chen is an Associate Professor and Clinical Mental Health Counseling emphasis area coordinator in the Counseling Program at Palo Alto University, USA. She is a bilingual (English and Mandarin) licensed professional clinical counselor in California, national certified counselor (NCC), and registered play therapist (RPT). With a specialization in clinical mental health and play therapy, she has worked with diverse populations in a variety of settings, including private practice, community agency, psychiatric hospital, and elementary schools. Her research and presentations focus on play therapy, play-based teacher intervention, multicultural issues in counseling and clinical supervision, and immigrants' mental health issues. Her most recent work is the application of humanistic play therapy to children exposed to attachment trauma, teacher-child relationships, and children's social-emotional and behavioral problems.

Chapter 12
The Spirit of Volunteerism: Supporting Young Children of Medical Workers During the COVID-19 Pandemic in the United Arab Emirates

Lawrence Meda

Abstract Medical workers have risked their lives by being at the forefront of treating and caring for people infected by the Coronavirus (COVID-19) pandemic. The majority of medical workers left their families with limited educational support so that they could treat COVID-19 patients. This resulted in some workers asking volunteers to help their children by supporting them with online learning while they were assisting COVID-19 patients in hospitals. The purpose of this study was to examine the nature of learning support which was provided by a university professor who volunteered to assist medical workers' three young children. The study was conducted using a qualitative case study within an interpretive paradigm. Vygotsky's theory of social constructivism and the Community of Inquiry framework were used as analytical frameworks for this study. Data was collected through the instructor's reflections and analyzed using content analysis. A significant contribution that emerges from this study is demystifying misleading thoughts that children in early childhood development cannot learn meaningfully online. It is concluded that instilling the spirit of volunteerism in the nation is a good thing as it promotes human rights and provides a milestone of achievement towards the attainment of the fourth Sustainable Development Goal of quality inclusive education during the unprecedented times of a global pandemic.

Keywords Volunteering, online learning · ECD · Collaborative learning

---

L. Meda (✉)
Sharjah Education Academy, University City, Sharjah, United Arab Emirates
e-mail: lmeda@sea.ac.ae

Introduction

The global pandemic caused by the Coronavirus (COVID-19) affected the education sector world-wide. Many schools and universities in different countries were forced to close as a preventative measure to reduce the spread of the deadly pandemic. In the United Arab Emirates (UAE), the Ministry of Education announced that all schools and institutions must be closed from 20 March 2020. This did not stop teaching and learning from happening in the country as institutions changed from face-to-face classes to online learning. The switch from regular face-to-face classes to online learning happened very fast and did not give students, teachers, and parents enough time to prepare for a new pedagogical approach (Cavanaugh & Deweese, 2020). Children in early childhood development (ECD) were among the worst affected by online learning as they depend on caregivers to help them set up technological devices and complete work assigned by teachers Saxena (2021) argues that ECD children require additional support with online learning in order to access it and engage meaningfully. This was a challenge for children whose caregivers were medical workers as they (children) were not getting the needed support to access and engage in online learning during the start of COVID-19. Children whose caregivers were medical workers were affected by online learning more than others as their parents/guardians were expected to work extra hours in healthcare institutions during the start of the global COVID-19 pandemic. Zaman (2020) concurs that children of medical workers were arguably the worst affected by the move to online learning during the time of COVID-19.

The purpose of this study is to examine the nature of learning support provided by a university professor who volunteered to assist three ECD children whose parents/guardians were medical workers during the start of COVID-19 in the UAE. The study was guided by one critical question: what is the nature of learning support which was provided to children of medical workers during the start of COVID-19 in the UAE? The paper begins by presenting a literature review which focused on unpacking key constructs of the study (spirit of volunteerism and supporting children of medical workers). This is followed by the context of the study and theoretical framework guiding the research. Methods are presented thereafter, followed by results and discussion which were presented concurrently. The study ends with a succinct conclusion and implications for further studies.

The Spirit of Volunteerism in the UAE

Volunteerism is conceptualized from Ryan and Deci's (2000) self-determination theory which foregrounds intrinsic and extrinsic motivation as major contributing factors. For a person to volunteer, there is a need for some internal drive (intrinsic motivation) which pushes him/her to be determined to completing a task even if he/she is not paid. A person will be intrinsically motivated to complete a task willingly to benefit other people or the environment. This concurs with NCVO's (2020), definition of volunteering: "any activity that involves spending time, unpaid, doing something that aims to benefit the environment or someone (individuals or groups) other than, or in addition to, close relatives." The most important part of volunteerism is that it is unpaid and a person does it willingly with the intention to help (Al Saraidi et al., 2020, p. 335). The definition of a volunteer articulated in law no. (5) of 2018 says a volunteer is "any person who, willingly and under no duress or coercion, dedicates himself to performing volunteer work without pay." According to Ryan and Deci (2000) extrinsic motivation is a great component of volunteering as someone may volunteer with the ultimate purpose of gaining new skills or getting a token of appreciation which does not necessarily have to be monetary. In the UAE, volunteering is mainly done to satisfy humanitarian obligation to help others, show concern for and worrying about a community, to gain skills and experience, and meeting the expectation of or getting the approval of significant others (Akintola, 2011, p. 55).

Volunteerism is very common in the UAE as it forms part of the culture of the country. Awofeso et al. (2017, p. 25) argue that the "Emirati people have always striven to offer help to others in times of difficulty and prosperity to strengthen the social ties and share life events with others." The spirit of giving and volunteering was inspired by the late Sheikh Zayed, forefather of the UAE, who believed in offering service freely for the growth and development of the nation and as part of promoting human rights (Awofeso et al., 2017). When COVID-19 started, the Ministry of Education in the UAE worked in collaboration with institutions of higher learning to offer learning support to children of medical workers since they were working extra hours with people infected with the virus. The Ministry collaborated with institutions of higher learning in the country and requested them to let faculty members and students volunteer to assist children in early childhood with online learning while their caregivers were helping to fight against the global pandemic of COVID-19.

Supporting Children of Medical Workers

Since the start of COVID-19 in 2019 in Wuhan, China, medical workers have risked their lives by being at the forefront of treating and caring for people infected by the pandemic. The majority of them left their families with limited educational support so that they could treat COVID-19 patients. During the time when COVID-19 started, children of medical workers needed a lot of support as they were at a greater risk of getting stressed and traumatized by the fact that their parents/guardians were vulnerable to contracting the virus since they were working as frontline staff to curb the virus (Skokauskas et al., 2020). The children were worried that their caregivers could be infected or die and they would then suffer the consequences. The medical workers were also worried about their health and more importantly their children whom they were leaving at home. This necessitated a need for people in different countries to help fight COVID-19 by helping families of medical workers so that they could work in hospitals without worrying about supporting their children with online learning. The World Health Organization (WHO) (2020) states that one way of supporting healthcare workers during the time of COVID-19 was by providing psychosocial support to their children. This includes providing online learning support to the children so that they do not miss anything when their parents/guardians are on duty.

Williams et al. (2020) contend that many countries across the globe had different ways of supporting children of medical workers during the time of COVID-19. Education was one of the ways children were supported by getting access to resources and additional instruction online. Children in ECD need someone to assist them setting up their devices in order to participate in online learning. They also needed someone to monitor them so that they remain focused and engaged on the teaching and learning activities planned by the teacher. There is a need for someone to collaborate with online instructors in order to enhance young children's online learning experiences. A collaboration of instructors and parents in Indonesian schools helped make online learning successful for children during the time when emergency remote teaching and learning were introduced as a preventative measure for reducing the spread of COVID-19 (Aliyyah et al., 2020). Collaboration is key in any form of learning; teachers will be in a better position to understand learners and be able to scaffold them successfully (Vygotsky, 1978; Shabani et al., 2010).

In ECD, learning requires collaboration and the use of games to enhance young children's learning experiences. This is because "children learn best through play and concentrate when they can be active through hands-on activities" (Kim, 2020, p. 156). Research shows that learning through play whether in face-to-face classes or online is very important as it enables children to better understand instruction (Rupere et al., 2013; UNICEF, 2018). Using online chats, video conferencing, online games and interactive cloud-based apps like Google docs can provide a richer online learning experience for learners (Lestiyanawati & Widyantoro, 2020). Lathifah et al. (2020) concur that the use of different apps, videos, pictures and audio help when teaching online. When different teaching activities are used and children are excited about online learning, it makes class management easy and allows effective learning to take place.

Context of the Study

When schools were closed in March 2020 in the UAE, learning did not stop as online learning commenced. Medical workers in the UAE expressed concern that their children (particularly in ECD) were lacking support during online learning. They were unable to offer help to the children as they were treating and caring for COVID-19 patients in hospitals. One health worker in the UAE said, "we have found remote learning to be a challenge because our daughters are both very young. They need constant support to get through the live sessions, then there are activities to complete afterwards" (Zaman, 2020). Similarly, Skokauskas et al. (2020, p. 1) postulate that "healthcare workers and first responders are appropriately concerned about their children. If they can have more confidence that practical support is available to support their children during these challenging times, it will inevitably improve their ability and willingness to work effectively during the COVID-19 pandemic." In response to this, the UAE health ministry collected names of all medical workers who had children who needed support with online learning. One federal university in the country offered to help medical workers by supporting their children with online learning. The university allocated all families to volunteering faculty staff and undergraduate students. Each volunteer was expected to contact the family and arrange with parents/guardians how they could support the children. The volunteering sessions ran from April to June. Each volunteer from the university who completed a minimum of 40 h of virtual academic support to children of medical workers was given a digital badge as a sign of acknowledging their contributions. The instructor whose reflections are provided in this study volunteered to offer learning support to children and exceeded the minimum of 40 h.

Theoretical Frameworks

Vygotsky's theory of social constructivism, the Community of Inquiry (CoI), and theory of connectivism were used as theoretical frameworks for this study. Vygotsky's (1978) theory states that children learn best when there is social interaction, when they are scaffolded in order to reach their zone of proximal development (ZPD) and when there is language development. These components were evident in this study as the instructor promoted active engagement with children through social interaction and knowledge was co-created by both parties. This concurs with Vygotsky (1978) who argues that in children's learning cognitive processes are developed through social interactions which take place between a learner and a more knowledgeable other. Medical workers' children were supported and scaffolded consistently in order to maximize their learning experiences and be able to reach their ZPD. According to Vygotsky (1978, p. 86) ZPD is:

> The distance between the actual development level as determined by independent problem solving and the level of potential development as determined through problem solving under adult guidance or in collaboration with a more capable peer.

ZPD was an important component of this study as children did not know a lot of content and the instructor spent a considerable amount of time supporting and scaffolding them to understand better. The theory was suitable for this study as it applies to digital learning. Fadeev (2019) concurs that Vygotsky's theory of mediation is suitable for use in a digital learning environment as it enables social interaction and scaffolding to occur.

Garrison et al. (2000) CoI Framework consists of three interconnected elements: social presence, cognitive presence, and teacher presence. The social presence entails human interaction within an online community (Garrison, 2015). It focuses on the social and emotional aspects which shows that there are real people participating in an online program. This is related to this study as the instructor established social interaction with each of the children during the time of online learning. The cognitive presence requires students to use their critical thinking skills to construct meaning through discourse and sustained reflection (Garrison et al., 2000). This is related to this study where children were challenged to use their cognitive skills to work out learning problems which were given. Teacher presence is the most critical elements as it combines both social presence and cognitive to give authentic learning experiences (Garrison et al., 2000). Teacher presence, as the name suggest involves a teacher being present in children's learning. An instructor was present throughout the time children were attending their online learning voluntary sessions.

Theory of connectivism was selected as it is a framework that is suitable for understanding learning in a digital age. Theories of behaviorism, constructivism, and cognitivism were developed before the era of technology. They are still essential theories which support teaching and learning, but in cases where technology is involved, it is better to include connectivism as it integrates different principles of learning in the digital era (Siemens, 2004). The study reports on volunteering teaching which happened online and that makes connectivism suitable to understand the main online principles which were used to enhance children's learning experiences.

Methods

The study was done using a qualitative case study within an interpretivist paradigm. A qualitative approach was selected as the researcher sought to obtain rich textual data about the phenomenon. Creswell and Creswell (2018) state that a qualitative approach is suitable for a study that seeks to focus on small scale textual data. An interpretivist paradigm was chosen as it is compatible with a qualitative approach. Lapan et al. (2012) contend that every qualitative approach has an element of interpretivism and the two can be used in a study that seeks to understand and interpret data using the researcher's subjective views. The study was done as a case study of a university professor from a federal university in the UAE who volunteered to offer online learning support to children of medical workers. A case study was selected as it enabled the researcher to undertake an in-depth investigation of the phenomenon (Yin, 2018) in order to understand the nature of support which was offered to children. Purposive sampling which is characterized by deliberate targeting of information rich participants (Cohen et al., 2017) was used to select a university professor who volunteered to offer online learning support to children of medical workers. The professor has more than ten years experience of teaching in institutions of higher learning. He was one of the professors who volunteered to offer support to children of medical workers. The professor was selected for this study as he volunteered to share his reflections on working with the children. There were three children of medical workers who were supported and their details are noted in Table 12.1.

Table 12.1 Details of Children who were Supported

Child No.	Age	Grade	Level	Duration of each class	Lesson focus
1.	4 years	Kindergarten	Early childhood education (birth – 8 years)	30 min	Based on parent's recommendation
2.	6 years	1		30 min	Based on what was learnt online with class teacher
3.	8 years	3		45 min	Based on what was learnt online with class teacher

Child 1 and child 3 were from the same family. They were brother and sister. Data was collected through reflections which were provided by the instructor who supported the children. The instructor selected a minimum of four lessons which he offered to the children and explained the nature of support that he provided. The reflections provided enabled the researcher to have in-depth understanding of support which was offered to the children. The study was done as a reflective analysis where the instructor provided a deep reflection of online classes which were offered, how they were offered, and support which was given to children to enhance their learning experiences. Reflections were preferred in this study as they allowed the participant to provide descriptive personal narratives about the phenomenon. They were also selected as they promoted self-assessment and analytical perspectives into the instructor's teaching methods and actions (Dervent, 2015). Data was analyzed using content analysis where the researcher began by firstly reading through all the reflections provided. The reflections were categorized according to lessons which were offered to the children. This was done to reduce similarities which were noted. For this study the researcher selected four lessons which were offered to child 1 and child 2 and eight which were offered to child 3. Child 3 had more lessons because the total number of classes where he was supported by the instructor was double the number of lessons offered to child 1 and child 2. Ethical issues were observed by using pseudonyms.

Results and Discussion

Results of this study are focused on the nature of learning support which was provided to children of medical workers during the time of COVID-19. The results are presented according to the nature of learning support which was given to each of the three children. Results and discussion are presented concurrently guided by theoretical frameworks of Vygotsky's theory of social constructivism, connectivism, and the CoI.

Learning Support Provided to Child 1

Four lessons offered to child 1 were reported in this section. The objective for the first lesson was stated as: 'by the end of the lesson, child should be able to spell the six words given.' The lesson was conducted synchronously using Zoom and an application called spelling training (spellingtraining.com). The mother of the child was at home shortly before the lesson started and she helped the child set up Zoom and get started with the spelling activity. The child was asked by the instructor to click a link where it says 'listen'.

The child listened to how each word was pronounced and spelt. She did the exercise by herself and got three spellings correct and the other three wrong. In order to practice the three spellings she got wrong, the instructor put the words on the spelling training app.

The words were put in such a way that the child learns each word in three steps:

- Step 1 – Child sees the word on the screen.
- Step 2 – Child was required to spell the word by clicking letters which the device was showing her on the keyboard. A keyboard was flashing the correct letter which the child had to choose.
- Step 3 – Child spells the word without any support. Steps 1 and 2 were removed.

At the end of the lesson, the child managed to spell all the six words correctly. The nature of support which was given to the child through the three steps of spelling training is consistent with Vygotsky's (1978) concept of scaffolding where a child gets support which will be gradually removed when he/she understands the concept. Acar et al. (2017) argue that scaffolding is indispensable in the teaching and learning of pre-schoolers as it enable children to get adequate learning support in order to understand the instruction. Similarly, Shabani et al. (2010) echoed the same sentiments that scaffolding is key as it enables children to understand the topic better and to be in a better position to actively participate in the co-creation of knowledge with teachers. The way in which the instructor taught the child resonates with both cognitive presence and teacher presence in Garrison et al.'s (2001) CoI. The child was challenged to use her cognitive skills to identify the words and spell them independently after the support was removed. Teacher presence was evident as the instructor selected the learning activities for the child and supported her to reach the ZPD. It is important to note that teacher presence was evident throughout the study as the instructor selected learning activities, conducted formative and summative assessments, and supported children during their entire learning process.

The next lesson's objective was for the child to be able to count from 8 to 12 since she was able to count from 0 to 7. Since the child's attention span was very low and she liked music, the instructor figured out that the best way to get her involved and attentive was by using a counting game that has music in it. A musical drumming link called pbskids.org (https://pbskids.org/daniel/games/feel-the-music/) was used to facilitate the lesson. The link enables children to make different types of sounds by simply clicking five different flowers (each has a different sound), drums, rattles and musical symbols. There is a bear dancing to the beat and each time a child clicks, there is a different sound. Child 1 was assisted by her brother (child 3) to set up the link and get started making different sounds. She was smiling and enjoying hearing a different sound each time she clicked an instrument and what made it more fun was a bear dancing to the beat.

The child was asked to count each time she clicked an instrument. The instructor was showing the numbers and the child was clicking an instrument and counting the number she clicked. She would say a number and click the instrument. Each time she clicked an instrument and counted correctly, the instructor would praise her by clapping hands (with her) and shouting yeeeeeee. The child managed to count from 1 to 12.

In the third lesson, the child was expected to count in twos. The concept of counting in multiples of two was taught and the instructor used pictures of bees, strawberries, lollipops, hockey sticks, bananas and balls which were all arranged in twos. The child did not get it at first, but she was supported and she played an online game of twos which made her develop an understanding of the concept.

Both lessons two and three which were administered with child 1 were successful because of the way games were used to enhance her learning experiences. The use of games in the child's learning made the social presence become more dominant as there was social interaction where emotions were involved (Garrison, 2007). The child was not just playing games for enjoyment purposes, but learning as she had to use her thinking skills to game the answers correct. The use of thinking skills in learning aligns with the cognitive presence. The game played required the child to use her mind. Rupere (2013, p. 247) said "Games are critical to early childhood learning as they develop a child to recall taught concepts and improve their learning." This is because games in ECD are associated with children's learning. Similarly, UNICEF (2018, p. 7) postulates that "play is one of the most important ways in which young children gain essential knowledge and skills." When children learn through games, it improves their socio-emotional competence and they (games) help them develop imagination and creativity skills (Parker & Thomsen, 2019). Learning through play is associated with interactive learning which is an integral part of Vygotsky's theory of social constructivism. Vygotsky (1978) believed that effective learning takes place when there is social interaction. This was evident in this study where the instructor and the child interacted extensively and participated in various learner-centered activities. Connectivism was evident as the child connected ideas through online games played and managed to use her critical thinking skills to solve problems paused. This is consistent with Siemens (2004) who states that connectivism is essential in digital learning as it makes learners connect ideas and apply their minds to figure out concepts.

The fourth lesson was a comprehension exercise where a Daniel stories link (https://pbskids.org/daniel/stories/neighborhood-clean-up/?language=en) was used. Child 1 was asked to press start and each time she clicked, there were cartoon pictures and narration of the story. Before moving to the next page, the child was asked to retell what the page was about. She did an excellent job by retelling the story, explaining why some characters behaved the way they did and how she would have reacted in specific cases which were presented. The child was able to navigate through lower order thinking skills to higher order thinking. This aligns with the cognitive presence as the child was using her critical thinking skills ranging from lower to higher levels (Garrison et al., 2000). This is consistent with Bloom's taxonomy which states that questioning and reasoning should progress from lower order to higher order thinking skills (Anderson & Krathwohl, 2001; Beck & Condy, 2017). Swart (2010) concurs that good questioning styles should challenge students to think from a lower order to a higher order. A famous theorist, Jean Piaget, supported the view that children should use their cognitive skills to learn. This is different from Vygotsky's theory where it is believed that learning takes place primarily through social interactions. The comprehension passages which were given to the child did not only challenge the child to exercise her thinking skills, but also language development. According to Vygotsky (1978), language development is essential as it is a great determinant of a child's performance in a subject. If a child struggles with language of instruction, that has a negative effect on academic performance (Green et al., 2012).

Learning Support Provided to Child 2

All the four lessons reported in this study were a follow-up of what child 2 studied with the schoolteacher in their online classes. This child was able to join Zoom classes with the instructor and complete online activities without a caregiver's help. The instructor was given access by the parent to see all the topics which the class teacher was uploading on Padlet (platform used by the teacher). The objective of the first lesson was that by the end of the lesson, the child should be able to write five sentences about a lion using the words can, teeth, fast, eat and jungle. When the child was asked what she knew about a lion, she only knew that it was an animal. The instructor showed the child a short clip about lions in the jungle hunting and killing other animals. After the clip, the child was asked to write what she saw lions doing in the clip. The child wrote three correct sentences about a lion with the words fast, eat and can. The instructor showed her pictures and cartoons of a lion opening its mouth and asked the child to write a sentence about the animal's teeth. She was asked to write a sentence about where a lion lives (jungle).

The second and third lessons focused on Mathematics and the objective was for the child to be able to add 10 to numbers between 1 and 120. The instructor created a number box and wrote 1–12 on the top row. He asked the child to fill in each column by adding 10 to all the numbers. The work was done on Google docs where the instructor could see what the child was typing and also see her doing the work on Zoom. She had difficulties with some numbers. The instructor supported her until she could complete the number chat by herself. An additional activity was provided where the instructor covered some numbers on the table and asked the child to figure out which numbers they were. It was like a game where the instructor asked the child to close her eyes, deleted some numbers on the table and asked her to figure out the missing numbers using the same concept of adding 10.

The fourth lesson was Mathematics homework about greater than, less than and equal to signs which the child was given by the class teacher to complete on an app called Seesaw. The mother wanted the child to be assisted with that homework, so she sent the instructor a link to the app along with login details. The instructor supported the child while she was completing the work. Before doing the homework, the instructor showed the child a YouTube video about a big alligator which was biting small fish. The video symbolized greater than, smaller than and equal to signs. After watching the video, the child was given an activity to complete which was related to the topic. When the instructor saw that the child understood the concept, he let her begin completing the homework activity. The child did it successfully with minimal support.

In all the lessons, the instructor did not disclose answers to the child, but showed her visuals and videos to help refresh her memory about the topics. The child could not have done the work successfully if it was not for the support and guidance she received. This resonates with Vygotsky's (1978) concept of the ZPD where a child develops problem-solving skills and the ability to work out answers under the guidance of an adult. Walker (2010, p. 712) conceptualizes ZPD as a critical concept which is fundamental in the learning of children as it enables the learner to "successfully complete tasks with the assistance of more capable other people." The concept is closely related to scaffolded learning as the two (ZPD and scaffolding) focus on assisting a learner to understand instruction. Affine (2012) argues that ZPD is a useful tool in early childhood as it can be integrated in various ways to enhance young children's learning experiences and ability to understand instruction. The instructor managed to provide more guidance to the child at first in order to develop the five sentences. The amount of support was gradually removed as the child understood the concept. This approach is consistent with the ZPD which requires an instructor to offer support and step back in order to give a learner the chance to do the work independently (Vygotsky, 1978; Affine, 2012).

All the three presences of the CoI were evident on the teaching of child two. Social presence emanated from the fact that the child and instructor had open communication where the child was free to express herself. Garrisson et al. (2001) contend that open communication and risk-free expression are critical elements of the social presence. The instructor triggered a child's response using different questions and challenged her to explore the topics in detail. This aligns with the cognitive presence which Garrison (2007) described as an essential element for information exchange. The teacher presence was evident as the instructor kept the discussions with the child focused (Garrisson et al., 2000). The child was supported using numerous resources which include visuals, audio, and videos. This relates to connectivism which supports visualizing as an integral social aspect of learning (Siemens, 2006).

Learning Support Provided to Child 3

All the lessons which were conducted with this child were a follow-up of what she studied with the schoolteacher in their online class. The child was able to join Zoom classes with the instructor and complete online activities without a caregiver's help. The child helped his younger sister (child 1) to set up for online support lessons with the instructor.

Child 3 had the greatest number of lessons with the instructor. This is because he was getting a lot of homework activities which had to be completed and submitted to the teacher. The content was a lot and could not be covered in a single lesson. Each lesson used a minimum of 45 min and maximum of 1 h. Among the eight lessons which were conducted with the child, only one was conducted asynchronously whereas the rest were conducted synchronously. For the lesson which was conducted asynchronously, the instructor used screencast-o-matic to record the lesson and send it to the child to watch and complete the activities related to homework which his class teacher wanted him to do. Some of the topics which the instructor covered with the child are on Table 12.2.

In all the lessons, the child was leading the discussion as he would have covered the topic with the teacher in class. The instructor was mainly there to offer guidance and support to the child. In some instances, the child indicated that he did not understand the online lesson with the class teacher. In that case, the instructor would use different examples and resources related to the topic to make it easy for him to understand. The child was very active, he spoke English eloquently and was very enthusiastic about learning using different technology. A variety of digital resources were used to enhance the child's learning experiences. This is consistent with Lestiyanawati and Widyantoro (2020) who contend that using different

Table 12.2 Topics covered

Topic	Resources used
Mathematics	
Multiplication and division	Multiplication table, screencast-o-matic, Kahoot
Mixed word problems	Google docs, Kahoot
Proper fractions, improper fractions and mixed numbers	Orange pieces, pizza slices for fractions
Adding and subtracting fractions	Digital interactive whiteboard (Google Jamboard)
Decimals	Pizza slices, Google docs
English	
Adverbs	YouTube, flash cards, workbook
Pronouns	
Science	
Differentiate the three structures of the earth (crust, mantle and core)	Boiled egg to illustrate the three structures of the earth
Seven landforms in the Philippines (mountain, hill, plateau, valley, peninsula, island, archipelago)	Images of different landforms from the Philippines online textbook about land forms

applications, games and resources help children understand instruction in online learning. It helps children connect ideas easily and understand instruction (Siemens, 2004, 2006).

There was high level of interaction with child 3 as he was very inquisitive. The level of interaction between the child and the instructor improved the quality of learning as the child could easily voice his ideas about a topic and the instructor would know where he needed support. Learning through social interaction is an integral component in Vygotsky's (1978) theory of social constructivism where it is believed that meaningful learning occurs through collaboration. Zisopoulou (2019) postulates that collaboration is a twenty-first century education trend which should be implemented when teaching early childhood learners. Akçay (2016) concurs that collaborative learning strategies such as the jigsaw method help children in preschool and primary school to understand instruction. The jigsaw method is a collaborative learning strategy where a teacher assigns children into groups. Each group gets a topic different from the other. Children will be required to research information about their topic so that they have comprehensive understanding of it. They will exchange groups and share information about their respective topics. The jigsaw method promotes collaboration among children (Akçay, 2016). Collaborative learning is essential as it improves social and cognitive skills (Garrison et al., 2000) of young children in the early childhood phase (Zisopoulou, 2019). Similarly, Kim (2020) concurs that "online teaching requires various tasks to be accomplished in the different phases of planning, implementation and refection. Critical thinking, creativity, collaboration and communication are always required no matter whether the class is taught online or offline" (p. 156).

Conclusion

The purpose of this study was to examine the nature of learning support which was provided by a university professor who volunteered to assist three ECD children of medical workers during the time of COVID-19 in the UAE. A significant contribution that emerges from this study is demystifying misleading thoughts that children in ECD cannot learn meaningfully online. The children benefit significantly from face-to-face learning as it helps them develop all the three domains of development (physical, cognitive, and socio-emotional). However, online learning also can enable children to learn effectively if the instructor uses a variety of teaching materials and engages children using games which are related to the topic. It is possible for collaborative learning to take place with young children online as long as play-based activities are included and learners are scaffolded in order to reach their ZPD. Considering the severity of COVID-19 and the way it has negatively affected education and all other sectors of the economy, inculcating the spirit of volunteerism is indispensable as it forms part of inclusive education. Instilling the spirit of volunteering in the nation is a good thing as it promotes human rights and provides a milestone of achievement towards the attainment of the fourth Sustainable

Development Goal (SDG) of quality inclusive education during the unprecedented times of a global pandemic. This is consistent with the UAE's Federal Law 29 of 2006 which categorically states that all students must be afforded equal opportunities to education as it is their fundamental human right. The attainment of that human right enables SDG four to be attained. Further studies can be conducted focusing on children's performance in online learning during the time of the COVID-19 pandemic. This implies collecting and analyzing data about children's assessments. The study recommends that learning institutions be in the forefront of promoting a culture of volunteerism as it helps build better communities where people show humanitarian obligation of helping others. Volunteerism plays a significant role in the current time of COVID-19 where all people can benefit from each other's help. The researcher found the experience of offering a service to children during the global pandemic not only a service related to the profession, but something fulfilling and worthwhile. Information which was taught to children contributed to the success of online teaching and learning.

References

Acar, I. H., Hong, S., & Wu, C. (2017). Examining the role of teacher presence and scaffolding in preschoolers' peer interactions. *European Early Childhood Education Research Journal, 25*(6), 866–884. https://doi.org/10.1080/1350293X.2017.1380884

Affine, T. A. (2012). *The zone of proximal development in early childhood education*. Thesis in Social Services: Laurea University of Applied Sciences. Retrieved from https://www.theseus.fi/bitstream/handle/10024/45477/Affine_Tigist.pdf?sequence=1&isAllowed=y

Akçay, N. O. (2016). Implementation of cooperative learning model in preschool. *Journal of Education and Learning, 5*(3), 83–93.

Akintola, O. (2011). What motivates people to volunteer? The case of volunteer AIDS caregivers in faith-based organizations in KwaZulu-Natal, South Africa. *Health Policy and Planning, 26*(1), 53–62. https://doi.org/10.1093/heapol/czq019

Al Saraidi, A. S., Awofeso, N., & Dolan, T. C. (2020). Volunteering in the United Arab Emirates' health system – Motivations and challenges. *Health, 12*, 334–352. https://doi.org/10.4236/health.2020.124028

Aliyyah, R. R., Rachmadtullah, R., Samsudin, A., Syaodih, E., Nurtanto, M., & Tambunan, A. R. (2020). The perceptions of primary school teachers of online learning during the Covid-19 pandemic period: A case study in Indonesia. *Journal of Ethnic and Cultural Studies, 7*(2), 90–109. https://doi.org/10.29333/ejecs/388

Anderson, L. W., & Krathwohl, D. R. (2001). *A taxonomy for learning, teaching and assessing: A revision of bloom's taxonomy of educational objectives: Complete edition*. Longman.

Awofeso, N., Guleid, M., & Bamidele, M. (2017). Perceptions and motivations of volunteers in the United Arab Emirates – Health services' implications. *World Wide Journal of Multidisciplinary Research and Development, 3*(9), 23–32.

Beck, S., & Condy, J. L. (2017). Instructional principles used to teach critical comprehension skills to a grade 4 learner. *Reading & Writing, 8*(1), a149–a157. https://doi.org/10.4102/rw.v8i1.149

Cavanaugh, C., & DeWeese, A. (2020). Understanding the professional learning and support needs of educators during the initial weeks of pandemic school closures through search terms and content. *Journal of Technology and Teacher Education, 28*(2), 233–238.

Cohen, L., Manion, L., & Morrison, K. (2017). *Research methods in education* (7th ed.). Routledge.

Creswell, J. W., & Creswell, J. D. (2018). *Research design: Qualitative, quantitative, and mixed methods approaches* (5th ed.). SAGE.

Dervent, F. (2015). The effect of reflective thinking on the teaching practices of pre-service physical education teachers. *Issues in Educational Research, 25*(3), 260–275.

Fadeev, A. (2019). Vygotsky's theory of mediation in digital learning environment: Actuality and practice. *Punctum, 5*(1), 24–44.

Garrison, D. R. (2007). Online community of inquiry review: Social, cognitive, and teaching presence issues. *Journal of Asynchronous Learning Networks, 11*(1), 61–72. https://doi.org/10.24059/olj.v11i1.1737

Garrison, D. R. (2015). *Thinking collaboratively: Learning in a community of inquiry*. Routledge. https://doi.org/10.4324/9781315740751

Garrison, D. R., Anderson, T., & Archer, W. (2000). Critical inquiry in a text-based environment: Computer conferencing in higher education. *The Internet and Higher Education, 2*(2–3), 87–105. https://doi.org/10.1016/S1096-7516(00)00016-6

Garrison, D. R., Anderson, T., & Archer, W. (2001). Critical thinking, cognitive presence, and computer conferencing in distance education. *American Journal of Distance Education, 15*(1), 7–23. https://doi.org/10.1080/08923640109527071

Green, L., Condy, J., & Chigona, A. (2012). Developing the language of thinking within a classroom community of inquiry: Pre-service teachers' experiences. *South African Journal of Education, 32*(3), 319–330.

Kim, J. (2020). Learning and teaching online during Covid-19: Experiences of student teachers in an early childhood education practicum. *International Journal of Early Childhood, 52*, 145–158. https://doi.org/10.1007/s13158-020-00272-6

Lapan, S. D., Quartaroli, M. T., & Riemer, F. J. (Eds.). (2012). *Qualitative research: Anintroduction to methods and designs*. Jossey-Bass.

Lathifah, Z. K., Helmanto, F., & Maryani, N. (2020). The practice of effective classroommanagement in Covid-19 time. *International Journal of Advanced Science and Technology, 29*(7), 3263–3271.

Law No. (5) of 2018. (2018). *Regulating volunteer work in the Emirate of Dubai*. The Supreme Legislation Committee in the Emirate of Dubai. Retrieved from https://www.cda.gov.ae/ar/aboutus/Documents/CDA-Volunteer-Work-in-the-Emirate-of-Dubai-EN.pdf. Accessed 3 June 2021.

Lestiyanawati, R., & Widyantoro, A. (2020). The strategies and problems faced by indonesian teachers in conducting e-learning during COVID-19 outbreak. *Journal of Culture, Literature, Linguistics and English Teaching, 2*(1), 71–82.

NCVO. (2020). *Volunteering*. https://www.ncvo.org.uk/policy-and-research/volunteering-policy

Parker, R., & Thomsen, B. L. (2019). Learning through play at school: A study of playful integrated pedagogies that foster children's holistic skills development in the primary school classroom. Lego Foundations. https://research.acer.edu.au/cgi/viewcontent.cgi?article=1023&context=learning_processes.

Rupere, T., Muzurura, O., Zanamwe, N., & Munyaradzi, M. (2013). Use of a game in teaching early childhood learners in Zimbabwe. *International Journal of Computer and Information Technology, 2*(2), 247–254.

Ryan, R. M., & Deci, E. L. (2000). Self-determination theory and the facilitation of intrinsic motivation, social development, and Well-being. *American Psychologist, 55*(1), 68–78. https://doi.org/10.1037/0003-066x.55.1.68

Saxena, A. (2021). Challenges and factors influencing early childhood education in Hong Kong during COVID-19: Teachers' perspective. Paper presented at the *International Conference on Advanced Learning Technologies* (ICALT).

Shabani, K., Khatib, M., & Ebadi, S. (2010). Vygotsky's zone of proximal development: Instructional implications and teachers' professional development. *English Language Teaching, 3*(4), 237–248.

Siemens, G. (2004). *Connectivism: A learning theory for the digital age.* Accessed 21 November 2021 https://www.academia.edu/2857071/Connectivism

Siemens, G. (2006, November 12). *Connectivism: Learning theory or pastime of the self-amused?* Retrieved from Accessed 2 July 2019 https://altamirano.biz/conectivismo.pdf.

Skokauskas, N., Leventhal, B., Cardeli, E. L., et al. (2020). Supporting children of healthcare workers during the COVID-19 pandemic. *European Child Adolescent Psychiatry.* https://doi.org/10.1007/s00787-020-01604-6

Swart, A. J. (2010). Evaluation of final examination papers in engineering: A case study using bloom's taxonomy. *IEEE Transactions on Education, 53*(2), 257–264. https://doi.org/10.1109/TE.2009.2014221

UNICEF. (2018). *Learning through play: Strengthening learning through play in early childhood education programmes.* UNICEF. Retrieved from https://www.unicef.org/sites/default/files/2018-12/UNICEF-Lego-Foundation-Learning-through-Play.pdf.

Vygotsky, L. S. (1978). *Mind in society: The development of higher psychological processes.* Harvard University Press.

Walker, R. A. (2010). Sociocultural issues in motivation. In P. Peterson, E. Baker, & B. McGaw (Eds.), *International encyclopedia of education* (3rd ed., pp. 712–717). Elsevier. https://doi.org/10.1016/B978-0-08-044894-7.00629-1

Williams, G. A., Scarpetti, G., Bezzina, A., Vincenti, K., et al. (2020). How are countries supporting their health workers during COVID-19? *Eurohealth, 26*(2), 58–62.

World Health Organisation [WHO]. (2020). *2019 novel coronavirus global research and innovation forum: Towards a research roadmap.* WHO.

Yin, R. K. (2018). *Case study research and application* (6th ed.). SAGE.

Zaman, S. (2020).Coronavirus: Children of healthcare workers face harder task with e-learning. *Gulf News.* Local newspaper in the UAE. 31 May 2020.

Zisopoulou, E. (2019). Collaborative learning in kindergarten: Challenge or reality? *Erken Çocukluk Çalışmaları Dergisi, 3*(2), 335–351. https://doi.org/10.24130/eccd-jecs.1967201932113

Dr. Lawrence Meda holds a PhD in Curriculum Studies. He is currently working as an Associate Professor and Director of Research at Sharjah Education Academy in the United Arab Emirates. He is a certified online instructor and very passionate about research. His main research interests are in Inclusive Education, Curriculum Studies, Educational Technology and Teacher Education. He has supervised Masters and Doctoral students and published in high impact accredited journals.

Chapter 13
Collaborative Roles of Rural Stakeholders to Benefit Learners Within Inclusive Education

Patrick Mweli and Ntombizandile Gcelu

Abstract The type of leadership and the role school managers play in rural schools is crucial in accommodating diverse learners' learning needs within inclusive education. Most literature indicates scanty information about how rural school managers craft knowledge in inclusive leadership and their collaborative management roles. This chapter explores how rural school managers' collaborative roles help learners cope with learning in an inclusive environment. The chapter hinges on collaborative leadership theory. The authors employed the interpretivism paradigm using a qualitative research approach to gather rural school managers' stories on how their collaborative roles influence learners' academic achievement. The overall finding of the study reveals that collaborative leadership is central to inclusive education and that learners' academic performance increase due to teacher-parent collaboration in education.

Keywords Collaborative roles · Inclusive education · Rural schools · School managers

Introduction

Suppose inclusion in education (Black-Hawkins & Florian, 2012) is an attitude, belief, or mindset. In that case, it could mean transcending learners with learning barriers mere inclusion within the classroom but inclusive education becomes a philosophical stance that shapes the ethos of leaders within schools. Hence, the successful implementation of inclusive education depends entirely on the collaborative roles of school managers in creating inclusive learning environments (Forlin, 2010). Furthermore, to ensure the success of inclusive education, a "collective effort is

---

P. Mweli (✉) · N. Gcelu
University of the Free State, Bloemfontein, South Africa
e-mail: mwelip@ufs.ac.za

© The Author(s), under exclusive license to Springer Nature Switzerland AG 2022
L. Meda, J. Chitiyo (eds.), *Inclusive Pedagogical Practices Amidst a Global Pandemic*, Inclusive Learning and Educational Equity 7, https://doi.org/10.1007/978-3-031-10642-2_13

integrally required to reflect on everyday practice to make sense of the effects of inclusivity on education and its effectiveness" (Whitburn & Plows, 2017, p. 4).

School managers (principals, heads of departments, and members of school governing body-parental components) play a crucial leadership role within inclusive education. In this regard, they provide guidance and training to teaching staff and other stakeholders to ensure that all learners feel valued and accepted by their learning environment regardless of physical, intellectual, social, emotional, cultural, or other conditions (Heyder et al., 2020). School leaders believe in and uphold the principle of diversity and inclusion (Roberson & Perry, 2021; van Knippenberg & van Ginkel, 2021 because they organize the learning environment to consider ideas and knowledge, perspective, and styles from all stakeholders within a school. Initially, Hlalele (2012) described rural schools as underdeveloped. After that, new studies contextualized the concept of rurality by describing it as demographic, geographic, and cultural (Roberts & Green, 2013). Within this context, we foreground our discussion on how collaborative rural school managers' roles assist learners within inclusive education to cope with the challenges of inclusive learning. Thus, learners within this context who come from socio-economic and politically disadvantaged are classified as having many exceptional barriers within education, such as access to technology (Hlalele, 2014), while this chapter focuses on the positives that school managers do to support inclusive learning through their collaborative management roles within rural schools.

Background

The study was conducted in two rural secondary schools, one at Ngqeleni district in the Eastern Cape Province and the other at Reddersberg in Free State province in South Africa. Learners attending these schools come from poverty-stricken communities. Most families within these areas depend on government grants for a living. Both schools have an under-resourced educational infrastructure. Literature from around the world indicates that school leaders play various roles in inclusive education (Ainscow & Sandill, 2010; Lambrecht et al., 2020; Khaleel et al., 2021; Setia et al., 2021). For example, the findings of Khaleel et al. (2021) in a study conducted in the United Arab Emirates (UAE) indicate that school administrators' support and attitude toward teachers, such as holding regular meetings, assigning learning support teams, and requesting special needs teachers to assist other teachers, had a significant impact on their engagement. Furthermore, in a study conducted in Canada, Sider et al. (2021) concurred with the findings mentioned above when they revealed that principals are critical human resources in interpreting and implementing inclusive policies. Their behaviour has significantly influenced what teachers do in the classroom and the frontline of service delivery. According to Mapiet (2016), in a study conducted in South Africa, school principals ensure that all learners receive dignified and respectful treatment.

Collaboration is vital for the effectiveness of any organization, including rural schools (Gcelu, 2019). Research has revealed that successful school principals rely on teamwork, encouraging their staff to collaborate (Pashiardis et al., 2011; Klar & Brewer, 2014). Collaboration improves the staff's motivation, morale, and job performance. This study is based on Chrislip and Larson's (1994) collaborative leadership theory, which the literature reviewed by the authors support. This theory is based on the idea that by collaborating, we can be more innovative, more creative, and have more control over what gets done. The argument made in this chapter is that collaborative leaders should concentrate on promoting and safeguarding the collaborative process, which includes keeping stakeholders at the table to make decisions during difficult times and recognizing small victories. Collaborative leadership theory is the most suitable theory for this study because of its vital principle of using a team approach and belief in action learning (Wachs, 2005; Broadhurst et al., 2021). Hence, for the school principal to be able to use their roles collaboratively, they should believe in teamwork, sharing ideas, and respecting the opinions of their subordinates. The theory is rooted in the belief that everyone within the team can achieve the organization's goals by allowing all to own school stakeholders' decisions, including parents who play a vital role in schools. A study conducted within rural schools in the Eastern Cape indicated a clear improvement in learners' academic performance (Gcelu, 2019).

The discussion above demonstrates the roles of rural school managers in promoting inclusive education to the benefit of the learners. More significantly, rural schools are educational institutions lacking educational resources (Hlalele, 2014). In this regard, school managers who follow collaborative leadership styles have a vision, inclusive values, motivation, autonomy, and trust in school staff members with whom they work (Sherab et al., 2015; Schuelka et al., 2019). Furthermore, the latter statement concurs with Shogren et al. (2015) argues that school leadership is crucial for implementing inclusive education. Thus, within this context, it is crucial to note the argument of Cameli et al. (2010) that inclusive leadership depends on the interaction between leaders and employees that is open, effective, and accessible. Hence, Collaborative leadership theory is rooted within the latter mentioned belief.

Moreover, Ryan (2007) indicated that inclusive leadership requires a collective leadership process and defines inclusive leadership in education as the presence of a learning leader. A learning leader is defined as a leader who puts themself in an equal position with fellow workers and considers their views and contributions as an exceptional value in the process (Ryan, 2007). In this paper, we used three conceptual lenses to foreground how learners benefit from the collaborative roles of rural school managers. The conceptual lenses used were leadership from inside out (Cashman, 2017), authentic relationships (Sisson, 2015), and commitment to the whole (Geare et al., 2009). The first conceptual lens emphasized less concern for personal power but more trouble for collective accomplishment. The second conceptual lens refers to a leader who values openness and engagement. In contrast, the third conceptual lens depicts a leader who creates conditions for team members to move from concern about themselves to passion for the whole group (Hurley, 2011).

Most researchers argue for an education system that promotes the participation of all stakeholders in education (Black-Hawkins & Florian, 2012; Spratt & Florian, 2015). Such a position advocates that a definition of inclusion based on the notion of disability (Ballard, 2002; Reindal, 2008; Anastasiou & Kauffman, 2013) is not sufficient in defining inclusion, a broader and more all-embracing concept of inclusion that promotes collaboration and full participation of all learners is needed. In this regard, Gudjonsdottir and Óskarsdóttir (2016) indicate that the impact of technical, social, and cultural changes has added new challenges to education throughout the world. These issues are the root causes for global countries to seek education systems that promote the full participation of all stakeholders in education. Environmental and cultural changes influence the new challenges within education in communities caused by the influence of technology within twenty-first-century education. In this regard, Meda and Makura (2017) concur with Pitikoe and Makhasane (2021) on the impact of technology on education. In the sense that its influence enables teachers to meet the current educational needs of twenty-first-century learners. Successful accommodation of these needs depends on inclusive leadership within schools. In this light, this chapter focuses on exploring collaborative roles school managers play to benefit learners within Inclusive Education. Hence, inclusive schools led by collaborative managers who value openness and engagement create conditions for team members to be more passionate about group achievement. Within the latter environment, learners are likely to be provided with all the educational assistance to achieve academic success.

Methods

The study used a qualitative approach which enabled an in-depth understanding of the phenomenon (Lambert, 2019; Matias, 2021). The authors also employed the Interpretivism paradigm (Creswell & Poth, 2016) to interpret rural school managers' stories on how their collaborative roles assist learners in coping with learning. Two schools were selected purposefully, as they are located in a rural area. The principal and two department heads (HoD) from each schools took part in the semi-structured interview session. In total there were six participants. The principal of school 1 was a female of 36 years old, spoke Sesotho and possessed a master's degree in management and leadership. She was born in the Free State province urban area and had move to lead the participating school situated in Eastern Cape province of South Africa. The two HoD participants were local males between the age of 35–50 years, and who spoke IsiXhosa, and both had Bed (hons) qualification. The principal of school 2 was a male born in the rural Eastern province area where the school is situated and spoke IsiXhosa language. He was between the age of 40–55 years. HoD participants were both locals and they were a male and female of between 35 and 40 years old. One of the HoD participant had a Bed degree and the other a higher education diploma. All participants were purposefully selected based of their previous involvement in activities to implement Inclusive education to the benefit of all learners and the geographical location of their schools in rural areasThe credibility of the findings was ensured by limiting the scope of the study to a case and the use of a theoretical framework, as lenses to understand and interpret the results (de Vos et al., 2014). Thematic data analysis (Clarke & Braun, 2014) was used to analyze the stories of rural school managers. To ensure that ethical considerations were considered, we first applied for an ethical certificate within the University and obtained approval from all other gatekeepers. Participants signed a consent form that permitted them to participate while also ensuring the anonymity and confidentiality of the data. The study intends to gather data that could answer the question of the collaborative roles school managers play to benefit learners within Inclusive Education. To illuminate the latter question interview participants were asked questions such as how do school managers' collaboration contribute to learners' academic performance within inclusive classroom? How do school managers collaborate with the parents to boost learners' academic achievement? and why is the collaboration between school managers and parents, important within inclusive classroom learning? Hence, thematic analysis of the data gathered provided us with results in the form of themes discussed in the following sections.

Results

Collaborative Leadership to Benefit Learners Within an Inclusive Classroom

Most school managers in rural schools believe that collaborating with all school stakeholders is the key to effective management that results in learners performing to their optimal academic abilities within inclusive education. School managers collaborate with stakeholders by making their voices heard and helping them feel that they belong and are respected within the institution. This finding is rooted in the following evidence reported verbatim from semi-structured interviews held with rural school Principals and School heads of departments from the two schools that participated in the study.

> Leadership is not about power but about working together as a team with colleagues and the learners' parents. They have learners who have different abilities, whom we cannot say we can be the only ones contributing to their learning. Parents must understand that as much as we must teach, they also have a role to play in teaching their children. Through working with parents, it was evident that some parents are better teachers than some of us (School principals).
>
> As a leader of the school management team, other members and I must identify learners with special learning needs. The principal, in this case, leads the session, although whatever is done depends on the ideas from other stakeholders within the school. As the school principal, I believe in leading with people (School principal).

> For the school to include the learners with challenges, they need to identify them and know their challenges. The learners' identification helps all teachers understand the strategy they can use in class based on their difficulties identified (School Head of department)
>
> There is no way I can benefit learners within inclusive education without identifying those learners with other school stakeholders. School stakeholders expect the principal to lead, but teachers and parents know learners better; hence, there is a need for collaboration in doing this duty (School principal)
>
> Not all teachers had training on inclusive teaching pedagogy, but after identifying the challenges facing us, seminars/workshops are organized twice a year to guide teachers in creating an inclusive classroom (School head of department)

The above excerpts indicate that inclusivity in education is intertwined with collaborative leadership with all stakeholders within the school. It is well documented that educating learners with challenges within an inclusive context comprises many contextual factors (Smit et al., 2020). Working together with rural school- managers and other school stakeholders helps everyone understand and promote the school's vision. Leadership from the inside out is evident when the school principal indicates less concern about his power as a leader and focuses on team members' collective achievement (Hurley, 2011; Dalton, 2021). Moreover, strong leadership within the school enables the propagation and implementation of an explicit school vision based on the view that all learners can learn (Govender & Jacobs, 2020). In this regard, learners could benefit from a conducive and inclusive learning environment created in the process. The participants mentioned above indicated that leading people collaboratively is vital within inclusive education. It ensures power-sharing and a clear educational vision, giving learners and other stakeholders a sense of belonging and acknowledging their ideas in the school's Administration (Miller & Miller, 2007). In this manner, authentic relationships are created in which the openness and engagement of all stakeholders are valued. Hence, the latter promotes a sense of belonging, motivating learners to actively participate in learning activities (Kwatubana & Makhalemele, 2015).

A Collaborative Effort Between Parents and School Managers

Participants indicated that parental involvement is key to the successful implementation of inclusive education. The parental role in education enables learners to achieve their full academic potential as the work done at school is reinforced at home, where parents assist with school homework. The following excerpts indicated how parents assist learners with their schoolwork to reach optimal academic performance (Hamidun et al., 2019). The latter is achieved through the collaborative working of school managers and parents.

> It is vital to note that parents also play a significant role in identifying learners with challenges. These parents, in most cases, come forward and alert the teachers on the status of their children with regards to learner learning challenges (School Head of department).

> Our school has awareness sessions on inclusivity where we invite parents and teachers to the school, and someone with expertise in dealing with learners' challenges comes to address them. We found that these sessions are essential for both teachers and parents. When these sessions occur, we include learners to understand the process and do not mock one another (School principal)

> Our school started to have good results when they realized that parents could teach by supporting learners at home (School principal).

> The parents are also trained to deal with their children at school and at home, as usual, no matter what challenges they might have observed from their behavior (School head of department).

Parental involvement is crucial in inclusive education and, more specifically, in identifying and dealing with learning barriers and challenges. Participants indicated a shared responsibility between parents and teachers in the above excerpts. In this type of relationship, parents would team up with teachers to promote quality teaching and learning within rural schools. Moreover, the responses point to parental involvement in the school governance and parental emphasis on education, which Tan et al. (2020) describe as associated with learners' academic achievement. Learners benefit from this relationship since both teachers and parents model good behavior in making education the center of their lives and aspire to be successful in life.

Furthermore, Christenson (2002) asserts that good educational outcomes in teacher-parent collaboration rely on shared responsibilities. The principal affirmed the latter assertion when he stated that the school began to see good results when they realized that parents could teach by supporting learners at home (Myende & Nhlumayo, 2020). The principal's version also emphasizes that parents are trained to deal with their children at school and home. Thus, in the above excerpt, 'authentic relationship' as defined by Hurley (2011) is evident where parents form part of the leadership team and are empowered with the necessary skills to perform their duties. According to Venter (2016), there should be an open collaboration with those who deliver an educational service at school and within the home environment, especially parents. Considering the principal's response, parents were taught about inclusivity and the tools they needed to help the learners with schoolwork at home. The latter is also an affirmation of authentic relationships, where the schools' leadership values teamwork and empowerment. The results of the study at hand are synonymous with the results of a study conducted by Adams et al. (2018, p. 67), which shows that teacher-parent collaboration provides the pathway to the achievement of inclusive classrooms; however, an education system consisting of inclusive classrooms remains the final step in an educational journey. The benefits to learners in this parent-teacher collaboration are invaluable because it can produce quality teaching and learning.

Discussion

The success of inclusive education is intertwined with collaborative leadership by school managers and implications for teaching and learning within the school. Collaborative leadership directly influences student learning growth (Hallinger & Heck, 2011). The earlier excerpt shows how collaboration between school administrators, teachers, and parents resulted in high-quality teaching and learning for learners. Learners' academic performance improved because of teacher and parent collaboration in education. Hence, collaborative leadership within inclusive schools could be regarded as an engine of change, student learning, and sustainable school improvement.

Collaborative leadership could be a norm to enhance team collaboration in teaching and learning to benefit all learners. Thus, Sterret et al. (2018) indicated that more collaborative initiatives in educational institutions are being implemented. As implied in the findings of this study, leading people in a manner that allows members to take part in decision-making indicates the need for school managers to share the power with all stakeholders in the organization. Thus, when members of the school management team actively collaborate amongst themselves and with the parents and learners, all stakeholders feel that they belong to the institution and are respected when their ideas are valued and implemented in the Administration and governance of the school. The latter statement promotes hard work, commitment, and dedication, producing high performance within the school. Such a situation is conducive to inclusive education and allows learners to learn better and be taught better (Paju et al., 2021).

Moreover, teamwork, exchange of experiences, school partnership, and developing positive relationships between all educational actors are vital in creating an inclusive learning environment from which learning can freely grow (Margaritoiu, 2010). When school leaders use collaborative leadership in their management approach and structure, the decision-making process in schools allows all members of staff, learners, parents, and other related stakeholders to share their vision and agree on ways to carry out the agreed-upon direction, policies, and procedures (Telford, 2003; Ricci et al., 2020). The School Governing Body (SGB) is an essential parents' committee tasked with school governance in this collaboration. Hence, commitment to whole school activities is ensured. In this commitment, all school members are passionate about achieving the entire school, and members contribute to the institution's common goals. The latter statement is also evident in literature by Chrislip and Larson (1994), whose research has been frequently used and applied by collaborative leaders. Their findings revealed that collaborative leaders were decidedly visionary. Still, this vision focused on how people could work together constructively rather than about a particular idea or solution for a specific issue. (Miller & Miller, 2007). It is worth noting that through collaboration, the following can be achieved: new ideas, improved learning, and teaching strategies, and monitoring learners' academic progress (Hansen et al., 2020; Posey et al., 2020; Paju et al., 2021).

Finally, learners get assistance in acquiring skills and academic knowledge at school and home. The study focused on the craft-knowledge of the school managers and identifying the good behavior that promotes inclusive education and ensures high academic achievement of all learners. Collaboration in leadership and parental participation in school activities that promoted their children's effective learning are two important aspects of this study. Hence, the findings confirm that collaborative leadership and parental involvement are intertwined with inclusive education. The latter has profound implications for teaching and learning within the school. In this case, teaching could occur; in a manner that promotes quality learning. Teachers will have more profound content knowledge and be highly motivated to teach well. Learning will be informed by quality teaching and promoted by parental participation and partnership in educating their children. Hence, there will be a strong link between the school and the home environment.

Conclusion

Most research has described rural schools (Hlalele, 2012; Akala, 2020; Myende & Nhlumayo, 2020). In these environments, teaching and learning have faced many challenges, such as infrastructure issues and access to technology (Namirembe, 2017; Saruchera & Makasi, 2017). The findings in this study revealed an essential aspect in rural education that could lead to overcoming several challenges. Collaboration between school leadership and parents and learners within the school has been highlighted to achieve better education for rural school learners. School managers within these schools demonstrated an openness to working together with other stakeholders in the school. It is also evident that parents play a crucial role in education. The latter affirmed the existence of authentic relationships between all stakeholders. However, there were some methodological limitations about the selection of the participating schools. Initially, authors intended to have four schools where the principal and one head of department should participate in the study. The total in this case were eight participants. In the process two schools rejected the invitation. The authors had to work with two schools. In this case we increased the number of HoD participants from one to two per school, which gave use the total of six participants.

Furthermore, findings revealed the significance of teamwork and commitment by all members to the overall development of the school. Participants expressed their willingness to share power and empower stakeholders to contribute to teaching and learning for the benefit of all learners. The argument presented in this project states that the key to a successful implementation of inclusive education is collaborative leadership, which recognizes that all learners can learn and achieve learning objectives at different rates. (Lyons & Arthur-Kelly, 2014). Finally, the collaborative role of rural school administrators in promoting inclusive education and the high academic performance of learners is essential in an environment marked by scarcity of resources and high poverty levels. The discussion and findings in this study reveal an authentic relationship between school managers and parents. Thus, the authors recommend further research in these areas with a special focus on rural schools that are led by principals and heads of departments from other ethnic groups such as Afrikaans population and other Asian groups. Such studies will provide adequate data to compare results from these different environmental settings within the South African context.

References

Adams, D., Harris, A., & Jones, M. S. (2018). Teacher-parent collaboration for an inclusive classroom: Success for every child. *MOJES: Malaysian Online Journal of Educational Sciences, 4*(3), 58–72.

Ainscow, M., & Sandill, A. (2010). Developing inclusive education systems: The role of organizational cultures and leadership. *International Journal of Inclusive Education, 14*(4), 401–416.

Akala, B. (2020). Gender, rurality, and education: A critical perspective on Kenya's education system. In A. P. Ndofirepi & A. Masinire (Eds.), *Rurality, social justice and education in sub-Saharan Africa* (Vol. I, pp. 193–216). Springer.

Anastasiou, D., & Kauffman, J. M. (2013). *The social model of disability: Dichotomy between impairment and disability.* Paper presented at The Journal of Medicine and Philosophy: A forum for bioethics and philosophy of medicine.

Ballard, K. (2002). Disability, inclusion, and exclusion: Some insider accounts and interpretations. In *Inclusive Education* (pp. 108–126). Routledge.

Black-Hawkins, K., & Florian, L. (2012). Classroom teachers' craft knowledge of their inclusive practice. *Teachers and Teaching, 18*(5), 567–584.

Broadhurst, K., Ferreira, J., & Berkeley, N. (2021). Collaborative leadership and place-based development. *Local Economy, 36*, 143–163.

Cameli, A., Reiter-Palmon, R., & Ziv, E. (2010). Inclusive leadership and employee involvement in creative tasks in the workplace: The mediating role of psychological safety. *Creativity Research Journal, 22*, 250–260. https://doi.org/10.1080/10400419.2010.504654

Cashman, K. (2017). *Leadership from the inside out becoming a leader for life* (3rd ed.). Berrett-Koehler Publishers.

Chrislip, D., & Larson, C. (1994). *Collaborative leadership*. Jossey-Bass.

Christenson, S. L. (2002). *Supporting home-school collaboration*. University of Minnesota: Children, Youth and Family Consortium.

Clarke, V., & Braun, V. (2014). Thematic analysis. In T. Teo (Ed.), *Encyclopedia of critical psychology* (pp. 1947–1952). Springer.

Creswell, J. W., & Poth, C. N. (2016). *Qualitative inquiry and research design: Choosing among five approaches*. Sage publications.

Dalton, C. (2021). Outside-in and inside-out. In C. Dalton (Ed.), *The integrated leader: A foundation for lifelong management learning* (pp. 1–9). Henley Business School.

de Vos, A. S., Strydom, H., Fouche, G. B., & Delport, C. S. L. (Eds.). (2014). *Research at grassroots for the social sciences and human service professions*. Van Schaik.

Forlin, C. (2010). Developing and implementing quality inclusive education in Hong Kong: Implications for teacher education. *Journal of Research in Special Educational Needs, 10*, 177–184.

Gcelu, N. (2019). The effectiveness of stakeholder collaboration in preventing learner pregnancy in secondary schools in the eastern cape, South Africa: Implications for leadership. *South African Journal of Education, 39*(3), 1–8.

Geare, A., Edgar, F., & McAndrew, I. (2009). Workplace values and beliefs: An empirical study of ideology, high commitment management, and unionization. *The International Journal of Human Resource Management, 20*(5), 1146–1171.

Govender, S., & Jacobs, M. K. (2020). Evaluation of the implementation of education E hite paper 6 in selected full-service schools in KwaZulu-Natal. *e-Bangi, 17*(3), 111–128.

Gudjonsdottir, H., & Óskarsdóttir, E. (2016). *Inclusive education, pedagogy, and practice* (pp. 7–22). Routledge.

Hallinger, P., & Heck, R. H. (2011). Collaborative leadership and school improvement: Understanding the impact on school capacity and student learning. In T. Townsend & J. MacBeath (Eds.), *International handbook of leadership for learning* (pp. 469–485). Springer.

Hamidun, R., Awang, M. M., Ahmad, A. R., & Ahmad, A. (2019). *Parent involvement in children learning to academic excellence.* Paper presented at The 2nd international conference on sustainable development and multi-ethnic society.

Hansen, J. H., Carrington, S., Jensen, C. R., Molbæk, M., & Secher Schmidt, M. C. (2020). The collaborative practice of inclusion and exclusion. *Nordic Journal of Studies in Educational Policy, 6*(1), 47–57.

Heyder, A., Südkamp, A., & Steinmayr, R. (2020). How are teachers' attitudes toward inclusion related to the social-emotional school experiences of learners with and without special educational needs? *Learning and Individual Differences, 77,* 101776.

Hlalele, D. (2012). Social justice and rural education in South Africa. *Perspectives in Education, 30*(1), 111–118.

Hlalele, D. (2014). Rural education in South Africa: Concepts and practices. *Mediterranean Journal of Social Sciences, 5*(4), 462–462.

Hurley, T. J. (2011). *Collaborative Leadership: Engaging collective intelligence to achieve results across organizational boundaries.* https://www.oxfordleadership.com/wp-content/uploads/2017/07/OL-White-Paper-Collaborative-Leadership.pdf.

Khaleel, N., Alhosani, M., & Duyar, I. (2021). *The role of school principals in promoting inclusive schools: a teachers' perspective.* Paper presented at the frontiers in education.

Klar, H., & Brewer, C. (2014). Successful leadership in a rural, high-poverty school. The case of line middle school. *Journal of Educational Administration, 52*(4), 422–445.

Kwatubana, S., & Makhalemele, T. (2015). Parental involvement in the process of implementation of the national school nutrition programme in public schools. *International Journal of Educational Sciences, 9*(3), 315–323.

Lambert, M. (2019). *Practical research methods in education: An early researcher's critical guide.* Routledge.

Lambrecht, J., Lenkeit, J., Hartmann, A., Ehlert, A., Knigge, M., & Spörer, N. (2020). The effect of school leadership on implementing inclusive education: How transformational and instructional leadership practices affect individualized education planning. *International Journal of Inclusive Education,* 1–15.

Lyons, G., & Arthur-Kelly, M. (2014). UNESCO inclusion policy and the education of school learners with profound intellectual and multiple disabilities: Where to now? *Creative Education, 2014.*

Mapiet, J. A. (2016). *Investigating the role of school management teams in implementing inclusive education at schools in the Mangaung metropolitan, municipal area in the Free State.* (Ph.D. Doctoral Thesis), Central University of Technology, Free State, Bloemfontein.

Margaritoiu, A. (2010). The partnership in inclusive school – Truth and challenges. *Educational Science Series, 62*(2), 115–119.

Matias, C. E. (2021). *The handbook of critical theoretical research methods in education.* Routledge.

Meda, L., & Makura, A. H. (2017). *Technology-driven curriculum for 21st century higher education learners in Africa.* Langaa RPCIG.

Miller, W. R., & Miller, J. P. (2007). *Leadership styles for success in collaborative work.* Paper presented at the Annual Conference of the Association of Leadership Educators.

Myende, P. E., & Nhlumayo, B. S. (2020). Enhancing parent-teacher collaboration in rural schools: Parents' voices and implications for schools. *International Journal of Leadership in Education, 25*, 490–514.

Namirembe, B. (2017). Teaching pre-service teachers to integrate technology for inclusive classrooms with deaf learners in Tanzania. In A. H. Makura (Ed.), *Technology driven curriculum for 21st century higher education learners in Africa* (p. 127). Langaa Rpcig.

Paju, B., Kajamaa, A., Pirttimaa, R., & Kontu, E. (2021). Collaboration for inclusive practices: Teaching staff perspectives from Finland. *Scandinavian Journal of Educational Research, 1–14.* https://doi.org/10.1080/00313831.2020.1869087

Pashiardis, P., Savvudes, V., Lytra, E., & Angelibou, K. (2011). Successful school leadership in rural contexts: The case of Cyprus. *Educational Management, Administration and leadership, 39*(5), 536–553.

Pitikoe, S., & Makhasane, S. D. (2021). The possibility of including herders in Lesotho's education provision through the use of information and communication technologies. In Z. L. Sosibo & E. Ivala (Eds.), *Creating effective teaching and learning spaces: Shaping futures and envisioning unity in diversity and transformation* (p. 147). Vernon Press.

Posey, K., McGrath, K., & Tobon, G. (2020). Collaboration. In D. M. Maggin & M. T. Hughes (Eds.), *Developing teacher leaders in special education* (pp. 117–131). Routledge, Routledge.

Reindal, S. M. (2008). A social-relational model of disability: A theoretical framework for special needs education? *European Journal of Special Needs Education, 23*(2), 135–146.

Ricci, L. A., Benis Scheier-Dolberg, S., & Perkins, B. K. (2020). Transforming triads for inclusion: Understanding frames of reference of special educators, general educators, and administrators engaging in collaboration for inclusion of all learners. *International Journal of Inclusive Education, 26.* https://doi.org/10.1080/13603116.2019.1699609

Roberson, Q., & Perry, J. L. (2021). Inclusive leadership in thought and action: A thematic analysis. *Group & Organization Management.* https://doi.org/10.1177/10596011211013161

Roberts, P., & Green, B. (2013). Researching rural places: On social justice and rural education. *Qualitative Inquiry, 19*(10), 765–774.

Ryan, J. (2007). Inclusive leadership: A review. *Journal of Educational Administration and Foundations, 18*(1–2), 92–125.

Saruchera, F., & Makasi, A. (2017). Prior access to modern learning technologies as a predictor of post-admission cognitive dissonance in African universities: Evidence from Namibia and Zimbabwe. In A. H. Makura (Ed.), *Technology driven curriculum for 21st century higher education learners in Africa* (p. 27). Langaa Rpcig.

Schuelka, M. J., Sherab, K., & Nidup, T. Y. (2019). Gross national happiness, British values, and non-cognitive skills: The role and perspective of teachers in Bhutan and England. *Educational Review, 71*(6), 748–766.

Setia, S., Leng, P., Mauliate, Y. E., Ekowati, D., & Ratmawati, D. (2021). The principal leadership in developing inclusive education for diverse learners. *International Journal of Emerging Issues in Early Childhood Education, 3*(1), 08–24.

Sherab, K., Dorji, K., Dukpa, D., Lhamo, K., Thapa, R., & Tshomo, S. (2015). Opportunities and challenges of implementing inclusive education in Bhutanese schools: A case study. *Retrieved from ResearchGate.* https://www.researchgate.net/publication/303661279_Title_Opportunities_and_Challenges_of_Implementing_Inclusive_Education_in_Bhutanese_Schools_A_Case_Study.

Shogren, K. A., McCart, A. B., Lyon, K. J., & Sailor, W. S. (2015). All means all: Building knowledge for inclusive schoolwide transformation. *Research and Practice for Persons with Severe Disabilities, 40*(3), 173–191.

Sider, S., Maich, K., Morvan, J., Villella, M., Ling, P., & Repp, C. (2021). Inclusive school leadership: Examining the experiences of Canadian school principals in supporting students with special. *Journal of Research in Special Needs, 21*(3), 233–241.

Sisson, D. C. (2015). *Authentic relationship management to heighten control mutuality in social media.* (Ph.D.), University of Carolina.

Smit, S., Preston, L. D., & Hay, J. (2020). The development of education for learners with diverse learning needs in the south African context: A bio-ecological systems analysis. *African journal of disability, 9*(1), 1–9.

Spratt, J., & Florian, L. (2015). Inclusive pedagogy: From learning to action. Supporting each individual in the context of 'everybody'. *Teaching and Teacher Education, 49*, 89–96.

Sterret, W. L., Parker, M. A., & Mitzner, K. (2018). Maximizing teacher time: The collaborative leadership role of the principal. *Journal of Organizational and Educational Leadership, 3*(2), 1.

Tan, C. Y., Lyu, M., & Peng, B. (2020). Academic benefits from parental involvement are stratified by parental socioeconomic status: A meta-analysis. *Parenting, 20*(4), 241–287.

Telford, H. (2003). *Transforming schools through collaborative leadership*. The Falmer Press.

van Knippenberg, D., & van Ginkel, W. P. (2021). A diversity mindset perspective on inclusive leadership. *Group & Organization Management*. https://doi.org/10.1177/1059601121997229

Venter, B. J. (2016). *The perceptions of stakeholders regarding the disciplinary system in a South African school*. MEd Thesis. The University of Free State.

Wachs, J. E. (2005). Building the occupational health team: Keys to successful interdisciplinary collaboration. *AAOHN Journal, 53*(4), 166–171.

Whitburn, B., & Plows, V. (2017). Making sense of everyday practice: By whom, for whom, for what? In V. Plows & B. Whitburn (Eds.), *Inclusive education: Making sense of everyday practice* (pp. 3–11). Sense Publishers.

Patrick Mweli is a lecturer at the University of Free State in the School of Education, specializing in Educational Psychology, and the highest qualification is a PhD (Educational Psychology). My research interest is Inclusive management, indigenous knowledge systems, decolonization in education and collaborative activities within inclusive education.

Ntombizandile Gcelu, started her academic career as a primary school teacher and later pursued her PhD in Walter Sisulu University and worked first as part-time lecturer and then a Post-Doctoral Researcher Fellow in the same institution. She is currently a Senior lecturer in the University of the Free State, in the School of Education Studies. Her research focuses on Management Education Leadership, Law and Policy, collaboration, and collaborative initiatives for sustainable leadership in rural schools and communities in deprived contexts. She is lecturing both undergraduate and postgraduate students with a teaching philosophy grounded on collaboration and ubuntu as a teaching approach. Her research methodologies are not limited to one methodology but include new methodologies. She is one of the three co-conveners of World Education Research Association (WERA) International Research Network (IRN) in Africa and a member International Mentoring Association. She has supervised and graduated both master's and PhD students.

Chapter 14
Teaching in a Global Pandemic: Experiences of Five Educators Supporting Students with Disabilities in Inclusive Classrooms in the United States

Adam Moore, Abigail Higgins, Carly Doulette, Kayla Hoff, and Simoneil Sarbh

Abstract The global coronavirus disease 2019 (COVID-19) pandemic has had an unprecedented impact on the learning of children around the world. This chapter explores five educators' experiences teaching and observing students with disabilities included in general education classrooms in the United States during the pandemic. Qualitative analyses revealed three salient components to championing inclusive practices during the pandemic: (a) focusing on social emotional wellbeing; (b) ensuring academic access; and (c) fostering family/caregiver partnerships. Practical examples and resources to guide educators in providing inclusive and equitable pedagogies during the pandemic are included.

Keywords COVID-19 · Inclusion · USA · Students with disabilities

Introduction

In the last 100 years, educators have never been faced with such an extraordinary event than that of the coronavirus disease 2019 (COVID-19) pandemic (i.e. Kaden, 2020; World Bank, 2020). Across the world devastating impacts on the economy (i.e. McKibbin & Fernando, 2020) and healthcare systems (i.e. Borges do Nascimento et al., 2020; Pokhrel & Chhetri, 2021) were felt. Educators in preK-12 settings were forced to adapt to teaching online at a moment's notice (Diliberti

---

A. Moore (✉) · A. Higgins · C. Doulette
Roger Williams University, Bristol, RI, USA
e-mail: amoore@rwu.edu

K. Hoff · S. Sarbh
Dr. William W. Henderson K-12 Inclusion School, Boston, MA, USA

© The Author(s), under exclusive license to Springer Nature Switzerland AG 2022
L. Meda, J. Chitiyo (eds.), *Inclusive Pedagogical Practices Amidst a Global Pandemic*, Inclusive Learning and Educational Equity 7,
https://doi.org/10.1007/978-3-031-10642-2_14

et al., 2021; Diliberti & Kaufman, 2021; Marshall et al., 2020; Peterson et al., 2020). From supporting students to have the materials necessary for distance learning to comforting frightened families, educators were asked to reinvent and adapt what they do and how they do it. Globally close to 2 billion people had their education interrupted as a result of the pandemic (United Nations, 2020).

Literature Review

In the United States (U.S.) alone, nearly a million people have perished from COVID-19 pandemic as of March 2022 (Johns Hopkins University, 2022). Parents, grandparents, siblings, and friends of preK-12 youth have died. These sobering facts, along with the additional trauma facing students who live in poverty; lack access to sufficient healthcare (Berube & Bateman, 2020), housing, and internet access (Stelitano et al., 2020); and face food insecurity (Enriquez & Goldstein, 2020; Hines et al., 2021)-COVID-19 has impacted essentially every student across the United States (i.e. Bansak & Starr, 2021; Kuhfeld & Tarasawa, 2020). Bailey et al. (2021) surveyed leading education researchers across the U.S. who forecasted a significant achievement gap between low- and high-income students in the United States as a result of COVID-19 learning disruptions.

Students of color and students living in poverty were adversely and disproportionately affected in the United States during the pandemic (Bauer et al., 2020; McKinney de Royston et al., 2020; Pokhrel & Chhetri, 2021; Samuels, 2020; United Nations, 2020). Mahajan and Larkins-Pettigew (2020) conducted a county-wide analysis of COVID-19 population and mortality rates by race in the United States. They found that that while only 22% of counties in the U.S. are predominantly Black, 58% of these counties account for COVID-19 diagnoses and 58% of deaths in the U.S. Other studies have found disproportionate mortality rates for Hispanic or Latino, non-Hispanic Black, and non-Hispanic American Indian or Alaskan Native people in the United States when controlled for age (i.e. Price-Haywood et al., 2020; Running Bear et al., 2021; Wadhera et al., 2020).

People with disabilities, like BIPOC (Black, Indigenous, and People of Color) communities, are expected to be adversely affected by the pandemic (den Houting, 2020; Pellicano & Stears, 2020; U.S. Department of Education, World Health Organization, 2020). Under U.S. federal legislation with the Individuals with Disabilities Education Act (IDEA) (2004), students with disabilities are entitled to a Free and Appropriate Public Education (FAPE), that is delivered in the least restrictive environment (LRE). According to federal legislation, preK-12 students across the United States are entitled to an education that meets their needs while ensuring they are taught in an environment most like that of their non-disabled peers as outlined in their Individual Education Program (IEP). Loss of in-person services (Hirsch & McDaniel, 2021), difficulty navigating virtual learning environments (Marshall et al., 2020; Tokatly Latzer et al., 2021), and the difficulty receiving inclusive supports (Hill, 2020) were all noted by students and families during the first months of the pandemic.

The pandemic created many barriers to ensuring that students with diverse learning needs were provided with the adaptations and services they were entitled to by law (Jameson et al., 2020). How did schools provide interventions to students to support their access to the general education curriculum? In what ways were students with disabilities being included in whole-class lessons? How were lessons differentiated for students during the pandemic?

This chapter will explore how preK-12 educators in the United States adapted to supporting students in remote, online, and hybrid learning environments to provide inclusive support to students with disabilities.

Methods

This project utilized the methodological approach of practitioner inquiry research, whereby educators are actively engaging in their own inquiry approaches to better understand educational problems of practice (Cochran-Smith & Lytle, 2009). While sometimes criticized for lack of generalizability, methodological approach, and following traditional forms of meaning making in research, Cochran-Smith and Lytle (2009) argue that teacher inquiry provides a unique and valuable contribution to gaining "new insights about teaching and learning; new knowledge about teacher inquiry, teachers' learning, and professional growth; and new knowledge about the relationships among teacher inquiry, knowledge, and school reform." The authors of this chapter posit that practitioner inquiry is a viable form of research, particularly conducting ethical and meaningful research during a global pandemic (DeMatthews et al., 2020; Lane et al., 2021).

The five authors narrated their own experiences in their respective roles during the COVID-19 pandemic to describe inclusive practices utilized to support students with disabilities within the United States. The authors used the following as part of their analysis: (1) notes and reflections on teaching since March 2020; (2) personal observations from the field; and (3) literature in both peer-reviewed publications and in educational news outlets. The authors met three times in the spring of 2021 to discuss and document their teaching experiences. Notes were taken as the group discussed their experiences during these meetings and were then organized based on themes. Only experiences that every author encountered were included in the list. A list of initial and thematic codes was developed in an iterative process so that all experiences that were faced by all authors were included in the qualitative analysis. Three salient categories of teaching students with disabilities in inclusive settings during the pandemic emerged from the data: (a) focusing on social-emotional learning; (b) ensuring academic access; (c) and fostering caregiver and family partnerships.

Three of the authors worked in the same classroom during the COVID-19 pandemic and were able to triangulate their experiences. Additionally, the first author

Table 14.1 Author Demographic Information

	Years teaching	Education attainment level	Current role	Teaching approaches used during pandemic
Author 1	17	Doctorate (Ph.D.)	Special Education Teacher Educator (University Professor)	Remote
Author 2	0	Master's Degree (M.A.)	Special Education Teacher Candidate	Remote
Author 3	0	Master's Degree (M.A.)	Special Education Teacher Candidate	In-Person, Remote, Hybrid
Author 4	7	Master's Degree (M.Ed.)	3rd Grade Teacher in Inclusive Co-taught Setting	In-Person, Remote, Hybrid
Author 5	5	Master's Degree (M.Ed.)	Special Education Teacher in Inclusive Co-taught Setting	In-Person, Remote, Hybrid

observed both teacher candidates teaching lessons in the field which provided additional context to reflect on inclusive practices utilized during the pandemic in these classrooms. The types of support the authors provided ranged from: (a) face-to-face instruction (students in a classroom); (b) remote instruction (students working at home via a computer); and (c) hybrid instruction (some students in the physical classroom and some at home on video technology). Table 14.1 provides demographic information about each of the authors.

Results and Discussion

Social-emotional learning, academic access, and family partnerships emerged as salient and imperative factors to successfully include students with disabilities during the pandemic for these educators. The subsequent section explicates each of the emergent categories replete with examples, resources, and strategies the educators utilized for including all learners during the pandemic.

Social-Emotional Learning

The Collaborative for Academic, Social, and Emotional Learning (CASEL), an organization based in the United States which focuses on evidence-based practices in the field, defines social-emotional learning (SEL) as "the process through which all young people and adults acquire and apply the knowledge, skills, and attitudes to develop healthy identities, manage emotions and achieve personal and collective goals, feel and show empathy for others, establish and maintain supportive relationships, and make responsible and caring decisions" (CASEL, 2021). Each of the authors noted social-emotional well-being to be a major component in successfully including all students during the pandemic. Students' social and emotional well-being was one of the biggest concerns of the authors which is consistent with experiences shared in practitioner publications (i.e. Hill, 2020; McKinney de Royston et al., 2020) as well as empirical research published since the global pandemic began (i.e. Duckworth et al., 2021; Mahapatra & Sharma, 2021).

The abrupt end to face-to-face instruction in March of 2020 in most preK-12 settings across the United States (Diliberti & Kaufman, 2021) especially took a toll on the social-emotional well-being of students. As previously noted, hardships were exacerbated for BIPOC and disability communities in the United States. Some schools sent only students with disabilities back to schools in the fall of 2020, so that their services could be provided in person. However, students who received inclusive support in a general education setting according to their IEP were not provided with these services, since their non-disabled peers were often not brought into the school. Each of these situations presented challenges, especially when thinking about how to include all learners. For example, students with disabilities were particularly isolated, as many were forced to learn in settings segregated from their peers without disabilities.

The COVID-19 pandemic forced educators to support students' social-emotional needs holistically, in part due to the emerging knowledge about the distress and trauma that the pandemic has caused for students all across the world (i.e. Collin-Vezina et al., 2020). Whole child education is a teaching philosophy that promotes thinking beyond the traditional academic needs of students (i.e. Taylor et al., 2017). Rather, a whole child approach to teaching pays particular focus on the social, emotional, and physical well-being of a student (Cohn-Vargas, 2020). In order to educate the whole child, it has become imperative that educators account for students' social and emotional well-being when navigating their instructional approach, bearing in mind that communication with students is dependent upon the age of the student (Dalton et al., 2021). Below are strategies the authors' noted as being successful pedagogies used in supporting the social-emotional needs of students.

Setting aside time to explicitly teach social-emotional strategies was vital to promote an inclusive classroom during COVID-19 pandemic. One practical way to teach students about how to identify and manage their emotions is through using the Zones of Regulation framework (Kuypers & Garcia Winner, 2011). This curriculum and approach focus on teaching students to become metacognitive of their feelings, responses, and internal dialogue. One approach that was effective when students were remote learning was through whole group instruction followed by small group meetings of students to practice the skills that were introduced in the whole-class instruction. One educator taught her students about the Zones of Regulation and practiced using different tools via breakout rooms on the video conferencing platform, Zoom. Students had access to a Bitmoji classroom, a cartoon avatar-based application, that focused on the Zones of Regulation and gave them strategies to practice recognizing when they were in a specific "zone." Students were able to access the Bitmoji classroom at any time and use a tool to get themselves back in the "green" zone, the emotional state that is ideal for learning. Students also benefited from being allowed to turn off their cameras and mute themselves as a way to regulate their emotions.

Exposure to self-monitoring strategies and providing opportunities to unpack various social scenarios was instrumental throughout the COVID-19 pandemic (Collin-Vezina et al., 2020). For example, the authors noted that students were provided with an opportunity to interact with their peers in virtual breakout rooms to support socialization through online learning. Though online learning presented a host of challenges (i.e. Mahapatra & Sharma, 2021), one unanticipated positive consequence on supporting the social emotional needs of some students by promoting self-regulation and self-monitoring coping strategies. For instance, students learned that turning off their camera for a brief moment to take a break was an effective de-escalation strategy. Encouraging students to know when to turn on their camera and microphones encouraged self-awareness, as well as self-regulation strategies. Engagement platforms such as Remind were utilized to involve families when a student was particularly overwhelmed; this was key to bridging the home-school landscape.

In addition to the challenges that students faced with being isolated from their peers and educators, many students were unable to take part in enriching experiences, such as end of the year field trips. Virtual field trips allowed students to experience visits to the zoo, museums, and historical sites that they would not have been able to otherwise take part in during the lockdown (e.g. Discovery Education, 2021).

Finally, educators also benefited from structured curricula that focused on SEL components. Through programs such as Second Step, students had an opportunity to identify their own emotions, as well as the emotions of those around them. Students engaged in problem solving, decision making, effective communication strategies, and self-regulation in this structured curriculum. For example, students in one school participated in Second Step twice a week, read aloud a book focused on SEL tenets once a week, had social time in a break out room with peers once a week, and shared "highs" of the week, as well as "shout outs" to peers as a group. As one author recalled, "these [daily] 30 minutes were imperative for students' emotional stability, social exposure, and their overall mental health." Table 14.2 provides an overview of resources to help educators with utilizing SEL in their classrooms.

Academic Access

Inclusive classroom settings require an emphasis on access and equity in meeting the needs of all learners. During the COVID-19 pandemic, educators found this to be especially true. Students learning in a variety of settings (remote learning, face-to-face, hybrid) meant that teachers needed to devote more time to plan for a myriad of contexts. The salient ways in which educators kept academic access and equity at the center of their pedagogical approaches are explored below.

Table 14.2 Social-emotional learning (SEL) resources

	Description	Website
The Collaborative for Academic, Social, and Emotional Learning (CASEL)	This organization collates evidence-based strategies, practical applications, and a framework for educators to use in supporting students' SEL.	www.casel.org
The Yale Center for Emotional Intelligence	Yale University's Center for Emotional Intelligence offers research and resources supporting the use of SEL, as well as a newly created online section that focuses on teacher well-being during the global COVID -19 pandemic.	https://www.ycei.org/
Second Step Social-Emotional Learning	The Second Step Social Emotional Learning program is a comprehensive curriculum that is designed to support students through grade 8 with developmentally appropriate activities, games, and media in their SEL.	www.secondstep.org
The Zones of Regulation	The Zones of Regulation offer a framework and curriculum for teaching students how to identify and manage their feelings. A specific area was added to this resource page to think about how to support students during the COVID-19 global pandemic.	www.zonesofregulation.com
Trauma Informed Instruction from Learning for Justice	From Learning for Justice, a Southern Poverty Law Center sponsored organization, this resource provides ideas, tips, and research linked to how educators can adopt trauma informed teaching.	https://www.learningforjustice.org/magazine/a-trauma-informed-approach-to-teaching-through-coronavirus
UNICEF Kid Power	UNICEF, an international organization, has created a platform of free videos that educators and families can use for movement breaks as well as teach students social-emotional learning concepts like resilience, while also benefiting children in poverty around the world.	www.unicefkidpower.org

Technology played a big part in providing access for students. In the United States there were a range of ways in which school districts tried to ensure students had access to computers and reliable internet access. While this issue existed before the global pandemic, in March 2020 access to technology became paramount. Perhaps one of the most daunting obstacles that educators had to address was ensuring equitable access to the resources needed for online learning. Particularly in March of 2020 when much of the world went into a "lockdown," educators were tasked with scrambling to find technology, access to the internet, and materials needed to continue learning (Dilberti & Kaufman, 2021). Once the materials that students needed for remote learning were acquired, the next question began to look at whether students on the margins were being provided with an equitable access to learning.

Prior to March 2020, assistive technologies were used within the classroom to provide youth with exceptionalities with an access point to the curriculum. But, the use of technology became an essential pathway for students to access their education during the COVID-19 pandemic (i.e. Romig & Alves, 2021). Many schools utilized Google Classroom to organize classes by topic, streamline assignments, and provide frequent feedback to students. Google Classroom also allowed teachers to make announcements on a class stream, post virtual assignments, and deliver feedback –all helpful in an inclusive online classroom. Assignments could be assigned to a whole class, to a group of students, or to individuals. This feature allowed for educators to easily differentiate assignments. Educators additionally had the ability to monitor student work in real-time. This allowed educators to efficiently identify students who were struggling and design targeted interventions.

Educators also had to think about how to engage students in responding to questions during distance learning. Barbetta and Morales (2021) suggest several low-tech strategies including choral responses, guided note taking, and response cards. Each of these ideas require the student to be an active part of the instruction happening during instruction, and can be modified to support a range of learners. Romig and Alves (2020) offer tech-based ideas on student responses when teaching via video conferencing software (i.e. Zoom, Microsoft Teams, Google Meets). They suggest the use of polling, a random name generator to call on students in an equitable manner, and use of reaction tools in video conferencing software for students to respond to teacher questions.

Online games were also used by educators as engaging ways for students to practice various academic skills and were used as a formative assessment tool. This allowed teachers to design questions to fit the content area and current unit of study in their classrooms. While it can be challenging to differentiate the types of questions (i.e. multiple choice, open response, fill-in-the-blank) and length of time questions are presented, some platforms, like Blooket and Gimkit, allow students to answer questions at their own pace. Students who benefitted from more time to think or have extended time to respond as an accommodation were better supported and included in whole group instruction with these platforms.

For educators who were lucky enough to work in co-taught classrooms with two educators, the approach for meeting all students' needs looked different during the pandemic. Some educators opted to have one professional teach students who were participating in distance learning, while the other teacher taught all of the students in the face-to-face classroom. This arrangement could lead to less inclusive settings if students were separated based on disability status. Additionally, related service professionals (i.e. speech and language pathologists, occupational therapists, physical therapists) who, before the pandemic, delivered their services in a general education classroom, might have been forced to provide individual or small group instruction. To address this issue, some professionals included students without disabilities in remote or face-to-face service delivery models. This approach maximized inclusive opportunities during extraordinary circumstances.

Few empirical studies have yet been published on the promising teaching strategies used during the pandemic. However, one study by Young Kim and Fienup

(2021) found that providing a contingency reward intervention for students with disabilities who missed assignments during remote learning instruction significantly increased their engagement in subsequent classwork. As more evidence becomes available, these practices will be crucial for educators to incorporate into their teaching.

Caregiver and Family Partnerships

The third inclusive category identified by the authors was caregiver and family partnerships. Caregiver collaboration is an integral part of an inclusive education (i.e. Flouri, 2006; McLeskey et al., 2017). The pandemic presented many challenges ensuring that caregivers of children with disabilities were included in their child's educational planning and daily communication with educators. Schools around the world adopted policies that limited the number of adults that could be admitted into a building. This unique situation forced many educators who were once reticent of adopting some technology, to fully commit to alternatives of face-to-face meetings.

Use of video platforms to hold meetings with families, as well as providing them more frequent communication were essential (i.e. Tremmel et al., 2020). Similarly, digital engagement platforms such as Remind, Clever, and Seesaw offered educators the ability to communicate with families through instant text-messaging. Likewise, providing families with visuals of what was happening in school through use of photos, slide shows, and short video clips were effective ways to ensure that caregivers and families were included.

Remote learning created various barriers for some of this country's most vulnerable students (Hill, 2020). In order to ensure equitable access, students with complex special needs in some districts were the first students to re-enter the building. These students included children with moderate and severe disabilities, students in foster care and families with multiple children video conferencing from the same home. Many of these students were not able to successfully learn from home. Teachers had to think creatively about ways to support these students during school closures. While some teachers dropped off materials to the homes of students who required manipulatives, other teachers met with students outside in parks and settings where social distancing could be practiced. Ensuring equitable access also required the distribution of appropriate technology. Schools supported families by dropping off computers, iPads, headphones, and wireless hotspots. Caregivers relied on district and school leaders to provide the technological support they needed to access remote learning. Many video conferencing programs included closed captions and visual support to assist caregivers with language barriers.

Finally, keeping consistent communication with caregivers and engaging them in remote learning was vital to the success of the most vulnerable students. Many teachers found success in using video recording platforms like Screencastify, FlipGrid, and SnagIt to record how-to videos and give support to families at home. Other schools held "Family Nights" on Zoom to give caregivers the opportunity to problem-solve together. Likewise, IEP meetings were held via video conferencing to support students with disabilities in meeting their benchmark goals and ensure the entire IEP team was working together.

What Will Schools Look Like After COVID-19?

Much talk has been centered around students' learning loss due to the global pandemic (i.e. Kuhfeld et al., 2020; Kuhfeld & Tarasawa, 2020). Some researchers have referenced other crises, such as natural disasters, that impacted the education of students. In 2005, Hurricane Katrina struck New Orleans, Louisiana, U.S.A., devastating the city and closing schools for months on end. The approach for how students were supported centered around remediation, such as holding students back from progressing to the next grade level due to learning loss. Instead, an approach that provides students access points to grade level the curriculum, through differentiation and designing instruction to support all learners is preferred by these authors. One framework for educators to utilize in the coming years is Universal Design for Learning (UDL), which asks educators to consider multiple means of engaging learners, representing instructional materials, and assessing competencies (Meyer et al., 2014). The Universal Design for Learning framework urges educators to consider how they can design their assignments, instruction, and activities to promote flexibility, learner autonomy, and transferability to other contexts. Rao et al. (2021) urge educators to consider UDL support through use of digital tools when teaching students in online environments. Similarly, Fritzgerald (2020) offers professionals strategies to implement antiracist pedagogies within a UDL framework (see Table 14.3 for more information about these recommended resources).

Will educators have to become skilled at addressing standards that are below their grade level to meet the needs of their students? How will schools determine which students need additional support? Will students be penalized and retained for not meeting grade level standards? Will schools adopt a more inclusive and equitable approach such as Universal Design for Learning following the end of the pandemic? These questions will be essential for all educators to consider in the years to come.

Conclusion

After over a year of strife, educators must pause and reflect on the lessons learned. As of the fall of 2021, there is much uncertainty about the global COVID-19 pandemic. While close to 55% of people older than 12 years of age in the U.S. are fully vaccinated as of October 2021, some individual communities in the U.S. have a much lower rate of vaccination (John Hopkins, 2021). Additionally, the variants that continue to circulate, along with some scientists' beliefs that climate change played

Table 14.3 Additional resources for supporting inclusive & UDL practices

	Description	Access
ARTICLE: Digital Tools and UDL-Based Instructional Strategies to Support Students with Disabilities Online (2021)	Rao, Torres, and Smith (2021) provide explicit ideas for utilizing UDL in online teaching.	Rao, K., Torres, C., & Smith, S. J. (2021). Digital tools and UDL-based instructional strategies to support students with disabilities online. Journal of Special Education Technology, 36(2), 105–112. doi: 10.1177/0162643421998327
BOOK: Antiracism and Universal Design for Learning: Building Expressways to Success (2020)	Andratesha Fritzgerald (2020) offers concrete and practical suggestions for becoming an antiracist educator who centers UDL in their pedagogical approach.	http://castpublishing.org/books-media/antiracism-universal-design-learning/
BOOK: The Blind Advantage: How Going Blind Made Me a Stronger Principal and How Including Children with Disabilities Made Our School Better for Everyone (2011)	Former Principal, Dr. Bill Henderson (2011), describes his journey losing his vision and leading a school that adopted a fully inclusive philosophy.	http://hepg.org/hep-home/books/the-blind-advantage_145
BOOK: What Really Works with Universal Design for Learning (2019)	Drs. Wendy Murawski and Kathy Lynn Scott (2019), editors of an 18-chapter text, provide novel and creative ways for educators to consider a UDL approach.	https://us.corwin.com/en-us/nam/what-really-works-with-universal-design-for-learning/book261998

a role in the current pandemic (i.e. Beyer et al., 2021) and could increase future infectious virus disease spread in the coming decades (i.e. Keesing et al., 2010; Thoradeniya & Jayasinghe, 2021), there is much to consider.

Educators across the globe will certainly be tasked with facing additional crises that will impact how students of all abilities are included and provided an equitable education (Grissom & Condon, 2021). In this study, centering social-emotional learning, ensuring all students had access to academic information, and finding innovative ways to connect with families were central to including students with disabilities. How will we continue to keep inclusive pedagogies central to our praxis? As practitioners and researchers, we have a responsibility to continue to learn from and investigate the experiences that educators, students, and families are facing during these trying times. Our proposed strategies offer insight into how educators can ensure all students are successfully included even during a global health crisis.

References

Bailey, D. H., Duncan, G. J., Murnane, R. J., & Yeung, N. A. (2021). Achievement gaps in the wake of COVID-19. *Educational Researcher, 50*(5), 266–275. https://doi.org/10.3102/0013189X211011237

Bansak, C., & Starr, M. (2021). Covid-19 shocks to education supply: How 200,000 U.S. households dealt with the sudden shift to distance learning. *Review of Economics of the Household, 19*, 63–90. https://doi.org/10.1007/s11150-020-09540-9

Barbetta, P. M., & Morales, M. (2021). Three low-tech active student responding strategies for inclusive online teaching. *Teaching Exceptional Children, 1–8.* https://doi.org/10.1177/00400599211025553

Bauer, L., Pitts, A., Ruffini, K., & Schanzenbach, D. W. (2020). *The effect of pandemic EBT on measures of food hardship.* Brookings Institution.

Berube, A., & Bateman, N. (2020). Who are the workers already impacted by the Covid-19 recession? *Report for Brookings.* Retrieved from https://www.brookings.edu/research/who-are-the-workers-already-impacted-by-the-covid-19-recession/

Beyer, R. M., Manica, A., & Mora, C. (2021). Shifts in global bat diversity suggest a possible role of climate change in the emergence of SARS-coV-1 and SARAS-CoV-2. *Science of the Total Environment, 767*(1), 145413. https://doi.org/10.1016/j.scitotenv.2021.145413

Borges do Nascimento, I. J., Cacic, N., Abdulazeem, H. M., von Groote, T. C., Jayarajah, U., Weerasekara, I., Esfahani, M. A., et al. (2020). Novel coronavirus infection (COVID-19) in humans: A scoping review and meta-analysis. *Journal of Clinical Medicine, 9*(4), 941. https://doi.org/10.3390/jcm9040941

Cochran-Smith, M., & Lytle, S. L. (2009). *Inquiry as stance: Practitioner research for the next generation.* Teachers College Press.

Cohn-Vargas, B. (2020, December 9). What educators are learning during the pandemic. *Edutopia.* Retrieved from https://www.edutopia.org/article/what-educators-are-learning-during-pandemic

Collaborative for Academic, Social, and Emotional Learning. (2021). *SEL is…* Author. https://casel.org/what-is-sel/

Collin-Vezin, D., Brend, D., & Beeman, I. (2020). When it counts the most: Trauma-informed care and the COVID-19 global pandemic. *Developmental Child Welfare, 2*(3), 172–179. https://doi.org/10.1177/2516103220942530

Dalton, L., Rapa, E., & Stein, A. (2021). Protecting the psychological health of children through effective communication about COVID-19. *The Lancet Child & Adolescent Health, 4*(5), 346–347. https://doi.org/10.1016/S2352-4642(20)30097-3

DeMatthews, D., Knight, D., Reyes, P., Benedict, A., & Callahan, R. (2020). From the field: Education research during a pandemic. *Educational Researcher, 49*(6), 398–402. https://doi.org/10.3102/0013189X20938761

den Houting, J. (2020). Stepping out of isolation: Autistic people and COVID-19. *Autism in Adulthood.* Advance online publication. doi:https://doi.org/10.1089/aut.2020.29012.jdh

Diliberti, M., & Kaufman, J. H. (2021). *Will this school year be another casualty of the pandemic? Key findings from the American educator panels fall 2020 COVID-19 surveys.* RAND Corporation, RR-A168-4, 2020. https://www.rand.org/pubs/research_reports/RRA168-4.html

Diliberti, M. K., Schwartz, H. L., & Grant, D. (2021). Stress topped the reasons why public school teachers quit, even before COVID-19. *RAND Corporation, 1–38.* https://doi.org/10.7249/RRA1121-2

Discovery Education. (2021). *Virtual field trips.* https://www.discoveryeducation.com/community/virtual-field-trips/

Duckworth, A. L., Kautz, T., Defnet, A., Satlof-Bedrick, E., Talamas, S., Lira, B., & Steinberg, L. (2021). Students attending school remotely suffer socially, emotionally, and academically. *Educational Researcher, 1–4.* https://doi.org/10.3102/0013189X211031551

Enriquez, D., & Goldstein, A. (2020). COVID-19's socioeconomic impact on low-income benefit recipients: Early evidence from tracking surveys. *Socius: Sociological Research for a Dynamic World, 6*, 1–17. https://doi.org/10.1177/2378023120970794

Flouri, E. (2006). Parental interest in children's education, children's self-esteem, locus of control and later educational attainment: Twenty-six year follow-up of the 1970 British birth cohort. *British Journal of Educational Psychology, 76*, 41–55.

Fritzgerald, A. (2020). *Antiracism and universal design for learning: Building expressways to success*. CAST Professional Publishing.

Grissom, J. A., & Condon, L. (2021). Leading schools and districts in times of crisis. *Educational Researcher, 50*(5), 315–324. https://doi.org/10.3102/0013189X211023112

Hill, F. (2020.) The Pandemic is a Crisis for Students with Special Needs. *The Atlantic*. Retrieved from https://www.theatlantic.com/education/archive/2020/04/specialeducation-goes-remote-covid-19-pandemic/610231/.

Hines, C. T., Markowitz, A. J., & Johnson, A. D. (2021). Food insecurity: What are its effects, why, and what can policy do about it? *Policy Insights form the Behavioral and Brain Sciences, 1–9*. https://doi.org/10.1177/23727322211032250

Hirsch, S. E., & McDaniel, S. C. (2021). Remote instruction and interventions: Considerations for students with disabilities. *Intervention in School and Clinic, 1–3*. https://doi.org/10.1177/10534512211001828

Individuals with Disabilities Education Improvement Act. (2004). PL 108-446, 20 U.S.C. § 1400.

Jameson, J. M., Stegenga, S. M., Ryan, J., & Green, A. (2020). Free appropriate public education in the time of COVID-19. *Rural Special Education Quarterly, 39*(4), 181–192. https://doi.org/10.1177/8756870520959659

Johns Hopkins University. (2022). *Coronavirus research center*. Retrieved from https://coronavirus.jhu.edu

Kaden, U. (2020). COVID-19 School closure-related changes to the professional life of a K–12 teacher. *Education Sciences, 10*(6), 165. https://doi.org/10.3390/educsci10060165

Keesing, F., Belden, L., Daszak, P., et al. (2010). Impacts of biodiversity on the emergence and transmission of infectious diseases. *Nature, 468*, 647–652. https://doi.org/10.1038/nature09575

Kuhfeld, M., & Tarasawa, B. (2020). The COVID-19 slide: What summer learning loss can tell us about the potential impact of school closures on student academic achievement. *NWEA*.

Kuhfeld, M., Soland, J., Tarasawa, B., Johnson, A., Ruzek, E., & Liu, J. (2020). Projecting the potential impact of COVID-19 school closures on academic achievement. *Educational Researcher, 49*(8), 549–565. https://doi.org/10.3102/0013189X20965918

Kuypers, L. M., & Winner, M. G. (2011). *The zones of regulation: A curriculum designed to foster self-regulation and emotional control*. Think Social Publishing, Inc.

Lane, K. L., Cabell, S. Q., & Drew, S. V. (2021). A productive scholar's guide to respectful, responsible inquiry during the COVID-19 pandemic: Moving forward. *Journal of Learning Disabilities, 1–12*. https://doi.org/10.1177/00222194211023186

Mahajan, U. V., & Larkins-Pettigrew, M. (2020). Racial demographics and COVID-19 confirmed cases and deaths: A correlational analysis of 2886 US counties. *Journal of Public Health, 42*, 445–447. https://doi.org/10.1093/pubmed/fdaa070

Mahapatra, A., & Sharma, P. (2021). Education in times of COVID-19 pandemic Academic stress and its psychosocial impact on children and adolescents in India. *International Journal of Social Psychiatry, 67*(4), 397–399. https://doi.org/10.1177/0020764020961801

Marshall, D. T., Shannon, D. M., & Love, S. M. (2020). How teachers experienced the COVID-19 transition to remote instruction. *Kappan, 102*(3), 46–50.

McKibbin, W., & Fernando, R. (2020). The economic impact of COVID-19. *Economics in the time of COVID-19*, CEPR Press.

McKinney de Royston, M., Lee, C., Nasir, N. S., & Pea, R. (2020). What is a good school: rethinking school, rethinking learning. *Kappan, 102*(3), 8–13.

McLeskey, J., Barringer, M.-D., Billingsley, B., et al. (2017). *High-leverage practices in special education*. Council for Exceptional Children and CEEDAR Center.

Meyer, A., Rose, D. H., & Gordon, D. T. (2014). *Universal design for learning: Theory and practice*. CAST Professional Publishing.

Pellicano, E., & Stears, M. (2020). The hidden inequities of COVID-19. *Autism, 24*(6), 1309–1310. https://doi.org/10.1177/1362361320927590

Peterson, L., Scharber, C., Thuesen, A., & Baskin, K. (2020). A rapid response to COVID-19: One district's pivot from technology integration to distance learning. *Information and Learning Science, 121*(5/6), 461–469. https://doi.org/10.1108/ILS-04-2020-0131

Pokhrel, S., & Chhetri, R. (2021). A literature review on impact of COVID-19 pandemic on teaching and learning. *Higher Education for the Future, 8*(1), 133–141. https://doi.org/10.1177/2347631120983481

Price-Haywood, E. G., Burton, J., Fort, D., & Seoane, L. (2020). Hospitalization and mortality among black patients and white patients with COVID-19. *New England Journal of Medicine*. https://doi.org/10.1056/NEJMsa2011686

Rao, K., Torres, C., & Smith, S. J. (2021). Digital tools and UDL-based instructional strategies to support students with disabilities online. *Journal of Special Education Technology, 36*(2), 105–112. https://doi.org/10.1177/0162643421998327

Romig, J. E., & Alves, K. D. (2021). Implementing individual opportunities to respond in online teaching environments. *Journal of Special Education Technology, 36*(2), 84–89. https://doi.org/10.1177/01626434211004120

Running Bear, C., Terrill, W. P. A., Frates, A., Peterson, P., & Ulrich, J. (2021). Challenges for rural Native American students with disabilities during COVID-19. *Rural Special Education Quarterly, 40*(2), 60–69. https://doi.org/10.1177/8756870520982294

Samuels, C. (2020, September 16). Fighting for fairness amid a pandemic. *Education Week*. https://www.edweek.org/ew/articles/2020/09/17/fighting-for-fairness-amid-a-pandemic.html

Stelitano, L., Doan S., Woo, A., Diliberti, M.K., Kaufman, J. H., & Henry, D. (2020). *The digital divide and COVID-19: Teachers' perceptions of inequities in students' internet access and participation in remote learning*. RAND Corporation. https://www.rand.org/pubs/research_reports/RRA134-3.html

Taylor, R. D., Oberle, E., Durlak, J. A., & Weissberg, R. P. (2017). Promoting positive youth development through school-based social and emotional learning interventions: A meta-analysis of follow-up effects. *Child Development, 88*(4), 1156–1171.

Thoradeniya, T., & Jayasinghe, S. (2021). COVID-19 and future pandemics: A global systems approach and relevance to SDGs. *Global Health, 17*, 59. https://doi.org/10.1186/s12992-021-00711-6

Tokatly Latzer, I., Leitner, Y., & Karnieli-Miller, O. (2021). Core experiences for parents of children with autism during the COVID-19 pandemic lockdown. *Autism, 25*(40), 1047–1059. https://doi.org/10.1177/1362361320984317

Tremmel, P., Myers, R., Brunow, D. A., & Hott, B. L. (2020). Educating students with disabilities during the COVID-19 pandemic: Lessons learned from commerce independent school district. *Rural Special Education Quarterly, 39*(4), 201–210.

U.S. Department of Education, Individuals With Disabilities Education Act. (2020). *Urging states to continue educating students with disabilities, secretary Devos publishes new resource on accessibility and distance learning options*. Retrieved from https://sites.ed.gov/idea/new-resource-accessibility-distancelearning-options-students-with-disabilities/

United Nations. (2020). *Policy brief: Education during COVID-19 and beyond*. United Nations. https://www.un.org/development/desa/dspd/wp-content/uploads/sites/22/2020/08/sg_policy_brief_covid-19_and_education_august_2020.pdf

Wadhera, R. K., Wadhera, P., Gaba, P., et al. (2020). Variation in COVID-19 hospitalizations and deaths across New York City boroughs. *Journal of the American Medical Association, 323*(21), 2192–2195. https://doi.org/10.1001/jama.2020.7197

World Bank. (2020). *The COVID-19 pandemic: Shocks to education and policy responses*. World Bank Group. https://openknowledge.worldbank.org/bitstream/handle/10986/33696/148198.pdf?sequence=4&isAllowed=y

World Health Organization. (2020). *Disability considerations during the COVID-19 outbreak*. https://www.who.int/docs/default-source/documents/disability/covid-19-disability-briefing.pdf

Young Kim, J., & Fienup, D. M. (2021). Increasing access to online learning for students with disabilities during the COVID-19 pandemic. *The Journal of Special Education, 1-9*. https://doi.org/10.1177/0022466921998067

Dr. Adam Moore is an Associate Professor of Special Education and Director of Special Education Graduate Programs at Roger Williams University in Bristol, Rhode Island, USA. A former National Board-certified Exceptional Needs Specialist in the Boston Public Schools, he earned his Ph.D. in Education from the joint doctoral program at the University of Rhode Island and Rhode Island College in 2013. He has 21 peer-reviewed publications, over 75 national or invited presentations, and over $125,000 in funding. Dr. Moore is involved in the Council for Exceptional Children (CEC) at the state and national level, serving on the CEC's Teacher Education Division Small Special Education Programs Caucus Executive Board. Dr. Moore's research in special education teacher preparation focuses on family-centered and inclusive practices, advocating for individuals with disabilities, and teaching for social justice.

Abigail Higgins is a graduate from the Special Education Graduate Program at Roger Williams University in Bristol, Rhode Island, USA. Throughout her experiences at Roger Williams University, Abigail has co-founded campus-wide organizations aimed at education and student activism. Abigail has additionally identified her future professional aspirations, which include becoming an ally, advocate, and educator of people with disabilities within inclusive classroom settings. Through her experiences within the field, Abigail has had several opportunities to engage with school communities that are dedicated to fostering inclusive educational experiences for all students. She has continued these experiences within her graduate residency in which she had an opportunity to engage virtually with an Inclusion School located within the Boston Public School District in Boston, Massachusetts. In addition to her desire to be within the field, Abigail has consistently engaged in service work focusing on supporting people with disabilities, activism for gender equity, addressing campus sexual assault and violence, and prompting gun violence awareness within educational settings.

Carly Doulette inclusive education experience began while she was earning her B.A. in Elementary Education from Roger Williams University. She completed her student residency at an inclusive school in Providence, RI. In these co-taught classrooms, the educators worked together to meet the needs of each and every student. The following year, while completing her M.A. in Special Education, she taught general education math as a member of the middle school multidisciplinary team at the aforementioned school. This experience opened her eyes to special education and began her passion for inclusive practices. Carly Doulette now serves as a special education inclusion teacher, in a co-taught math classroom, on the same multidisciplinary team. She looks forward to creating a classroom environment that supports the learning and development of every student.

Kayla Hoff As a longtime attendee and graduate of the Massachusetts Public School System, it's no surprise that **Kayla Hoff**, decided to teach at an inclusion school within the City of Boston. She understands the importance of providing all students with an equitable and accessible education. While studying at University of Massachusetts Amherst, Kayla focused on communication and education while student teaching in the area. Following her undergrad, Kayla moved to Boston where she received her Master's in Education while joining the, Teach Next Year program through University of Massachusetts Boston. Kayla has been at her current school since 2014 and recently switched roles from Special Education Teacher to General Education Teacher. In 2014, she was trained and certified through Wilson Reading Program, which has allowed her to use this multi-sensory reading approach to support students with reading disabilities. Kayla began her role as the Elementary Math Facilitator where she leads data meetings and professional development opportunities while supporting teachers use of a variety of blended learning tools. In 2018, Kayla received the Fund for Teachers Grant and traveled to Kenya to learn alongside other teachers from an inclusion school in Nairobi.

Simoneil Sarbh is a Special Education teacher at an Dr. William W. Henderson K-12 Inclusion School in Boston Massachusetts, U.S.A. She grew up in India where she experienced an Indian elementary education and then moved to an American School in India where she had a different educational experience. The contrasting styles of education got Simoneil interested in improving the overall educational system. At college at Wesleyan University she focused on developmental psychology and sociology of education where she explored the inequality of education and strived to close the gap. After college she worked at a nonprofit after school program where she shadowed Special Education teachers and found her calling. She then proceeded to get her Masters of Education with a focus in Special Education from Simmons College. She has taught in self-contained classrooms with students with reading disabilities and currently teaches in an inclusion classroom.

Chapter 15
Educators Coming Together to Empower Learners, Families, and Teachers in Developing Culturally Responsive/Sustaining Postsecondary Transition Plans During COVID-19

Rebekka J. Jez, Keitha Osborne, and Clara Hauth

Abstract Students around the globe benefit from the community coming together to support them in developing into adulthood. Educators have a legal and ethical responsibility to provide a well-rounded education that guides learners as they move through school. The earlier they start this process the better. Since the onset of the COVID-19 global pandemic many students, families, and teachers have encountered unexpected challenges to their education, health, and mental health. The current study attempted to assess teachers' knowledge and perspectives around culturally responsive/sustaining postsecondary transition and then train them using remote pedagogical practices. This multinational study recruited 21 primary and secondary teachers from Jamaica and the United States to participate in a Presurvey, workshop, and Postsurvey to explore how educators could empower learners and their families in developing culturally responsive/sustaining postsecondary transition plans. Three outcomes of this work indicated that students, families, and educators were able to build community relationships; teachers learned about more culturally responsive/sustaining transition practices, strategies, and resources; and learners were given the opportunity to explore self-awareness, self-determination skills, and healing skills.

R. J. Jez (✉)
University of San Diego, San Diego, CA, USA
e-mail: rjez@sandiego.edu

K. Osborne
The Mico University College, Kingston, Jamaica

C. Hauth
Marymount University, Arlington, VA, USA

Keywords Culturally responsive/sustaining postsecondary transition · Global pandemic · Family engagement · Teacher professional development · Self-determination

Introduction

A major factor exacerbating the already challenging life transition between secondary school and adulthood in both Jamaica and the US is the COVID-19 global pandemic. In June–July 2020, the United Nations International Children's Emergency Fund (UNICEF) and the Caribbean Policy Research Institute (CAPRI) examined the impact of COVID-19 on school age children. After the school doors were closed and learning moved online, Jamaicans reported a lack of access to online classes and devices, nutritional concerns, health concerns (ex. being asthmatic), and a deep awareness of the major economic downturn across the country. Similarly, in the US, citizens reported a myriad of challenges such as anxiety and stress, loss of access to mental health and medical supports, lack of access to and/or familiarity with technology, caregiver job loss, housing insecurities, fear for the health and safety of themselves and others, and a heightened risk of sexual and identity harassment and abuse (Barnum & Bryan, 2020; Lazzell et al., 2020; Office of Civil Rights, 2021). Herburger et al. (2020) highlighted six barriers related to the disruption in schooling: (1) evaluating student focus and engagement, (2) addressing social emotional needs, (3) managing student workload, (4) supporting students' processing and retention, (5) assisting with technology, and (6) facilitating family engagement. Researchers in both countries recommended using trauma-informed practices, referred to as healing skills, with students, families, and teachers (Crosby et al., 2020; UNESCO, 2021).

Furthermore, although inclusive education promotes quality of life for students of all ages around the globe, many educators are not equipped with the skills, time, and resources needed to support learners through life transitions in ways that value the cultural, ethnic, and linguistic diversity (CELD) of students and their families. Additionally, many governmental policies, which were created to support learners' transition into adulthood, are not always enacted as they are written. There are legal and ethical benefits for students and families when teachers use culturally responsive/sustaining transition practices to prepare students for adulthood (Jez, 2014; Suk et al., 2020) and collaborate with stakeholders to meet students' goals for life after secondary school (Kohler et al., 2016). Students and families also benefit when teachers intentionally include them throughout a child's educational transitions (Achola & Greene, 2016).

According to the United Nations Educational, Scientific, and Cultural Organization's (UNESCO) Caribbean Symposium on Inclusive Education and Jamaican Disabilities Act (2020), Jamaica advocates for a system where all children are permitted to learn together (UNESCO, 2007) and mandates that persons with dis/abilities are treated with equity. Although the Disabilities Act (2020) gives persons with dis/abilities the right to postsecondary education/training and employment (Ministry of Education, 2015), fewer than 1% of people identified as having a disability were employed in 2001 (World Bank, 2016). At this time, the Jamaican parliament has not ratified the draft Special Education Policy that will ensure persons with dis/abilities have "equity and access to educational opportunities," although the document was submitted to the cabinet in 2018, the country is still awaiting approval (Ministry of Education, Youth, and Information, 2018a, b, para. 4). Furthermore, the Jamaican government has been developing initiatives to support children with dis/abilities such as training and hiring of qualified special education teachers for every school and the launch of the Alternative Pathway to Secondary Education (APSE) program. APSE allows for educational support for struggling students from specialized educational coaches (Ministry of Education, Youth, & Information, 2018a, b).

In the United States (US), inclusive education is outlined in two major educational policies: Individuals with Disabilities Education Improvement Act (IDEIA, 2004) and Every Student Succeeds Act (2015). IDEIA (2004) provides funding for additional educational services for Transitional Kindergarten to 21 year old students who have been identified as having a disability, ensuring that they have access to "free appropriate public education…designed to meet their unique needs and prepare them for further education, employment, and independent living" (para. 1). Subsequently, the Every Student Succeeds Act (ESSA, 2015) established clear provisions that educators are to support students' success in college and career readiness. Yet only 18% of persons with dis/abilities were employed in 2020, which was much lower than the 62% of people without dis/abilities (US Bureau of Labor Statistics, 2021). Even with governmental policies, people with dis/abilities in both Jamaica and the US experience lower rates of postsecondary education and employment when compared to their non-dis/abled peers (US Bureau of Labor Statistics, 2021; Gayle-Geddes, 2016).

Beyond the legal mandates concerning students' success, educators have ethical responsibilities to consider as well. Suk et al. (2020) suggested that CELD students and families benefit when transition planning is done with cultural competence in mind. The current researchers furthered this idea by developing a culturally responsive/sustaining transition workshop and planning tool for teachers to address transition with students and families from CELD backgrounds during the COVID-19 pandemic and throughout their career. Culturally responsive/sustaining transition is based on cultural proficiency work, which asks teachers to begin with an examination of their personal assumptions and then commit to learning practices that not only serve, but promote, the educational needs and success of students from all cultural groups (Center for Culturally Proficient Education Practice, 2018; Gorski, 2016; Lindsey et al., 2018). Equipped with this knowledge, educators can use components of Gay's (2013) culturally responsive teaching to improve educational outcomes by framing learning through students' culture and prior experiences; connecting with learners, families, and community; and integrating assets-based instructional materials and techniques that empower learners while also allowing students to critically examine inequities within their own experience. However, educators cannot stop here. Culturally responsive/sustaining transition calls for schools to recognize that cultural and language identities continue to evolve; therefore, they need to be accountable to the community with continuous teacher professional development (e.g., to learn about transition practices/resources and opportunities to examine implicit biases) and providing resources and supports to students and families that reflect values based on collective communities rather than autonomous, Eurocentric values (Paris, 2012). Educators' practices need to empower and sustain (rather than dismantle) multilingualism and multiculturalism to ensure access and opportunity for CELD students and families, especially those who historically have been negatively affected by the dominant societal power structures (Paris & Alim, 2014).

Culturally responsive/sustaining transition tasks educators to uncover biases and intentionally implement responsive teaching practices that will result in positive social transformation and addressing transition goals of their students and families. Transition research (Kohler et al., 2016) has identified five effective practices when implementing transition-focused education called the Taxonomy of Transition 2.0. These practices include: (1) student-focused planning, (2) student development (3) family engagement, (4) program structures, and (5) interagency collaboration. Although these research-based practices for supporting CELD youth and families during transition have been shared, Gothberg et al. (2018) found teachers needed training on cultural competence, support in implementing transition practices, and access to resources.

Background

Prior to the pandemic, educators were asking for training on transition practices and ways to connect with their students and families in both Jamaica and the US (Hull et al., 2020; Trainor, 2017). Even when educators are equipped with the predictors of post-school success that clearly outline steps schools could take to increase graduation numbers, school climate, and transition services, such as those found in the Taxonomy of Transition 2.0, many teachers report they have not received training in these areas (Jez, 2014; Kohler et al., 2016; Morningstar et al., 2016; National Technical Assistance Center on Transition, NTACT, 2019). To address this lack of training since the pandemic moved instruction to remote platforms, local and global educational organizations began to promote the use of effective inclusive practices (Herburger et al., 2020; Schleicher, 2020; UNESCO, 2021). For example, the Collaboration for Effective Educator Development, Accountability, and Reform (CEEDAR) and Center and the Council for Exceptional Children (CEC) urged educators to integrate high leverage practices (HLP) to increase accessibility, engagement, and students' learning during remote learning (CEEDAR, 2020; Herburger et al., 2020; McClesky et al., 2017).

Reimers and Schleicher (2020) echoed the call for building capacity and creating a space for innovation and accessibility for learners and families that focuses on real-life experiences using a variety of modalities. Schleicher (2020) found an increase in the types of platforms used for learning, such as television, radio, the internet, tutors, and self-paced formalized lessons. While Daniel (2020) described the importance of increasing the partnership between schools and families, Reich et al. (2020) warned educators to closely examine equity issues when working with families that are dealing with technological or socioeconomic challenges. They recommended providing non-digital alternatives. Consequently, educators were tasked with finding ways to empower their students, families, and communities by leveraging more intentional engagement between the school and students and families (Borup et al., 2020). Because many culturally, linguistically, and socioeconomically diverse families report frustration with their postsecondary transition experience, training and supporting teachers in culturally sustaining inclusive practices during transition benefit all stakeholders (Achola & Greene, 2016; Jez, 2014; Jez & Luneta, 2018; Kohler et al., 2016).

The current study attempted to bridge research-based transition practices with the lessons learned about remote teaching to connect teachers with their students and families to plan for adulthood in a culturally responsive/sustaining manner. The Culturally Responsive/Sustaining Student Transition Portfolio (CRSTP) is a research-based template that teachers can use when doing transition planning with elementary and secondary learners (Jez, 2014). The CRSTP uses student-centered and family-centered transition strategies (Achola & Greene, 2016; Bui & Turnbull, 2003; Division for Career Development and Transition, DCDT, 2019), recommendations from the Taxonomy of Transition 2.0 (Kohler et al., 2016), and tenets of culturally responsive and sustaining pedagogy (Gay, 2013; Paris & Alim, 2017). This research-based tool was chosen for this study because the template is user friendly and can be easily adapted to meet the context of the community (Jez, 2014). Also, the prompts provide a starting point for teachers to begin conversations with students and families about multiple areas of postsecondary success that confront the Eurocentric values often found in postsecondary transition tools (e.g. encouraging the traditional 4-year college pathway). Additionally, student and family voices are validated and empowered through the process, which speaks to the importance of honoring familial values during the transition process (Jez, in press). As demonstrated by the negative postsecondary statistics reported over the last 30 years, many students and communities have been hurt by the current school systems (Harvey et al., 2020; Lipscomb et al., 2017). Culturally sustaining pedagogy aims to foster and sustain cultural knowledge and experience from communities who have been historically marginalized (Suk et al., 2020; Trainor, 2017). The CRSTP does this by engaging the student and family in transition planning; creating an environment where students are provided with skills and resources necessary for postsecondary success (ex. self-determination/self-advocacy skills); facilitates cultural competence to empower linguistic, literate, and cultural pluralism; and assists learners in developing sociopolitical and critical consciousness to ensure societal change as they move into adulthood (Creighton Thompson & Hauth, 2015; Jez, 2014; Paris & Alim, 2017). The CRSTP template allows teachers the unique opportunity to adapt postsecondary transition tools and resources based on individual and community context.

The purpose of the study was to increase educators' knowledge and skills of culturally responsive/sustaining transition practices. This was done by first assessing teachers' knowledge and perspective of student transition supports. Based on the results of the assessment, a teacher training workshop was designed with culturally responsive/sustaining postsecondary transition planning tools and resources educators could use when working with learners and families remotely during the global pandemic of 2021. Finally, the researchers assessed changes to teachers' knowledge, perspectives, and skills around transition practices.

Methods

Two White, female American teacher education faculty members from two universities in the United States and one Black, female Jamaican teacher education faculty member from a university college in Jamaica collaborated on this multinational research study. All of the researchers have been working in the education field for over 20 years, both locally and globally. The researchers were interested in learning more about how teachers across the globe could apply the knowledge and skills necessary to support students and families in preparing for postsecondary transition during the global pandemic. They began by surveying participants about what they knew about transition, what they were currently doing with students, and asked them to identify transition areas they felt would benefit their students. An asynchronous professional development video and materials were curated based on their responses (Appendix). Additionally, teachers were encouraged to adapt the materials presented in the workshop for their context using the multimodal resources and shared experiences.

Research Approach

A mixed methods approach (Creswell, 2014) was used to describe the impact of the online culturally responsive/sustaining transition workshop (Fig. 15.1). The study triangulated data from the Presurvey, Postsurvey, and document analysis. The mixed method approach was chosen so we could expand our understanding of the

Fig. 15.1 Descriptive mixed methods research design to assess the impact of the culturally responsive/sustaining transition workshop

quantitative data, understand any contradictions between the qualitative and quantitative responses, and give voice to the participants' experiences. First, participants shared information about the current transition planning practices, culturally sustaining practices, and impact of COVID-19 on postsecondary planning (Fowler, 2014) in the Educator Transition Planning Presurvey. A professional development workshop was developed based on the results of the Presurvey. The workshop included a recorded training video that reviewed transition policies and practices and provided a template that teachers could use with students. The template focused on three areas the participants identified in the Presurvey: (1) Students' strengths, preferences, interests, and needs; (2) Self-determination: self-advocacy and decision making; and (3) Healing strategies. Participants were asked to choose a learner between the ages of 5–22, adapt the CRSTP template using the resources presented in the workshop, and reflect on the experience in the Educator Transition Postsurvey.

Research Design

To address challenges due to the global pandemic the descriptive research design relied heavily on online technologies to complete a mixed method research design to learn more about the impact of a transition workshop using a presurvey and postsurvey (Creswell, 2014). An email was sent out to recruit educators from both countries. In Jamaica, educators were also sent the materials using WhatsApp to address challenges with internet access and devices. The study employed a presurvey, workshop (intervention), and a follow-up survey. The 10-min surveys (pre and Post) were intentionally developed online and participants were given the option of uploading the completed CRSTP to ensure convenience of access, anonymity of their students, and safety during the global pandemic (no personal contact). The workshop was recorded so that educators could watch the video at a time convenient for them and when they had access to the internet. The topics of the intervention workshop provided participants with information about transition mandates, supports, and resources available (CRSTP) to the teachers. Finally, because past research identified teachers' lack of training regarding transition and resources, the CRSTP was developed to provide a template that educators could use remotely, with students and families using evidence-based transition practices. The researchers realized that not all educators may have access to the online resources, so the CRSTP template was provided in multiple formats (Google slidedeck, PowerPoint, one-page handout, and four-page activity sheet) within the training documents.

Context of the Study Since the onset of COVID-19 and the subsequent move to remote teaching and learning across the globe, educators have searched for ways to engage learners and families while preparing students with the skills necessary to be successful in life. Although Jamaica and the United States have different policies and procedures around inclusive education, students with dis/abilities often experience negative postsecondary outcomes in both countries. The researchers focused on examining educators' experiences with CELD students with dis/abilities because these groups have been historically marginalized during the postsecondary transition phase, and in turn, have more significant challenges after secondary school. Also, many educators are working with more diverse populations, however, they often lack the training and support in effective strategies. The collaborative study attempted to capture similarities between educators' experiences with postsecondary training, resources, and supports. The study provided the educators with evidence-based transition practices to support learners with transitional planning for ages 5–22, the ages outlined for eligibility under IDEIA (2004). These resources, tools, and strategies are applicable for children with or without dis/abilities and can be adapted for a multitude of settings.

Participants Forty general and special educators (20 from Jamaica and 20 from the US) were recruited for this study. A convenience sample of 20 participants from each country was used: five primary special education teachers, five primary general education teachers, five secondary special education teachers, and five secondary general education teachers (Johnson & Christensen, 2017). Twenty-one educators responded to the pre survey; eleven from the US and ten from Jamaica. The educators identified as either primary/elementary (n = 13) or secondary/middle or high school teachers (n = 8). They reported teaching in special education (n = 12), general education (n = 7), and dual education (n = 2) classrooms. Although eight had taught for less than 2 years, the majority (n = 13) would be considered veteran teachers because they had taught for over 5 years and up to 30 years. Eighteen identified as female and two identified as male. The Postsurvey yielded a smaller number of responses – ten from Jamaica and four from the US. Nine worked in primary/elementary grades while five worked in a secondary classroom. Respondents (13 female and one male) reported they assisted students in receiving education in special education (n = 7), general education (n = 3), and dual (n = 4) classrooms. Three (two American and one Jamaican) teachers had taught for less than 5 years and eleven had taught for over 5 years.

Data Collection After ethics approval from the Institutional Review Board in the United States and Jamaican Ministry of Education Youth and Information: Planning and Development Division, an email solicitation was sent out to 40 educators. Once the participants completed the Educator Transition Planning Presurvey, the workshop entitled Educators Coming Together to Empower Learners, Families, and Teachers in Developing Culturally Sustaining Postsecondary Transition Planning During COVID-19 was developed based on the results of the survey. Educators were asked to watch the prerecorded video training workshop and then adapt the CRSTP to meet the needs of their community context and individual learners' needs. The CRSTP version developed for this workshop focused on students' self-awareness, self-determination skills, and skills around healing. After viewing the recorded training video, educators were asked to implement the CRSTP with a student between the ages of 5–22. They selected resources from the workshop and adapted CRSTP prompts based on the individual, family, and community needs. Finally, participants were asked to complete the Educator Transition Postsurvey.

Instruments An overview of the instruments and the workshop are described below. Appendix lists the resources presented in the workshop.

Educator Transition Planning Presurvey. The pre survey included five demographic questions (questions about number of years taught and gender were open-ended to allow educators flexibility with their response), nine Likert-type items, one rank order, and seven open-ended questions to ask about the current transition planning practices, culturally sustaining practices, and impact of COVID-19 on postsecondary planning in Jamaica and the US. Examples of questions asked included: "How have you assessed your students' transition goals for their future (ex. educational, employment, and independent living) since the onset of the global pandemic?" "Select the TOP FOUR topics you believe are most important for your learners to develop in order to be successful adults." and "To what extent do you feel prepared to assist your students in meeting their future goals since the onset of the global pandemic?"

Transition workshop. Based on the results of the pre survey, the 38-min video workshop, Educators Coming Together to Empower Learners, Families, and Teachers in Developing Culturally Sustaining Postsecondary Transition Planning During COVID-19, was designed to address the knowledge and challenges identified by educators. Topics included an overview of Jamaican and US educational policies, the need for trauma-informed practices since the onset of the global pandemic, trauma-informed strategies and effective transition practices for families and educators, and a description of the adapted CRSTP template with resources, assessments, tools, and examples to support completing it. Within the video description of the CRSTP template, educators were encouraged to choose resources and modify prompts based on their individual context. For example, they were given a choice of format (online or paper), they could change the wording of the prompts/questions they asked their students, or they could choose which resources they felt would best support their learners.

Educator Transition Postsurvey. Once the participants completed the pre survey, watched the recorded transition workshop, and implemented the CRSTP, they were asked to complete the Postsurvey. The Postsurvey included the same five demographic questions as the pre survey, seven Likert-type items, seven open-ended questions, and the option to upload their adapted CRSTP (without identifying information). The Postsurvey asked educators to share what they have learned, how they will continue to work with families and students, and changes they made to how they support learners using both online and face-to-face support.

Validity and Reliability The current study was completed in June of 2021 using email, video, and online links to documents to ensure all participants received the same information to increase reliability and reduce the influence of external factors. June marked the end of the academic school year in both the United States and Jamaica and many teachers were unable to participate as they were closing down their classrooms for the year. Due to COVID-19, the Institutional Review Board (IRB) process was delayed, which affected the recruitment of teachers and decreased the sample size. Because of the small sample size from the pre survey and Postsurvey, only descriptive statistical analyses (mean, mean difference, variance, standard deviation, and standard deviation difference) were possible; therefore, the claims are not generalizable. The researchers assessed the data for internal consistency by triangulating the data with a comparison of qualitative and quantitative responses and requesting participants share their completed CRSTP. To address reliability challenges within the data, the researchers used interrater reliability when analyzing qualitative responses. All three researchers read and coded responses, when there was discrepancy in coding, the team discussed the response until 100% agreement was met.

Although the external validity was affected by the small sample size, the information gained from the participants is still useful. Internal validity was demonstrated in the thoughtful design of what to measure and how it was measured. The topics within the surveys and CRSTP were intentionally defined and piloted with experts in the field of transition and culturally responsive/sustaining practices along with educators to ensure they addressed their intended content. Demographics were collected with anonymity protected. Participants were able to select from Likert-type responses to identify their knowledge of transition policies, resources, and family involvement and open-ended questions supported their responses. Finally, by including items about remote teaching, educators were able to share about their challenges and successes using online technologies.

Data Analysis The quantitative-qualitative data analysis was completed using Creswell (2014) mixed methods research design to triangulate the descriptive information in order to have a more complete understanding of teachers' experience with transition during the global pandemic. The qualitative and quantitative survey data were analyzed using Google Sheets and the document analysis was used to provide evidence of the themes that emerged from the data analysis (Bowen, 2009). The mean and standard deviations from the Likert-type items on the Educator Transition Planning Presurvey and the Educator Transition Postsurvey were calculated using Google Sheets. Next, the variance was calculated to determine changes from the pre survey to the Postsurvey. The sample size was too small, and the sample sizes were unequal from the pre survey to the Postsurvey to calculate the p-value (the probability that the difference in scores could have occurred by random chance). The qualitative data analysis followed Creswell's (2014) six steps of qualitative data analysis: (1) organized, (2) read and identified trends, (3) created labels (themes), (4) coded for themes (by all three researchers), (5) discussing findings, and (6) interpreting data. Document analysis is an iterative process examining content and themes through reviewing the words and pictures used in the documents (Bowen, 2009). The researchers looked at each CRSTP provided, appraised the work for evidence of transitions information and resources presented in the workshop and within the Postsurvey responses. Next, a synthesis of the data was organized through content analysis. Inter-rater reliability was obtained with 100% consensus through team discussion.

Ethical Considerations Ethics approval was obtained from the Institutional Review Board in the United States and Jamaican Ministry of Education Youth and Information: Planning and Development Division. All participants were given adequate opportunity to ask questions prior to enrolling in the study and they were given a copy of the consent form. No identifying information was included in the data collection tools, and responses were organized by numbers and demographic information. Only members of the research team had access to the data.

Results and Discussion

The results of this study indicate the teachers learned more about inclusive and culturally responsive/sustaining transition practices, strategies, and resources. This section discusses how teachers' responses shifted concerning current transition planning policies and resources, culturally responsive/sustaining transition practices, and impact of COVID-19 on postsecondary planning in Jamaica and the US before and after the workshop. As seen in Table 15.1, the mean and mean difference (MD) for each Likert-type survey item increased between the pre survey and the Postsurvey for each of the areas. The researchers used the variance to determine the average of all the scores and the standard deviation to determine how far the individual responses differed from the mean (smaller standard deviation indicates similarity teachers' responses).

Transition Planning Policies

Educators' knowledge of transition planning policies and student assessment increased after the study as seen in the results of the pre survey to Postsurvey. To establish teachers' knowledge about transition policies, the researchers asked them to rate their familiarity with policies and access to transition resources using a 5-point Likert-type scale (1 = no familiarity and 5 = very familiar). In the pre survey, respondents said their knowledge was below average (33%), average (48%), and above average (19%). In the Postsurvey, familiarity increased as seen by the numbers – below average (7%), average (43%), above average (43%), and far above average (7%). As seen in Table 15.1, teachers' knowledge of transition policies (IDEIA, 2004; ESSA, 2015; Jamaica Disabilities Act, 2020; UNESCO, 2007) did not change much (MD = +0.64) from the pre survey (m = 2.86) to Postsurvey (m = 3.50). This was expected because most of the participants were veteran teachers (having over 5 years in the field).

Table 15.1 Descriptive statistics of the educators' transition planning since COVID-19 presurvey (n = 21) and postsurvey (n = 14)[a]

Likert-type survey item	Mean				SD[b]	
	Pre	Post	MD[c]	Variance	Pre	Post
Familiarity with transition policies	2.86	3.50	+0.64	+0.21	0.73	0.76
Student involvement in the planning process	1.14	2.43	+1.29	+0.83	1.01	0.51
Collaboration with outside agencies	2.37	3.71	+1.34	+0.91	1.12	1.14
Teacher prepared to assist students with transition	2.76	4.14	+1.38	+0.95	1.04	0.77
Engagement of students and families in transition planning	2.71	3.86	+1.15	+0.65	1.15	0.95
Families are prepared to assist their children with transition	1.76	2.07	+0.31	+0.48	0.94	0.73
Schools provide transition information to families	2.86	3.07	+0.21	+0.23	1.15	1.14
Prepared to teach remotely when the pandemic began	2.35	n/a	n/a	n/a	1.27	n/a

[a]Fewer respondents completed the Postsurvey
[b]SD = standard deviation
[c]MD = mean difference

Notably, one area of transition planning that varies across settings is assessment. Teachers were asked how they assess their students' transition goals in the pretest and many teachers (38%) responded that they did not assess learners and the teachers who did report assessing students (29%) used diagnostic assessments from their school or informal observations. After the workshop, more educators (64%) reported assessing their learners using the tools described in the training. For example, they used student assets-inventories on strengths, interests, and needs inventories; using self-determination assessments; evaluating "their emotions and what motivates them" (Appendix). The CRSTP documents that were uploaded by participants demonstrated the teachers were able to apply the knowledge, skills, and materials presented in the workshop. Participants were given virtual transition tools to supplement their workshop training.

Culturally Responsive/Sustaining Transition Practices

Educators reported four major shifts in culturally responsive/sustaining transition practices in this study. First, teachers identified additional skills and access to online resources that assist students in transition planning (Jez, 2014; Suk et al., 2020). Second, educators committed to collaborating more with outside agencies after the workshop (Kohler et al., 2016). Third, an increase in student-centered transition planning was reported (Bui & Turnbull, 2003). Fourth, educators highlighted more engagement with families regarding their child's transitions (Achola & Greene, 2016). Using the pre survey, Postsurvey, and adapted CRSTP document, the researchers worked to understand teachers'use of culturally responsive/sustaining transition practices. The researchers adapted the workshop and CRSTP template based on the pre survey results. Interestingly, the elements of transition the educators requested to learn more about in the workshop were in line with current research in the area of culturally responsive/sustaining transition (Achola & Greene, 2016; DCDT, 2019; Jez, 2014; Kohler et al., 2016; Paris & Alim, 2014: 1) identifying strengths, preferences, interests, and needs (71%); 2) teaching self-determination skills such as self-advocacy and decision-making (74%), and healing skills such as self-awareness, being proactive, perseverance, and emotional coping strategies (57%). The professional development workshop and CRSTP were developed to explicitly address these skills by providing information and resources to the teachers.

When probed about the transition resources teachers had access to at their school in the pre survey, 34% said none, 24% mentioned career or college seminars, 19% mentioned life skills books and programs, 15% said work experience, and 10% identified campus visits. After the workshop and implementation of the CRSTP, all of the teachers were able to identify additional resources they could use during transition planning. For example, half of the teachers said they would use student and family inventories, questionnaires, and worksheets such as self-advocacy sheets, Zarrow Center for Enrichment transition materials, self-determination scale, family interviews, etc. Thirty-six percent of teachers mentioned growth mindset, social emotional learning skills, healing/trauma-informed practices, and culturally responsive/sustaining teaching strategies and practices. They mentioned "teaching and encouraging listening skills to address biases," "teaching mistakes are okay," and integrating "healing skills" into their practice. These moves reflect adherence to policy recommendations for promoting access, equity, and inclusion in society (Jamaican Disabilities Act, 2020), intentionally planning for transition (ESSA, 2015; IDEIA, 2004) and integrating research-based practices during transition (Achola & Greene, 2016; Jez, 2014; Kohler et al., 2016; Hull et al., 2020; Morningstar et al., 2016; NTACT, 2019; Trainor, 2017).

After the workshop, four areas where teachers reported the most change were feeling prepared to assist students with transition since COVID-19 (MD = +1.38), collaborating with outside agencies such as employment services and transition support people (MD = +1.34), including students in the planning process (MD = +1.29), and engaging of families in transition planning (MD = +1.15). Quite a few teachers (38%) admitted that they had not used any transition-focused curriculum or activities since the onset of the global pandemic and moved to remote learning, while others mentioned activities such as career planning (e.g. "researching jobs in the field"), academic strategies (eg. "ASPE curriculum"), and independent living skills (e.g. "teach them about financial matters"). For those who were attempting to assist students in planning for life after secondary school (19%), they said they taught students about problem solving, parenting, decision making, and coping skills. After the workshop, teachers reported feeling more confident about their postsecondary transition skills and were able to provide more detailed examples of developing goals with learners (36%), using social emotional learning skills (36%), and getting to know their students holistically (14%). One teacher plans to "learn student strengths, preferences, interests, and needs inventories to get to [learners] as a whole…and develop lessons for engagement." Another mentioned the need to "develop decision making skills and to build and maintain relationships with others."

Research (Herburger et al., 2020; Kohler et al., 2016; NTACT, 2019) encourages teachers to collaborate with outside agencies. When teachers were asked about the extent to which they have collaborated with outside agencies and community organizations when planning students' transitions while working remotely, majority of the respondents in the pre survey said sometimes (25%), rarely (40%), or never (20%), with only a few reporting very often (10%) or always (5%). In the Postsurvey, teachers' responses indicated a desire to become more collaborative (29% always, 29% very often, 36% sometimes, and 7% never). Educators were excited to share ways they planned to do this in the future, such as, "Set up a structured transition team [including] the parent, child, guidance counselor, and student's vocational [support people]" and to "work with students and families in connecting them to community organizations, businesses, non-profits, to make sure students and families are getting what they need, which is essential in student success."

The theme of involving students really shifted through this study. Prior to the workshop, more than half (52%) of teachers reported their students were not involved in transition planning, 33% said students were somewhat involved, and only 10% said the students were very involved. Whereas after the workshop, all of the teachers planned to follow evidence-based practices by involving their students in planning for life after high school such as co-developing their education plan's goals and participating in the meetings (Achola & Greene, 2016; Bui & Turnbull, 2003; Kohler et al., 2016; NTACT, 2019; Trainor, 2017). The fourth important aspect of culturally responsive/sustaining transition, engaging students and families in the transition planning process, also had an impressive positive shift (mean difference + 1.15). Although 50% of the teachers indicated that families were engaged in assisting their children in meeting their future goals in the pretest, that number rose to 94% in the posttest. Teacher's confidence in their ability to engage families increased after working with them on postsecondary planning. Teachers shared examples of how they included families in transition planning since the pandemic teachers such as discussing the child's choices, attending online meetings, hosting career-focused events, and connecting with specialists. After the workshop, they reported more research based practices like having the family work to assess the student; follow up phone calls, emails, and meetings; providing the families with resources and documentation; and creating a collaborative team of support that includes outside agencies and support persons (Creighton Thompson & Hauth, 2015; Herburger et al., 2020; Jez, 2014; Kohler et al., 2016; Hull et al., 2020; NTACT, 2019; Paris & Alim, 2014; Trainor, 2017).

Impact of COVID-19 on Postsecondary Planning

Similar to the literature found around the globe on the impact of COVID-19 on students, families, and educators (Barnum & Bryan, 2020; CAPRI & UNICEF, 2020; Crosby et al., 2020; Lazzell et al., 2020; Reimers & Schleicher, 2020; Reich et al., 2020; UNESCO, 2021), the teachers reported similar challenges since the onset of the global pandemic such as lack of preparation, technological resources, support, and opportunities for engagement with students and families. In the pre survey, the educators reported they did not feel prepared to teach remotely prior to the pandemic ($M = 2.35$, $SD = 1.27$). Based on the responses from the initial survey about transition activities during remote teaching indicated that although teachers supported the move to online platforms, they did not feel prepared to do so adequately. Since the onset of COVID-19 and the move to remote learning, teachers shared that their primary activities revolved around video lessons (38%) and virtual synchronous meetings (33%), followed by online assessments (14%). Also noted 19% of teachers shared they had not attempted to implement any transition-related activities during remote learning due to the pandemic.

When asked how remote teaching has affected engagement and interaction with families since the onset of the global pandemic, they replied there was a lack of student engagement (38%) and many families were stressed by new technologies (38%). With little to no family engagement, teachers struggled to interact and engage learners (38%). This led to the final question in the survey which asked teachers to share how accessibility to technology (virtual communication, networks, etc.) impact your interactions with students and families. Most teachers shared that accessibility was an issue (67%), over half of the teachers stated that lack of accessibility and funding for technology somewhat or greatly affected interactions with students and families during the pandemic. In the Postsurvey, only one US teacher mentioned her students were more engaged because students have their own computers which were provided by the school.

In the Postsurvey, teachers reported they planned to continue to plan transition with students and families, increase the use of technology, and use the CRSTP template in the future. Respondents wrote they want their "students to be more vocal and express their feelings" and they would "use the CRSTP as an ongoing project for students to create a PowerPoint presentation and present them when complete." Some positives of the move to remote platforms included the increase in family interactions and involvement. One respondent wrote, "There is more interaction with families because families now realize the challenges we the teachers face with their child/children. Therefore, they become more interested in ways they can reach their child/children." On the flipside, teachers also noted some challenges including families that struggle with technology, feeling isolated, students needing to babysit siblings, conflicting schedules, and students needing additional support. A teacher wrote, "It is really difficult to monitor every single child in class, to be certain that everyone is actually on task, and many students are dealing with mental health issues related to remote learning that affect their engagement."

Conclusion

Preparing youth for their future weighs heavy on everyone in society, especially as the world is recovering from the global pandemic. Through this study the researchers aimed to assess teachers' knowledge and perspective of student transition supports, train and support the educators in working remotely during the global pandemic of 2021 with learners and families using culturally responsive/sustaining postsecondary transition planning tools and assess any changes to their knowledge and perspective about transition practices. There are things teachers and families can do with children of all ages in order to support them as they grow. Some hopeful shifts that teachers shared through the course of this study included a desire to involve students, families, and outside agencies in the transition planning process. The increase in collaborative efforts not only provides opportunities for the community to assist learners in developing skills, knowledge, and dispositions that aid in becoming productive members of society, but address the inclusive education laws, mandates, and statutes currently held in both countries. Another area evidenced by this study is the enthusiasm teachers described when integrating the transition resources and materials. Educators prepared students for life's transition by explicitly teaching them to learn about and value their own self-awareness, self-determination skills, and healing skills. In addition to a lack of time and resources, many teachers report a lack of training prevents them from implementing culturally responsive/sustaining teaching practices. By providing training and support materials as educators integrate new information, students and families benefit. Thus, the current study highlighted the need for additional time and support for teachers to engage in collaborative efforts with families and outside agencies.

Another major area explored in this study was the impact of the COVID-19 global pandemic. The move to remote learning and teaching exposed inequities within systems such as access to technology and the impact of traumatic events. Yet, some students, families, and educators were able to identify creative solutions and healing practices to support their communities through these changes. Explicitly working with learners on developing healing skills using SEL lessons could be a hopeful response to a devastating experience. Future teacher education and training should encourage the inclusion of virtual and in-person culturally responsive/sustaining practices with transition services for learners with special needs and their families. Recognizing the potential outcomes for greater collaboration with teachers and families in this endeavor is paramount for our global educational systems. More research could be done to learn about students' experience and outcomes after culturally responsive/sustaining transition practices were integrated into their school experiences.

Appendix

Resources from the CRSTP Video Training

Policies

Jamaica Disabilities Act (2020)
(Drafted) Special Education Policy (2015)
Individuals with Disabilities Education Improvement Act (2004)
Every Student Succeeds Act (2015)

Resources

Trauma-Informed Practices
UNICEF (2020)
Essential Components Effective Transition Programs (Morningstar & Mazzotti, 2014)

Workshop Supports for Teachers

Area# 1 – Students Strengths, Preferences, Interest and Needs Assessments
Elementary Picture Interest https://www.jist.com/content/picture-interest-career-survey-third-edition
Link to Age Appropriate transition assessments https://nextsteps-nh.org/resources/transition-assessment/
https://www.ou.edu/education/centers-and-partnerships/zarrow/self-determination-assessment-tools/air-self-determination-assessment
Self-Determination Assessment https://www.ou.edu/education/centers-and-partnerships/zarrow/self-determination-assessment-tools/air-self-determination-assessment
Zarrow Center for Learning Enrichment https://www.ou.edu/education/centers-and-partnerships/zarrow/transition-education-materials-transition-resources

Area #2: Self-Determination: Self-Advocacy and Decision Making Resources
Self-advocacy sheet https://www.ou.edu/education/centers-and-partnerships/zarrow/transition-education-materials/me-lessons-for-teaching-self-awareness-and-self-advocacy
Accommodations and modifications sheet (from your IEP/504/ISP) https://www.understood.org/articles/en/common-classroom-accommodations-and-modifications
Assistive technology (devices and services)
https://www.understood.org/en/school-learning/assistive-technology/assistive-technologies-basics/assistive-technology-what-it-is-and-how-it-works

https://adayinourshoes.com/self-advocacy-iep-goals
https://www.smartkidswithld.org/getting-help/raising-independent-kids/self-advocacy-strategies-ages/
CEC's DCDT Self-Determination/Self-Advocacy https://higherlogicdownload.s3.amazonaws.com/SPED/34aee1c1-7ded-4d59-af82-da4af08d5fc4/UploadedImages/DCDT_Fast_Facts/Self-Determination_and_Self-Advocacy.pdf

mindfulschools.org
https://www.edutopia.org/take-chance-let-them-dance

Area #3: Healing Strategies Resources
CASEL.ORG
Emotion Chart (to identify and discuss feelings) https://thechalkboardmag.com/the-feelings-circle-chart-emotional-communication
Video: teen's emotional intelligence https://youtu.be/gqAZuOqBXgw
Ohio Emotional IntelligenceActivities https://ong.ohio.gov/frg/FRGresources/emotional_intellegence_13-18.pdf
Self-Determination/Self-Advocacy https://higherlogicdownload.s3.amazonaws.com/SPED/34aee1c1-7ded-4d59-af82-da4af08d5fc4/UploadedImages/DCDT_Fast_Facts/Self-Determination_and_Self-Advocacy.pdf
Mindfulness Resources http://www.heardalliance.org/wp-content/uploads/toolkit/promotion/PAMF_Fliers-_Mindfulness_Resources-_K-8.pdf
Resilience Curriculum Activities https://strongkids.uoregon.edu/strongteens.html
Growth Mindset Resources https://www.edutopia.org/article/growth-mindset-resources
Gratitude https://ggsc.berkeley.edu/images/uploads/GGSC_Gratitude_Curriculum_MS_HS.pdf
Art as Empowerment https://www.youtube.com/watch?v=bPszGBfjuOY
Art therapy https://www.verywellmind.com/what-is-art-therapy-2795755

Implementing CRSTP
CRSTP Google Slidedeck template
https://docs.google.com/presentation/u/1/d/10aUjq6zoTzkEXHF-qG7_IZbVd2yFuwuFraVaBSoMuJw/edit?fromCopy=true
CRSTP PowerPoint template https://drive.google.com/file/d/1DkgX0FXfapt9k0EMCCX1aCESzog_-mMr/view
CRSTP PDF template
https://drive.google.com/file/d/1SEog-hxo4NKnq_4rAnro5UcZ9FH7Bgw_/view?usp=sharing

References

Achola, E., & Greene, G. (2016). Person-family centered transition planning: Improving post-school outcomes to culturally diverse youth and families. *Journal of Vocational Rehabilitation., 45*(2), 173–183. https://doi.org/10.3233/JVR-160821

Barnum, M., & Bryan, C. (2020, July). *America's great remote-learning experiment: What surveys of teachers and parents tell us about how it went*. Retrieved from https://www.eschoolnews.com/2020/07/22/americas-great-remote-learning-experiment-what-surveys-of-teachers-and-parents-tell-us-about-how-it-went/

Borup, J., Jensen, M., Archambault, L., Short, C. R., & Graham, C. R. (2020). Supporting students during: Developing and leveraging academic communities of engagement in a time of crisis. *Journal of Technology and Teacher Education, 28*(2), 161–169.

Bowen, G. A. (2009). Document analysis as a qualitative research method. *Qualitative Research Journal, 9*(2), 27–40.

Bui, Y. N., & Turnbull, A. (2003). East meets west: Analysis of person-centered planning in the context of Asian American values. *Education & Training in Developmental Disabilities, 38*, 18–31.

Center for Culturally Proficient Education Practice. (2018). *Who we are*. Retrieved from https://ccpep.org/home/about-us/who-we-are/

Collaboration for Effective Educator Development, Accountability, and Reform. (2020). *Effective remote instruction pd pack*. Retrieved from https://ceedar.education.ufl.edu/portfolio/effective-remote-instruction/

Council for Exceptional Children's Division of Career Development and Transition Publications Committee (DCDT). (2019). *Fast facts: Culturally responsive transition Practices*. Retrieved from https://dcdt.org/dcdt-fast-fact-sheets

Creighton Thompson, C., & Hauth, C. (2015). *The survival guide for new special education teachers*. Council for Exceptional Children.

Creswell, J. W. (2014). *Research design: Qualitative, quantitative and mixed methods approaches* (4th ed.). Sage.

Crosby, L. M. S. W., Shantel, D., Penny, B., & Thomas, M. A. T. (2020). Teaching through collective trauma in the era of COVID-19: Trauma-informed practices for middle level learners. *Middle Grades Review, 6*(2), 5.

Daniel, S. J. (2020). Education and the COVID-19 pandemic. *Prospects, 49*, 91–96. https://doi.org/10.1007/s11125-020-09464-3

Every Student Succeeds Act, 20 U.S.C. § 6301. (2015). Retrieved from https://www.congress.gov/bill/114th-congress/senate-bill/1177

Fowler, F. J. (2014). *Survey research methods*. SAGE Publications.

Gay, G. (2013). Teaching to and through cultural diversity. *Curriculum Inquiry, 43*(1), 48–70.

Gayle-Geddes, A. (2016). *Disability and inequality: Socioeconomic imperatives and public policy in Jamaica*. Palgrave MacMillian.

Gorski, P. C. (2016). Poverty and the ideological imperative: A call to unhook from deficit and grit ideology and to strive for structural ideology in teacher education. *Journal of Education for Teaching, 42*(4), 378–386.

Gothberg, J. E., Greene, G., & Kohler, P. D. (2018). District implementation of research-based practices for transition planning with culturally and linguistically diverse youth with disabilities and their families. *Career Development and Transition for Exceptional Individuals, 43*(2), 77–86. https://doi.org/10.1177/2165143418762794

Harvey, M. W., Rowe, D. A., Test, D. W., Imperatore, C., Lombardi, A., Conrad, M., … Barnett, K. (2020). Partnering to improve career and technical education for students with disabilities: A position paper of the division on career development and transition. *Career Development and Transition for Exceptional Individuals, 43*(2), 67–77.

Herburger, D., Holdheide, L., & Sacco, D. (2020, September). Removing barriers to effective distance learning by applying the high leverage practices. *Collaboration for effective educator development, accountability, and reform*. Retrieved from https://ceedar.education.ufl.edu/wp-content/uploads/2020/10/CEEDER-Leveraging-508.pdf

Hull, D. M., Powell, M. G., Fagan, M. A., Hobbs, C. M., & Williams, L. O. (2020). Positive youth development: A longitudinal quasi-experiment in Jamaica. *Journal of Applied Developmental Psychology, 67*, 101118.

Individuals with Disabilities Education Improvement Act 20 U.S.C. § 1400. (2004). Retrieved from https://sites.ed.gov/idea/

Jamaica Council for Persons with Disabilities. (2020). *The disabilities act*. Retrieved from https://jcpdja.com/the-disabilities-act

Jez, R. J. (2014). Empowering postsecondary transition planning for culturally and linguistically diverse students with disabilities by giving a voice to the family. In D. Michael & L. Lo (Eds.), *Promising practices to empower culturally and linguistically diverse families of children with disabilities*. Information Age Publishing Inc.

Jez, R. J. (in press). Involving at-promise youth, families, and schools in culturally responsive transition.

Jez, R. J., & Luneta, K. (2018). Effective teacher training on inclusive practices: Using needs and interests to design professional development and follow-up support in South Africa. *Asian Journal of Inclusive Education., 6*(1), 21–47.

Johnson, B. R., & Christensen, L. B. (2017). *Educational research: Quantitative, qualitative, and mixed approaches* (6th ed.). SAGE Publications.

Kohler, P. D., Gothberg, J.E., Fowler, C., & Coyle, J. (2016). *Taxonomy for transition programming 2.0: A model for planning, organizing, and evaluating transition, services, and programs*. Western Michigan University. Retrieved from https://transitionta.org/taxonomy-for-transition-programming-2-0/

Lazzell, D. R., Jackson, R. G., & Skelton, S. M. (2020). *Inequalities in online classrooms: How do we bridge the distance (learning)?*. Equity Digest. Retrieved from https://greatlakesequity.org/sites/default/files/202016092341_equity_digest.pdf

Lindsey, R. B., Nuri-Robins, K., Terrell, R. D., & Lindsey, D. B. (2018). *Cultural proficiency: A manual for school leaders*. Corwin Press.

Lipscomb, S., Hamison, J., Liu Albert, Y., Burghardt, J., Johnson, D. R., & Thurlow, M. (2017). *Preparing for life after high school: The characteristics and experiences of youth in special education. Findings from the National Longitudinal Transition Study 2012. Volume 2: Comparisons across disability groups*. Full Report. NCEE 2017–4018. National Center for Education Evaluation and Regional Assistance.

McLeskey, J., Barringer, M.-D., Billingsley, B., Brownell, M., Jackson, D., Kennedy, M., … Ziegler, D. (2017). *High-leverage practices in special education*. Council for Exceptional Children & CEEDAR Center.

Ministry of Education, Youth and Information. (2015). *Draft special education policies*. Ministry of Education.

Ministry of Education, Youth and Information. (2018a). *Special education policy to be submitted to cabinet*. Retrieved from https://moey.gov.jm/special-education-policy-to-be-submitted-to-cabinet/

Ministry of Education, Youth and Information (2018b). *Multiple education pathways at secondary level*. Ministry of Education. Retrieved from https://moey.gov.jm/multiple-education-pathways-secondary-level.

Morningstar, M. E., & Mazzoti V. (2014). *Teacher preparation to deliver evidence-based Transition planning and services to youth with disabilities*. Retrieved from https://ceedar.education.ufl.edu/innovation-configurations/

Morningstar, M. E., Lee, H., Lattin, D. L., & Murray, A. K. (2016). An evaluation of the technical adequacy of a revised measure of quality indicators of transition. *Career Development and Transition for Exceptional Individuals., 39*(4), 227–236. https://doi.org/10.1177/2165143415589925

National Technical Assistance Center on Transition (NTACT). (2019). *Predictors implementation school/district self-assessment.* Retrieved from https://transitionta.org/wpcontent/uploads/docs/toolkit_ResourceMapping_Predictor_Self-Assessment_2019-04.pdf

Office of Civil Rights. (2021). *Education in a pandemic: The disparate impacts of COVID-19 on America's students.* Retrieved from https://www2.ed.gov/about/offices/list/ocr/docs/20210608-impacts-of-covid19.pdf

Paris, D. (2012). Culturally sustaining pedagogy: A needed change in stance, terminology, and practice. *Educational Researcher, 41*(3), 93–97.

Paris, D., & Alim, H. S. (2014). What are we seeking to sustain through culturally sustaining pedagogy? A loving critique forward. *Harvard Educational Review, 84*(1), 85–100. https://doi.org/10.17763/haer.84.1.982l873k2ht16m77

Paris, D., & Alim, H. S. (Eds.). (2017). *Culturally sustaining pedagogies: Teaching and learning for justice in a changing world.* Teachers College Press.

Reich, J., Buttimer, C. J., Fang, A., Hillaire, G., Hirsch, K., Larke, L. R., ... & Slama, R. (2020). Remote learning guidance from state education agencies during the COVID-19 pandemic: A first look. EdArXiv. doi:https://doi.org/10.35542/osf.io/437e2

Reimers, F., & Schleicher, A. (2020). *Schooling disrupted, schooling rethought. How the COVID-19 Pandemic is Changing Education.* Retrieved from https://globaled.gse.harvard.edu/files/geii/files/education_continuity_v3.pdf

Schleicher, A. (2020). *The impact of COVID-19 on education insights from education at a glance 2020.* Retrieved from https://www.oecd.org/education/the-impact-of-COVID-19-on-education-insights-education-at-a-glance-2020.pdf.

Suk, A. L., Sinclair, T. E., Osmani, K. J., & Williams-Diehm, K. (2020). Transition planning: Keeping cultural competence in mind. *Career Development and Transition for Exceptional Individuals, 43*(2), 122–127.

Trainor, A. A. (2017). *Transition by design: Improving equity and outcomes for adolescents with disabilities.* Teachers College Press.

United Nations Educational, Scientific, and Cultural Organization (UNESCO). (2007). *Inclusive education.* Caribbean Symposium on Inclusive Education. Retrieved from http://www.ibe.unesco.org/sites/default/files/Kingston_IE_Final_Report.pdf

United Nations Educational, Scientific, and Cultural Organization (UNESCO). (2021). *Education transforms lives.* Retrieved from https://en.unesco.org/themes/education.

United Nations International Children's Emergency Fund (UNICEF) and the Caribbean Policy Research Institute (CAPRI). (2020). *The effect of the COVID-19 pandemic on Jamaican children: Preliminary results.* Retrieved from https://www.unicef.org/jamaica/reports/effect-COVID-19-pandemic-jamaican-children-preliminary-results

United States Bureau of Labor Statistics. (2021, February). *Persons with a disability: Labor force characteristics summary.* Retrieved from https://www.bls.gov/news.release/disabl.nr0.htm.

World Bank. (2016). *Acting on disability discrimination in Jamaica.* Retrieved from https://www.worldbank.org/en/news/feature/2016/04/18/acting-on-disability-discrimination-jamaica

Dr. Rebekka J. Jez is an Assistant Professor at University of San Diego's School of Leadership and Education Sciences (SOLES) in the Department of Learning and Teaching where she teaches, researches, and supports educators from around the world in assisting their learners using culturally responsive, sustaining, and healing inclusive practices. Dr. Jez is also the Director of the Academy of Catholic Teaching (ACT) program which supports teachers in Catholic schools. She has worked on contributing to the field of education through scholarship on culturally responsive/sustaining inclusive practices, trauma-informed/healing practices, holistic assessment of learners, postsecondary transition for K-12 learners, and collaboration for learners, families, educators, and communities both locally and globally. She serves on the Board of Directors for the Division of International Special Education and Services, Balang Foundation (South African Literacy Non-Profit Organization), and Nativity Preparatory School. She is a co-editor of Teacher Education

Quarterly. Dr. Jez represents USD as an invited member of the national Collaboration for Effective Educator Development, Accountability, and Reform (CEEDAR). Dr. Jez co-leads and organizes the DLT #BLM Social Justice and Advocacy Series monthly events.

Dr. Keitha Osborne has over 30 years of experience in teaching at the primary, secondary and tertiary levels. She began her pedagogical trajectory as a Home Economics teacher and later transitioned into the field of Special Education. Currently a Senior Lecturer at The Mico University College in the Special Education Department. Dr. Osborne is a council member of the Jamaican Association on Intellectual Disabilities (JAID) and the Association for Supervision and Curriculum Development (ASCD), and of CEC: DISES and DCDT. She is passionate about her job as a teacher educator and takes her responsibilities as the special education department evening school program coordinator seriously. She is an advocate for her students and believes in promoting students' satisfaction. Keitha Osborne enjoys research, traveling, sharing her knowledge, and advocacy for children with special needs.

Clara Hauth, PhD is an Associate Professor at Marymount University where she is the program lead for their Educational Leadership and Organizational Innovation EdD. With a background in K-12 classroom instruction, special needs intervention research, global education and educational leadership, she examines current trends in education in the US and abroad. Her research focus is on three main areas: special education teacher preparation, educational leadership, and inter-professional global competencies. She currently supports global projects with schools in Panama and engages in educational inter-professional research in Jamaica, Ecuador, and South Africa. She is the co-author of the book *The Survival Guide for New Special Education Teachers* and is an active member of the Council for Exceptional Children's Division of International Special Education and Services (DISES).

Chapter 16
Understanding Life in Lockdown for Autistic Young People in Northern Ireland

Gillian O'Hagan and Bronagh Byrne

Abstract As COVID-19 continues in Northern Ireland (NI), there is limited understanding of how this will impact the lived experience of children and young people with disabilities. In particular, autistic children in mainstream schools in NI have limited access to critical statutory support. This, combined with transitions to remote learning, is especially distressing. School learning support teams are attempting to support online learning for autistic young people during lockdowns. However, this is potentially exacerbated by the autistic students' abilities to identify or express how lockdown restrictions are having an impact on their capacity for coping with remote learning. Through co-research with an autistic young people's advisory group, this chapter explores the impacts of COVID-19 on online learning experiences of autistic young people in post-primary schools. The research specifically considers the challenges experienced by autistic young people during lockdown; the coping strategies developed by autistic young people during lockdown; recommendations for helping autistic young people manage in similar situations in the future. Photovoice is the participatory arts-based method (Wang & Burris, 1997), used in this study to capture autistic students' (11–18) lives during lockdown as they learn at home. Their experiences are documented using smartphones enabling each young person to present insight into how lockdowns impacted their experiences. The young people's advisory group then assisted the adult researchers with a thematic analysis of the Photovoice data. They provided guidance to ensure future online learning programs are accessible to autistic young people by presenting evidence-informed recommendations for education policymakers, schools, and parents.

Keywords Autism · Young people · Photovoice · Lockdown

G. O'Hagan (✉) · B. Byrne
Queen's University Belfast, Belfast, UK
e-mail: gcurran04@qub.ac.uk

© The Author(s), under exclusive license to Springer Nature Switzerland AG 2022
L. Meda, J. Chitiyo (eds.), *Inclusive Pedagogical Practices Amidst a Global Pandemic*, Inclusive Learning and Educational Equity 7,
https://doi.org/10.1007/978-3-031-10642-2_16

Introduction

The rights of children and young people with disabilities are clearly stipulated under both the United Nations Convention on the Rights of the Child (United Nations, 1989) and the United Nations Convention on the Rights of Persons with Disabilities (United Nations, 2006) and include the substantive rights to education, health services, play, rest, and leisure. Children with disabilities have the right to appropriate support to enable them to achieve their fullest possible individual development and are not to be discriminated against. When decisions are being made for children with disabilities, their best interests should be the primary consideration and due weight must be given to their expressed views during decision making processes. This includes being provided with disability and age-appropriate support for expressing their views.

The COVID-19 pandemic has deepened inequalities for children with disabilities making it increasingly challenging for countries aspiring to ensure that the rights of children are realized effectively (Couper-Kenney & Riddell, 2021). In 2020, the United Nations Committee on the Rights of the Child (the Committee) expressed serious concern at the undoubted adverse effect of the pandemic on marginalized children and young people. As such, the Committee (2020) has called on governments to address how pandemic restrictions have impacted the health, social, educational, economic, and recreational rights of the child and that planning for any future restrictions be proportionately imposed and only when absolutely necessary. While acknowledging the limited availability of financial resources due to the pandemic, the Committee (2020) calls upon countries to ensure that the allocation of resources reflects the principle of the best interests of the child.

The extent to which children, including children with disabilities, are able to enjoy their right to education, play, rest, and leisure is implicated by the COVID-19 pandemic. The Committee (2020) urged governments to ensure that plans to provide education solely online does not exacerbate existing inequalities among children. Furthermore, remote learning should not be equated to nor be intended to replace student-teacher interaction. It acknowledges that online learning is a purposeful and creative alternative to classroom learning, but one which poses challenges for children who experience digital poverty (Ferguson, 2021) or who do not have adequate parental support. Alternative solutions should be provided for these children so that they can continue to benefit from the guidance and support provided by their teachers. Finally, the Committee (2020) emphasized that governments should explore innovative solutions enabling children to resume their enjoyment of their rights to rest, leisure, recreation. This should include the provision of child-friendly cultural and artistic activities on TV, radio, online and supervised daily outdoor activities that respect physical distance and hygiene protocols.

A nascent body of work is examining the impact of the pandemic on children's rights such as the global survey of over 26,000 young people from across 137 countries about their "Life Under Coronavirus" (Lundy et al., 2021). However, there is limited research that specifically explores the impacts of the pandemic on the rights and experiences of children and young people with autism. Yet there is anecdotal evidence suggesting that autistic children and young people are no longer able to meaningfully access their critical statutory health and educational support (Crane et al., 2021). This, combined with changes to 'normal' routines, restricted movement, and profound uncertainty, can be especially distressing for autistic young people, with many finding it difficult to express the extent of their distress. The primary focus of this small study was on the experiences and impacts of COVID-19 on autistic young people in post-primary education settings in Northern Ireland.

Background

Inclusion in education is a fundamental right of all learners and of all ages, but definitions of inclusion vary and its practice is often more tokenistic than genuinely inclusive (Byrne, 2013). This is particularly true of children and young people with disabilities whose inclusion in education is largely decided by adult stakeholders, professional and parental. While the importance of inclusive education is underpinned in Article 24 of the UNCRPD (Couper-Kenny & Riddell, 2021), the social injustice concept of childism is often imposed on children and young people, considering them limited in their capacity to make informed decisions about their education (Adami & Dineen, 2021; Lundy, 2018). Children and young people with disabilities are more often than not regarded as "less than" others which further perpetuates their limited input into shaping their education (Byrne & Kelly, 2015).

The voice of children and young people with disabilities is quite often omitted from decision making processes in education and this pertains to epistemic injustice that is both testimonial and hermeneutical (Byrne, 2019; Kotzee, 2017; Fricker, 2007). In the context of education, testimonial injustice uses status identifiers to construct power imbalances between the speaker and the hearer. In education, the imbalance is between the student and the educator, with the educator assuming they have more knowledge and power than the student and thus disregarding the student's views, perspectives, or wishes. Hermeneutical injustice is epitomized in education when the means by which student voice is explored by stakeholders is inaccessible to the student, making it difficult for them to convey their experience or perspective in a meaningful way.

In the context of autism, which is indicated on schools' special educational needs registers in Northern Ireland as a communication and social interaction difficulty (Department of Education, 2019), epistemic injustice is easily outlined. Testimonial injustice occurs when there is an assumption by the educational stakeholder that the autistic student cannot accurately articulate their views on their education and so the autistic student is misheard. Hermeneutical injustice occurs when educational stakeholders seek autistic students' views through means which create barriers to their ability to communicate rendering the autistic student voiceless, for example conducting a face to face interview with an autistic student who finds face to face interactions extremely challenging. In short, an autistic student's view is fundamental in understanding how to support their learning and the channels of illuminating their perspective should be explored with and guided by the autistic student. If education is to be inclusive, it must uphold children's rights and seek to avoid such instances of epistemic injustice, both of which underpin the conceptual framework of this research.

Dimitrellou and Male (2020) presend an analysis of multiple educational research studies, all upholding the inclusion of pupil voice in education and including pupils with additional needs. Therefore, it appears obvious to include the perspectives and views of children and young people when constructing an online/remote learning curriculum during a pandemic rather than imposing a structure composed by adults alone. However, with the abrupt onset of the first lockdown in March 2020, schools scrambled to consistently support children and young people who needed to continue learning with limited means and time. Due to the challenges faced, schools were perhaps exonerated, to an extent, for limiting student input to new home learning approaches (Couper-Kenny & Riddell, 2021). Nonetheless, this first period of remote learning further exposed global issues of inclusion in education for children and young people with disabilities (Masonbrink & Hurley, 2020) and provided an opportunity to explore how remote learning could be made more inclusive should a second lockdown occur.

Considering how bespoke curricula becomes in the physical classroom and bearing in mind the mental health impact of the current imposition of restrictions on more vulnerable learners, the curation of remote learning programs must respond individually to each child with additional needs by including and reflecting their voices. However, the unprecedented nature of the pandemic limits the research that marries these concepts. Through the CovidUnder19 initiative, Lundy et al. (2021) recently published their global survey on "Life Under Coronavirus" communicating the views of 26,258 children across 137 countries through a child's rights based approach. Stated among their findings is a clear indication of the effect of COVID-19: "The pandemic has had a direct impact on children's ability to exercise their right to an effective education." (Lundy et al., 2021, p. 269).

In the United Kingdom, Ferguson (2021) effectively combined the inability to access online education and the lack of appropriate support for special educational needs during the pandemic as fundamental factors to the academic and social exclusion of children and young people with disabilities from their right to education during the lockdown. Crane et al. (2021) further demonstrated this notion finding in England, that the majority of decision making for education during the pandemic was centered around mainstream schooling contexts with limited consideration given to the continuation of education for autistic students in special schools. In Scotland, Couper-Kenny and Riddell (2021) made similar assertions demonstrating the variation in the allocation of educational support staff and services for children and young people with disability during the pandemic.

Northern Ireland remains in a state of flux regarding the education of autistic children and young people. The Department of Education's (2016) implementation of the Special Educational Needs and Disability Act of Northern Ireland (the 2016 Act) has been stalled due to the temporary absence of the Northern Ireland Assembly (devolved nation's government), the emergence of the pandemic, and public SEND consultation. As such, until the 2016 Act is fully implemented, education for children and young people with disabilities in Northern Ireland remains guided by the Northern Irish Special Educational Needs and Disability Order of 2005 and the Autism Act of 2011 which stipulates the inclusion of the voice of the child regarding educational decision making (Department of Education, 2005; 1.18–1.20). In Northern Ireland, and similarly in Scotland, England, and Wales, the basis of school placements for autistic students is in mainstream schools where in 2015, 73% of children with autism had a mainstream placement (National Autistic Society NI and Autism NI, 2015). In May 2020, the Department of Health concluded that 4.2% of NI school-aged children had a diagnosis of autism, meaning that by that point 12,544 autistic children in NI had experienced their first lockdown and two months of remote online learning. Of these autistic children, 37% belonged to the most deprived category, where digital poverty is also at its greatest.

Methods

The combination of an epistemic injustice framework with child's rights based research situates this study within the transformative paradigm where the voices and experiences of autistic young people are not solely heard, but are acted upon by focusing on the emancipation of its research participants. In line with this concept, autistic children and young people in this research were encouraged to convey their experiences during lockdown, but the method by which this is achieved circumvented possible barriers to the verbal articulation of their lived experience. Furthermore, where autistic children and young people are encouraged to illuminate their experiences and to realize their rights, their participation must result in meaningful action by gatekeepers who play an active role in decision-making for autistic children and young people.

Photovoice is a participatory arts-based method (Wang & Burris, 1997) that potentially fulfils the requirements of this paradigm. It affords autistic children and young people a conduit for illuminating their experiences through documentary photography and bypasses barriers to variable language competence. The presentation of thematically grouped photographs urges gatekeepers and in this case, stakeholders within education, to respond meaningfully through tangible action to improve life for autistic children and young people.

Young People's Advisory Group (YPAG)

The primary focus of this small research study for the Centre for Children's Rights at Queen's University Belfast was the experiences and impacts of COVID-19 on autistic young people in post-primary education settings in Northern Ireland. Using a child-rights based approach (Lundy & McEvoy, 2012) for the purpose of foregrounding autistic voices, the project was guided by a group of 4 young autistic advisors from across Northern Ireland aged between 11 and 15 years of age.

The YPAG and researchers refined the project aims and developed the questions that would be used to visually capture their peers' experiences during lockdown. An introductory zoom meeting between the researcher and each young advisor verified their understanding of the aim of the study and confirmed their participation within the YPAG. Three subsequent group online zoom meetings followed, two preceding the data collection and one after. Agendas for each meeting were sent in advance so each young advisor would know what to expect.

During the first YPAG meeting, the current issues facing autistic young people were explored and this culminated in devising three research questions:

Question 1: What were your experiences and emotions during lockdown?
Question 2: How have you adjusted to lockdown during this time?
Question 3: What have adults done that has helped you during lockdown?

Photovoice was then introduced as a potential method for data collection. Photovoice is a particularly useful and rich method for accessing the perspectives of autistic young people (O'Hagan, 2020; Teti et al., 2016) and requires only a basic knowledge of photography while opportunistically aligning itself with adolescent use of smartphone photography. Sample Photovoices were presented to the YPAG to ascertain if they concurred with its proposed use for this study. For the second meeting, the YPAG created their own Photovoices to trial this method confirming its suitability for this study. This activity built YPAG's capacity in understanding Photovoice supporting them in their later analysis and interpretation of the research data. This meeting also explored discussion points to cover with research participants during their post-Photovoice interview. The final YPAG meeting involved the analysis and interpretation of each participant's photographs using the platform Padlet to group photographs into themes and this analysis is presented in the discussion section.

Research Participants

Ethical approval for the study was received from the School of Social Sciences, Education and Social Work Ethics Committee in May 2020. Following this, post-primary aged participants (11–18) were sought from all school sectors (mainstream and special). The study had nine participants; three girls and six boys, from post-primary mainstream education in Northern Ireland. Participants were recruited through an email-drop to the Autism Advisory and Intervention Service (AAIS) and various Special Education networks across NI. A poster advertising the research project was widely shared through the online platforms of Facebook and Twitter. Young people and their parents who expressed interest were provided with accessible information sheets and consent forms and all participants who returned completed forms were included in the research.

This small study, while highly ethnographic, recognized the limitations of its reach in that it did not capture the experiences of autistic children and young people from non-mainstream schools. It is also limited to autistic participants who have access to digital technology and is therefore not representative of all autistic children and young people in post-primary school in NI.

Data Collection

Data collection took 6 weeks to complete by which point lockdown restrictions were beginning to ease for the first time in Northern Ireland. The research team designed three PowerPoint presentations to guide participants through the project. Once recruited, each participant was emailed the first presentation which introduced the research team, explained the purpose of the study and introduced the concept of Photovoice. Participants were asked to email the research team to confirm they had read and understood the PowerPoint and were encouraged to ask any further questions to clarify their understanding. Following this the second PowerPoint was emailed. This was a short accessible guide to documentary photography which highlighted how the composition of photographs could be used to portray meaning. Once participants emailed to confirm they had read and understood this guide to photography, the third and final PowerPoint was emailed. This contained the research questions and detailed instructions of the Photovoice task.

Participants were then asked to document the realities of their life under lockdown using their smartphones and to send their photographs to the research team with a short description of their reason for taking the photographs. Follow up individual interviews were then conducted with each participant over Zoom by the adult researchers to discuss the meaning of each photograph.

Results and Discussion

The Photovoice resulted in 43 photographs being submitted by 9 participants and were thematically grouped by the YPAG at the final group meeting using the platform Padlet. In turn, each advisor randomly selected a number and the corresponding photograph and quote was presented on screen. The advisor who selected the photo then led the discussion with the YPAG about how each photo should be categorized and this was done for all photos until six categories were identified. Once complete, a wider discussion on the findings of the research took place culminating in the YPAG making three recommendations as a result of the Photovoice.

Main Findings

The six main findings were divided into two themed sub-sections. The first section related to the challenges that young people experienced since the emergence of the pandemic; the second set of themes related to the coping strategies and supports that young people identified as being helpful.

Challenges

The first section of the findings depicted the challenges faced by the participants during their time in lockdown. These were divided into three sub-sections: isolation and space; uncertainty and the pressures of home-schooling.

Isolation and Space

Young people told us of their isolation during lockdown and their experiences of 'somber' and 'depressed' mood. For the young people in this study, the isolation manifested itself in the amount of time they now spent alone, often in their bedrooms. Furthermore, spending all of the time at home during lockdown heightened already existing stress and anxiety for some. Young people in the study were perhaps not used to spending so much time with their family in restricted spaces and so felt that having their own space was a necessity. It was not necessarily something they wanted to do but in the case of Ellen, was deemed to be necessary in order to keep bubbling anxiety under control (Fig. 16.1).

'I'm usually in my room all day. I know if I come downstairs to socialize with everybody I would get stressed. Sometimes my stress and anxiety take over and it makes me say things I don't mean'. (Ellen).

Joe shared how he struggled to keep himself occupied in the absence of his daily school routine (Fig. 16.2).

The object of the picture had a deeper meaning for him: 'how I've been feeling during lockdown. At times it can feel a bit sluggish, nothing much changes and usually I'm okay with that but it's starting to get a bit monotonous.' (Joe) (Fig. 16.2).

Eimhear presented herself as feeling very small in the face of something that was overwhelming, comparing the coronavirus to a seagull 'because I sometimes feel like lockdown is eating up all my social life.' (Eimhear) (Fig. 16.3).

As lockdown restrictions eased, some young people were able to go out however this continued to contribute to anxiety when adults did not appear to take social distancing measures seriously (Fig. 16.4).

'…The stress of catching Covid-19…and that Mummy could potentially die. There were situations when I was going to Gaelic even the coaches were standing

16 Understanding Life in Lockdown for Autistic Young People in Northern Ireland 271

Fig. 16.1 On my own

Fig. 16.2 Feeling sluggish

Participant 6

Fig. 16.3 No social life!

Fig. 16.4 Covid-life or death!

shoulder to shoulder. I was so annoyed as I had gone there in confidence thinking social distancing like a sort of lockdown. I found it very difficult at times. The gravestone represents the danger of not being careful.' (Sam) (Fig. 16.4).

Uncertainty

Many of the young people referred to the uncertainty caused by the pandemic. Like all young people, the participants in this study were worried about what was going to happen and how long the pandemic was going to last (Fig. 16.5).

'The beach goes out a bit so you can't really see what's at the end, this is like my current situation and the world's current situation, we don't know what's at the end and we don't know what's coming for us and what's coming for me. I don't really know what's at the end of the road. It's uncertain.' (Darach) (Fig. 16.5).

Some participants tried to regain control of this uncertainty by implementing new routines (Fig. 16.6).

'When we had school at the start, I found it quite hard. I needed routine and I needed structure. I needed to know. I'm not the sort of person who can do school

Fig. 16.5 Uncertainty

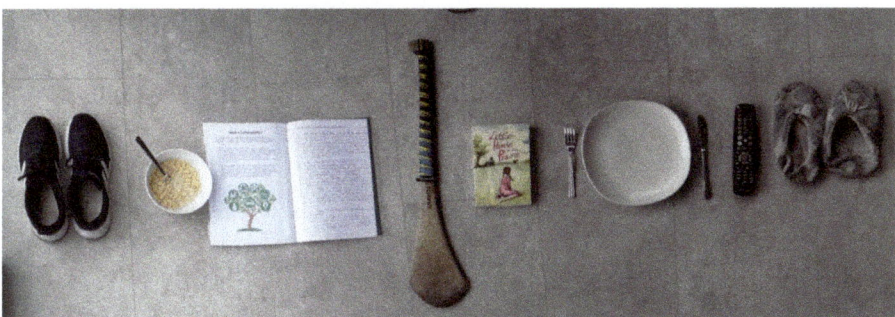

Fig. 16.6 My routine

one day at 9 am and then 4 pm the next day. I need things to be the same and predictable. These are all the objects of my routine.' (Patricia) (Fig. 16.6).

Pressures of Home-Schooling

The young people of the study consistently referred to the pressures and stresses associated with home-schooling and engaging with new educational platforms across multiple subjects could be overwhelming at times (Fig. 16.7).

Fig. 16.7 The stress of online learning

'That's google classroom and these are some of my classes but my book is closed because I'm trying to represent that I've been finding work really stressful and I haven't been able to do it. I've been able to do the stuff that I find easy but I find math and science really stressful.' (Ellen) (Fig. 16.7).

James confirmed this by stating that not having his learning support teacher made it impossible for him to do math at home due to his dyscalculia while Jarlath used a photograph to demonstrate just how much homework was part of his life during lockdown (Fig. 16.8).

This feeling of not quite knowing what to prioritize or what to focus on is shared by another young person. Sam, for example, shared a picture of books and pens covering each other (Fig. 16.9).

'It's as if you are covered by all the books, like they're traps. I was finding it very difficult with all the work coming in. All the writing and reading coming in was overwhelming and there was no clarity.' (Sam) (Fig. 16.9).

Broader research confirms these challenges with Masonbrink and Hurley (2020) citing as critical the loss of resources and in-person education for children and young people. Crane et al. (2021) demonstrate how education has been significantly compromised for children with disabilities in multiple and intersecting ways and this intersection is reiterated through Adami and Dineen's (2021) discourse on childism and ableism. Ferguson (2021) notes that the absence of young people's voices during this pandemic is tantamount to exclusion from their education, therefore, the presentation of these experiences is crucial in understanding the

Fig. 16.8 Homework, homework, homework!

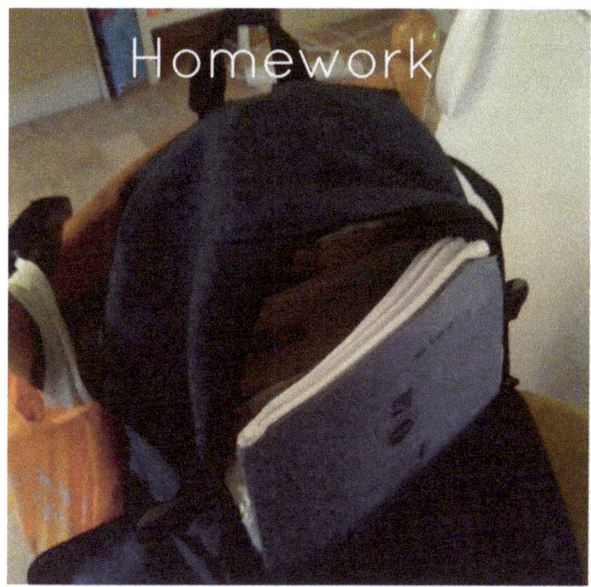

Fig. 16.9 Overwhelmed by Work

challenges, loneliness and uncertainty faced by these autistic young people during the first lockdown in Northern Ireland and should be acknowledged by all educational stakeholders going forward.

Coping Strategies

The second part of the findings focuses on the coping strategies that young people found helpful during lockdown when adapting to a 'new normal'. These are divided into three sub-sections: relationships, hobbies and the importance of being outdoors.

Relationships

Families were usually the first and sometimes only point of contact for young people in the study. Young people shared their anxieties with parents who were able to provide reassurance and help the young people navigate the challenges that arose (Fig. 16.10).

'I chat with my Mum on a day to day basis. She knows what would make me anxious most of the time, she can almost predict when I'm going to be anxious. If I'm worried about something, I can just talk to her about it and she can help me. My mum can calm me down, give me a hug, get the weighted blanket or go on the swings.' (Patricia).

Pets were also perceived as a central part of family lives and a key source of comfort and companionship during what was an isolating time (Fig. 16.11).

'Lennie has helped me through lockdown. It's hard not being able to see my friends but I have been able to take Lennie for a walk everyday'. (Stephen).

Other young people found it helpful to talk to professionals. However, the now virtual nature of this support brought its own challenges and made it more difficult to engage with counsellors, etc. (Fig. 16.12).

'My therapist phones me every week or every two weeks. Talking… is problem solving. It's more than just conversation. If I have a problem or am worried about something I talk to her and come up with the solution. But on the phone you can't see her reaction. You can only hear it, normally I would have a bit of time to catch up with her but it's harder to talk on the phone than in person. The phone calls are shorter than normal appointments so you can't go into as much detail.' (Patricia).

Fig. 16.10 Anxietea!

Fig. 16.11 Lennie

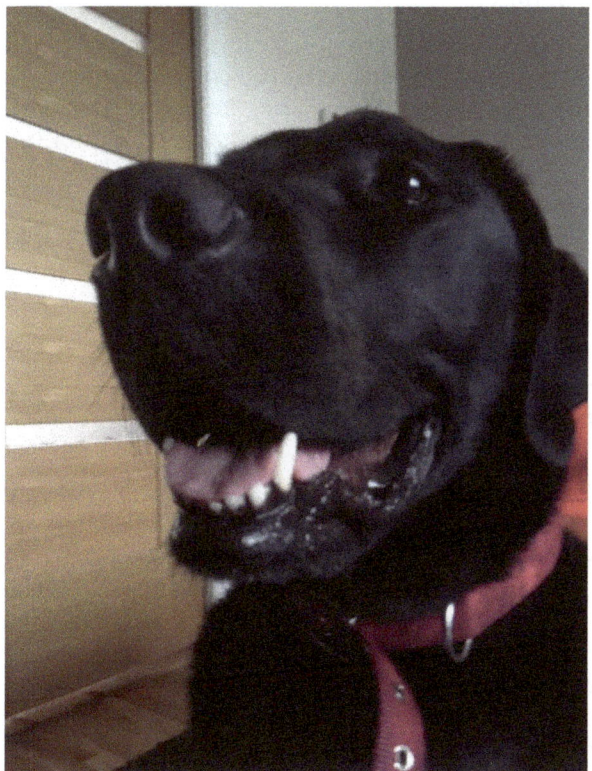

Fig. 16.12 Phone therapy

Hobbies

All young people in the study had drawn on existing hobbies or developed new hobbies as a coping strategy during lockdown. This provided a source of distraction, routine and instilled a sense of calmness (Fig. 16.13).

'Baking helps me relax and it helps me forget about the things I'm worrying about. I've been worrying a lot.' (Ellen).

Eimhear enjoyed the baking packs sent out by the autism family support group in her area while James described how lockdown gave him more time for gardening (Fig. 16.14).

Being Outside

Having time outside everyday as a way of alleviating stress during lockdown. Time outside was built into the new routine of their days and was a welcome and necessary reprieve to online learning and being confined to home. Each participant has clearly identified the therapeutic aspect of being outside (Fig. 16.15).

"This place is a sanctuary for me." (Darach).

"I've been trying to get out every day because I feel like it clears my head. My dog is just in front of that cornfield and everyday when I cycle past, I look up and I see it getting bigger every day. I don't think I am growing as much intellectually but the cornfields will keep growing. (James) (Fig. 16.16).

16 Understanding Life in Lockdown for Autistic Young People in Northern Ireland 279

Fig. 16.13 Baking distractions

Fig. 16.14 Family support groups

Fig. 16.15 Gardening to cope

Fig. 16.16 Sanctuary

"I do think I prefer being outside a lot of the time, it clears your head. When you're outside there's not lots of noise, bright light or tons of people." (Patricia).

Finally, Sam very clearly articulated the therapeutic benefits of being outdoors (Fig. 16.17):

"It's blurred in the background and pixelated in areas because at times I have found myself very, very stressed and there was a lot of frustration and anger building up. The bike is very clear because I find a lot of solace or it'll be like a great escape to go on a bike ride. It was so good to have my bike to have the opportunity to escape from all the school work (Fig. 16.18).

Fig. 16.17 Trapped by the spokes

Fig. 16.18 The calm outside

Fig. 16.19 Escape!

Masonbrink and Hurley (2020) urged educators to address the psychological impact of the pandemic on children and young people. A starting point for this is identified by the autistic young people in this study. Acknowledging their perspective has the potential to empower these young people (Dimitrellou & Male, 2020) while also helping to rectify their futures (Couper-Kenney & Riddell, 2021). This study's findings align with Couper-Kenney and Riddell (2021) on the importance of parent-child relationships and outdoor activity during the first lockdown. In support of this, Crane et al. (2021) propose the adoption of a holistic approach to education that ultimately reflects the needs of more vulnerable learners either in class or at home (Fig. 16.19).

In line with the principles of Photovoice (Wagner, 2007) and in recognition of the need and fundamental right for consideration of children's views when decisions are being made for them (Lundy et al., 2021; Couper-Kenney and Riddell, 2021), the findings and recommendations of this research were presented to the Education Committee of the Northern Ireland Assembly in December 2020, just three weeks before a second closure of schools in Northern Ireland. During this second lockdown, the recommendations were also published in a Northern Irish teachers' union magazine 'PrintOut' and distributed to every union member in February 2021. Finally, the findings of this study are posted on the website for the Centre for Children's Rights at Queen's University Belfast.

Conclusion

Autistic young people's experiences of lockdown were more negative than positive. This study demonstrated a shared urgency to illuminate their challenges so that, in the event of a future lockdown, these stressors could be taken into account when making lockdown arrangements for autistic young people.:

"There is not one cure for this, we need to look at things individually and figure out things for each different person." (Joe- YPAG).

Recommendations

Recommendation 1

Autistic young people rely on extended family networks, voluntary groups and statutory services that provide support that may not exist within a closed family unit. By restricting contact with these wider key people, levels of isolation and loneliness soar contributing to poor mental health, an adverse factor already associated with autistic young people. The substitution of online social/clinical interactions does not adequately take the place of face-to-face interactions for both personal/social engagement and clinical therapeutic interventions. Therefore, any future lockdown restrictions should aim to give specific considerations to autistic young people in terms of movement restrictions within wider family circles and prioritize appropriate face to face access to the services designed to support autistic young people.

Recommendation 2

With regards to home-schooling and online learning, there are several points which autistic young people wish to be considered. In schools, learning for autistic young people is usually scaffolded by key learning support staff: e.g. classroom assistants and through differentiation by the class teacher within the classroom. Curricular accommodations also enhance learning for autistic young people. The closure of schools during lockdown replaced these supports with inconsistently used learning platforms where tasks appeared ambiguous for the autistic young person in terms of structure, length, duration and deadlines. Furthermore, there was limited acknowledgement of the additional time required to navigate these platforms and complete the assignments set resulting in some participants engaging in school days of 12 h. Young people felt their teachers overloaded their classes with work showing no regard for students already overwhelmed by the volume of work set.

Therefore, future lockdown learning should focus on quality over quantity. Learning tasks should be meaningful, adding to learning in a systematic and scaffolded way, and mindful of the fact that learning new concepts online is a much slower process for autistic students, and indeed all students, than it would be in the classroom. The volume of work assigned should be monitored in terms of setting a time limit for school-work when students are learning from home. Time limits should reflect the additional time required to coordinate learning online with the subsequent submission of work. In some instances, it may be inappropriate to set tasks in all classroom based subjects and a core set of subjects should be prioritized. It should be made explicit to autistic young people that a stipulated amount of time for school-work is sufficient each day rather than a stipulated amount of school-work.

Recommendation 3

It is very clear from this study that autistic young people need time to engage with their hobbies and the outdoors in order to mitigate against the negative aspects of life in lockdown. This time should not be seen as simply recreational, but rather a meaningful way of improving mental health wellbeing when other usual supports and clinical services are no longer available. Mental health wellbeing should be formally included as part of the school curriculum when homeschooling/online learning is taking place and there should be discrete time for this included in the time budgets for each school day.

This recommendation clearly supports all students in a lockdown, but has particular relevance for autistic young people who may struggle with lack of consistent routines and daily predictability of lockdown education. Prioritizing mental health wellbeing during lockdown will make it easier for the autistic young person to re-engage with learning on return to school. Rather than experiencing protracted disaffection from online learning, a positive home school learning experience where autistic young people have continued support for their mental health coupled with realistic demands of school work makes for a much smoother transition back into classroom education.

Concluding Statement

While the scope of this research is limited to a post-primary, Northern Irish context, our autistic young people have demonstrated through this research that home learning was disproportionately difficult for them compared to their peers and contributed to their isolation and loneliness in lockdown. Autistic young people devised their own coping strategies for the inordinate stress and pressure they felt during this time, coupled with the removal of the key support networks they usually rely on. In moving forward there is one clear and consistent message from our autistic young people with regard to the specific consideration that must be given to shaping lockdown for autistic young people:

"During a pandemic, you cannot leave people with autism without help, without support." (Eimhear – research advisor).

Acknowledgements Particular acknowledgement goes to the four young advisors Darach, Eimhear, Joe and Patricia who worked tirelessly on this project.

We are also grateful to the School of Social Sciences, Education and Social Work at Queen's University Belfast (QUB) for funding this research project.

References

Adami, R., & Dineen, K. (2021). Discourses of Childism: How covid-19 has unveiled prejudice, discrimination and social injustice against children in the everyday. *The International Journal of Children's Rights, 29*(2), 353–370. https://doi.org/10.1163/15718182-29020001

Byrne, B. (2013). Hidden contradictions and conditionality: Conceptualisations of inclusive education in international human rights law. *Disability & Society, 28*(2), 232–244.

Byrne, B. (2019). How inclusive is the right to inclusive education? An assessment of the UN convention on the rights of persons with disabilities' concluding observations. *International Journal of Inclusive Education*, 1–19. https://doi.org/10.1080/13603116.2019.1651411

Byrne, B., & Kelly, B. (2015). Special issue: Valuing disabled children: Participation and inclusion. *Child Care in Practice, 21*(3), 197–200. https://doi.org/10.1080/13575279.2015.1051732

Couper-Kenney, F., & Riddell, S. (2021). The impact of COVID-19 on children with additional support needs and disabilities in Scotland. *European Journal of Special Needs Education, 36*(1), 20–34. https://doi.org/10.1080/08856257.2021.1872844

Crane, L., Adu, F., Arocas, F., Carli, R., Eccles, S., Harris, S., … Wright, A. (2021). Vulnerable and forgotten: The impact of the COVID-19 pandemic on autism special schools in England. *Frontiers in Education, 6*, 629203. https://doi.org/10.3389/feduc.2021.629203

Department of Education. (2005). *Code of practice on the identification and assessment of special educational needs*. Bangor.

Department of Education. (2016). *The special educational needs and disability act* (Northern Ireland) 2016 (the 2016 Act). DoE.

Department of Education. (2019). *Recording SEN and medical categories: Guidance for schools*. DOE.

Department of Health. (2020). *The prevalence of autism (including Asperger's syndrome) in school age children in Northern Ireland*. DoH.

Dimitrellou, E., & Male, D. (2020). Understanding what makes a positive school experience for pupils with SEND: Can their voices inform inclusive practice? *Journal of Research in Special Educational Needs, 20*(2), 87–96. https://doi.org/10.1111/1471-3802.12457

Ferguson, L. (2021). Vulnerable children's right to education, school exclusion, and pandemic law-making. *Emotional and Behavioural Difficulties, 26*(1), 101–115. https://doi.org/10.1080/13632752.2021.1913351

Fricker, M. (2007). *Epistemic injustice: Power and the ethics of knowing*. Oxford University Press.

Kotzee, B. (2017). Education and epistemic injustice. In I. J. Kidd, J. Medina, & G. Polhaus (Eds.), *The Routledge handbook of epistemic injustice* (1st ed., pp. 324–335). Routledge.

Lundy, L. (2018). In defence of tokenism? Implementing children's right to participate in collective decision-making. *Childhood, 25*(3), 340–354. https://doi.org/10.1177/0907568218777292

Lundy, L., & McEvoy, L. (2012). Children's rights and research processes: Assisting children to (in)formed views. *Childhood, 19*(1), 129–144. https://doi.org/10.1177/0907568211409078

Lundy, L., Byrne, B., Lloyd, K., Templeton, M., Brando, N., … Wright, L. H. V. (2021). Life under coronavirus: Children's views on their experiences of their human rights. *International Journal of Children's Rights, 29*(2), 261–285. https://doi.org/10.1163/15718182-2902001

Masonbrink, A. R., & Hurley, E. (2020). Advocating for children during the covid-19 school closures. *Pediatrics, 146*(3), 1–6.
National Autistic Society Northern Ireland (NI) and Autism NI. (2015). *Broken Promises*. National Autistic Society.
O'Hagan, G. (2020). *Missing voices: The educational experiences of girls with Autism*. Unpublished EdD thesis: Queen's University Belfast.
Teti, M., Cheak-Zamora, N., Lolli, B., & Maurer-Batjer, A. (2016). Reframing autism: Young adults with autism share their strengths through photo-stories. *Journal of Pediatric Nursing, 31*, 619–629. https://doi.org/10.1016/j.pedn.2016.07.002
United Nations. (1989). *United Nations convention on the rights of the child*. United Nations.
United Nations. (2006). *Convention on the rights of persons with disabilities (CRPD)*. United Nations.
United Nations Committee on the Rights of the Child. (2020). *Statement on Covid-19*. United Nations.
Wagner, J. (2007). Observing culture and social life: Documentary photography, fieldwork and social research. In G. Stanczak (Ed.), *Visual research methods: Image, society and representation* (pp. 23–60). Sage Publications.
Wang, C., & Burris, M. (1997). Photovoice: Concept, methodology, and use for participatory needs assessment. *Health Education and Behavior, 24*(3), 369–387.

Dr. Gillian O'Hagan is an Associate lecturer in 'Autistic Voice and SEN Practice', at St Mary's University College, Belfast and a Researcher at Queen's University Belfast. Dr O'Hagan's background is in researching with autistic young people particularly focusing on advancing understanding of autistic girls. She specializes in Photovoice research. Dr O'Hagan is also a Senior Teacher and Learning Support Coordinator in Aquinas Diocesan Grammar School, Belfast.

Dr. Bronagh Byrne is Co-Director of the Centre for Children's Rights and Senior Lecturer in Social Policy at Queen's University Belfast, UK. Her research expertise lies in the rights of children and young people with disabilities generally and the right to inclusive education in particular. Dr Byrne sits on the editorial board of the International Journal of Disability and Social Justice.

Chapter 17
Inclusive Educational Practices in Turkey During the Period of COVID-19

Ismail Hakki Mirici

Abstract The COVID-19 pandemic caused fundamental changes in most educational institutions globally regardless of the educational level from pre-school to university. The main shift was the transition from onsite face to face education to online teaching in distance. Majority students in Turkey, especially in rural areas, had huge challenges. The study aimed to investigate how inclusive education was provided for students in Turkey during the COVID-19 pandemic period. In other sense, it was aimed to find out how students were included in the educational implementations offered by the Ministry of Education in Turkey regardless of their location and their economical conditions. In the study, phenomenological research design, a qualitative method, was adopted. The participants of the study comprised randomly selected 50 volunteer teachers (40 females, 10 males), and 70 volunteer students and their parents. The data were collected via a structured 5 point Likert type teacher questionnaire, a semi-structured student & parent interview both of which were developed by the researcher; and using governmental documents related to the "Emergency Distance Education" practices in schools. The data from the participant teachers, students and parents and were analyzed using qualitative data analysis methods, such as descriptive statistics of percentage and frequency, and coding based on the common themes of the respondents; as well as through document analysis. The results revealed that the participant students were not satisfied with the distance education program offered in terms of neither materials and implementation nor testing and assessment. Likewise, their parents and the participating teachers were of the opinion that the Emergency Distance Education in Turkey was not truly inclusive or effective at all.

Keywords COVID-19 · Emergency distance education · Inclusive education · Effectiveness in education

---

I. H. Mirici (✉)
Hacettepe University, Ankara, Turkey

© The Author(s), under exclusive license to Springer Nature Switzerland AG 2022
L. Meda, J. Chitiyo (eds.), *Inclusive Pedagogical Practices Amidst a Global Pandemic*, Inclusive Learning and Educational Equity 7,
https://doi.org/10.1007/978-3-031-10642-2_17

Introduction

Emerging in China in late 2019, the COVID-19 pandemic made countries adopt urgent policies, and made people reframe their socio-economic life. Social life had limitations in terms of social interaction, habits, leisure activities, visits of all sorts, and travels. Likewise, most businesses have experienced serious setbacks due to closures or loss of clients. Upon the pandemic declaration of the World Health Organisation (WHO, 2020), a new approach in education has been introduced, namely the "Emergency Distance Learning" or the "Emergency Remote Teaching". By locking down the schools, distance education has become an alternative system to face-to-face education.

This sudden situation forced countries, institutions, and individuals to reconsider the educational needs of students and teachers in accordance with the new conditions. Initially the aim of preventing the rapid spread of the Coronavirus meant that educational activities were ceased globally, and then, after determining precautions, restarted gradually. The first step of restarting entailed that classes were organized using "Emergency Distance Learning" or "Emergency Remote Teaching" activities, and then, face to face education in schools were rescheduled in accordance to pandemic cases in each setting. At this point, the main issue to consider was an inclusive education in an effective way. Researchers have long been discussed the significance of an inclusive education for a peaceful and sustainable global society (Carrington et al., 2013; Nind, 2014).

It is widely known that there is a positive relationship between the learning of students and excellence of designing online teaching (Bao, 2020; İpek et al., 2020; Çalık & Altay, 2021). Nations have shifted to distance education with certain precautions and identical implementations considering the needs of the children in their own context and Turkey has also had to adapt to the unexpected pandemic situation with no predetermined distance education strategy, which has the key role for an inclusive education during a pandemic.

Background

According to the 2019–2020 statistics reports released by the Ministry of Education (MoNE), Turkey has a student population of more than 18 million in its seven geographical regions. Out of these students; about 15 million are enrolled in state schools, about 1.5 million in private schools, and more than 1.5 million in open schools. The number of boys in state schools is 7, 781; and girls 7, 408, 87 (MoNE, 2020a). Each region has its own socio-economic realities, educational opportunities, and facilities. Therefore, in Turkey, the adaptation process was a true dilemma for parents, students, and teachers, as well as policy makers in school education and higher education. For example, in the metropolitan of Turkey, in Istanbul, refugee children had additional challenges in the early period of the Emergency Distance

Education process besides their adaptation problems (SPI, 2020). Majority of these disadvantaged children did not have any technological devices, such as a television, computer or a mobile phone to follow the distance classes. Likewise, the number of preschool children affected by the disruption of education in Turkey is 1,326,123 (UNESCO, 2020). The preschool curriculum approved by the Ministry of Education was based on in-class, face to face education. However, the pandemic required a complete distance educational implementation. The distance program for these children should have been designed in order to consider their emotional, cognitive and psychomotor development facts. Besides this, academics experienced challenges in performing their lectures and research activities, just as in any part of the world (Brammer & Clark, 2020). Immediate actions for an inclusive education were needed to support every stage and in every field of education, such as pre-school, primary school, secondary school, high school, special education, vocational education, and higher education.

Just after the first COVID 19 incident in Turkey on March 11, 2020, the MoNE declared the measures that had to be taken, and announced that education in schools would be implemented via intensive distance education during the pandemic period at all levels of school education, from kindergarten to High School (MoNE, 2020b). In 2012, the Ministry of Education, set up an information network called Education Informatics Network (in Turkish: EBA), a technological platform, for both students and teachers to access. In the Emergency Distance Education period, the ministry utilized that platform via EBA TV accessible at https://www.eba.gov.tr. Similarly, the Council of Higher Education, Turkey (CoHE) announced an online education model on 18 March 2020, based on the experiences and practices of some leading universities in order to avoid the risk of interruption in education (YÖK, 2020). Accordingly, the "Digital Transformation Commission in Higher Education", which was composed of subject matter faculty members from various universities, had prepared the Pandemic Distance Education Applications Roadmap, which was approved by the CoHE executive committee. These were some of the concrete efforts of the education authorities to provide an inclusive education for all regardless of their location to access online classes and digital materials.

This study aimed to seek answer to the main research question; "What are the inclusive educational practices like in Turkey during the period of COVID-19?" Based on this main research question, the sub-research questions were formulated as in the following:

1. Are the educational materials and facilities accessible for all students regardless of their locations and economical conditions during COVID-19 Pandemic?
2. What are the viewpoints students about their inclusion in the educational process during COVID-19 Pandemic?
3. What are the viewpoints of the parents about the inclusion of their children in the educational process during COVID-19 Pandemic?
4. What are the viewpoints of the teachers about the students' inclusion in the educational process during COVID-19 Pandemic?

Method

Study Design

In this study, which aimed to scrutinize the inclusive education practices in Turkey during the COVID-19 pandemic, phenomenological research design, a qualitative method, was utilized. In phenomenological research, data sources consist of individuals or groups who experience the phenomenon which the research focuses on and which can express this phenomenon (Buyukozturk et al., 2018; Creswell, 2020). In addition, phenomenological research helps to make better understandings and to recognize the phenomenon to be investigated (Yildirim & Simsek, 2016).

Participants

The participants of the study were composed of 50 teachers and 70 students and 70 parents. The participant teachers were from different subjects of education and taught different grades in different schools in different geographical regions in Turkey. They were selected randomly and took part in the study voluntarily.

Some demographic information about the participant teachers is presented in Table 17.1.

As Table 17.1 illustrates, most of the teachers teach at a primary school; the technology literacy level of the majority is moderate; most of the teachers have 6-10 years of teaching experience; most of them teach for 16-20+ hours a week; the majority of them are female; more than half of them have teaching experience in distance learning; and none of them knows how to teach during a pandemic. It is also understood that the fields of expertise of the respondent teachers are Elementary Education, Social Sciences, Math, Natural Sciences, and Fine Arts.

Demographic information about the participant students is illustrated in Table 17.2 below.

In Table 17.2 below, it is seen that the participant students comprise all school levels from primary school to high school. The number of primary school students in the 3rd and 4th grade s and the secondary school 8th graders is higher than the other groups. Majority of them do not own a personal computer of their own, and have siblings who are also students and need to study online. Therefore, although they are able to connect to the internet at home, they find themselves in the situation of sharing the only computer available. Table 17.2 also shows that the family income of the majority of participants is between 3001 and 4000 TL, which means they are not from wealthy families .

Table 17.1 Demographic information about the participant teachers

Items	Responses											
Type of the institution	Primary school		Secondary school		High school							
	N	%	N	%	N	%						
	33	66	10	20	07	14						
Technology literacy level	Low		Moderate		High							
	N	%	N	%	N	%						
	04	08	40	80	06	12						
Years of teaching experience	1–5		6–10		10+							
	N	%	N	%	N	%						
	00	00	35	70	15	30						
Weekly teaching hours	5-10		11–16		16–20+							
	N	%	N	%	N	%						
	00	00	10	20	40	80						
Gender	Male				Female							
	N	%			N	%						
	10	20			40	80						
Teaching experience in distance	Yes				No							
	N	%			N	%						
	20	40			30	60						
Knowledge about how to teach during a pandemic	Yes				No							
	N	%			N	%						
	00	00			50	100						
Teaching branch	Classroom teacher		Social science		Math		Natural sciences		Fine arts		Sports	
	N	%	N	%	N	%	N	%	N	%	N	%
	05	10	12	24	13	26	09	18	11	22	00	00

Data Collection Tools and Analysis of the Data

All the following forms were developed by the researcher.

Personal Information Form was developed for students and teachers and is composed of questions related to the demographic information of the respondents.

The Teacher Interview Form which comprises open ended questions aiming to gather teachers' opinion about teaching methods, materials, testing and assessment implementation, and the students' needs during the pandemic in Turkey. In addition, teachers are invited to reflect their viewpoints about how inclusive the Emergency Distance Learning process is within their own context.

The Student & Parent Interview Form is composed of open ended questions in order to obtain students' and their parents' opinions related to distance learning, the access to materials, access to the Internet, possessing a personal computer or a tablet, getting feedback from teachers and their opinions on their inclusion in educational processes in general during the COVID 19 pandemic period. In the development of the interview questions, the reports released by the government were made use of.

Table 17.2 Demographic information about the participant students

Items	Responses										
School type	Primary school			Secondary school			High school				
	N		%	N		%	N	%			
	32		45.71	23		32.85	15	21.42			
Age	06–09			10–13			14–17		17+		
	N		%	N		%	N	%	N	%	
	32		45.71	23		32.85	13	18.57	02	2.85	
Gender	Boy						Girl				
	N			%			N		N		
	28			40			42		60		
Grade	1	2	3	4	5	6	7	8	9	10	11	12
	N	N	N	N	N	N	N	N	N	N	N	N
	2	8	10	12	04	05	05	09	06	04	02	03
Possessing a personal computer	Yes						No				
	N			%			N		%		
	09			12.85			61		87.14		
Having a sibling	Yes						No				
	N			%			N		%		
	58			82.85			12		17.14		
Internet access	Yes						No				
	N			%			N		%		
	70			100			00		00		
Sharing the computer at home	Yes						No				
	N			%			N		%		
	49			70			21		30		
Monthly income of the family	Less than 1000 TL		1001–2000 TL		2001–3000 TL		3001–4000 TL		4001 + TL		
	N	%	N	%	N	%	N	%	N	%	
	00	00	02	2.85	11	15.71	49	70	08	11.42	

Upon developing the questions in relation to the aim of the study, the interview forms were sent to 4 academic experts for their opinions. One was in the Psychological Guidance and Counselling Department, one was in the Department of Statistics, and two were in the Department of Educational Sciences. Based on the experts' feedback, the forms were finalized. Then the Personal Information Forms and the Interview Forms were converted to Google Forms, and the links were accessible to school teachers via social media tools, such as LinkedIn and Facebook, and were emailed to volunteer students and their parents who were selected randomly.

All of the data obtained were analyzed using the descriptive statistics of percentage and frequency, and via coding method based on the common themes of the respondents.

Findings

The findings of the study are based on the results of the descriptive statistics and the qualitative data analyses. The viewpoints of teachers, students and their parents constitute the backbone of the research findings. In order to find out the answer to the main research question, the findings referring to each sub-research question are presented in the related table or via some direct quotations as in the following:

Sub-research Questions 1 & 2: How effective was the implementation of the educational programme during the pandemic? & How much are.

the students' needs considered during the pandemic in Turkey?

The students' and their teachers' responses are presents in the Tables 17.3 and 17.4.

As it is seen in Table 17.3, the participating students are not satisfied with the educational facilities offered during the pandemic. The majority of them are of the opinion that their needs are not taken into consideration, materials are not

Table 17.3 Students' responses

Theme	Categories	Statements	Frequency (N)	Percentage (%)
Distance education	Needs	My needs for learning in distance are considered.	05	7.14%
		My possession of a personal computer or a tablet is considered.	02	2.85%
	Materials	Materials are suitable for my age and my interests	41	58.57%
		I am informed about how to study in online classes.	02	2.85%
		My access to the teaching materials is taken into consideration.	32	45.71%
	Testing and assessment	Testing and assessment tools are appropriately administered to show my performance and my achievements.	27	38.57%
		I cannot perform well in the testing and assessment process.	65	92.85%
	Technology	I have no difficulty in connecting to the internet	68	97.14%
		Having a personal computer is not important to follow the classes.	03	4.28%
		Internet connection does not affect my success.	01	1.42%
	Implementation	I received regular feedback from my teachers.	04	5.71%
		The distance education program is effective enough to learn the content of the lessons.	23	32.85%

Table 17.4 Teachers' responses

Theme	Categories	Statements	Frequency (N)	Percentage (%)
Distance education	Needs	The needs of students for learning in distance are considered.	10	20%
		Students' possession of a personal computer or a tablet is considered.	03	6%
	Materials	Materials are suitable for the students' age and interests	05	10%
		Students are informed about how to study in online classes.	03	6%
		Students' access to the teaching materials is taken into consideration.	05	10%
	Testing and assessment	Testing and assessment tools are appropriately administered to help students show their performance and achievements.	07	14%
		Students cannot perform well in the testing and assessment process.	43	86%
	Technology	Students have no difficulty in connecting to the internet	08	16%
		Having a personal computer is not important to follow the classes.	07	14%
		Internet connection does not affect the success of students.	01	2%
	Implementation	Students received regular feedback from teachers.	03	3%
		The distance education program is effective enough to teach the content of the lessons.	11	22%

accessible, they are not well-informed about distance education, testing and assessment practices are not student friendly and the program which is offered via distance learning is not effective enough.

As Table 17.4 illustrates, the participating teachers do not find the Emergency Distance Education program during COVID-19 pandemic in Turkey effective or successful. This is consistent with the responses of the majority of the students and most of them believe that the needs of the students are not considered, testing and assessment practices are not good enough, the teaching materials are not effectively used, and the students are not well-informed about distance education.

The findings related to the other sub-research questions are discussed under each related research question below:

Sub-research Question 3. What are the viewpoints of Turkish students about their inclusion in the educational process during COVID-19 Pandemic?

Some direct quotations of the participating students are as follows:

In My Opinion the Program Is Inclusive Because......

S1- we are all invited to watch the lessons on EBA TV.
S2- our teachers do their best to teach the lessons.

In My Opinion the Program Is Not Inclusive Because......

S3- We do not know how to take classes in distance.
S4- Most of our friends do not have computers or internet connections.
S5- I never feel myself in a classroom with my friends.
S6- The classes are not interesting or attractive for me.
S7- We are not given any chance to say what we want.

It can be seen that the students emphasize the necessity of inclusion and state that their personal ideas and needs should be considered for effective and inclusive education. They also draw attention to the fact that the fundamental requirements for an inclusive distance education program are possessing a personal computer and having access to the internet, which most of their friends do not have.

Sub-research Question 4. What are the viewpoints of the students' parents about the inclusion of their children in the educational process during COVID-19 Pandemic?

In My Opinion the Program Is Inclusive Because......

P1- my daughter has attended the classes as much as the other students.
P2- the program offered has been presented to all students with no exception for any student groups.
P3- our sons do not complain about any kind of an exclusion.
P4- the teachers who we contact never complained about exclusion of students.
P5- I trust our government about inclusion of every student.

The statements of these parents are evidence of the fact that they are actually not aware of the level of inclusion of the program. They only develop the idea in connection with the reflections of their children or the teachers.

In My Opinion the Program Is Not Inclusive Because......

P6- our child's technological needs are not considered at all. During the pandemic period I have lost my job, and I have no chance to afford a laptop or a mobile phone for my son to follow the classes online. He sometimes studies with his friends, which is not enough to learn the lessons.

P7- in some regions of the country there is no strong internet connection. The students in those regions are definitely disadvantaged and are not included in the educational implementations.

P8- mostly students are excluded due to poor Wi-Fi signals in their home, lack of financial support, or sharing a computer of a tablet with siblings.

P9- the Ministry of Education cannot manage the process successfully.

P10- the program delivered via EBA TV and the expected educational outcomes do not overlap. My daughter will definitely have serious problems in the exams.

From the parents' responses above, it is safe to deduce that the technological infrastructure, financial situation and the policy of the Ministry of Education might cause the lagging behind of children in Turkey, with regards to inclusive education.

Sub-research Question 5. What are the viewpoints of the teachers about the students' inclusion in the educational process during COVID-19 Pandemic in Turkey?

In My Opinion the Program Is Inclusive Because......

T1- we are doing our best to reach every single child at our best capacity as much as the facilities are provided. Every child is the same for me.

T2- The contents of the education programs are definitely suitable for all students.

In My Opinion the Program Is Not Inclusive Because......

T3- the classes presented on the EBA TV are not equivalent to the objectives of the curriculum. They are too simple, short, and boring.

T4- majority of the students do not or cannot attend online classes. We have lost almost 2 years of education.

T5- the Ministry of Education cannot set up an understandable policy. They intent to open the schools, then they say the schools are closed. They give a date for exams, then the exams are cancelled. It has become a chaotic period for most of the students.

Although they say they are doing their best to ensure inclusive education, the teachers' viewpoints above do not seem to be in favor of the educational implementations. They are of the opinion that the Emergency Distance Education implementations are not inclusive or successful because of several reasons, such as students' access problems, irrelevanance and boring content, students' loss of interests, and the contradictory and inconsistant attitude of the Ministry of Education.

Discussion and Conclusion

In this study, conducted to determine the educational inclusion of school children in Turkey during COVID-19 Pandemic, students', parents, and teachers' points of view are utilized as important indicators. Therefore, the data of the study has been obtained from these groups via specifically developed interview forms. The concept of educational inclusion mainly refers to inclusion of disadvantaged students, such as children with special needs, children of immigrant families, and today children who need to access education via limited sources or time. It can then be argued that when the facilities to foster inclusion in education are considered, educational consultancy, social interaction, and the educational facilities provided can be seen as some of the fundamental ways of inclusion (Heward, 2013; Friend & Bursuck, 2012). However, results of this investigation shows that during the COVID-19 period, although Emergency Distance Education has been offered by the Ministry of Education in Turkey, almost 60% of students have signing on problems due to poor internet connection or have no personal computer. Furthermore, there has been no official data about how much of the course content is effectively planned, how many students are able to follow these courses properly, or whether parents are able to support their children's learning (İpek et al., 2020).

If governments do not manage the process sufficiently during the Emergency Distance Teaching period, or do not provide essential educational facilities, due to their roles in education, teachers' responsibilities increase. In that case, their professional qualifications play a significant role for the success of all kinds of educational practices. At this point it can be inferred that pre-service teachers' simultaneous or asynchronous study skills in accordance with individual differences have a significant place (Karsak & Yurtçu, 2021). Likewise, it can be stated that both pedagogical and technological skills are essential skills for teachers, in the face of any situation that requires online teaching in distance learning (Frankel et al., 2020). Some researchers recommend that teacher education programs be revised, the TPACK model elements be evaluated, and the prospective teachers' program content and objectives be updated (Gözüm & Demir, 2021). Since the program offers more theory than practice, a change in the "theory and practice" approach seems to be inevitable (Taşçı, 2021).

To sum up, it can be stated that the process of Emergency Distance Education in Turkey has not been managed successfully by the Ministry of Education since there is no consistency regarding the decisions and precautions taken against the risks of losing time, not meeting the syllabus objectives, and excluding the majority of students from the implementation of the educational programme. Millions of students do not have personal computers, those students who have siblings have to share the computer at home, students feel that their needs are not considered at all, and they are not offered an inclusive education. Teachers, likewise, are not satisfied with the educational implementations during this period, and do not believe in the effectiveness of the program they have been offering. Parents, on the other hand, do not know how they can help their children in terms of educational inclusion, and teachers. All these show that the Ministry of Education in Turkey has not set up an urgency plan for such an unexpected situation, the facilities they have invested in for many years seem to be ineffective and unrealistic, the informatics infrastructure of the ministry needs urgent development, and the children of millions of families living in the rural areas or those in crowded families with two or more siblings may not have the internet access or facilities to follow the courses offered in distance learning programs. However, even the Ministry itself voices the need for such ideal educational implementations such as "Blended Learning", "Flipped Classroom", or "Distance Education". Then it is time to start sustainable development for innovative education in the country.

Recommendations

The experiences during the COVID-19 pandemic period shows that educational policy and practices in Turkey need to be reconsidered and restructured. Even after the pandemic there should be blended education models in practice at every level of education to make sure that the system may switch into an online model whenever necessary. Likewise, teacher education programs should employ hybrid education models, the accomplishments of the prospective teachers should be reconsidered and they should be introduced to the technology of distance education via smart classes. Education administrators should be trained in accordance with the realities of distance education, and to make sure about parental support and involvement in the educational process parents should be provided with seminars about how to support their children in the distance education periods.

The study shows that the majority of students may be excluded from the educational implementation of distance learning. This is a big risk for the future of a country. The loss of time in education should be compensated for via some remedial or after school teaching models. It is not realistic to plan a period of a few months for the loss of almost 2 years. When face to face education starts again, the normal curricula should be put aside, students should be provided with supportive education via a few hours of additional face to face classes after school, plus some distance education opportunities over weekends until they gain the educational objectives they have missed during the pandemic. For this purpose, the Ministry of Education may make use of the technological facilities at hand and may encourage schools and teachers to collaborate for the inclusion of all students, especially, those who are in the disadvantaged excluded group.

References

Bao, W. (2020). COVID-19 and online teaching in higher education: A case study of Peking University. *Hum Behav & Emerg Tech., 2*(2), 113–115.

Brammer, S., & Clark, T. (2020). Covid-19 and management education: Reflections on challenges, opportunities, and potential futures. *British Journal of Management, 31*(3), 453–456.

Buyukozturk, S., Kilic Cakmak, E., Akgun, O. E., Karadeniz, S., & Demirel, F. (2018). *Scientific research methods in education*. Pegem.

Çalık, E. Ö., & Altay, İ. F. (2021). Analysis of English lesson broadcasts during emergency remote teaching from pedagogical, instructional and technical aspects. *International Journal of Education, Technology and Science, 1*(2), 71–87.

Carrington, S., MacArthur, J., Kearney, A., Kimber, M., Mercer, L., Morton, L., & Rutherford, G. (2013). Towards an inclusive education for all. In S. Carrington & J. MacArthur (Eds.), *Teaching in inclusive school communities*. John Wiley.

Creswell, J. W. (2020). *Qualitative inquiry & research design: Choosing among five approaches*. Siyasal.

Frankel, A. S., Friedman, L., Mansell, J., & Ibrahim, J. K. (2020). Steps towards success: Faculty training to support online student learning. *The Journal of Faculty Development, 34*(2), 23–32.

Friend, M., & Bursuck, W. M. (2012). *Including students with special needs: A practical guide for classroom teachers*. Pearson.

Gozum, A. İ., & Demir, Ö. (2021). Technological pedagogical content knowledge self-confidence of prospective pre-school teachers for science education during the COVID-19 period: A structural equational modelling. *International Journal of Curriculum and Instruction, 13*(1), 712–742.

Heward, W. L. (2013). *Exceptional children: An introduction to special education*. Merrill Prentice Hall.

İpek, D. S., Çetinkaya, G. A., Çelikdemir, K., Celep, N. D., & Suna, S. (2020). In E. Karip (Ed.), *COVID-19 sürecinde eğitim: Uzaktan öğrenme, sorunlar ve çözüm önerileri*. TEDMEM.

Karsak, H. G. O., & Yurtçu, M. (2021). The effects of pre-service teachers' extracurricular study habits and emotion regulation on lifelong learning tendencies in COVID-19 process. *International Journal of Curriculum and Instruction, 13*(1), 334–342.

Ministry of Education (MoNE). (2020a). *National Education Statistics Formal Education 2019-2020*. MoNE Publications.

Ministry of Education (MoNE). (2020b). *Bakan Selçuk, koronavirüs'e karşı eğitim alanında alınan tedbirleri açıkladı*, Retrieved from http://www.meb.gov.tr/bakan-selcuk-koronaviruse-karsi-egitim-alaninda-alinan-tedbirleri-acikladi/haber/20497/tr

Nind, M. (2014). Inclusive research and inclusive education: Why connecting them makes sense for teachers' and learners' democratic development of education. *Cambridge Journal of Education, 44*(4), 525–540. https://doi.org/10.1080/0305764X.2014.936825

SPI (Small Project İstanbul). (2020). *Covid-19 Sürecinde İstanbul'un farklı yerleşimlerinde çocukların haklarına erişimi araştırması. Araştırma Ön Raporu*, Retrieved from https://drive.google.com/file/d/1ZXwPwkMO3VtHnLHe9Sn_uY5iIdcIuVcW/view

Taşcı, G. (2021). The impact of COVID-19 on higher education: Rethinking internationalization behind the iceberg. *International Journal of Curriculum and Instruction, 13*(1), 522–536.

UNESCO. (2020). *Startling digital divides in distance learning emerge*. Retrieved from https://en.unesco.org/news/startling-digital-divides-distance-learning-emerge

WHO (2020). *WHO Director-General's opening remarks at the media briefing on COVID-19*. Retrieved from https://www.who.int/dg/speeches/detail/who-director-general-sopening-remarks-at-the-media-briefing-on-covid-19-11-march-2020

Yildirim, A., & Simsek, H. (2016). *Qualitative research methods in the social sciences*. Seçkin.

YÖK. (2020). *Basın açıklaması – (18 Mart 2020) President of CoHE Prof. Dr. M. A. Yekta Saraç*. Retrieved from https://www.yok.gov.tr/Sayfalar/Haberler/2020/universitelerde-uygulanacak-uzaktan-egitime-iliskin-aciklama.aspx.

Prof. Dr. Ismail Hakki Mirici, full-time Professor at Hacettepe University, is the ELP National Contact Person of the Turkish Ministry of Education in the Council of Europe. He is also the Past President (2011–2013) of the World Council for Curriculum and Instruction (WCCI), and the Founder of the WCCI Turkish Chapter. He has been lecturing at universities for about 35 years. He used to be the Dean of Education Faculty of Near East University in Northern Cyprus. He also worked at Gazi University, Kirikkale University, Akdeniz University and Hacettepe University as the Coordinator of English Language Preparatory Classes, the Director of Foreign Languages Research and Practice Center, the Director of Vocational College, and the Chair of Foreign Languages Department. He was the Education Attaché of Turkish Consulate in Chicago between the dates of March- September 2017. He has about 20 books and more than 50 articles published in national and international academic journals. He has coordinated or participated in the steering committees of several national and international education projects. His main fields of studies are English Language Teaching, Teacher Training and Curriculum and Instruction.

Chapter 18
Inclusive Pedagogical Practices Amidst a Global Pandemic: Lessons Learnt from Across the Globe

Jonathan Chitiyo and Lawrence Meda

The COVID-19 global pandemic has challenged teachers to reimagine new ways of teaching to ensure the diverse learning needs of children are catered for. Various inclusive pedagogical practices were implemented to enhance the learning experiences of children. This chapter provides concluding remarks of the issues presented in the book. The book covered a range of topical issues relating to inclusive teaching during the time when the education sector was affected by the COVID-19 global pandemic.

According to a report by the United Nations International Children Emergency Fund (UNICEF), more than a billion children are now at risk of falling behind in their education because of the COVID-19 pandemic. Schools across the globe closed their doors and transitioned to online learning with the hope of containing the spread of the virus. Schools used platforms such as Zoom, Webex, Google meet and Microsoft teams to support synchronous online instruction. However, this transition had consequences for students and families. The switch from regular face-to-face classes to online learning happened very fast and did not give students, teachers, and families enough time to prepare for a new pedagogical approach. In some contexts, teachers had difficulties adjusting to a new pedagogical approach. That made it hard for them to cater for the diverse learning needs of all students especially those with special learning needs. Will (2020) argues that students with exceptional learning needs bore the brunt of the transition (from face-to-face to online learning) as

---

J. Chitiyo
University of Pittsburgh Bradford, Bradford, PA, USA
e-mail: chitiyoj@pitt.edu

L. Meda (✉)
Sharjah Education Academy, University City, Sharjah, United Arab Emirates
e-mail: lmeda@sea.ac.ae

© The Author(s), under exclusive license to Springer Nature Switzerland AG 2022
L. Meda, J. Chitiyo (eds.), *Inclusive Pedagogical Practices Amidst a Global Pandemic*, Inclusive Learning and Educational Equity 7, https://doi.org/10.1007/978-3-031-10642-2_18

special education services and accommodations are difficult to provide in online environments. UNICEF (2021) states that over 900,000 children with disabilities lost out on education during the COVID-19 pandemic.

A common theme that emerged from all the chapters is that the COVID-19 pandemic presented an unprecedented challenge to the education sector. That challenged teachers to step up their creativity and innovative teaching skills to be able to achieve learning outcomes in an environment where online learning was dominant. Daniel (2020) postulates that although the COVID-19 pandemic was the greatest challenge to education systems across the globe, various inclusive pedagogical practices were implemented to support teaching and learning.

It was also found that developed nations had adequate resources to meet the needs of their learners compared to developing countries even though the transition to online learning was abrupt. As a result of the limited resources in developing countries, many children received limited instruction, feedback, or interaction with their teachers. It was also found that even in developed countries, families that were in the low socio-economic class of their societies had problems securing digital devices and accessing fast internet connectivity for students to connect with their teachers. This further widen the already existing achievement gap between students who come from middle to high income households and those coming from low-income households. Research has consistently shown that students from low-income households perform less well than students from high income households on all measures of academic success (Reardon, 2013). The COVID-19 pandemic has further exposed this ugly truth.

As a way forward, it is recommended that governments across the globe provide financial and other resources to schools for them to procure adequate learning technologies (i.e. computers, iPads, tablets, radios, cellphones that can connect to the internet) that is needed to deliver instruction to students. Secondly, it also important for digital literacy to be prioritized in teacher training programs. Research has consistently shown that pre-service teacher training is one of the predictors of teacher competency in using innovative educational techniques such as technology (Chitiyo et al., 2019). In addition to offering courses focused on technology, teacher preparation programs should also place their teacher candidates for field placements in schools or settings where technology is utilized. Immersing teacher candidates in settings where technology is used to deliver instruction will provide them with practical experience related to using technology and this may in turn enhance their confidence. Consequently, when teachers are adequately trained in the use of technology, they will be prepared to provide online instruction to students in the event of another wave of COVID-19 or any pandemic which forces schools to go online. In addition, it is also necessary to provide in-service training/professional development centered on technology to teachers who are already on the job as some of them may not have had such training during their teacher training. So, the in-service professional development will make up for that deficit. Pancsofar and Petroff (2013) found that after controlling for demographic variables (i.e., years of teaching experience, job position) teachers who had access to professional development were more confident with using innovative educational practices compared to teachers who did not have such training. So, if teachers are adequately prepared to cater for the diverse learning needs of children in both online and face-to-face classes, that will be a big step towards the attainment of the fourth Sustainable Development Goal of quality inclusive education.

References

Chitiyo, J., May, M. E., Mathende, A. M., & Dzenga, C. G. (2019). The relationship between school personnel's confidence with using the school-wide positive behavior intervention support model and its sustainability. *Journal of Research in Special Educational Needs, 19*(3), 232–240.
Daniel, S. J. (2020). Education and the Covid-19 pandemic. *Prospects, 49*, 91–96.
Pancsofar, N., & Petroff, J. G. (2013). Professional development experiences in co-teaching: Associations with teacher confidence, interests, and attitudes. *Teacher Education and Special Education, 36*(2), 83–96.
Reardon, S. F. (2013). The widening income achievement gap. *Educational Leadership, 70*(8), 10–16.
United Nations International Children Emergency Fund [UNICEF]. (2021). Children with disabilities: Ensuring their inclusion in Covid-19 response strategies and evidence generation: Children with disabilities: Ensuring their inclusion in COVID-19 response strategies and evidence generation – UNICEF DATA
Will, M. (2020, March 25). *Teachers in limbo as districts rush to boot up online learning.* https://www.edweek.org/ew/articles/2020/03/25/teachers-in-limbo-as-districts-rush-to.html

Dr. Jonathan Chitiyo holds a PhD in Special Education from Southern Illinois University Carbondale, USA. He is currently working as an Associate Professor of Special Education and Director of Teacher Education at the University of Pittsburgh at Bradford, USA. His research interests include the implementation of different school-based practices, factors affecting the education of vulnerable children, and the development of special education systems in developing countries, especially in Africa.

Dr. Lawrence Meda holds a PhD in Curriculum Studies. He is currently working as an Associate Professor and Director of Research at Sharjah Education Academy in the United Arab Emirates. He is a certified online instructor and very passionate about research. His main research interests are in Inclusive Education, Curriculum Studies, Educational Technology and Teacher Education. He has supervised Masters and Doctoral students and published in high impact accredited journals.

List of Reviewers

1. Adrianne Colquitt, PhD candidate. Tennessee Technological University, USA
2. Alfred Makura, PhD. Central University of Technology, Free State, South Africa
3. Allen Mathende, PhD. Tennessee Technological University, USA
4. Andrew Chindanya, PhD. Great Zimbabwe University, Zimbabwe
5. Areej ElSayary, PhD. Zayed University, UAE
6. Argnue Chitiyo, PhD. Ball State University, USA
7. Asiana Banda, PhD. The Copperbelt University, Zambia
8. Candice Livingston, PhD. Cape Peninsula University of Technology, South Africa
9. Cara Williams, PhD. Emirates College for Advanced Education, UAE
10. Christina Gitsaki, PhD. Zayed University, UAE
11. Cina Mosito, PhD. Nelson Mandela University, South Africa
12. Daniel Sukowski, PhD Candidate. Tennessee Technological University, USA
13. Fanny Saruchera, PhD, University of the Witwatersrand, South Africa
14. Francina Mahlo, PhD. University of South Africa, South Africa
15. Gordon Brobbey, PhD. University of Washington, USA
16. Hugh Mangeya, PhD. Midlands State University
17. Jacob Mapara, PhD.
18. Janet Condy, PhD. Cape Peninsula University of Technology, South Africa
19. Joyce West, PhD. University of Pretoria, South Africa
20. Kinsey Porter, PhD candidate. Tennessee Technological University, USA
21. Laila Mohebi, PhD. Zayed University, UAE
22. Lwazi Sibanda, PhD. National University of Science and Technology, Zimbabwe,
23. Marlana Smith, PhD candidate. Tennessee Technological University, USA
24. Mike Litrell, PhD. Tennessee Technological University, USA
25. Mohamed Fteiha, PhD. Abu Dhabi University, UAE
26. Muna AlHammadi, PhD. Zayed University, UAE

© The Author(s), under exclusive license to Springer Nature Switzerland AG 2022
L. Meda, J. Chitiyo (eds.), *Inclusive Pedagogical Practices Amidst a Global Pandemic*, Inclusive Learning and Educational Equity 7, https://doi.org/10.1007/978-3-031-10642-2

27. Najwa Norodien-Fatar, PhD. Cape Peninsula University of Technology, South Africa
28. Naseema Shaik, PhD. Cape Peninsula University of Technology, South Africa
29. Nomakhaya Mashiyi, PhD. University of the Fort Hare, South Africa
30. Oliver Mutanga, PhD.
31. Prabitha Singh, PhD. Stadio College, South Africa
32. Sandra Baroudi, PhD. Zayed University, UAE
33. Sekitla Makhasane, PhD. University of the Free State, South Africa
34. Silas Mangwende, PhD, Women's University in Africa, Zimbabwe
35. Wayne Brinda, Ed.D. University of Pittsburgh Bradford, USA
36. William Clark, Ed.D. University of Pittsburgh Bradford, USA
37. Womack Payton, PhD candidate. Tennessee Technological University, USA
38. Zachary Pietrantoni, PhD. California State University Eastbay, USA

Index

A
Abu Dhabi, 136
Achievement gap, 226, 302
Adaptive systems, 121
Advocacy skills, 87, 89, 92, 181
Africa, 37, 43
Anguilla, 50, 51
Annual teaching plan (ATP), 101, 109, 111
Antigua, 51, 58
Anxiety, 45, 56, 99, 103, 107, 110, 136, 152, 160, 161, 173, 183, 184, 186–188, 242, 270, 276
Arabic, 70, 72, 74
Argentina, 51, 53–56
Arithmetic fluency, 17
Art, 3, 86, 135, 160–174, 258
Aruba, 51
Assessment, 13, 15, 19, 23–25, 51, 55, 56, 59, 65, 101, 109–111, 122, 126, 151, 181, 184, 186, 202, 208, 232, 246, 249, 251, 252, 255, 257, 291, 293, 294
Autism, 2, 4, 12, 13, 87–91, 265, 267, 268, 278, 285
Autonomy, 2, 66, 213, 234

B
Bahamas, 51, 52, 54, 58
Barbados, 51, 55, 58
Barbuda, 51, 58
Belize, 51, 54, 58
Black, Indigenous, and People of Color (BIPOC), 226, 229
Black Lives Matter, 117
Bolivia, 51, 54–58
Brazil, 51, 53–56
British Virgin Islands, 51

C
California, 84
Canada, 2, 160, 161, 164, 168, 172, 212
Caribbean, 2, 50–59, 242
Case study, 38, 103, 160, 164, 200
Cayman Islands, 51
Centre on Child Protection and Wellbeing, 36
Chile, 51, 53–58
Chinese, 2, 3, 81–93
Classroom, 4, 21, 35, 40, 50, 53, 55, 58, 66, 91, 98–111, 116, 117, 119, 121–123, 133, 135, 136, 143, 151, 152, 160–162, 164, 165, 167, 168, 170, 172, 173, 180–182, 185, 186, 189, 211, 212, 215–217, 225–235, 248, 250, 264, 266, 283, 284, 291, 295, 298
Cognitive interest, 20
Collaboration, 3, 4, 102, 103, 105, 106, 108, 110, 120, 135, 144, 150, 152, 160, 171, 174, 178–181, 184, 185, 187, 188, 190, 197–199, 207, 213–219, 233, 244, 252, 256
Collaborative leadership, 4, 213, 215–216, 218, 219
Colombia, 51, 53, 55, 56, 58
Commissions, 15, 50, 51, 57, 289
Community activist, 119–121
Community involvement, 84
Content analysis, 201, 250–251

Conventional education, 152
Coronavirus (COVID-19), 1–5, 8, 34–45, 50–59, 64–68, 72, 75, 82, 83, 85, 86, 91, 98–111, 132–154, 160–174, 178, 183–185, 187, 189, 190, 196–208, 225–227, 229–232, 234, 242, 243, 247–253, 255, 256, 264–267, 289, 290, 293–298, 301, 302
Costa Rica, 50–53, 55–57
Critical discourse analysis (CDA), 118
Critical literacy, 66
Cross sectional, 19, 134
Cuba, 51, 53, 57, 58
Culturally and/ linguistically diverse, 82
Culturally-Sustaining Pedagogy, 117, 245
Curaçao, 51
Curriculum, 3, 11, 14, 15, 18, 50, 52, 55, 58, 59, 77, 98, 100–103, 105, 106, 109–111, 117, 121, 122, 126, 127, 132, 133, 136, 146, 149–153, 181, 186, 187, 190, 227, 229–232, 234, 253, 258, 266, 284, 289, 296, 298

D
Deficit model, 135
Depression, 99, 160, 161, 173, 183
Deprived children, 34, 35, 37–39
Descriptive statistics, 13, 140, 141, 252, 292, 293
Developmental, 8, 9, 11–13, 15, 19, 21, 22, 26, 91, 181
Diagnostic education, 10, 11, 15
Diagnostic role, 18
Differentiation, 132, 133, 164, 234, 283
Digital landscape, 37
Digital tools, 23, 150, 234, 235
Discrimination, 11, 23, 57
DisCrit classroom, 117, 124, 127
Diverse education, 10
Diversified education, 10, 11, 15
Dominica, 50, 51, 57
Dominican Republic, 51, 55, 56

E
Early childhood development (ECD), 4, 196, 198, 203, 207
Ecuador, 51–55, 57, 58
Educational Information System, 10, 12, 13
Effect size, 15, 17, 20, 21
El Salvador, 51, 53, 55, 56, 58
Emergency Distance Learning, 288, 291
Emotional disorder, 160

Emotional learning, 162, 228, 231, 253
Empirical, 11, 14, 19, 38, 164, 229, 232
English as foreign language, 68
Entropy, 134
Epistemic injustice, 265–267
European culture, 16
Every Student Succeeds Act (ESSA), 243, 251, 253, 257
Evidence based practice, 164, 185, 228, 254
Experiential learning, 121

F
Free and Appropriate Public Education (FAPE), 226

G
Global pandemic, 1–5, 178, 196, 197, 208, 225–235, 242, 246, 247, 249, 250, 253, 255, 256, 301–303
Google classrooms, 65, 83, 232, 274
Grenada, 51
Guatemala, 51, 53, 55, 56, 58
Guyana, 51, 53

H
Haiti, 50, 51, 53, 56
Harmonized education, 10, 11, 22
Honduras, 51, 53, 55, 56

I
Inclusion, 1–5, 14, 24, 34–45, 50–59, 76, 98, 102, 107, 115–127, 133–136, 142, 144, 147–150, 152–154, 160, 161, 165–167, 173, 188, 211, 212, 214, 253, 256, 265–267, 289, 291, 295–298
Inclusive culture, 3, 13, 15, 25, 132–154
Inclusive education, 2, 4, 8–12, 14, 18, 23–26, 54, 59, 77, 92, 132, 134–140, 142–154, 207, 208, 211–220, 233, 242, 243, 247, 256, 265, 288–290, 295, 296, 298, 303
Independent readers, 68
Individualized education program (IEP), 82, 85, 89, 183, 185, 186, 226, 229, 234, 257
Individuals with Disabilities Education Act (IDEA), 82, 83, 178, 183, 185, 226
Integration, 8, 10, 14, 18, 22, 24, 132, 133, 149, 161
Intellectual disability, 2, 12, 13, 18, 87, 91

Index 311

United Nations Educational, Scientific, and Cultural Organization's (UNESCO), 34, 50–55, 57–59, 64, 68, 102, 109, 132, 242, 244, 251, 255, 289
United States, 2–4, 82, 115, 118, 178, 225–235, 243, 246–249, 251
Universal Design for Learning (UDL), 116, 234, 235
Uruguay, 50, 51, 53, 55–58

V

Validity, 69, 105, 118, 134, 140, 164, 249, 250
Venezuela, 51, 53, 57, 58
Verbal communication, 163
Virtual-based learning, 2, 34–45

Volunteerism, 4, 196–208
Vulnerable children, 34, 36, 37
Vygotsky, 198, 199, 201–205, 207

W

Western Cape, 98, 104, 105
World Bank, 37, 41, 51, 225, 243
World Health Organization (WHO), 42, 99, 107, 198, 226, 288

Z

Zone of proximal development (ZPD), 199, 202, 205, 207
Zoom, 65, 73, 85, 162, 202, 204, 206, 229, 232, 233, 268, 269, 301

Milton Keynes UK
Ingram Content Group UK Ltd.
UKHW020112280923
429512UK00001B/12